Crafting & Decorating Made Simple

1 Table Toppers for All Occasions

2 Fun & Easy Gifts

3 Original Wraps & Cards

4 Decorative Home Furnishings

5 Creative Wall Accents

6 Finishing Touches for the Home

7 Wonderful Walls & Windows

8 Clever Fix-Ups

9 Holidays & Celebrations

10 Specialties from the Kitchen

11 Techniques & Tools

12 Patterns & Templates

The Crafting & Decorating Made Simple series consists of 12 groups, each featuring a variety of craft projects to make for your home, family, or friends. This sample index, arranged by group, is designed to help you quickly locate cards contained in your Crafting & Decorating Made Simple collection and give you a preview of future shipments. To try Crafting & Decorating Made Simple in your home, see the enclosed letter for details.

☑ CARDS CONTAINED IN THIS PACKAGE
☑ CARDS YOU WILL RECEIVE WITH YOUR INTRODUCTORY PACKAGE

1 Table Toppers for All Occasions

2 Fun & Easy Gifts

3 Original Wraps & Cards

4 Decorative Home Furnishings

5 Creative Wall Accents

6 Finishing Touches for the Home

CRAFTING & Decorating MADE SIMPLE

7 Wonderful Walls & Windows

8 Clever Fix-Ups

9 Holidays & Celebrations

10 Specialties from the Kitchen

11 Techniques & Tools

12 Patterns & Templates

☑ CARDS CONTAINED IN THIS PACKAGE
☑ CARDS YOU WILL RECEIVE WITH YOUR INTRODUCTORY PACKAGE

135 26001 400

Table Toppers for All Occasions

Table dressings to complement any event and every occasion

1

TABLE TOPPERS FOR ALL OCCASIONS

CARD 1

Shaping Centerpieces to Their Settings

The shape of a floral centerpiece is as important as the type and color of flowers used within the arrangement.

Like the table linens, china, and menu you select, the centerpiece must fit the occasion and meet the requirements of the table setting–either formal or informal, large or small. In the photo above, the arrangement set on a small dining table is low enough to see over, but high enough at the bottom to leave table space beneath it. The centerpiece, made up of roses and wax flowers, is gracefully arranged in a ceramic bowl. For another occasion, a long buffet table may demand a long and narrow arrangement.

Roses, available all year 'round, offer many options in a floral centerpiece. In the top arrangement, yellow roses, ranuncului, and asters are used in a simple, clean design with galax leaves. The elegant centerpiece with red roses is set in a silver compote and features button chrysanthemums, fern fronds, and salal leaves.

When making a floral centerpiece, choose flowers with long sturdy stems. If using chrysanthemums, be sure each flower has at least a 3" stem, so that each individual flower can be used. If not, group the mums into a cluster.

Roses are always an elegant choice for a centerpiece. They grow in a variety of colors and can be combined with many other flowers, such as mini-carnations, tulips, and alstroemerias.

Floral Arrangement Guidelines
Some arrangements can be made the night before, then stored in a cool place overnight.

- Cut floral foam to fit container, then submerge foam in water and soak for 15 minutes.
- Prepare flowers by removing lower leaves on each stem.
- Recut stems to desired length, then place tallest top flower at center, adjusting height to your liking.
- Place flowers on each end to determine width of arrangement. Build in through middle, using all available flowers; even buds can be utilized.
- Fill container with water, then mist lightly if storing centerpiece overnight.

You'll Need

- ***Floral foam***
- ***Wax flowers***
- ***Salal leaves***
- ***Ceramic vase***
- ***Roses***
- ***Fern fronds***
- ***Knife***

1 Cut floral foam to fit inside ceramic vase. Fit smaller pieces around edges to fill in and secure main piece, but leave foam loose enough to expand when filled with water. Round off edges of foam.

2 To establish shape of arrangement, alternate salal leaves and fern fronds along bottom edges of foam, just above lip of container.

3 Remove lower leaves from stem of each flower. Place first flower in center of arrangement, adjusting it to desired height.

4 Cut stems of 8 flowers to equal length. Space them evenly around lower edge just above leaves, angling them so each blossom faces out.

5 Cut 4 more roses to same length as previous roses. Insert them in between center and ring of roses already in place; stems should cross each other to maintain even shape.

6 Select another 3 roses and cut stems a little shorter than top roses. Place them in and around arranged flowers.

7 Position remaining flowers so final effect is balanced from all sides. Remember, however, shape need not be perfectly uniform.

8 Fill in empty spaces with rose leaves or greenery so floral foam is covered and does not show through foliage.

Crafter's Secrets

Once floral foam is soaked and allowed to dry out, it can never be soaked again. Therefore, when preparing a floral arrangement, cut the foam to the size needed for your container and store the remaining pieces in a cool, dry place to keep the moisture out. The stored foam can be used at another time for your next centerpiece.

9 Starting at edges and working towards middle, fill in bare spots with sprays of wax flowers. Be sure to cover all open areas.

Try This!

This lovely basket arrangement with the fresh scent of summer is made with freesias, tulips, chrysanthemums, asters, and salal leaves. Try to create a natural, wild-garden look by selecting greens and field flowers that grow locally. Dried or fresh weeds often lend a refreshingly casual quality to the total effect, but must be changed frequently as they have a tendency to fade quickly. When selecting fresh flowers, do not allow strong fragrances to overpower the savory flavors of the foods to be served on the same table.

Making a Long Centerpiece

When creating an arrangement for a buffet or a large, sit-down dinner party, an oblong shape may be the best choice. The flowers can be elongated by leaving the stems full length and using long greenery such as fern leaves and tall grasses. By working in a raised vase with the flowers arranged in a row, you can create an arrangement that appears in proportion to your large table, but does not take up a lot of table space. Use the greenery to determine the horizontal length of the arrangement.

The long centerpiece in the setting above consists of roses, tulips, carnations, and sprays of lady's mantel, plus croton leaves, palm leaves, fern-palm fronds, and sprigs of berries.

If you need a long, low arrangement with trailing greens that can touch the table, try stalks of wheat, cattails, or bittersweets for an autumnal mood. The plants used in the arrangement above include gladioli, wild ferns, asparagus ferns, bear grass, yellow tulips, and sweet williams.

1 To establish width of arrangement, insert a fern-palm frond, 2 croton leaves, and 4 small palm leaves into each side of floral foam.

2 Center a carnation to establish height, then fill in arrangement with 8 tulips, 11 more carnations, 6 roses, sprays of lady's mantel and sprigs of berries.

1

TABLE TOPPERS FOR ALL OCCASIONS

CARD 5

Creating Accents with Ribbon Roses

Set a stunning table with a centerpiece of exquisitely crafted roses. Luxurious wire-edged ribbons fashioned into petals and leaves are bound together to create each sensational rose.

Flower lovers will delight in making and arranging these beautiful blooms. Because they are easy to make from ribbons, the colors can be chosen to celebrate holidays and the changing seasons. Try red at Christmas, soft pastels at Easter, golds and russets in the fall.

Ribbon roses make beautiful and versatile floral accents. Display single stems in a bud vase or use them to make napkin rings. Add the flowers to a wreath or swag or use them as curtain tiebacks.

Place ribbon roses of uniform color in a crystal vase filled with glass marbles for a simple yet formal arrangement. For a more casual look, mix roses of various hues in a wicker basket.

For an arrangement to look its best, use a great number of flowers. Mix small and large roses with buds and leaves for the most realistic effect. Use eight petals to make a small ribbon rose; 16 to make a large, full-blossomed rose. Vary the number of petals to vary the size of the bloom. For instructions to make a rosebud see the back of Group 1, Card 6. Make leaf stems with three leaves and tape them to the flower stems if desired.

Tips for Making Ribbon Roses
Maintain a sharp edge to scissors for cutting ribbons and floral tape.

- Wind floral tape tightly around petals and stems to neatly and securely hold them in place.
- Vary petal colors for a more natural look.
- When creating an arrangement, insert a piece of floral foam into container to securely hold flowers and leaves in place.

You'll Need

- ***Wire-edged taffeta ribbons: 1½"- & 2¼"-wide mauve & pink for buds & full roses; 1½"-wide ombre green for leaves***
- ***Yellow floral stamens***
- ***Floral wire: covered 16- or 18-gauge for stems; 26- or 28-gauge for assembly***
- ***Floral foam & tape***
- ***Needle-nose pliers, wire cutters, & scissors***
- ***Ruler or tape measure***
- ***Knitting needle (size 5) or bamboo skewer***
- ***Hot-glue gun & glue sticks***
- ***Container***

Making Rose Ribbons

1 To make small roses, cut 1½"-wide mauve or pink ribbon into 8 (5") pieces; for large roses cut an additional 8 (6") pieces from 2¼"-wide ribbon. Fold each cut ribbon piece in half widthwise with raw edges aligned.

2 To create curls on underside of petal, lay knitting needle or skewer diagonally across 1 folded corner of petal. Roll ribbon firmly around tool, curling corner to center of ribbon width. Slide tool out of curl and repeat on other corner.

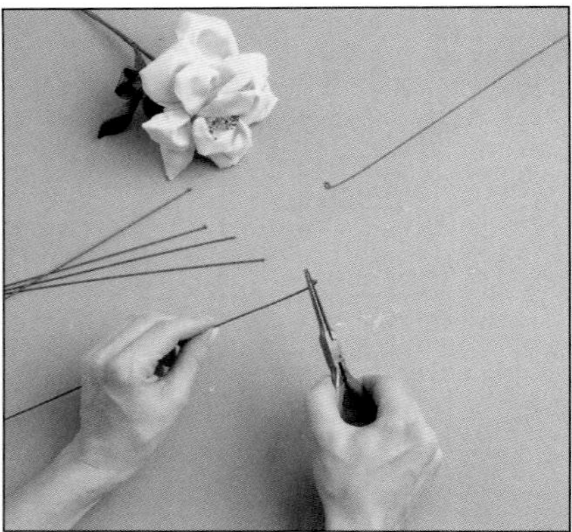

3 Cut piece of covered stem wire to desired length. Using needle-nose pliers, form small loop at 1 end of cut stem wire to make base for flower head.

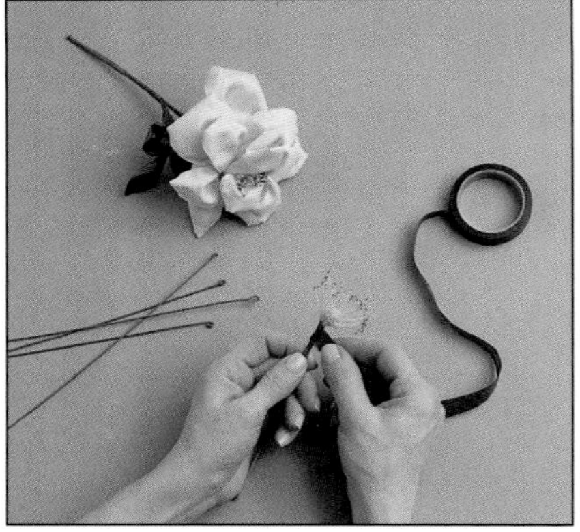

4 Insert floral stamens into looped end of stem wire. Wrap thinner wire around stamens and stem wire to hold stamens in place. Wrap with floral tape to cover wires.

5 Pinch raw end of 1 (1¼"-wide) petal around top of stem to cover stamens. Secure to stem with wire. Repeat, overlapping second and third petals. Wire in place to complete flower center and first round of petals.

6 Continue adding petals singly or in pairs. For small 8-petal rose add a round of 5 petals, centering each on 2 from previous round and overlapping evenly around stem. Wire ends of petals over wired raw ends of first round.

7 For large 16-petal rose, wire a round of 4 evenly spaced 2¼"-wide folded and curled ribbon petals, centering each on 2 petals from previous round. Repeat with another round of 4 large petals.

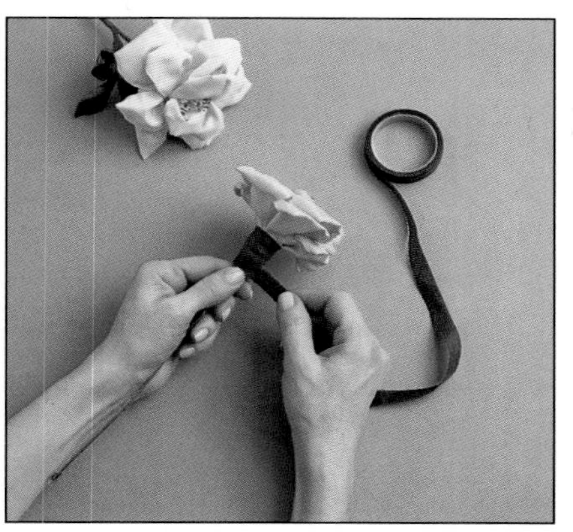

8 Wrap floral tape around base of ribbon petals, just below flower head. Continue wrapping over bottom of petals to cover wire and raw edges of ribbons, and around top of stem wire.

Making Leaves

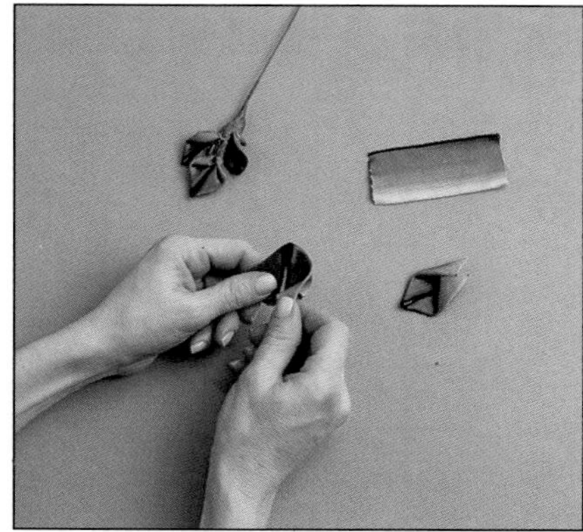

1 Loop 1 end of 6" piece of covered stem wire as for roses. Cut green ribbon into 3 (3") pieces. Fold top corners down to center of bottom edge, forming triangle. Fold bottom points of triangle to center; pinch bottom together

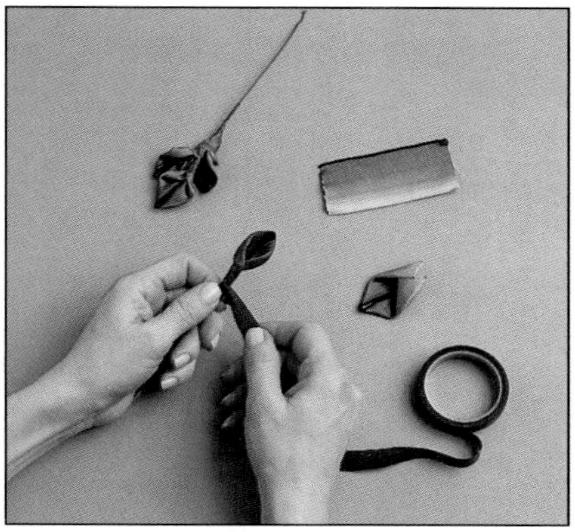

2 Put loop end of stem at bottom of leaf and wrap with floral tape. Form 2 more leaves and tape to each side of stem just below first leaf. Tape 1 or 2 of these leaf stems to each flower stem.

Try This!

Make this elegant napkin ring for your next dinner party, using a single ribbon rose and leaf. Hold the stem of one rose and one leaf together and twist them into a 2"-diameter circle. Wrap the circled stem with floral tape, then wind a length of ribbon around the entire taped ring to cover it. Tie the ribbon into a lush bow and arrange it beneath the bloom.

Making Ribbon Rose Buds for a Candle Ring

A ring of lovely ribbon rose buds and blooms creates a beautiful base for a candle. The floral candle ring can be made to fit around any size candle base—from a small taper to the tallest and thickest pillar.

Make ribbon rose blooms and leaves, then fashion ribbon rose buds, following steps at right. Insert rose blooms into a floral foam ring, angling extra roses on 3" stems in a circle around the foam ring. Fill in spaces with the ribbon leaves and buds.

To make festive candleholders for the holidays or special occasions, add seasonal decorations to appropriate colored flowers. For example, combine small gold balls with red roses and green or white candles at Christmas. For Easter, wire small eggs and insert them into a ring of pale pink and yellow roses surrounding lavender candles. Set a wedding table with white ribbon roses and buds around white candles.

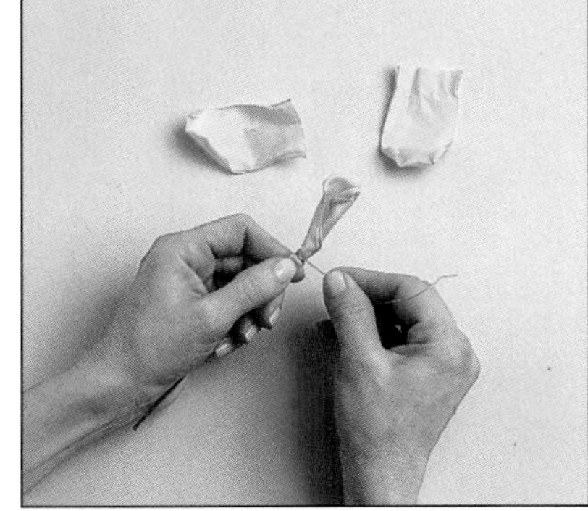

1 To make rosebud, cut, fold, and curl 3 (1½"x3") pieces of ribbon to form petals same as for roses. Loop 1 end of 6"-long covered stem wire, and pinch raw end of 1 petal around top of stem. Secure to stem with thinner wire.

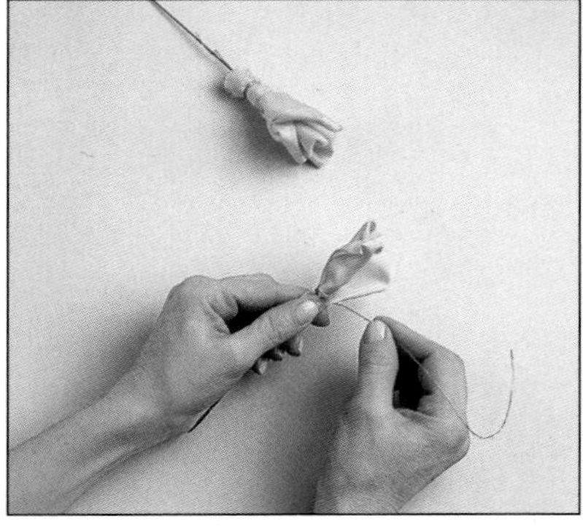

2 Insert second petal against stem, pinching raw edge to cup petal around stem; wire in place. Repeat with third petal to form complete bud. To form fuller bud add 1–3 more petals to stem.

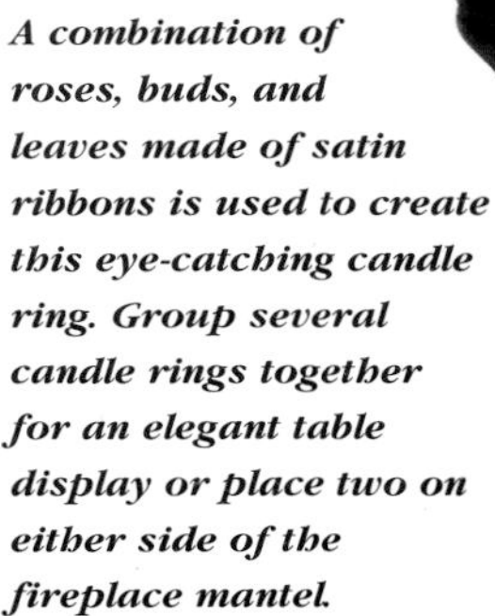

A combination of roses, buds, and leaves made of satin ribbons is used to create this eye-catching candle ring. Group several candle rings together for an elegant table display or place two on either side of the fireplace mantel.

3 Wrap floral tape around base of ribbon petals and continue wrapping downward, covering bottom of petals, wire, raw edges of ribbons, and top of stem wire.

Using Fruits and Vegetables as Accents

Floral arrangements are key elements to a party setting and nestling fruits and vegetables among the flowers gives the centerpiece a new twist. Their unusual shapes and colors are sure to spark your imagination.

While flowers form the basis of any arrangement, the addition of fruits and vegetables creates a visual surprise by introducing unexpected colors, shapes, and textures.

Think of the smooth skins of succulent grapes, the sheen of a purple eggplant, the earthiness of a forest mushroom. These fruits and vegetables have a beauty that rivals any flower. Combining edibles with florals highlights the uniqueness of each and creates a dramatic display.

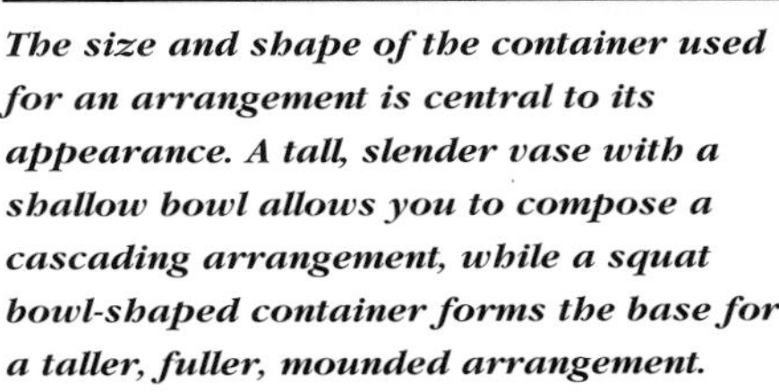

The size and shape of the container used for an arrangement is central to its appearance. A tall, slender vase with a shallow bowl allows you to compose a cascading arrangement, while a squat bowl-shaped container forms the base for a taller, fuller, mounded arrangement.

The look of an arrangement depends on the creative use of the shapes, colors, and sizes of its components. Fruits and vegetables mixed in with flowers and leaves increase your options.

Arrangement Guidelines

Because fruits and vegetables are heavier than flowers and leaves, select a stable container that is large enough to accommodate all the materials.

- Purchase thin plastic liners at a flower shop or nursery to insert into containers and baskets that might leak or are made of silver, which may be damaged by minerals in water. Take container along when shopping to be sure of choosing right size.
- Although tallest flowers in arrangement are usually one and a half times height of container, other scales can be very effective.
- To secure fruits and vegetables, insert one end of toothpick or piece of spooled floral wire into produce, or wrap wire around stem. Insert other end into floral foam, and hide wire behind leaves.

You'll Need

- ***Container***
- ***Plastic wrap***
- ***Floral foam***
- ***Serrated knife, pruning shears, or scissors***

For fan arrangement
- ***Fritillarias, budding celusias, astilbes, lilies; bear grass, emerald & eucalyptus leaves; dark grapes***

For round arrangement
- ***Tulips, ranunculi, orchid sprays, anemones; savoy cabbage leaves; mushrooms & small peeled onions***
- ***Spiked flower holder (for shallow bowl)***
- ***Floral clay***
- ***Toothpicks & green floral wire***

Making a Fan-Shaped Arrangement

1 Line container with piece of plastic wrap. Using serrated knife, trim floral foam to fit snugly inside container with about 3" extending above rim. Insert foam, pressing it firmly into container.

2 Trim foam extending above rim into a rounded shape. Notch out a small opening on side of foam, just above container rim, through which finished arrangement can be watered.

3 Place stems of eucalyptus horizontally on either side of foam just above rim, so they cascade over rim. Next add bear grass fronds at either side. Place emerald leaves in center front of foam.

4 Place 1 fritillaria stem about ½" forward from center back of foam to set tallest point of arrangement. Add 3 more fritillaria stems of descending heights on either side of first, forming an open fan shape across back of foam.

5 Insert celusia stems between fritillaria. Insert a row of astilbe between fritillaria stems about ½" in front of celusias, positioning astilbe heads so they are lower than fritillarias and celusias.

6 Center 3 large lilies in front of astilbes so they cover any exposed foam. Wrap wire around main stem of a bunch of grapes and add to arrangement so grapes cascade over container.

US P 8801 12 004 Printed in U.S.A.

Packet 4

Making a Mounded Arrangement

1 Place a spiked flower holder in container, securing it with floral clay. Push a shaped piece of floral foam onto holder. Insert 3 savoy cabbage leaves in foam to drape over edges of container.

2 Insert 4 tulips in center of foam. Working down and around sides, add ranunculi, more tulips, and sprays of orchids, inserting stems at angles so flowers cascade over leaves.

3 Add anemones. Using toothpicks inserted into mushrooms and onions, nestle vegetables among flowers.

Try This!

Make a mounded centerpiece featuring clusters of flowers mixed with strawberries and grapes. Arranged around a trio of protea, the clusters of carnations, roses, ranunculi, anemones, miniature mums, and green leaves form bold blocks of color, which are echoed by the fruits. An arrangement such as this can be viewed from all sides, making it perfect for a buffet table.

Crafter's Secrets

To make an arrangement last longer and look fresher, mist it frequently with water from a spray bottle. The water will form little dewlike drops on the flowers, fruits, vegetables, and leaves and keep them looking freshly picked. Moisten the floral foam at the same time you spray the leaves, but do not overwater.

Arranging on a Tiered Stand

A rarely used tiered stand can become the background for an artful arrangement. A few well-chosen flowers and greenery tucked in among succulent fruits forms a composition that delights the senses. Allow some stems and small fruits to extend beyond the dishes to unify the various levels.

Vegetables can also be used to create a striking display. Cauliflower and broccoli can be separated into small florets and added to an arrangement in the same manner as flowers. Cherry tomatoes, radishes, and hot peppers can be used in place of flower buds. Carrots, with their tops, peas in their pods, green beans, artichokes, all can be used to create interesting effects.

Be sure to select the ripest, most richly colored fruits and vegetables you can find, and consider using chickory, kale, lettuce leaves, or herbs, such as chives, parsley, and dill, for the necessary touches of green.

An antique two-tiered stand, originally used for serving sweets, makes an excellent foundation for a luscious still life of temptingly ripe fruits and brilliant flowers that is perfect for a buffet table or sideboard.

1 Place a spiked flower holder on 1 side of bottom tier of stand, securing it with floral clay. Secure a second spiked holder on opposite side of upper tier. Push a rounded piece of floral foam onto each spiked holder.

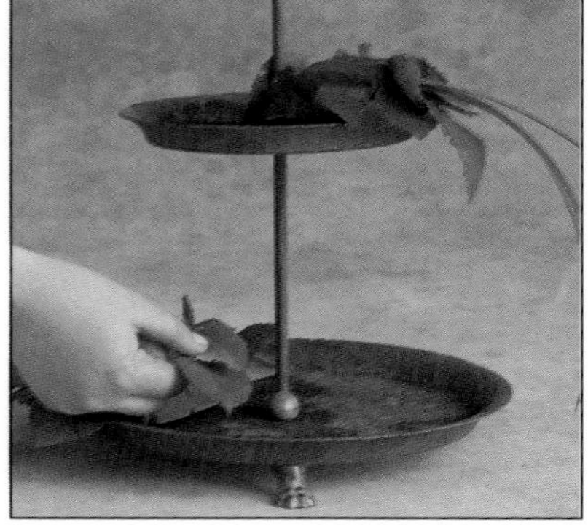

2 Insert some galax leaves into sides of each foam piece, covering sides of foam and draping leaves over edge of each tier. Add several bear grass fronds to top tier, letting them cascade over edge.

3 Place ladies' mantle, roses, ranunculi, and a sunflower in foam on each tier. Place grapes, strawberries, lemons, and pears next to flowers. If needed for stability, insert a toothpick in fruit, then insert other end of pick into foam.

TABLE TOPPERS FOR ALL OCCASIONS

CARD 11

Embroidering White on White

Patterns & Templates

White embroidery on white table linen is so refined in its simplicity yet has an heirloom quality that makes even an ordinary table look like company is coming.

Lend your needle skills to this Old World technique, which involves embroidering with white yarn or thread on white fabric. Characteristic of this traditional method is the use of varied stitches to create a raised design. The earliest of these designs were geometric, following the threads in the fabric, but any desired pattern can be transferred to the fabric.

This technique can be worked on small pieces, such as the table mat shown, or on larger pieces, such as a table runner or tablecloth.

For a contemporary look, the bread basket liner features white-on-white geometric designs. The stylized sliced fruit motif is made with a variety of stitches to create a raised design.

Patterns & Templates

Use the templates from Group 12, Card 6 to create the patterns for the white-on-white embroidery. Enlarge or reduce the templates as needed for your particular piece of linen.

An even-weave fabric, such as linen, is the usual choice for the background, but cotton fabrics work well too. Use yard goods or plain, store-bought table linens with finished edges. Select embroidery floss, thread, or Persian yarn for the stitching.

Transferring Pattern Guidelines

Before embroidering, carefully transfer patterns to cloth using fabric transfer paper and a ballpoint pen or a pencil.

- Place sheet of transfer paper face down on fabric and traced pattern over transfer paper.
- To transfer pattern to fabric, outline pattern with pen or pencil. Markings from transfer paper will wash out.

Embroidering Guidelines

Use an embroidery hoop to keep the fabric taut while embroidering.

- If hoop is not large enough to take in entire pattern, embroider a single motif at a time.
- Do not end yarn when working different stitches in same motif. Let yarn continue from stitch to stitch on back of fabric. When finished, secure yarn by running it through a few stitches on back of fabric before cutting off.

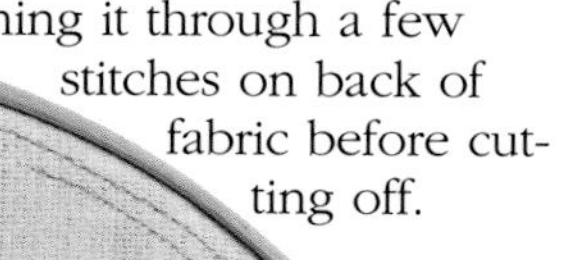

You'll Need

- White linen fabric
- Single-ply white embroidery thread
- Embroidery hoop & needle
- Transfer paper
- Ballpoint pen or pencil
- Scissors

1 Cut piece of white linen large enough to fit entire pattern, plus an additional 2" around. Transfer templates from Group 12, Card 6 to fabric using transfer paper and pen.

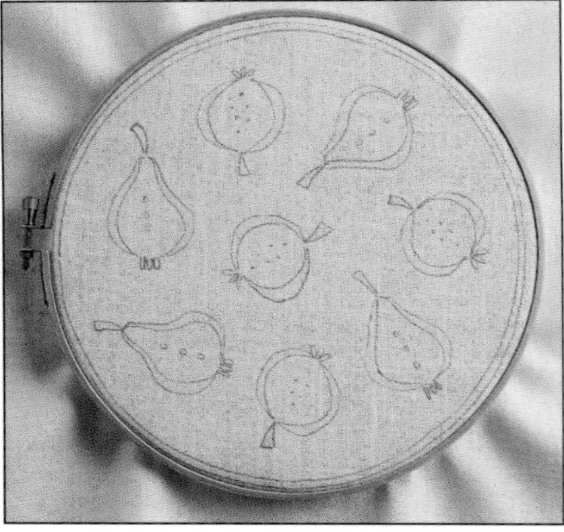

2 With pattern side facing up, place fabric over inner ring of embroidery hoop, centering motifs. Fit outer ring over inner ring; stretching fabric taut, turn screw on outer ring to firmly secure hoop rings together.

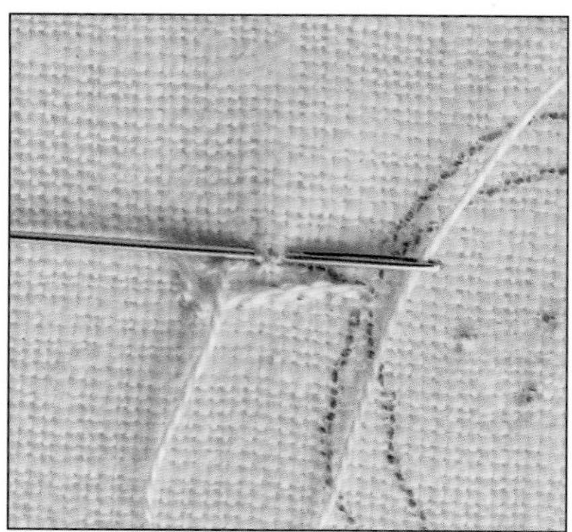

3 For stem, use *stem stitch*: Bring needle up, leaving a 1" tail; insert needle back down 1/8" farther along line. Bring back up midway between needle points, keeping thread below needle. Repeat, inserting in middle of last stitch.

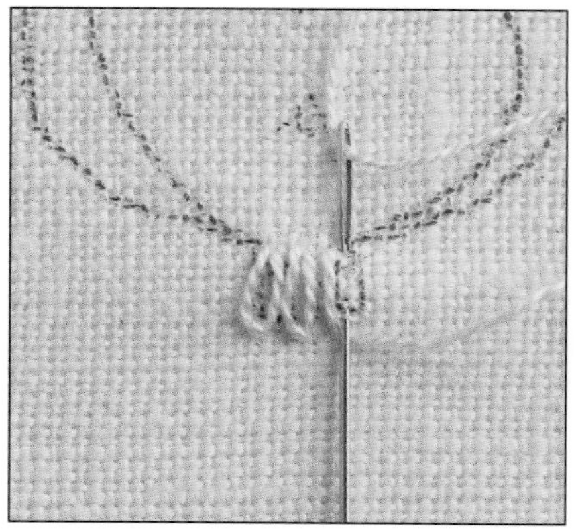

4 For buds, use *lazy daisy stitch*: Bring thread up at narrow end of bud. Insert needle at entry point and bring up at opposite end of bud, keeping thread under needle. Insert needle back into fabric over loop end of stitch. Repeat for 3 stitches.

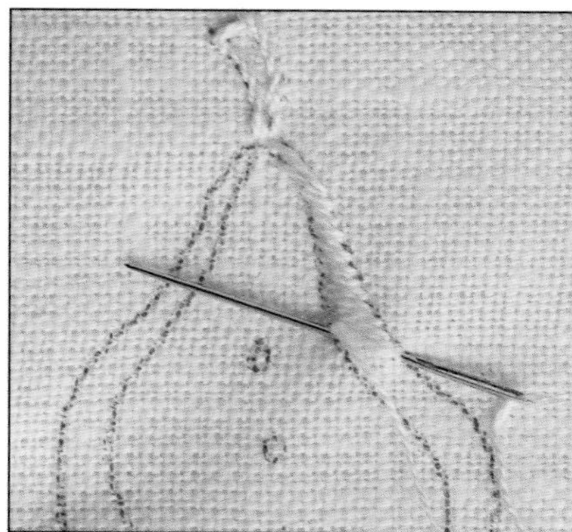

5 Embroider fruit outline with *satin stitch*: Bring needle up through fabric at inner edge of fruit body. Insert needle at opposite, outer edge. Bring needle up next to previous stitch at inner edge. Repeat, forming close parallel stitches.

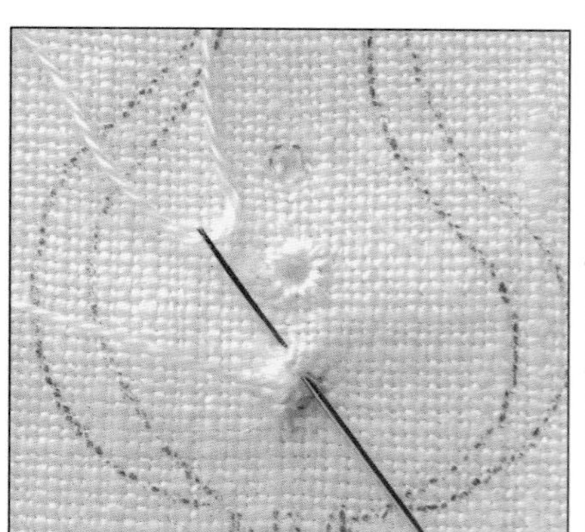

6 Embroider pear seeds with a series of small straight stitches radiating out from center of seed circles. For each radiating stitch, bring needle up in same spot at center of seed to form a hole in center.

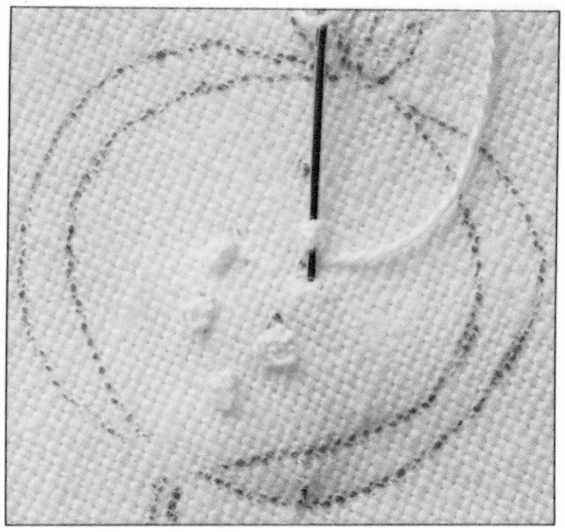

7 Embroider apple seeds with *French knots*: Bring needle up through fabric, wrap thread tightly around needle twice, and insert needle back down into fabric next to entry point. Pull to tighten knot.

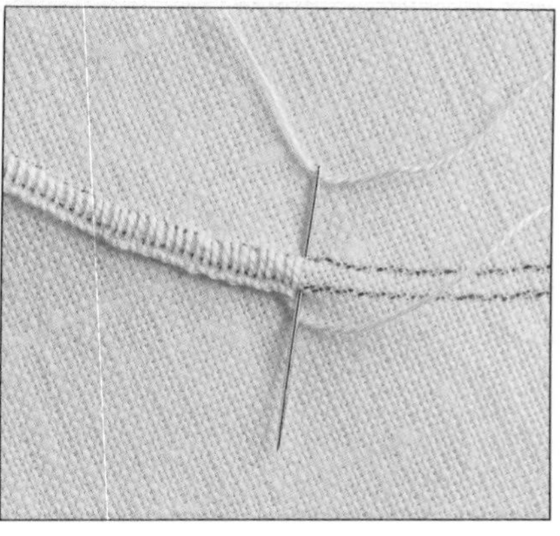

8 Embroider border with *buttonhole stitch*: Working from left to right, bring needle up at outer line, back down at inner line, then back up at outer line, keeping thread loop under needle. Repeat, making stitches close together and parallel.

Crafter's Secrets

Using the same color-on-color embroidery method, save a favorite tablecloth or blouse by satin-stitching a small motif, such as an initial, a flower, or shell, directly over a stain or spot. Match the yarn to the fabric for a discreetly embroidered pattern, or use a contrasting color to show off your needlework.

9 Remove fabric from hoop; trim away excess fabric along outer border line using small but very sharp scissors. Take care to avoid cutting stitches. Wash and press finished piece.

Try This!

Sew a simple white-on-white monogrammed motif on a pillowcase, a sheet, or hand towels for a gift that is certain to become a treasured heirloom. If desired, use colored yarn or thread to match the color scheme of the decor. A delicate heart surrounded by leafy vines, as shown here, is an appropriate motif for almost any occasion.

Making Cards with Embroidery

If you like to take your needlework with you, these little embroidered linen pieces are portable, quick, and easy to do in front of the TV, standing in line at the bank, or waiting to pick the kids up at school. When they're done, trim them and mount them with fabric glue to the front of folded card stock or medium-weight cardboard for a personalized greeting card that is an artistic gift in itself.

For the best effect, select paper, fabric, and yarn or thread in colors that work well together. Make sure the card is large enough to act as a frame for the embroidery and to write a message inside.

These motifs are done in a satin stitch, which can be used on almost any fabric. The stitch can be worked straight or at an angle. If you are embroidering without a hoop, do not pull the stitches too tight or the fabric and the design will pucker.

Brightly colored geometric motifs embroidered on contrasting, colored fabric give these greeting cards a contemporary look. Use the templates provided in Group 12, Card 6, or create your own. Make several cards to have on hand for whenever you need to send a personal note.

1 Cut thin card stock to desired size with craft knife. Mark center of stock on inside for foldline of card and lightly score with back of craft knife. Fold card along scored line, pressing firmly for a sharp crease.

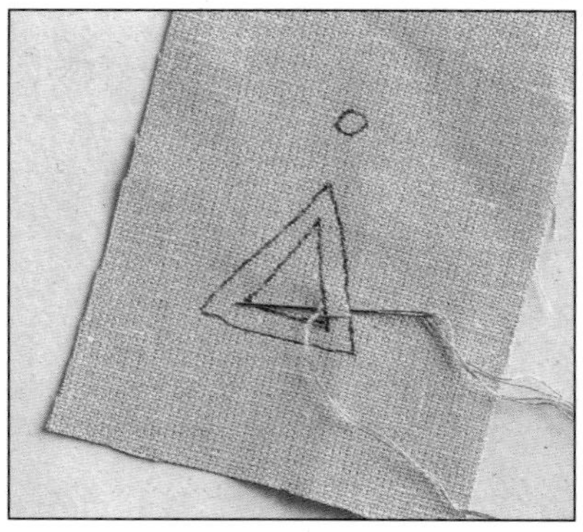

2 Cut colored linen fabric slightly smaller than front of card. Transfer templates from Group 12, Card 6 to fabric using paper and pen. With contrasting-color thread, embroider pattern using satin stitch.

3 Press embroidered piece; trim any loose threads from outside edges of fabric. Coat wrong side of embroidered piece with fabric glue; center on front of card, then smooth in place.

TABLE TOPPERS FOR ALL OCCASIONS

CARD 13

Patterns & Templates

Making Cutwork Table Accessories

Set an elegant table using linen finery trimmed with cutwork stitching. A sewing machine lets you create this delicate Old World hand embroidery technique in a fraction of the time.

The enduring charm of European cutwork is the open and stitched designs that decorate crisp linen fabric, adding a soft sheen and texture. Traditionally a pattern is outlined with hand-sewn button-hole stitches, usually done in white on white, then certain background areas of the design are cut away.

This modern version of the simple lily motif uses contrasting machine stitching, which enables you to create an heirloom floral design in a timely fashion.

Smaller accessories, such as these contemporary coasters and shelf doily, stitch up quickly. Try nontraditional color combinations, such as pastel fabrics with matching stitching or pastel stitching on a white background.

Patterns & Templates *Use the templates from Group 12, Card 24 to render the motifs for all the featured cutwork projects.*

For a true cutwork look, the best fabric to use is even-weave linen or cotton cambric. However, synthetic fabrics can be used and may make caring for the finished piece easier.

Cutwork Guidelines

Before starting a cutwork project, launder the fabric to preshrink, then lightly starch and press it.

- Cut two pieces of water-soluble stabilizer 2" wider than stitching area and fuse together between two presscloths. Place fused layers under fabric when stitching to provide firm base.
- To sew cutwork motif, several machine stitches are used, including straight, zigzag, and satin (formed by stitching with close, medium-width, zigzag stitches).
- In order to achieve raised cutwork motif, an initial line of stitching, called padstitching, is sewn with either straight or narrow zigzag. Then satin stitching is sewn over it.

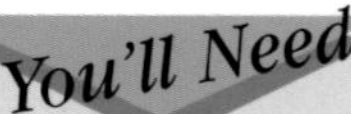

- ***2 yds. 70"-wide handkerchief linen for 54"x54" tablecloth***
- ***1½ yds. water-soluble stabilizer***
- ***Iron & 2 presscloths***
- ***8 spools of gold-colored silk or machine embroidery thread***
- ***Spray starch***
- ***Embroidery scissors***
- ***Water-soluble marking pencil***
- ***7"-diameter spring embroidery hoop***
- ***Sewing machine with embroidery foot***

1 Cut linen to 60" square. Place pattern under fabric and trace tablecloth motif onto each corner, using water-soluble marking pencil and leaving 3" margin at edges. Mark areas to be cut out with small Xs. Trace scallops between corners.

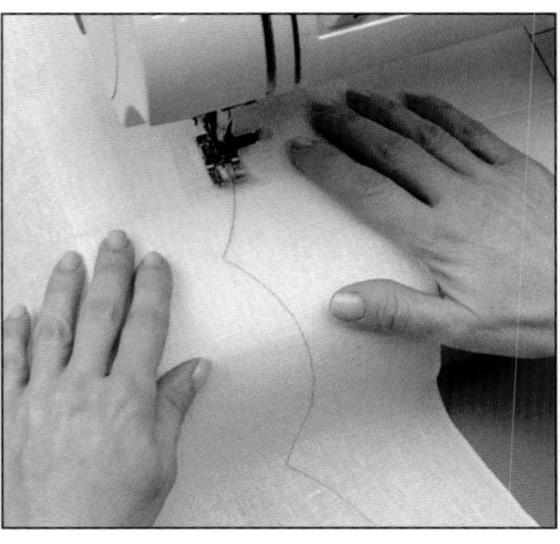

2 With embroidery thread on top and in bobbin of machine, sew over marked scallop lines of borders using short straight stitches (13 stitches per inch); pivot at points. Satin-stitch over straight-stitched scallop lines.

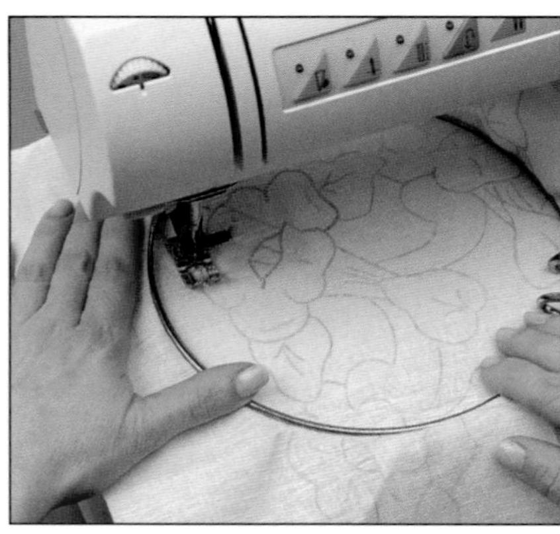

3 Place fused stabilizer under motif of fabric; fit both taut into hoop so fabric is flat against machine bed and design is facing up. Using narrow zigzag, padstitch along all design lines except bar lines running across areas marked to be cut.

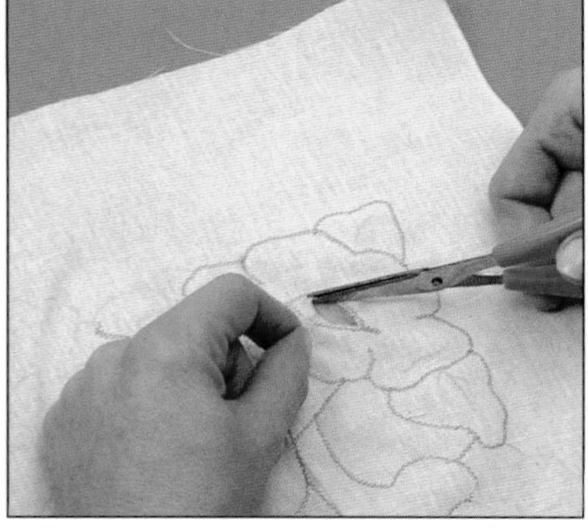

4 Using embroidery scissors, carefully cut away each area of fabric marked with X. Do not cut through stabilizer; leave it in place until stitching is completed. Cut carefully to avoid cutting into stitching.

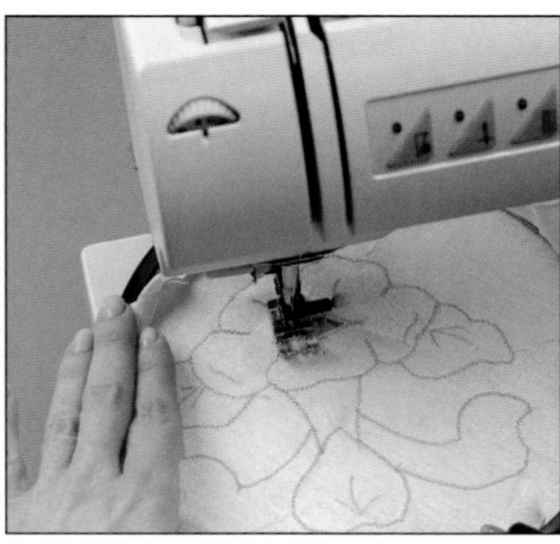

5 On stabilizer, mark position of bars that cross open areas. Using short straight stitches, padstitch over length of each bar with 3 lines of stitching placed right next to each other.

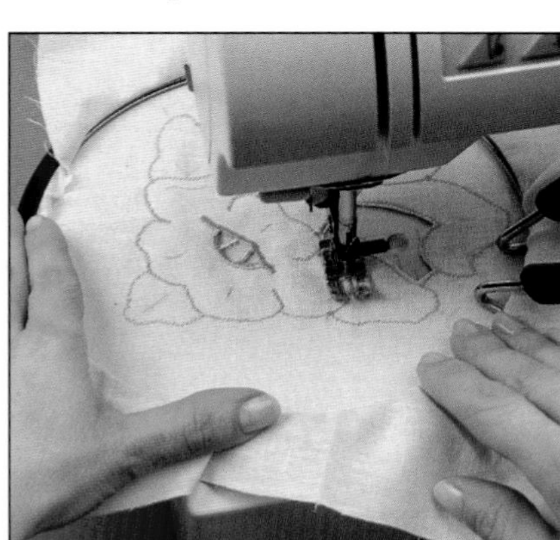

6 Satin-stitch over each bar, covering padstitching. Satin-stitch over zigzagged padstitching lines to create dimensional motif: Stitch bottommost design lines first, then subsequent layers, stitching over ends of bars to secure.

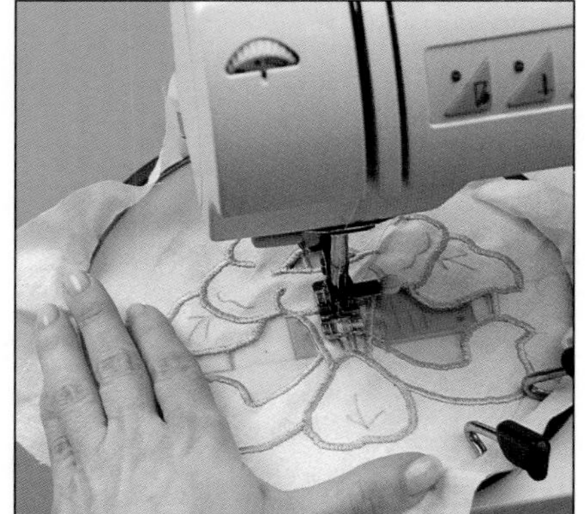

7 Stitch over detail lines with short, straight stitches. Pull thread ends to back and tie off. Trim away excess stabilizer. Soak fabric in cold water 5–15 minutes to remove remaining stabilizer. Trim fabric from scalloped edges.

Crafter's Secrets

Fine embroidered heirloom-quality linens require special care and handling to ensure generations of use. Wash them in warm water with a gentle non-detergent soap recommended for fine linens. Soak any stains and avoid rubbing the fabric together. Dry flat, away from direct sunlight, until just damp, or roll in a towel to remove excess moisture. If desired, starch before ironing. To iron linens while still slightly damp, place face down on a padded surface, such as a folded towel. Using a presscloth, press on the wrong side of the fabric. Store away from direct heat or sunlight. If desired, wrap in acid-free tissue paper, and to avoid creases, store linens rolled around a cardboard tube.

Try This!

Stitch a dainty calla lily design in one corner of an 11"x 14" vanity cloth made from linen or cotton. Finish the edges and remaining corners with satin-stitched scallops. Choose either matching or contrasting thread color to stitch the cutwork design.

Making Cutwork Shapes

Give your ready-made table linens the look of hand cutwork by cutting out individually stitched cutwork shapes and appliquéing them onto napkins, place mats, and tablecloths. With some creative folding and stitching, the shapes can become decorative three-dimensional motifs that can be used on table accessories, such as the informal napkin rings shown here.

This casual approach to cutwork presents lots of options. For example, you can purchase extra napkins to make cutwork cutouts that match, or use contrasting colors or prints. Choose any color embroidery thread that works well with the overall table setting.

Use the graceful fan template provided or make your own pattern. Simple shapes are the best motifs. Be sure to starch the cutout shape, so it will keep its contours when folded.

Create coordinating napkin rings with folded-fan cutwork shapes. Pick 1"-wide grosgrain ribbon to match the stitching and fuse two 5"– 6" lengths of ribbon together. Glue the ends into a ring and glue the cutwork on top.

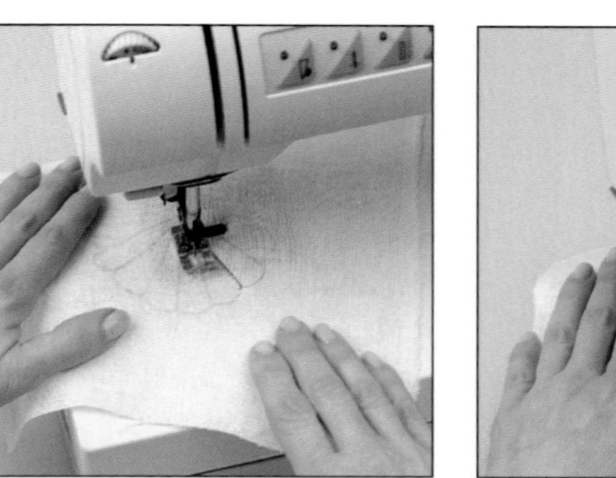

1 Using disappearing fabric marker, outline individual motif onto fabric, leaving 3" margins around design. Use contrasting thread and small straight stitch to padstitch along each line.

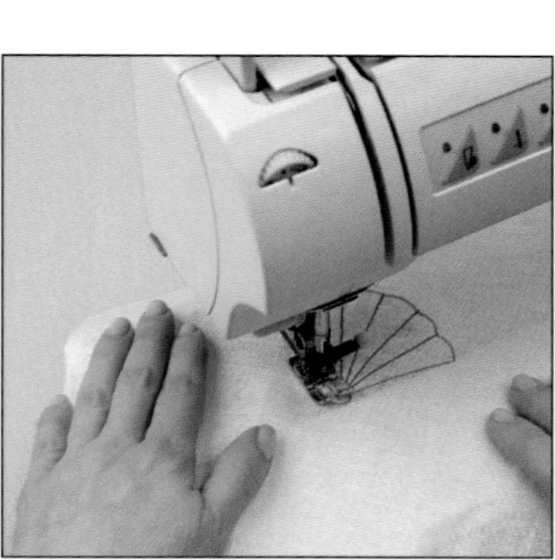

2 Satin-stitch over padstitching along outer edges of design only; pivot at inner corners with needle down for well-defined corners.

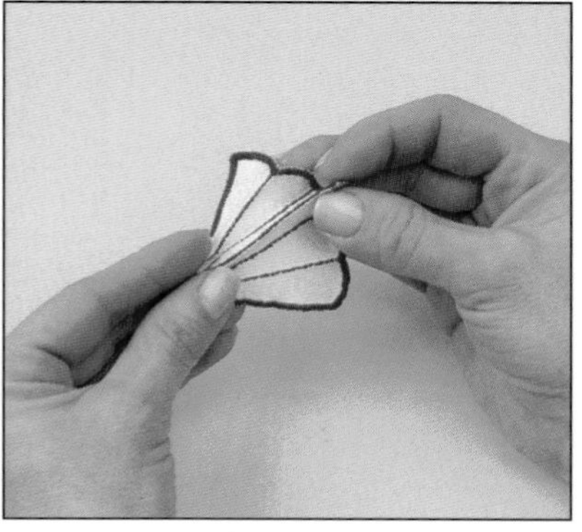

3 Cut out entire shape, without cutting outer satin stitches. Spray starch over cut shape. Fan-fold along stitched inner lines and finger-press to add dimension to shape. Glue fan over ends of ribbon ring with fabric glue.

Making Garlands from Fresh Flowers

Romantic candlelight and fresh flowers turn a graceful candelabra into a lavish floral display befitting the most elegant dinner table.

Bedeck your best silver candelabra in a lush garland and wreath made of carnations, sweet william, sea lavender, lady's mantel, and ferns. Select flowers in colors appropriate to the occasion—all white blossoms for a wedding breakfast or rich red blooms and bright green leaves for a Christmas Eve celebration, for example.

Use cuttings from your own garden if possible. It will save on decorating expenses, make your garden rebloom, and result in a very personal arrangement.

Garlands can grace a table in several ways. Entwined in a candelabra, pansies and asters predominate in an ensemble that features the cool tones of purple. A nosegay of roses anchors a floral swag that drapes around the table.

A candelabra festooned with a wreath of flowers at its base is a perfect centerpiece for an elegant party table. With the profusion of flowers available at all times, you can combine those of the same hue, complementary shades, or a kaleidoscope of colors.

Garland and Wreath Guidelines

Select flowers of approximately same size for balance. Add texture by mixing petal shapes and combining lacy flowers, such as statice, with solid flowers, such as roses.

- To make bouquets, cut stems of flowers for each bouquet to about 2"-3", then wrap with spooled floral wire.
- When attaching flowers to candelabra or to wreath form, wire large or heavy flowers, such as peonies, individually.
- Attach flowers directly to arm of candelabra using spooled wire. Or attach flowers to a vine-shaped wire form and drape over candelabra.

You'll Need

- ***Floral wire: heavy-gauge & spooled***
- ***Green floral tape***
- ***Wire cutters; scissors or pruning shears***

For candelabra:

- ***Flowers and greenery: miniature carnations, sweet william, sea lavender, lady's mantle (flowers & leaves); fern leaves***

For swag:

- ***Flowers & greenery: roses, sweet william, baby's breath, lady's mantle (flowers & leaves); lemon & gaultheria leaves***
- ***Small ball of floral foam***
- ***Spiked floral coupling***

Making a Wreath for a Candelabra Base

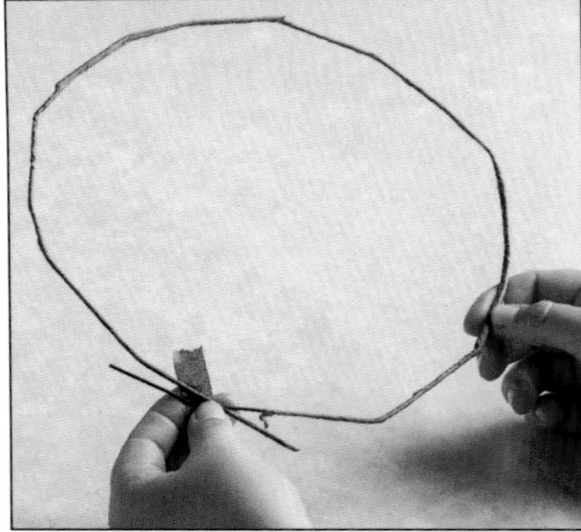

1 From heavy wire, make a ring that will fit around base of candelabra. Clip ends and twist to secure. Beginning at joined ends, wrap floral tape around wire ring, covering it completely.

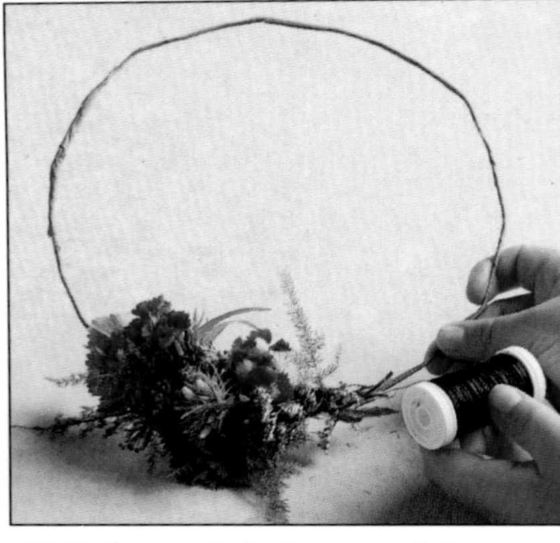

2 Twist spooled wire around ring several times to secure. Place a small bouquet of flowers and leaves against wire ring, just above wrapped ends, and secure by wrapping with spooled wire.

3 Continue to attach bouquets, placing each addition over stems and tight against flower heads of previous bouquet, until entire ring is covered. Place finished wreath around base of candelabra.

Festooning the Candelabra

1 Twist spooled wire several times around arm of candelabra to secure. Attach a small cluster of ferns and sea lavender to arm directly under candle cup; secure with spooled wire.

2 Add more bouquets across front and back of arms, placing each addition over stems and tight against flower heads of previous bunch. Wrap with spooled wire until candelabra arms are covered.

Making a Removable Festoon

Cut a piece of heavy floral wire and bend it around candelabra's arms. Wrap wire with floral tape. Attach bouquets with spooled wire to cover form. Place finished festoon on candelabra.

A garland can take many forms. Here it becomes a grand floral swag, draped around the front of the table. The nosegays of roses and sweet william are arranged on a ball of floral foam that is inserted into a spiked floral coupling. The swags are attached through eyelets on each side of the coupling. The ends of the garland are pinned or stitched to the tablecloth.

Making a Garland Swag

1 Wrap heavy floral wire with floral tape. Twist wire to form loops at ends. Attach to floral coupling with wire. Wire on leaf cluster, baby's breath, and more leaves to fill form.

2 Insert a rose in center of floral foam. Working around rose, add more roses and other flowers to form a tight nosegay. Insert gaultheria leaves to form a collar around nosegay.

Try This!

Decorate each place setting with flowers used in the garlands. For example, tuck a single rose into a rolled napkin so that it peeks out from the folds. Or place a small bouquet tied in ribbon on each plate. Petals strewn across the tablecloth or arranged on a silver platter with the heads of flowers and a swirl of matching ribbons makes the table look even more romantic.

Making a Tabletop Garland

A garland of lush pink, red, purple, and white blooms makes an opulent tabletop arrangement. Peonies and roses, mums and hydrangeas, sweet william and sea lavender form a graceful curve at the center of the table or mark the place setting of very special guests.

Begin by wiring a thick covering of grasses and green leaves onto heavy-gauge floral wire bent into shape. Make the form thicker in the center, tapering to the ends. Add flowers to one half of the garland at a time, working from the middle out to one end. Wire on individual peonies and clusters of large flowers and leaves first, decreasing the size of the clusters as you near the end. Repeat for the other half of the garland. Because the garland will rest on the table, only the top side has to be full and tightly packed with flowers. Finish with lemon leaves and a large satin bow on each end.

1 Cut a piece of heavy floral wire twice garland's length and fold in half to double. Cover wire form with bunches of leaves wrapped with spooled wire; make center of garland thicker than ends.

2 Working half of garland at a time, use spooled wire to attach small premade bouquets of flowers and leaves to form, beginning in center of form and working toward end.

3 Wire on additional bouquets directly under previously attached bunches, keeping large flowers and clusters, like peonies and mums, in center of garland, and smaller clusters of flowers tapering toward end.

4 About 6" from end, begin wiring a shaft of lemon leaves around entire form: Surround form with bunches of leaves, wrap twice with spooled wire; continue adding leaves and wiring, tapering to end.

TABLE TOPPERS FOR ALL OCCASIONS

CARD 17

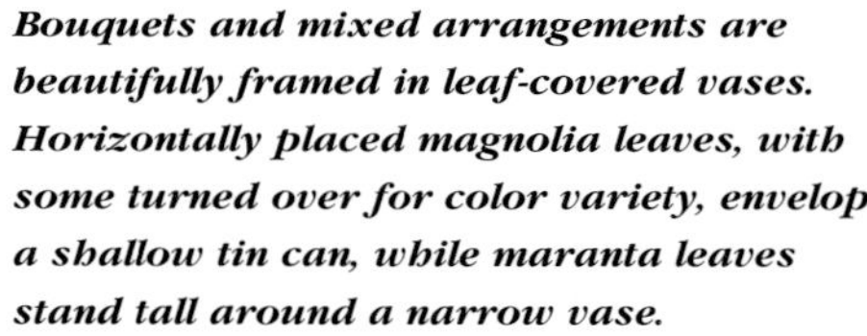

Making Leaf-Covered Pots and Vases

Cover just about any vase, jar, bowl or clay terra-cotta pot with real leaves to create unusual plant and flower containers for the dining table or side bar. It's a simple and unique way to make the ordinary extraordinary.

A leaf-covered vase is easy to make and the technique can be used with most containers. A minimum of equipment and a little imagination are all it takes.

Use common leaves, such as the coltsfoot leaves that were used to cover the flower pot. Or seek out more exotic varieties of leaves at your local flower shop. Then vary the placement of the leaves over the container to create your own little work of art.

Bouquets and mixed arrangements are beautifully framed in leaf-covered vases. Horizontally placed magnolia leaves, with some turned over for color variety, envelop a shallow tin can, while maranta leaves stand tall around a narrow vase.

When covering a pot with leaves, use a container that you don't want to use again, because the leaves are permanently attached. If you don't want the leaves permanently applied, so you can replace them with fresh leaves when they dry out, tie them on with spooled floral wire, then hide the wire with ribbon.

Leaf-Wrapping Guidelines

Select leaves at their prime and cut the stems off at the base of the leaves before beginning the project.

- Make sure leaves are absolutely dry before gluing, but not brittle.
- Use a glue gun to apply leaves to glass or aluminum; for pottery, use craft or wood glues.
- Vary arrangement by placing some leaves with back sides facing out to give a soft, matted look to pot's surface. Distribute leaves evenly over surface or overlap them as desired.
- After gluing leaves to vase, wrap with gauze or cheesecloth strips if you want leaves to set flat over container and not curl when drying.

You'll Need

For Clay Pot:

- ***Coltsfoot leaves***
- ***Clay pot***
- ***Wood glue***
- ***Household sponge***
- ***Scissors or craft knife***
- ***Gauze or cheesecloth & pins***

For Cookie Tin:

- ***Magnolia leaves***
- ***Aluminum cookie tin***
- ***Hot-glue gun, & glue sticks***

For Glass Jar:

- ***Maranta leaves***
- ***Glass jar***
- ***Spooled floral wire***

Gluing Leaves to a Clay Pot

1 Wash and dry a terra-cotta pot. Dip a piece of household sponge into wood glue and apply glue to front side of coltsfoot leaf.

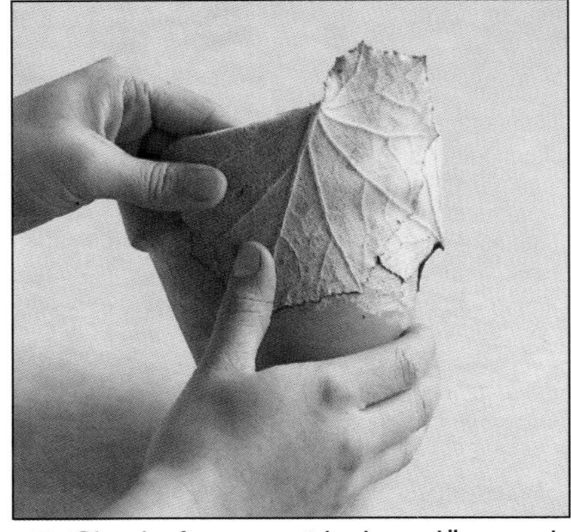

2 Glue leaf to pot with about 1" extending above rim; push gently with thumbs from leaf center outward so leaf lies smoothly. Fold leaf over rim of pot.

3 Continue gluing leaves to pot, overlapping them around rim. Glue a round of leaves to overlap first so pot does not show through. Trim leaves flush with bottom of pot using scissors or knife.

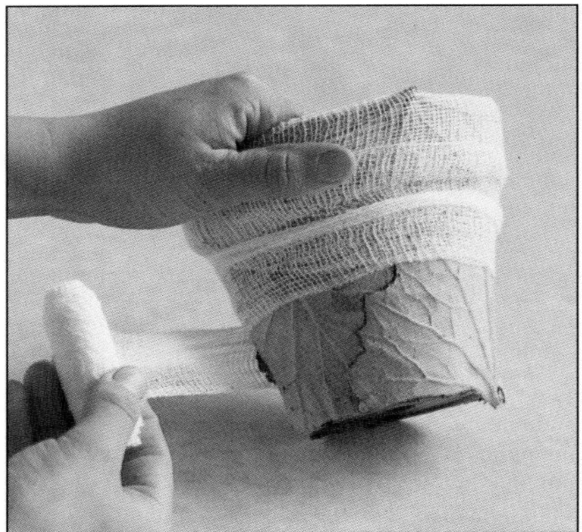

4 Wrap pot tightly with gauze strips and pin to secure. Leave gauze on for 2–3 hours, until glue is set; remove gauze.

Gluing Leaves to a Cookie Tin

1 Using glue gun, glue magnolia leaves horizontally onto can, alternating front and back sides of leaves for an interesting shaded effect. Allow leaves to overlap so none of metal shows.

2 Glue a round of leaves over rim of can, attaching them to both inside and outside of can; push down on leaves gently to help them lie flat.

Tying Leaves to a Glass Jar

1 Wrap spooled wire around jar a few times to anchor. Overlap several maranta leaves vertically around jar, then holding leaves in place, wrap them with wire. Continue, covering jar.

2 When entire jar is covered, place several leaves around jar, overlapping horizontally. Wrap with spooled wire. Cut wire, leaving a 1" long tail.

Crafter's Secrets

It is important to use the right kind of glue when attaching leaves to the container surface. When gluing large or stiff leaves, apply glue directly over the surface of the leaf for better adhesion. For smaller leaves, apply a thin layer of glue over the entire surface of the pot, then attach leaves.

3 Wrap a slender leaf or thick blade of grass around jar to hide wire; overlap ends on top of wire tail. Push tail through leaf ends and bend flat to secure leaf. Fold leaf over to hide tail wire.

Try This!

Besides leaves, many different vegetables can be used to create an exciting foundation for a centerpiece. For example, try using long, colorful hot peppers or freshly cut asparagus. String the vegetables through their centers onto a steel wire and twist the ends of the wire together around the pot. Cover the wire with some decorative twine or raffia.

Enclosing a Bouquet with Stalks

When you can't find the right size vase to make a floral centerpiece, make a "fence" with stalks of vegetables to create an entirely new covering for a jar, vase, or other container.

Stalks of red and green amaranths, rhubarb, celery, tulip stems, or even rose stems—thorns and all—make visually exciting cases for a vase. Select stalks of about the same thickness and trim them to a uniform length before stringing so the finished container will stand straight and steady.

The "fence" can be made thick or thin, tall or short, depending on the stalks used and the look desired. Make sure that the stalks are bound tightly. For a finishing touch, tie a ribbon or piece of twine around the casing.

Stalks of red and green amaranths form an unusual enclosure that frames a bouquet of pink dahlias in a plain glass vase. Vases decorated with stalks make uncommon table arrangements and also make beautiful gifts.

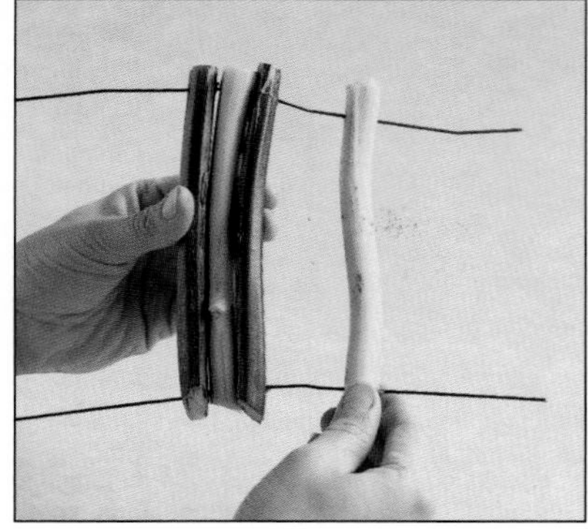

1 Cut stalks to a uniform length that is about 2" taller than vase or jar. Cut 2 lengths of heavy-gauge wire to reach around the vase plus 2". Push wires through stalks about 1" from top and bottom.

2 Continue threading stalks onto wires until vase is completely surrounded. Twist wire ends together to secure "fence" in place.

3 Tie a piece of twine around stalk "fence" to make sure that stalks do not shift out of position and to add a final decorative touch to vase.

Fun & Easy Gifts

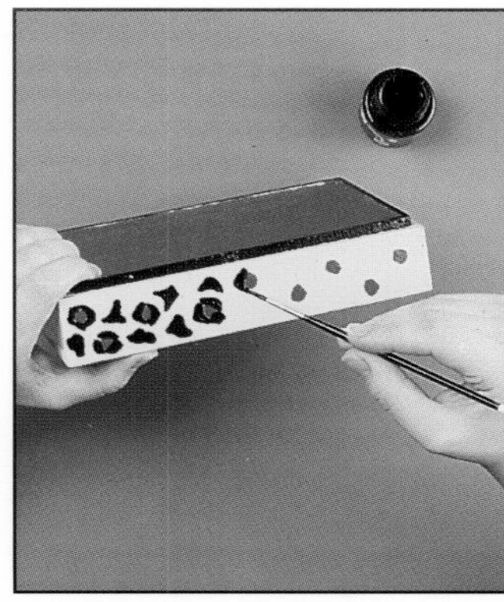

Simple-to-make presents for family and friends

2

FUN & EASY GIFTS

CARD 1

Creating No-Sew Scented Sachets

Tuck a personal sachet into a drawer, closet, or suitcase to evoke the fresh scent of a pine forest or the sweetness of a rose garden.

These simple no-sew sachets can be created in minutes using fusible web and a glue gun. Select fabrics and potpourri scents that enhance one another and complement your decor. For example, a woodsy plaid is ideal for a pine-scented sachet, while an elegant embroidered fabric is perfect for a feminine, floral sachet. Just be sure the weave of the fabric is loose enough to fringe.

Pick decorations, such as pinecones and flowers, that reflect the bouquet of the potpourri. Ribbons, charms, and shells can lend additional finishing touches.

For a Victorian sachet roll, use a rectangular vintage doily and fuse it to a bit of fabric. Follow steps 1–4 to create the roll, but without fringes. Weave ribbons through the lace to gather roll ends, then attach charms. To form a tiny hanging sachet pillow, fuse two Battenburg lace doilies together and trim with silk flowers and dainty pearls.

Fragrant sachets that are plump with potpourri can be made in a jiffy without taking a single stitch. Fusible web is the secret. When used with the heat of an iron, the web permanently bonds fabric to fabric in seconds. Available by the piece or as tape, the web comes in several weights. Be sure to follow each manufacturer's instructions.

A second no-sew shortcut is to fringe, rather than to hem the fabric edges. To create the fringe, use a pin to remove the horizontal threads of the fabric one at a time.

Lace-Dying Technique

The Battenburg doilies used for the pictured sachet were tea-dyed for an antique look.

- Simply soak doily in a cup of strong tea until desired depth of color is achieved.
- Rinse in clear, cold water. Dry, then press doily before making sachet.

You'll Need

For Sachet Roll:

- ***12"x13" fabric***
- ***½ yd. ¾" fusible web (heavy-duty)***
- ***Potpourri***
- ***2 rubber bands***
- ***Ties: 1 yd. leather shoelace or 6 yds. natural raffia***
- ***Trims: 2 sprigs treated pine, 4 small pinecones, or 10 dried roses***
- ***Glue gun & sticks***

For Battenburg Sachet:

- ***2 (4"-square) Battenburg doilies***
- ***3 small silk flowers with leaves***
- ***8"x10" piece fusible web***
- ***½ yd. ⅜" fusible web***
- ***Potpourri***
- ***½ yd. 4mm pearls***
- ***½ yd. ⅛" silk ribbon***
- ***Jewel craft glue***

SACHET ROLL

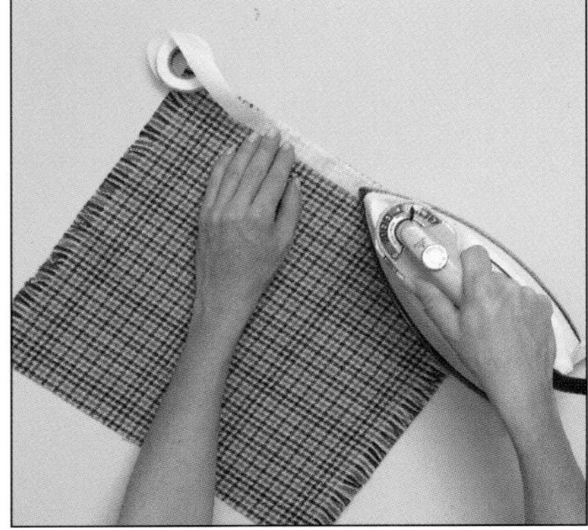

1 Remove horizontal threads at each short end of fabric piece to make a ½"-deep fringe. Fuse strip of fusible web to right side of 1 long fabric edge.

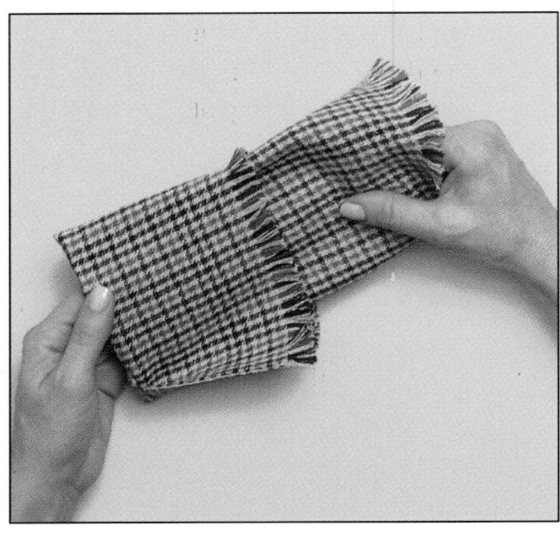

2 With right sides together, fold fabric in half, matching long edges. Press to fuse 2 long edges together. Let cool and turn roll right side out. Gather roll tightly 3" from 1 end; secure with rubber band.

3 Fill roll with potpourri up to 3" from opening. Gather open end and secure as before. Cut 4 (9") lengths of leather ties or 6 (1 yd.) lengths of raffia.

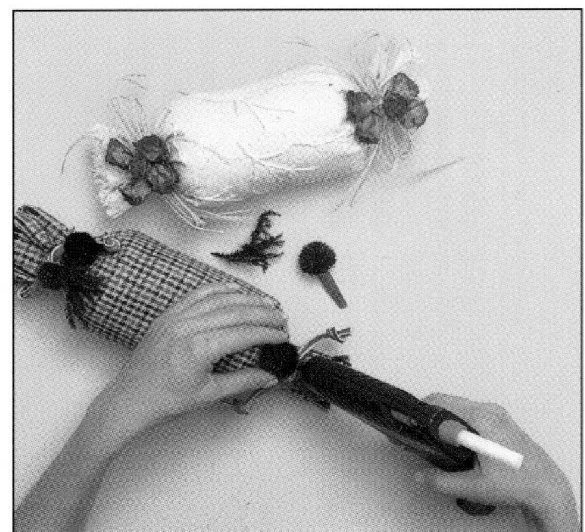

4 Tie each end with set of 2 leather ties; knot ends. Or tie each end with set of 3 raffia lengths; form bows; trim ends. Hot-glue pinecones and sprigs over leather ties, or dried roses over raffia.

BATTENBURG SACHET

1 Fuse web to wrong side of flowers and leaves. Arrange them over right side of 1 doily; fuse in place. Fuse tape to wrong side of borders on second doily. Wrong sides facing, fuse doilies together on 3 sides.

2 Fill with potpourri. Fuse last side together. Glue 6 pearls to centers of flowers. Glue pearls along border. Cut 6"-length ribbon; loop and glue to 1 corner of sachet. Make bow and glue to loop corner.

For further information: Crafting & Decorating Made Simple™ International Masters Publishers, 444 Liberty Ave., Pittsburgh, PA 15222-1207 1-800-527-5576

Making Traditional Nosegays

Re-create romantic floral fancies with these charming little bouquets that evoke the gentility of the 18th and 19th centuries.

These small, hand-held bouquets were carefully created with flowers of contrasting colors and varied shapes arranged in rows of concentric circles, worked out from and around a center bloom.

Today, they are just as appealing displayed in vases, given as tokens of friendship, or carried proudly down the aisle.

Select flowers that blend well in size and color, such as tea roses, miniature carnations, ranunculi, and hydrangea blossoms. Larger flowers will result in a more dramatic composition.

These variations on the basic theme include rounds of leaves as well as flowers. While still arranged in a circle, the flowers are added in bunches rather than individually, giving the nosegay a more informal, less structured look.

The secret to creating a perfect nosegay is to select the right flowers that will complement each other in color and shape.

General Guidelines

The flowers selected for a nosegay should have blooms of approximately the same size.

- Avoid mixing small and delicate flowers, such as primroses, violets, sweet peas and lavender, with larger flowers, such as roses and carnations.
- Condition flowers before starting nosegay by soaking them in cold water right up to base of calyx for several hours.
- Strip all leaves from flower stems with sharp knife to make assemblage easier and to enable flower heads to be bundled more tightly.
- A finishing row of large green leaves provides nice contrast and helps to keep flower heads in place.
- To make everlasting nosegays, follow same directions using silk or dried flowers.

You'll Need

- ***Flowers: grape hyacinths, roses, miniature carnations, & ligularia leaves***
- ***Raffia***
- ***Sharp knife (to strip leaves)***
- ***Pruning shears or scissors***

1 Hold 1 stem of grape hyacinth just beneath bloom. Cluster 2 more stems, 1 in front and other in back of center stem, to form core of bouquet.

2 Continue to add more hyacinth stems, alternately placing each stem in front and back of first 3 clustered stems, to form compact and circular-shaped central cluster.

3 Add individual rose blooms around half of bouquet's center to begin first ring of contrasting flowers. Maintain firm hold on stems already clustered to keep flower heads in tight bunch.

4 Place more roses around other half of bouquet's center to complete tight ring of blooms around center stems. Use length of raffia to secure gathered stems in place.

5 Add miniature carnations to form next ring of tight blooms around bouquet. Maintain round shape by turning bouquet as flowers are added. Tie carnation stems in place.

6 Add another ring of roses around last ring of flowers. Note how colors and different-shaped flowers form bouquet's special style of concentric rings.

7 Add another ring of grape hyacinths to bouquet, placing them as close together as possible with blooms laid almost horizontally out from edge of bouquet.

8 Finally, add ring of ligularia leaves or some other type of large green leaves. Place leaves tightly up against last ring of grape hyacinths, so blooms of nosegay are forced upright and kept in place.

Try This!

To present the nosegay as a gift, wrap it in a sheet of clear cellophane. Cover the bouquet loosely and gather the cellophane under the flower heads, tying it around the stems with raffia or string. Cut a 2 yd. length of 1" wide double-faced satin ribbon. Center it over the raffia and wrap it around a few times to cover. Twist the ribbon steamers around on themselves and tie them into a bow over the cellophane at the top of the nosegay. Trim ends as desired.

9 Tie nosegay stems together with raffia at base of blooms, wrapping it several times around all stems. Knot raffia securely to keep nosegay compact.

10 Trim ends of all stems to about 4" long. Select vase or pitcher to hold nosegay. Fill with warm water and add some sugar or fresh-flower preservative to lengthen life of bouquet.

Crafter's Secrets

When selecting roses for an old-fashioned nosegay, choose open blooms rather than buds, so that the look of the finished bouquet will be maintained. Since the flowers are held tightly together, the petals will stay in place and not droop. Long-lasting flowers, such as roses, carnations, and ranunculi, will look fresh for up to 2 weeks.

Making a Romantic Sectioned Bouquet

Roses, ranunculi, freesias, and asters are combined in related shades of pink and red to form this lush composition. Each flower type is gathered into little bunches, surrounded by large green leaves, then added to the bouquet one group at a time. The contrast of leaves and flowers creates undulating lines, almost like ruffles, and results in an arrangement that is less traditional than that of the formal concentric circles and the dramatically contrasting purple hyacinths and orange tones in the nosegay featured in Group 2, Card 2.

Frame the nosegay in a ruff made from two rectangular place-mat-size doilies (about 12"x16"). Gather the long width of each doily together with your fingers, a little above the center. Place one doily on either side of the nosegay, with the shorter ruffled ends on top. Tie them securely with a length of raffia, and fold the top ruffle down over the bottom one, forming a double tier of lace edging.

1 Strip leaves from all flower stems. Hold 1 rose stem just beneath bloom. Put second stem in front and third stem in back of first stem. Continue with 2 galax leaves, alternating them front and back as with blooms.

2 Create balanced bouquet by placing groups of flowers diagonally against each other as each new group is added. Use leaves to separate flowers into an alternating pattern of different groups.

3 Build bouquet by turning cluster as you add more flower groups. Keep flowers grouped tightly together and maintain rounded shape. The green leaves will set off blended colors of flower groups.

Patterns & Templates

Dressing Up Hangers and Towels

It's the little extra touches that make life so special. Perfect for gift-giving, these lovely covered hangers and smart monogrammed towels turn the mundane into something beautiful.

Hand-gathered ribbons slipped over a padded dress or coat hanger create a dressed-up finish for a commonplace object. The ribbon coverings stitch up quickly, making these hangers ideal gifts or projects for fund-raising bazaars.

Personalizing bath linens with monograms formed with bias tape adds a sophisticated look to plain towels. Bias tape is easily maneuvered around curves, which makes creating the letters a cinch. Zigzag stitching anchors them in place.

Plain wooden coat hangers get an instant makeover with fused plaid fabric and matching ribbon and braid trim. For a personalized bath set, apply a single monogrammed letter to the hand towel.

Patterns & Templates *Use the alphabet templates from Group 12, Card 7 for monogramming. The template letters provided are for a small hand towel. If desired, design a unique monogram by enlarging or reducing selected letters.*

Everybody loves receiving gifts that are especially made for them. These monogrammmed towels and boudoir hangers are no exception.

Tips for Covering Hangers

Select ribbons, fabric, and tape in colors or patterns appropriate to the taste of the receiver.

- Wrap batting around hanger about five times for padding.
- Choose soft ribbon, such as satin or silk, for gathering.

Tips for Monogramming

Use double-fold bias tape, which is easy to shape and doesn't require finishing of raw edges.

- Use contrasting thread to highlight monogram. Ribbon can be used for straight letters.
- Try using fabric glue to hold letter in place before stitching.

You'll Need

For padded hanger:

- ***Ribbons: 2 yds. 2¼"-wide for arm of hanger; 1 yd. ⅝"-wide for hook***
- ***2 (8") batting squares***
- ***Wooden dress hanger***
- ***Tape measure & scissors***
- ***Hand-sewing needle & sewing threads***

For monogrammed towel:

- ***Hand or bath towel***
- ***1 pkg. double-fold bias tape***
- ***Graphite paper, white paper, & pencil***
- ***Transparent tape***
- ***Iron & ironing board***
- ***Sewing machine & contrasting sewing threads***

Making Padded Hangers

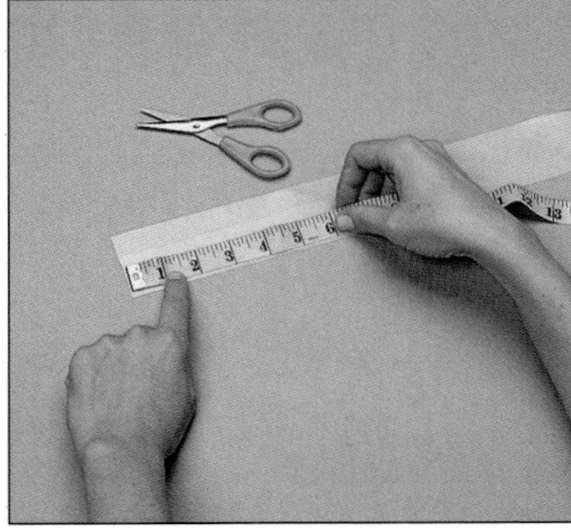

1 Measure wooden section of hanger from base of hook to 1 end of hanger. Multiply this measurement by 4 and cut 2 pieces of 2¼"-wide ribbon to this final measurement.

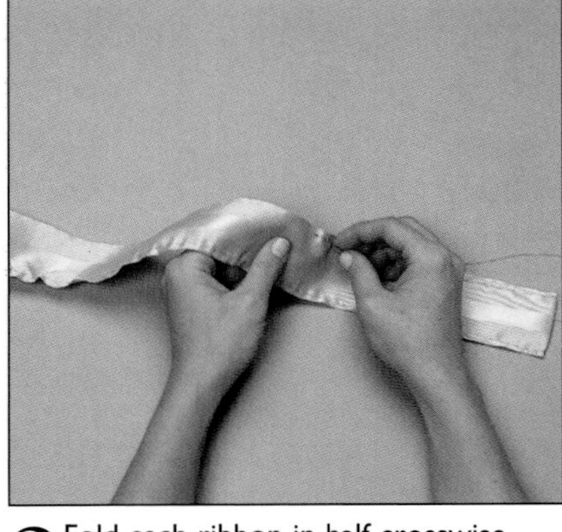

2 Fold each ribbon in half crosswise. Starting at folded end, hand sew a line of ⅛" running stitches through layers of ribbon about ⅛" from long edges to create a "sleeve" for each hanger "arm."

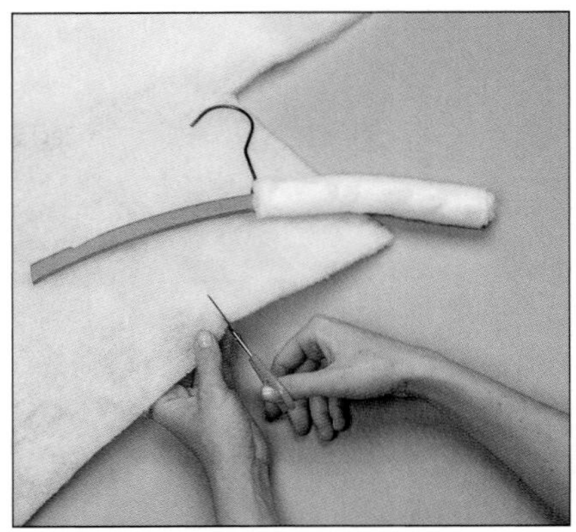

3 Tightly wrap 1 (8") square of batting around each hanger arm, extending batting slightly beyond end of wood. Secure edge of batting with basting stitches.

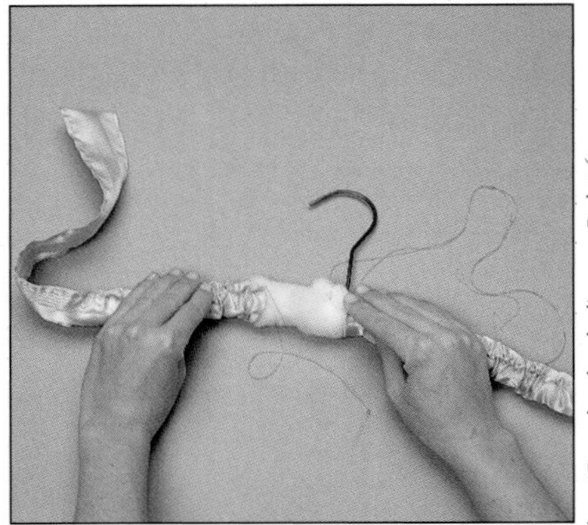

4 Slide a ribbon sleeve over each end of padded hanger. Pull sleeve on with sewn edges of ribbon along center front and back of arm, gathering ribbon and ending at center of hanger.

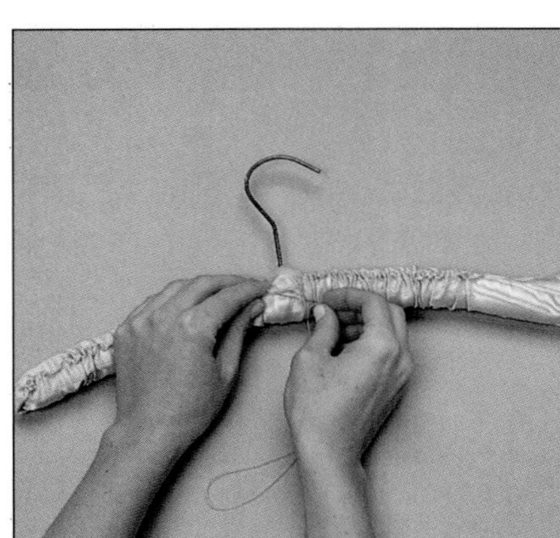

5 Tuck under ¼" along raw edge of each ribbon sleeve. Slipstitch folded edges together at center of hanger, catching stitches to batting to secure ribbon on hanger.

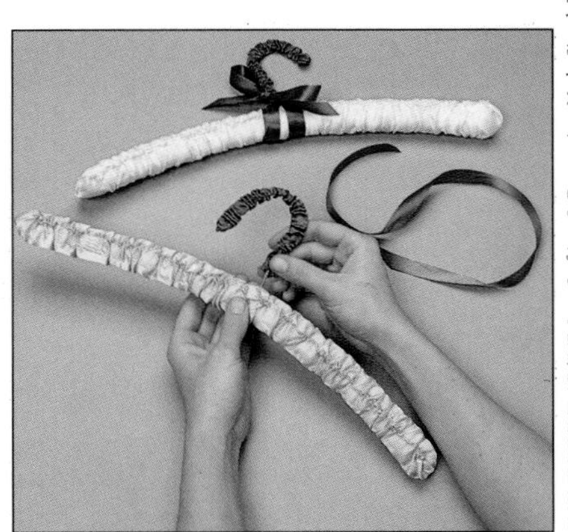

6 Measure entire length of hanger hook; multiply by 4; cut 1 length of ⅝"-wide ribbon to final measurement. Fold ribbon in half and sew along edges. Slide onto hook, gathering to fit. Tack end to arm of hanger. Tie bow at hook base.

Monogramming Towels

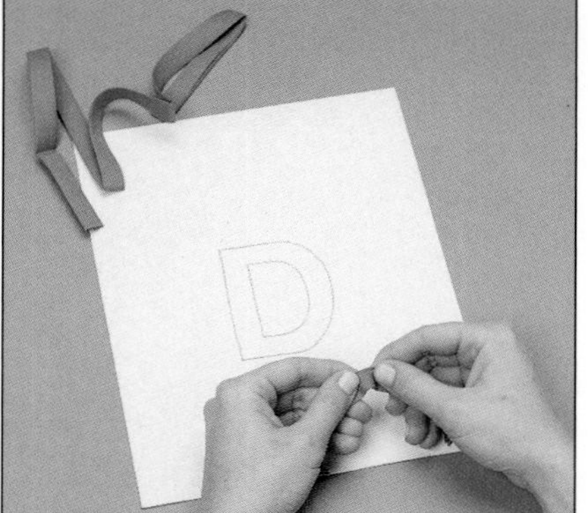

1 Trace letter outlines. Cut bias tape to form letter over outline. Steam-iron pieces to fit curves, stretching tape as needed. Cut straight pieces to overlap curved ends at corners; pin. Trim ends.

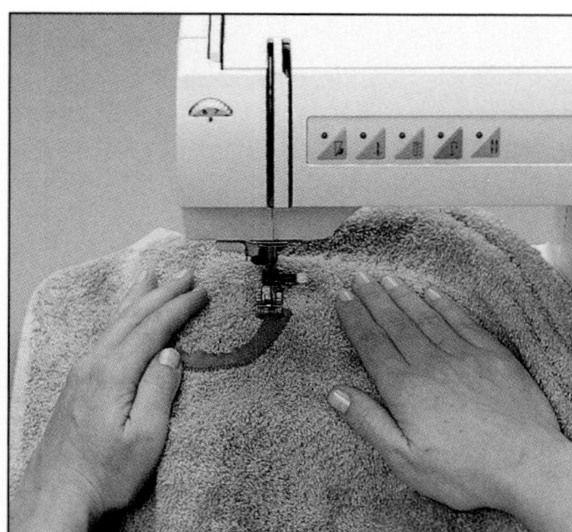

2 Remove bias-tape letter from outline; reassemble and pin letters to towel, centering them about 6"-8" from bottom of towel. Sew edges of tape pieces using medium zigzag or machine satin stitch.

Crafter's Secrets

When working curved letters, shape bias tape into curves by steaming. Place iron on one end of tape and shape it by pulling and turning the tape, then applying steam. If you intend to zigzag over edges there is no need to finish the ends. If desired, finish by edgestitching or satin stitching.

Monograms can be made from various braided trims, as long as they can be easily curved. Draw a freehand script letter with chalk or disappearing fabric marker onto towel. Pin or use fabric glue to hold braid in place. Hand stitch in place with matching thread, then whipstitch over top with ⅛"-wide silk embroidery ribbon. Use liquid fray preventer on ends to avoid unraveling.

Covering Hangers with Fabric

Wooden hangers covered with bias-cut fabric in a rich print, plaid, or paisley make a great gift for a male friend. Give a pair—one for slacks and one for a jacket—as a matched set.

The trick to covering the hangers is to fuse heavyweight paper-backed fusible web to bias-cut fabric, then fuse the fabric to the wooden surface of the hanger. The fabric can also be applied to the hanger with fabric glue.

To find the true bias on your fabric, fold the fabric diagonally so selvage and cut edge are even. Mark the diagonal to give the true bias. Plaid fabric makes this step easier because the fabric pattern will guide you.

To reduce bulk after fusing the fabric to the hanger, trim corners before turning the ¼" seam allowance to the sides. Use fabric glue to apply braid or grosgrain ribbon. Apply liquid fray preventer to the ends of the decorative braid.

Wooden coat hangers get a total makeover with fabric covers. These are easy to finish and require almost no sewing. Paper-backed fusible web is the secret to fast construction, and glued-on trims add the finish.

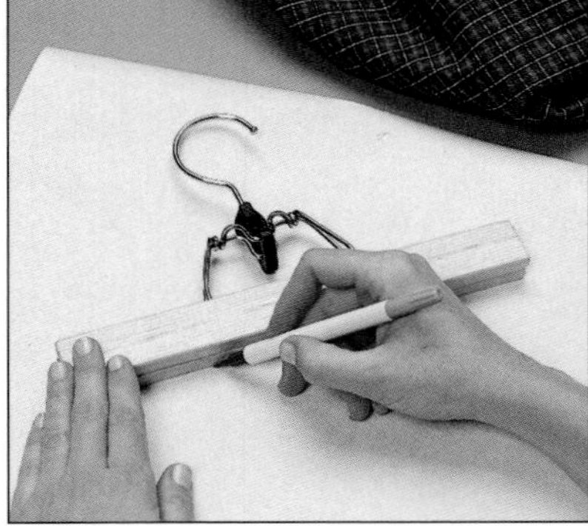

1 Lay hanger on paper side of fusible web. Using marking pen, outline entire shape of wooden section of hanger. Add extra ¼" along all edges and cut out web. Repeat for a total of 2 web cutouts.

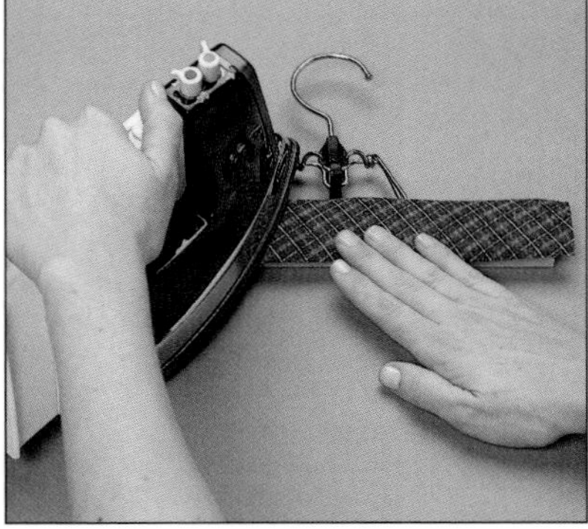

2 Place pattern on bias, on wrong side of fabric, and fuse. Cut out fused piece, peel off paper, and place, fusible side down, on flat surface of hanger, ¼" extending at edges; fuse. Repeat for other side of hanger.

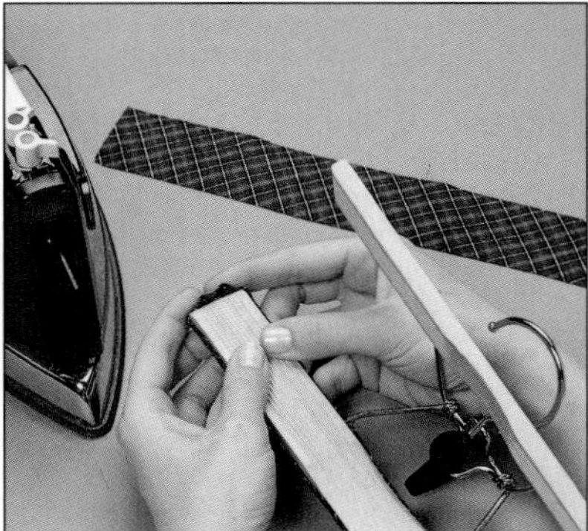

3 Fold and fuse ¼" edges around to sides of hanger, clipping curves and trimming corners as needed for tight fit. Use fabric glue to attach decorative braid along edges of hanger to cover edges of fused fabric.

Making Padded Photo-Album Covers

Patterns & Templates

Keep memories of special events in a photo album with its own theme cover, decorated with fabric and trims that let you know at a glance the people and occasion commemorated inside.

For a gift that will be cherished by a new bride and groom, choose elegant moiré, brocade, or satin for the album cover, and trim it with appliqués of church bells cushioned with soft fleece underneath.

Start with a new photo album of desired size, then cover it with fabric and decorations appropriate to the person or event. You can even give new life to a tattered school binder by dressing it up with motifs of local sports teams and their mascots.

Pad the front of baby's first photo album and decorate with fused or glued velvet and felt animal appliqués. Cover a looseleaf binder with a distinctive animal print for a special teenager and add an inside pocket as shown in Group 2, Card 7.

Patterns & Templates *Use the templates provided from Group 12, Card 9 to make patterns for embellishing the wedding and baby albums. Enlarge or reduce them on a photocopy machine as desired.*

Simple, quick cut-and-paste techniques are used to produce these distinctive albums. Or use fusible web and fleece to iron fabrics to the covers.

Guidelines for Covering Albums
Iron fabric before applying to prevent bubbles or puckering after being glued or fused.

- If gluing, select craft glue that dries clear. Apply in thin, even coat with flat artist brush.
- If using fusibles, choose fabrics and trims that can withstand heat needed to melt glue.

- ***11"x12" photo album***
- ***Iron, scissors, ruler, permanent marker, & tracing paper***
- ***½ yd. fleece or batting***
- ***Lightweight cardboard: 2 (11"x12") pieces & 2 (7"x10") pieces***

For Wedding Album:

- ***Fabric: 1 yd. cream moiré & ¼ yd. textured pale pink fabric***
- ***2 yds. ⅞" sheer ribbon***
- ***2 (⅝"-diameter) half pearls & (¾"-diameter) gold-painted wood disks for bell clappers***
- ***White craft glue & flat brush***

For Pocket:

- ***10½"x9¾" fusible fleece***
- ***12"x12" fabric***
- ***1 yd. fusible tape***
- ***1 yd. piping***

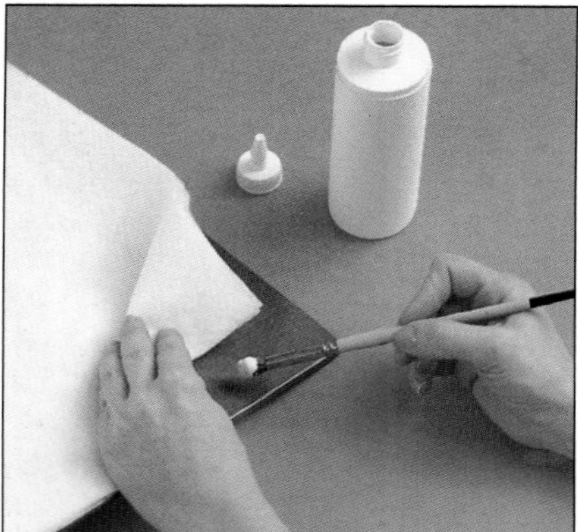

1 Place opened album on fleece and outline cover; add 1" at each end; cut along outline. Glue fleece to cover along spine; close cover to check fit, then glue to front and to back. Trim excess fleece.

2 Cut piece of moiré 2" larger all around than album cover. Glue wrong side of fabric to fleece checking fit as before. Fold and glue fabric edges to inside of cover, trimming as needed.

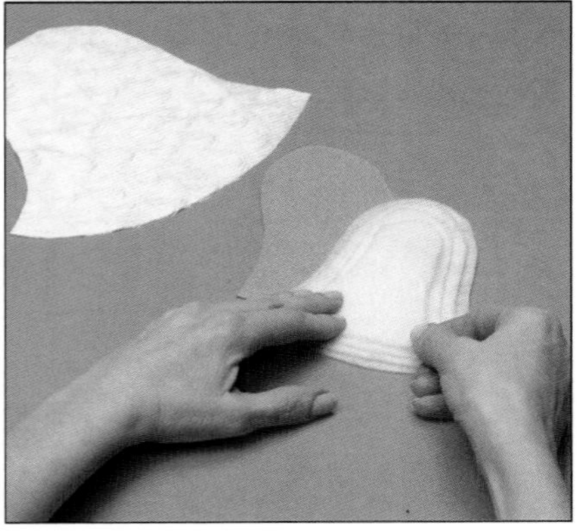

3 Trace template bells; outline on 7"x10" cardboard; cut 2 bells in each size. For each bell, cut 3 bells from fleece in decreasing sizes. Stack and glue fleece, in decreasing sizes, onto cardboard. Cut 1 appliqué for each bell 1" larger all around.

4 Place cardboard bell, fleece side down, onto wrong side of fabric bell. Firmly pull fabric edges around to back and glue in place, clipping fabric along curves so edges lie flat.

5 Cut 2 cardboard pieces 3/16" smaller than cover on all sides. Cut 2 pieces of moiré 1" larger. Glue cardboard to center of wrong side of fabric. Glue fabric to back. Glue linings to inside covers, inserting 2 (18") ribbon ties at center edge of album.

6 Center and glue 1 small bell on each large bell; glue bells on cover as shown on front of card. Glue a pearl in center of each painted disk, then glue onto each bell for clapper. Tie 2 ribbon bows and glue at top of each bell.

Adding Inside Pockets to Animal-Print Album

1 Place fusible fleece on wrong side of pocket piece so 1½" fabric extends at top and ¾" extends at bottom and sides; fuse. Fold and fuse side, bottom, and top hems, mitering corners.

2 Fold and press ¾"-deep pleat along each side of pocket. Unfold pleats. To eliminate bulk at bottom corners, cut away hemmed sections of pleated areas.

3 Refold pleats; fold up bottom hem and fuse. Iron fusible tape to piping; fuse piping around pocket on wrong side, extending it about ¼" beyond edges. Fuse pocket to inside cover on 3 sides.

Crafter's Secrets

Protect the outer surfaces of binders that are handled a lot, such as recipe albums and school looseleafs, with fusible vinyl. Available at craft shops and sewing centers, fusible vinyl is applied to the right side of a fabric, and is particularly useful for corners and edges, which wear easily.

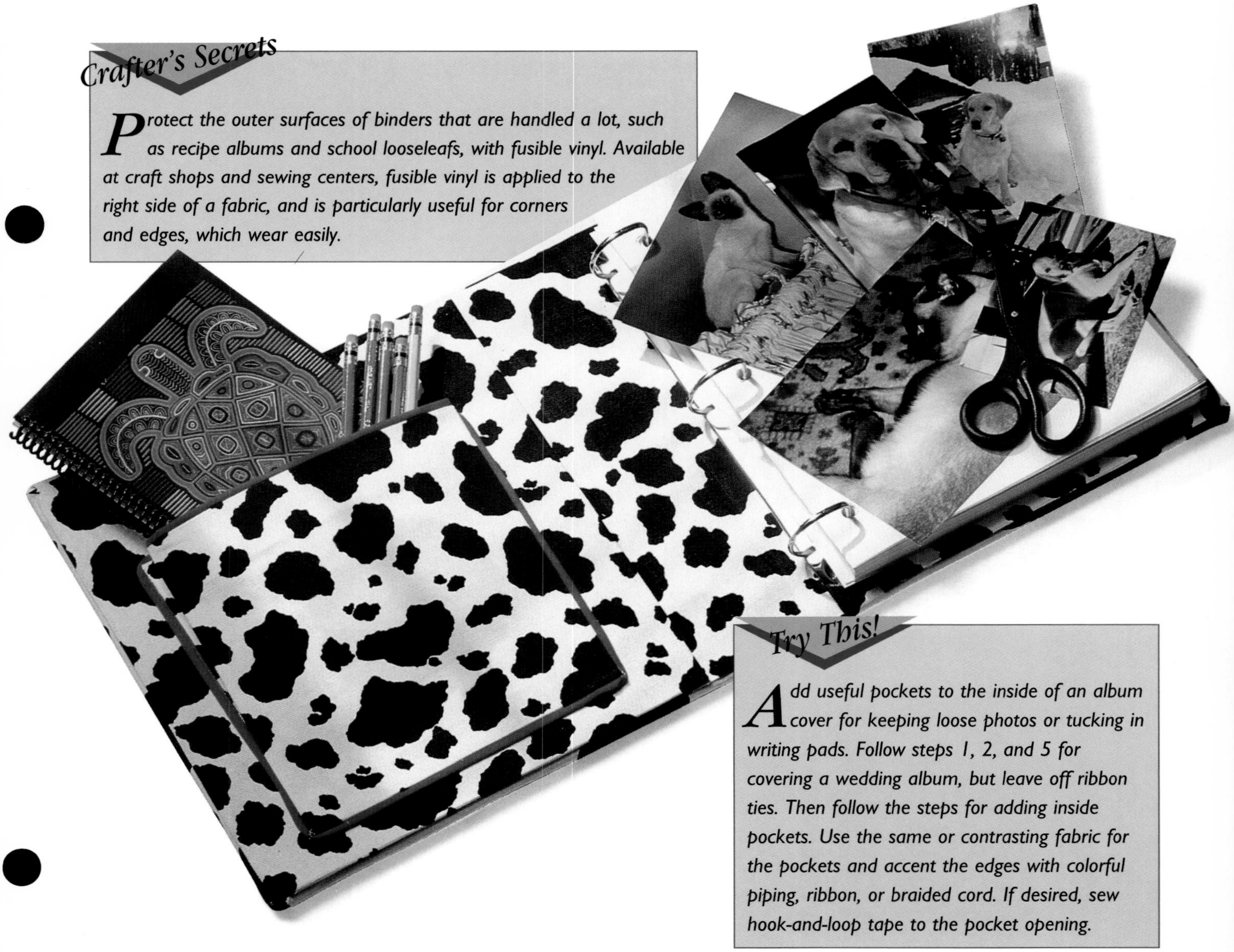

Try This!

Add useful pockets to the inside of an album cover for keeping loose photos or tucking in writing pads. Follow steps 1, 2, and 5 for covering a wedding album, but leave off ribbon ties. Then follow the steps for adding inside pockets. Use the same or contrasting fabric for the pockets and accent the edges with colorful piping, ribbon, or braided cord. If desired, sew hook-and-loop tape to the pocket opening.

Covering an Oversized Album

A grand coffee-table album covered in a rich fabric is an elegant way to show off your largest photographs, portfolio art pieces, or even event programs. Look for large-size binders at office or art supply stores, where you can also find the insert pages.

Choose large prints or patterns to coordinate the album cover with the decor of your room. Heavier-weight decorating fabrics, such as brocade, velvet, tapestry, and damask, are excellent choices.

If using a print with a large motif, such as the brocade covering the photo album at right, be sure to center the motif on the cover. Opulent trims, such as silk or satin braided cord, are suitable finishes. Use heavy-duty fusibles with these heavier fabrics and several layers of fleece for added plushness.

The tone-on-tone design of the regal-looking brocade covering this oversized album provides a dramatic focus for the coffee table. The matching upholstery cording trim adds yet another sumptuous note.

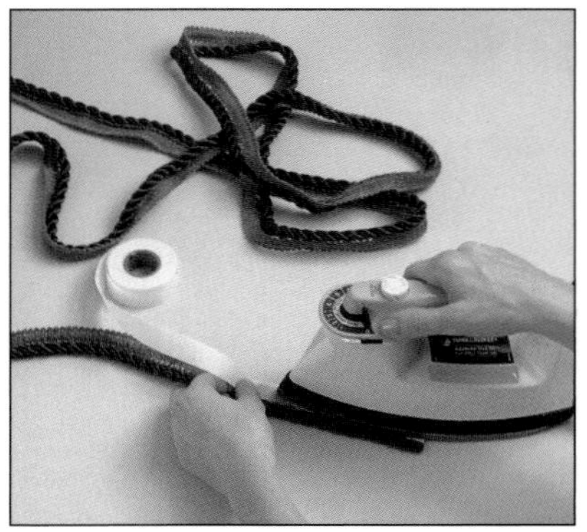

1 Iron heavy-duty fusible tape to 1 side of flange on decorative upholstery cording.

2 Iron several layers of fusible fleece to album front, then cover with brocade fabric, following directions for wedding album. Peel off paper from fusible web on cording and fuse cording along inside edges of entire cover.

3 Cut 2 cardboard pieces to fit inside album covers. Cover cardboard pieces with brocade to make inside linings. Hot-glue linings in place over cording edges.

Making Teddy Bears with Pile Fabric

Patterns & Templates

Teddy bears, in all their different forms, are loved the world over. Make a family of soft and cuddly bears for play or display.

Dressed in their finery or presented naturally "bear," there is something about these winsome creatures that tugs at the heartstrings of young and old alike.

Here's a chance to make a teddy tribe of your own. This huggable trio is fashioned from just a few pattern pieces cut from fake fur. But you can make your own teddy bear in the size, color, and fabric of your choice. Embroider or appliqué the facial features and dress mama, papa, and baby bear in standard doll clothes to bring the bear family to life.

There are many ways to add facial features and character to handmade teddies. While specialty craft eyes are very lifelike, embroidery is quick and easy, and felt appliqués, glued and then stitched in place, add graphic dimension.

Patterns & Templates *Use the templates provided in Group 12, Card 10 to make this adorable bear family. The templates are sized for a 9" bear. Enlarge or reduce the templates on a photocopy machine as desired.*

Trace the patterns onto heavy paper, including all markings. For side head, ear, body, arm, and leg pattern pieces that require two or more pieces, flip pattern over to cut matching pieces. Transfer markings to the wrong side of the fabric.

Use fake fur to re-create the plushness of real fur. Polar fleece and corduroy are other cuddly fabric choices.

Fake Fur Guidelines

All fake fur pieces should be cut with the pile running down the body to avoid mismatched shading.

- With pattern pieces pinned to fabric backing, cut one layer of fabric at a time, snipping only fabric backing, not fur.
- Depending on fabric weight, use a #14 or #16 needle, with cotton-wrapped polyester or heavy-duty cotton thread. Set stitch length at 8–10 stitches per inch. All seam allowances are ¼".

You'll Need

- ***Fabrics: ½ yd. fake fur & felt remnants***
- ***Matching threads***
- ***Sewing machine***
- ***Hand needles***
- ***Scissors***
- ***Polyester fiberfill***
- ***Embroidery floss: brown***
- ***Craft eyes***
- ***Clothing items: 10" square of calico fabric for shawl & 12" length plaid ribbon for tie; purchased baseball cap & reading glasses***

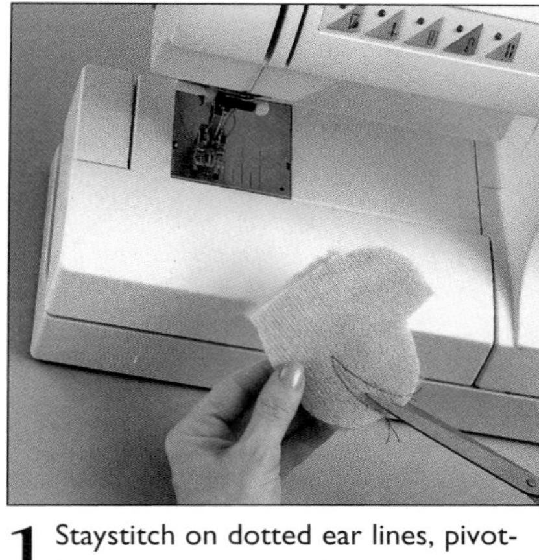

1 Staystitch on dotted ear lines, pivoting at x; cut along solid line. Staystitch along dotted lines at bridge of nose; clip to o. With right sides facing, stitch head sections together along center front from neck edge to o, pivoting at nose.

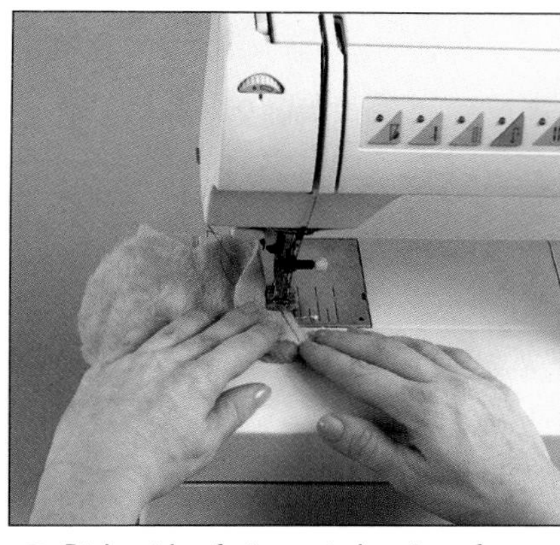

2 Right sides facing, stitch pairs of ear pieces together; leave lower edges open; turn right side out. Gather lower edges. Pin 1 ear to right side of ear opening; adjust gathers, baste. Stitch opening closed with ears encased in seam.

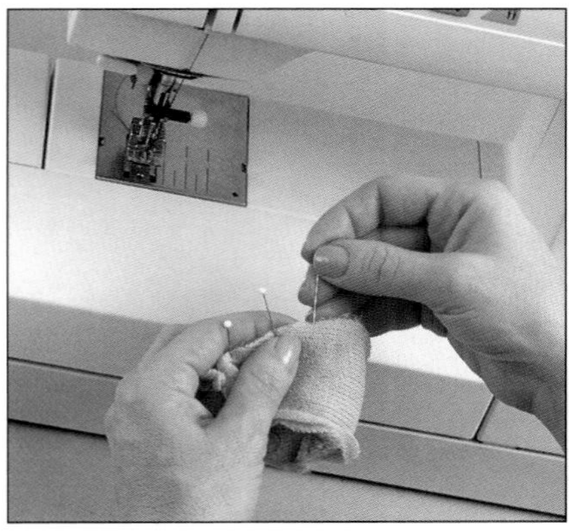

3 Pin both sides of gusset to head, from center front nose bridge to back neck; clip head-piece seams to fit. Stitch gusset in place, pivoting at large o. Turn head right side out. Finger press lower edge to wrong side, hand baste in place.

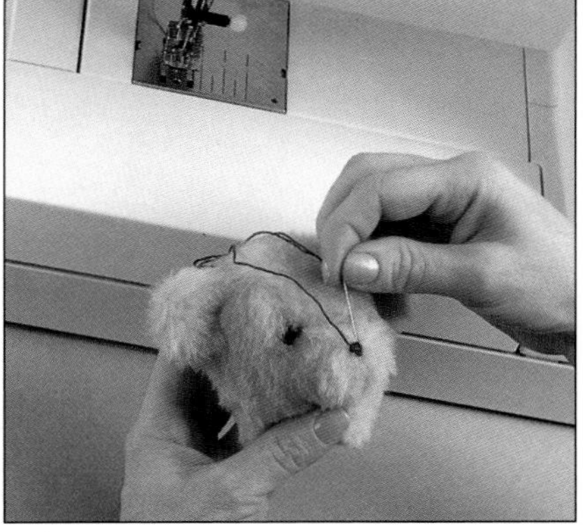

4 Insert craft eyes following instructions on package. Stuff head with fiberfill. Embroider nose and mouth using 6 strands brown embroidery floss: Use satin stitch to create nose and backstitch to create mouth.

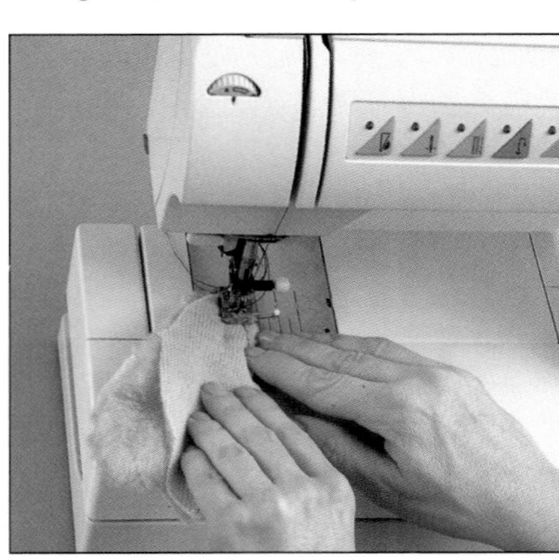

5 To reinforce body pieces, stitch along dotted lines at arm and leg openings; clip to •'s. Stitch center back dart; finger press flat. Sew arm pieces with right sides together; leave open between both sets of •'s. Turn right side out.

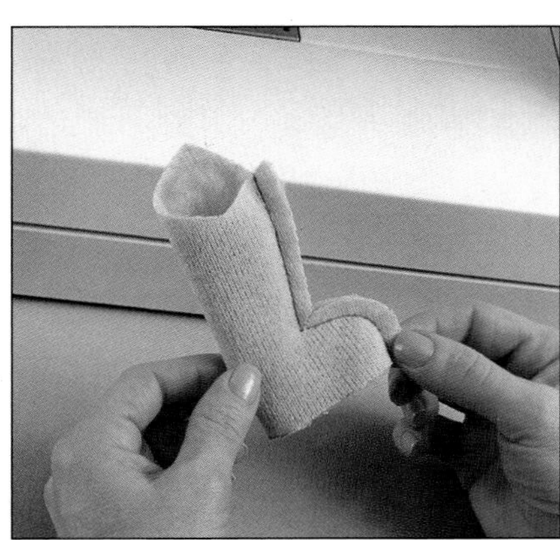

6 Pin each arm to body at arm opening, matching x's and encasing arm in seam; stitch. Reinforce legs by stitching along dotted lines. Stitch front leg seam with right sides together, pivoting at corner o's; clip at corner.

7 With right sides together, pin sole to lower opening of each leg, matching o's at heel; clip leg to fit, if necessary; stitch. Turn legs right side out; stuff with fiberfill to fill line. Baste top of leg closed.

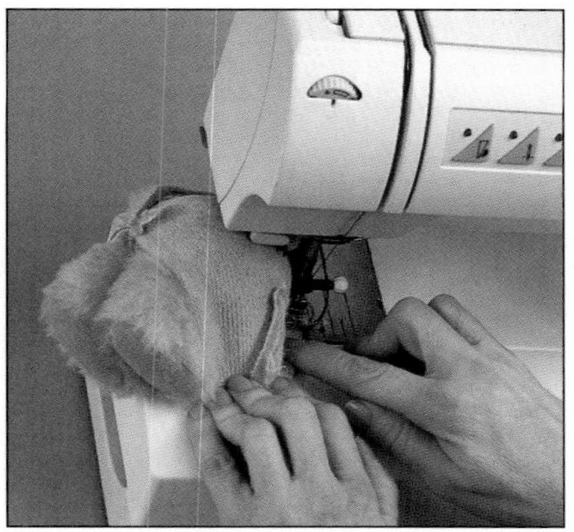

8 Pin each leg to body at leg opening, matching •'s and encasing leg in seam; stitch between •'s. Right sides facing, stitch body sections together at center front and back, matching notches; leave open at back and at head position.

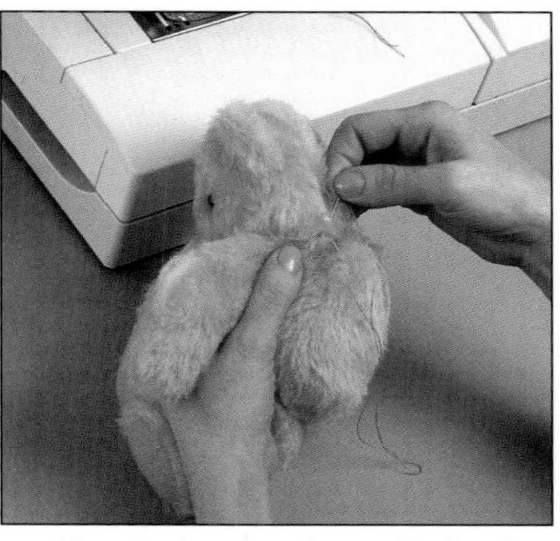

9 Turn body right side out. Pin head to body, keeping center front and center back aligned. Hand sew body to head with small stitches and heavy thread. Stuff arms and body; slipstitch openings closed.

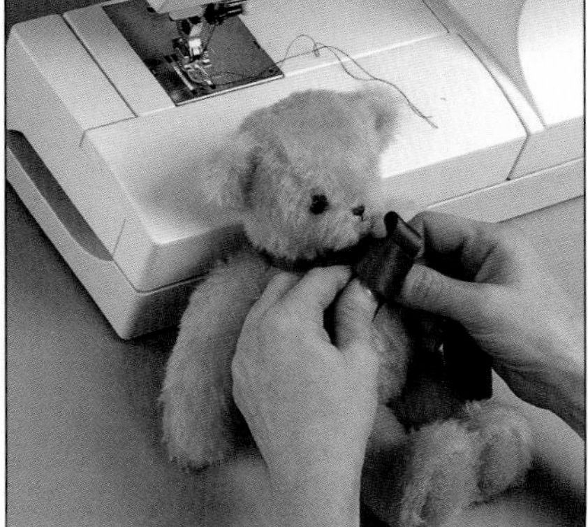

10 Add a purchased baseball cap to baby bear. Fringe a 10" square of calico for mother bear's shawl. Knot a 12" length of plaid ribbon around father bear's neck and trim ends in a V. Add a pair of purchased reading glasses.

Try This!

For a quick teddy bear, use the bear-shaped template in Group 12, Card 10 to cut two pieces of fabric. Right sides together, sew outline of bear, leaving an opening for turning and stuffing. Turn right side out, stuff bear, then slipstitch opening closed. Glue on eyes and nose; embroider mouth. Add a ribbon bow at the neck.

Crafter's Secrets

Fill bears firmly to achieve a good shape and feel. Stuff both legs and arms simultaneously to ensure equal amounts of stuffing in each pair. For tightly filled toys, allow stuffing to settle before closing; add more filling as necessary. If desired, add fabric weights or small coins inside arms and legs to give bear a heavier feel.

Making a Plush Panda

The bamboo-eating antics and roly-poly shape of the panda has made it a favorite animal of children of all ages.

Create your own version of the ever-popular critter by using the templates in Group 12, Card 10. If desired, enlarge the pattern pieces for a larger panda.

The panda's familiar black-and-white coat is re-created with fake fur—the legs, soles, arms, and ears are cut from black fur; the body, side head, and gusset pieces are cut from white fur. Black patches are added to the head to make the distinctive panda eyes.

To begin, follow steps 1–3 for making the teddy bear's head. Once the head is complete, refer to step 1 shown here to create panda's eye patch. Finish the bear following the remaining steps shown on Group 2, Card 10 and the front of this card.

The gentle appeal and quiet charm of the panda is evident even in this stuffed version. While fake fur is the obvious fabric of choice, this plump animal can be just as cuddly made in corduroy, velvet, fleece, or cotton flannel.

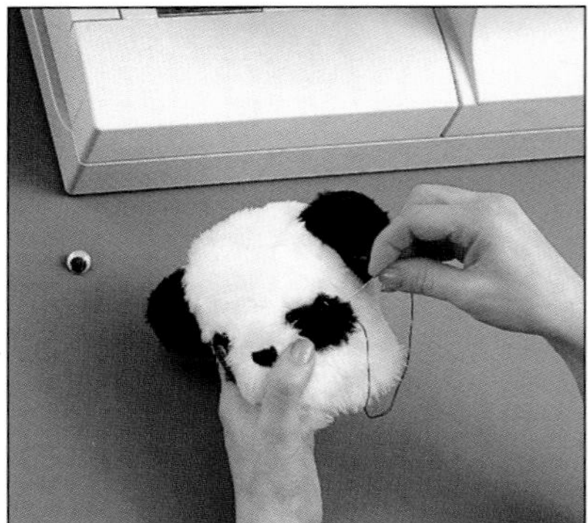

1 Cut 2 (1") square pieces of black fur for eyes; trim to round corners. Turn edges under and finger press. Slipstitch patches onto head, referring to photo for placement. Attach craft eyes over patches.

2 Hand sew completed, stuffed white fur head to white fur body, using heavy thread and small stitches. Keep center front and center back aligned. Stuff arms and body, then slipstitch opening closed.

3 Insert needle threaded with 2 strands of heavy thread at outside of 1 eye. Run thread through center of head, pulling needle out near other eye. Pull thread to sink eyes and add shape and dimension. Knot thread to secure.

2

FUN & EASY GIFTS

CARD 12

Fabric-Painting Children's T-Shirts

Patterns & Templates

Turn a plain T-shirt into a one-of-a-kind designer creation for your favorite youngster. Brilliantly colored fabric paints make it easy.

Picture your favorite child scooting around in his car shirt or standing in the middle of her own little garden of flowers. You don't need any special artistic skills to create these unique shirts. Just trace and transfer a motif from Group 12, Card 5 onto a T-shirt, then fill in with fabric paints and—*voila!*—the shirt is ready to wear.

Fabric paints are widely available in squeeze bottles, with and without applicator tips, and in a wide array of colors with flat, glossy, and glitter finishes. Mix and match the paints to create your own designs.

Paint a small lady bug emerging from a pocket to add an adorable accent design to a shirt. Use the tulip template as a stencil, or transfer the design and paint the flowers one by one. Either way you'll have a colorful ring of posies around the shirt.

Patterns & Templates

Use the templates from Group 12, Card 5 to create the darling T-shirt designs shown here. You can enlarge them, if desired, to fit a larger-size shirt.

The following tips for using fabric paints will help you get the best results.

Fabric-Painting Guidelines

Always read the manufacturer's instructions before using fabric paints.

- Use a ceramic or plastic plate as a palette for paints. Because fabric paint is water soluble before it is cured, it can be rinsed from plate when painting is completed.
- Always slip a piece of coated cardboard or shirt cardboard covered with plastic wrap into shirt before painting to prevent excess paint from bleeding through onto other side of shirt.
- While fabric paints with applicator tips, called *paint writers,* are easy to use, they require practice. Try them out on a piece of paper or scrap fabric before using on shirt.
- Do not wash finished shirt for at least 72 hours after painting to allow paint to cure and become waterproof and colorfast, or follow manufacturer's instructions for setting paint.

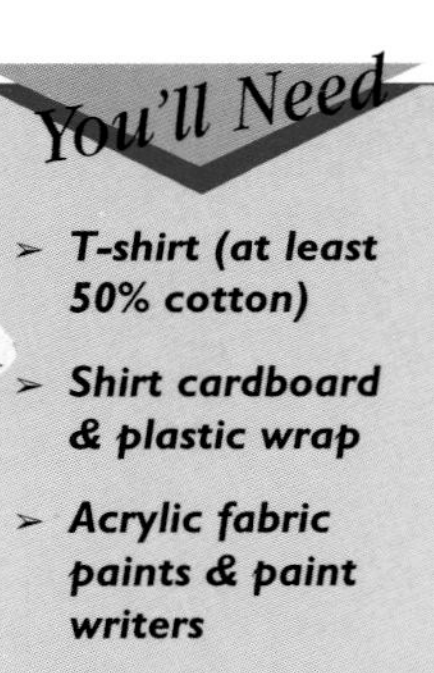

You'll Need

- **T-shirt (at least 50% cotton)**
- **Shirt cardboard & plastic wrap**
- **Acrylic fabric paints & paint writers**
- **Brushes: pointed & flat**
- **Tracing paper, graphite transfer paper, & pencil**
- **T-pins or tape**
- **Small plate**

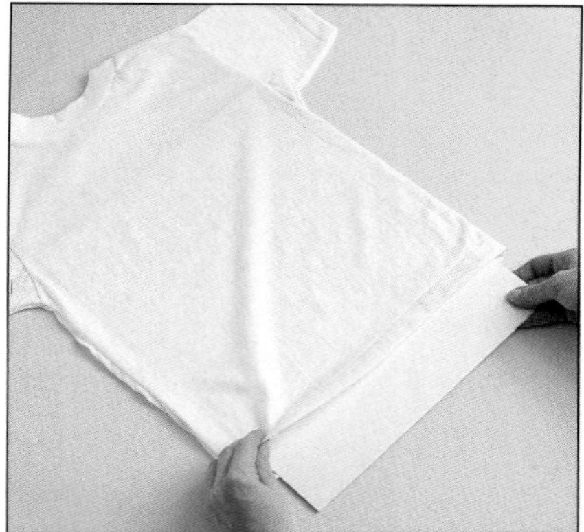

1 Wash T-shirt to remove sizing and prepare fabric for painting. Insert cardboard covered with plastic wrap into shirt, placing it between fabric layers to prevent paint from seeping through onto second layer.

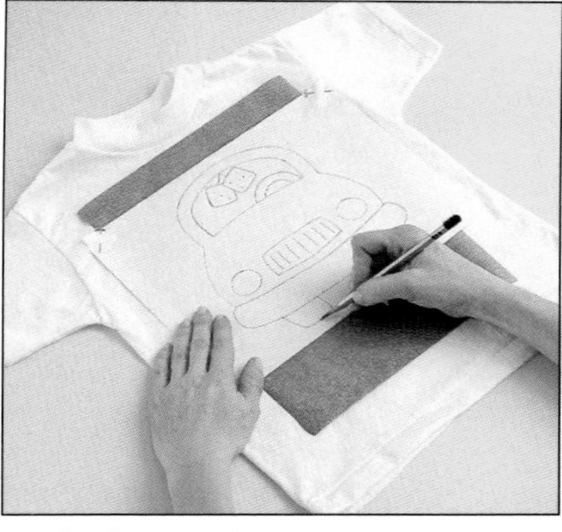

2 Outline car design onto tracing paper. Place graphite paper, carbon side down, on front of T-shirt. Center traced pattern on top of graphite paper; secure with T-pins or tape. To transfer drawing, trace over pattern with pencil.

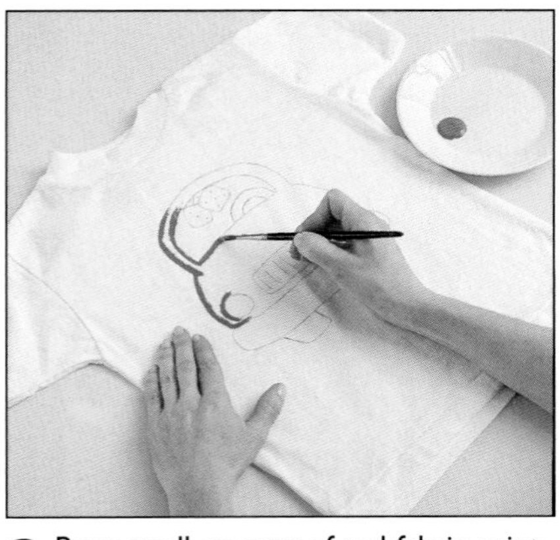

3 Pour small amount of red fabric paint onto plate. Using pointed artist's brush dipped into paint, outline largest area of design to be colored.

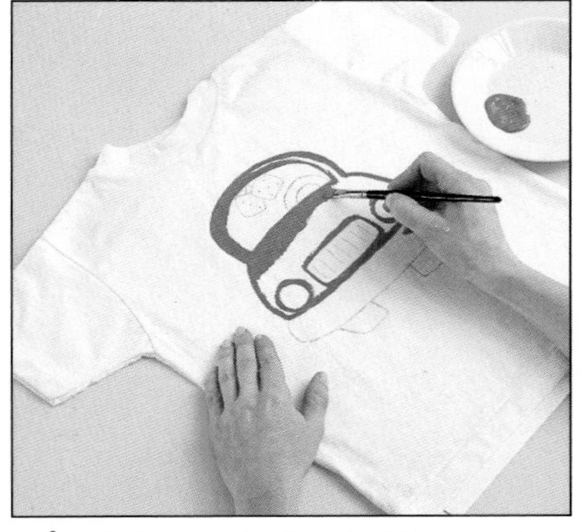

4 Switching to flat brush, fill in remainder of red area, working carefully inside painted outlines; avoid applying too much paint or fabric will be stiff when dry. Let paint dry.

5 Pour blue paint onto plate. Use clean pointed brush to outline and fill in shapes of fender and steering. Let paint dry completely.

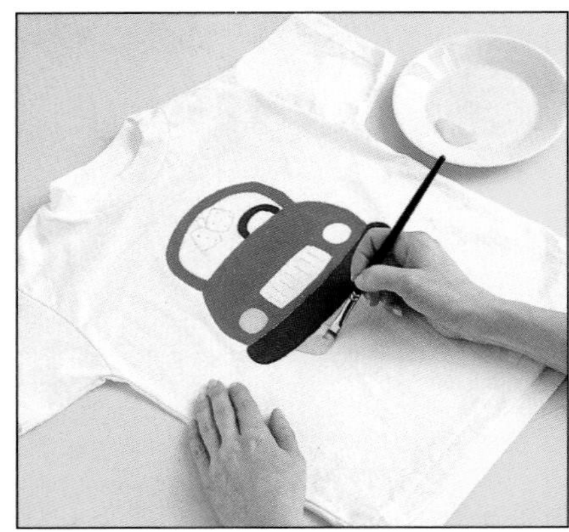

6 Pour yellow paint onto plate. Using edge of flat brush, pull yellow paint around edges of circular shapes for headlights and tires.

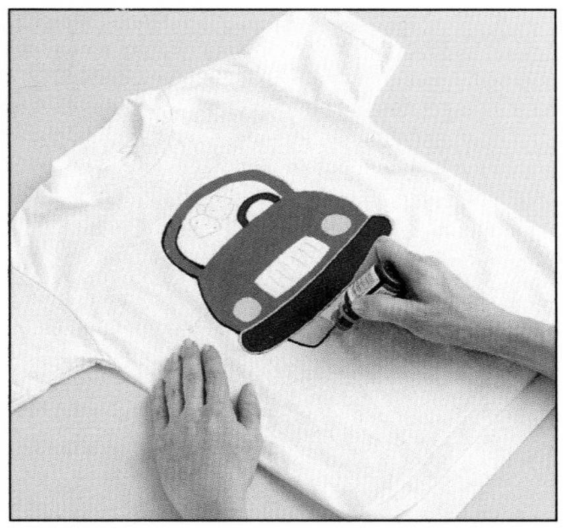

7 Using paint writers in contrasting colors, outline painted areas with pointed tips. Tap tip of bottle against flat surface before each painting stroke to remove any air bubbles in bottle and to help paint flow smoothly.

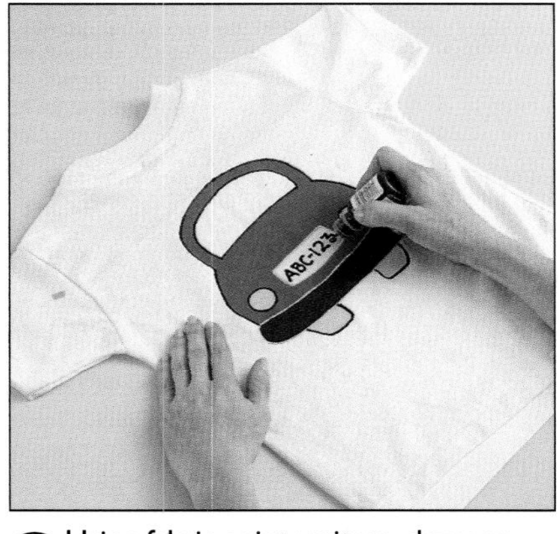

8 Using fabric paint writers, draw or letter any remaining fine lines or design details. Allow paint to dry at least 72 hours before washing, or follow manufacturer's instructions.

Crafter's Secrets

To transfer patterns to fabric without tracing, photocopy the chosen motifs from Group 12, Card 5 at regular size or reduce or enlarge them if desired. Then place the photocopy face down on the shirt and iron over it to transfer the lines from the design onto the fabric. Because a mirror image of the original design will result, this technique is not appropriate for designs with lettering or designs that are not symmetrical.

Try This!

If you are making this knit set for a small child, use the footprint template provided or capture his or her own footprints—or handprints—on the "canvas":

- *Have child stand barefoot on a piece of paper large enough to contain both feet (or hands). Trace around each of the child's feet or hands with a pencil.*
- *Cut out patterns and pin to shirt where desired for placement only.*
- *Insert cardboard between layers of T-shirt.*
- *Squirt paint onto a plate large enough to fit child's hand or foot. Spread paint evenly over plate with a brush.*
- *Beginning at top of shirt, lift first pattern piece.*
- *Place child's corresponding hand or foot straight down into paint, then lift it up. Press hand or foot firmly down onto shirt in selected spot; lift it off shirt.*
- *Repeat for remaining hand or foot, then alternate left and right.*

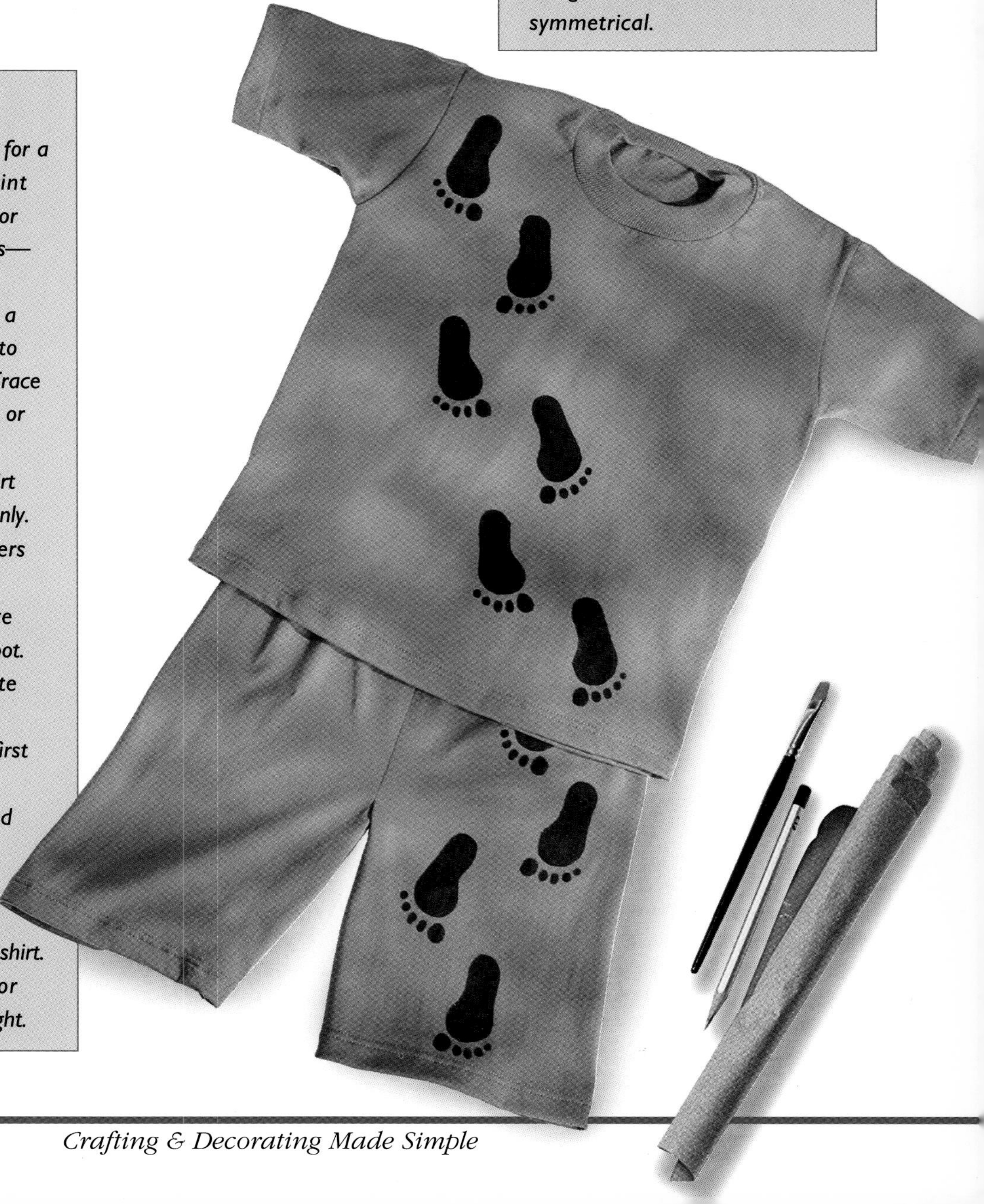

Sponging Design onto a T-shirt

Stenciling a design onto a T-shirt with a sponge creates a "dappled" and more muted painted effect, which gives the impression that some of the color has been washed away.

A synthetic sponge works best, as the holes are smaller and more even in size than those of a natural sponge.

Cut the sponge into small rectangles, one for each paint color. Dip a damp piece of sponge into a small amount of fabric paint; remove the excess by dabbing it on a plate. Then dab the paint onto the shirt where desired with a quick up-and-down motion.

If the shapes within the design are positioned very close together, you may wish to cover the areas not being painted with paper cut into the shape and attached with masking tape.

Stencil a little sailboat onto a colored T-shirt using pieces of sponge and fabric paints. Your little one will love dabbing on the paint himself and enthusiastically showing off his own creation.

1 Insert shirt cardboard covered with plastic wrap between fabric layers. Trace design onto paper, then cut along outlines to make stencil. Place stencil on front of shirt and tape in place across corners.

2 Cut sponge into small pieces. Dip damp sponge into paint, then, beginning at top of design, dab sponge onto fabric through space on stencil, filling in area of stencil and along edges for a sharp painted line.

3 Using clean sponge to apply each paint color, work from top of design down to avoid smudging colors with arm. Remove stencil. Let paint dry at least 72 hours before washing, or follow manufacturer's instructions.

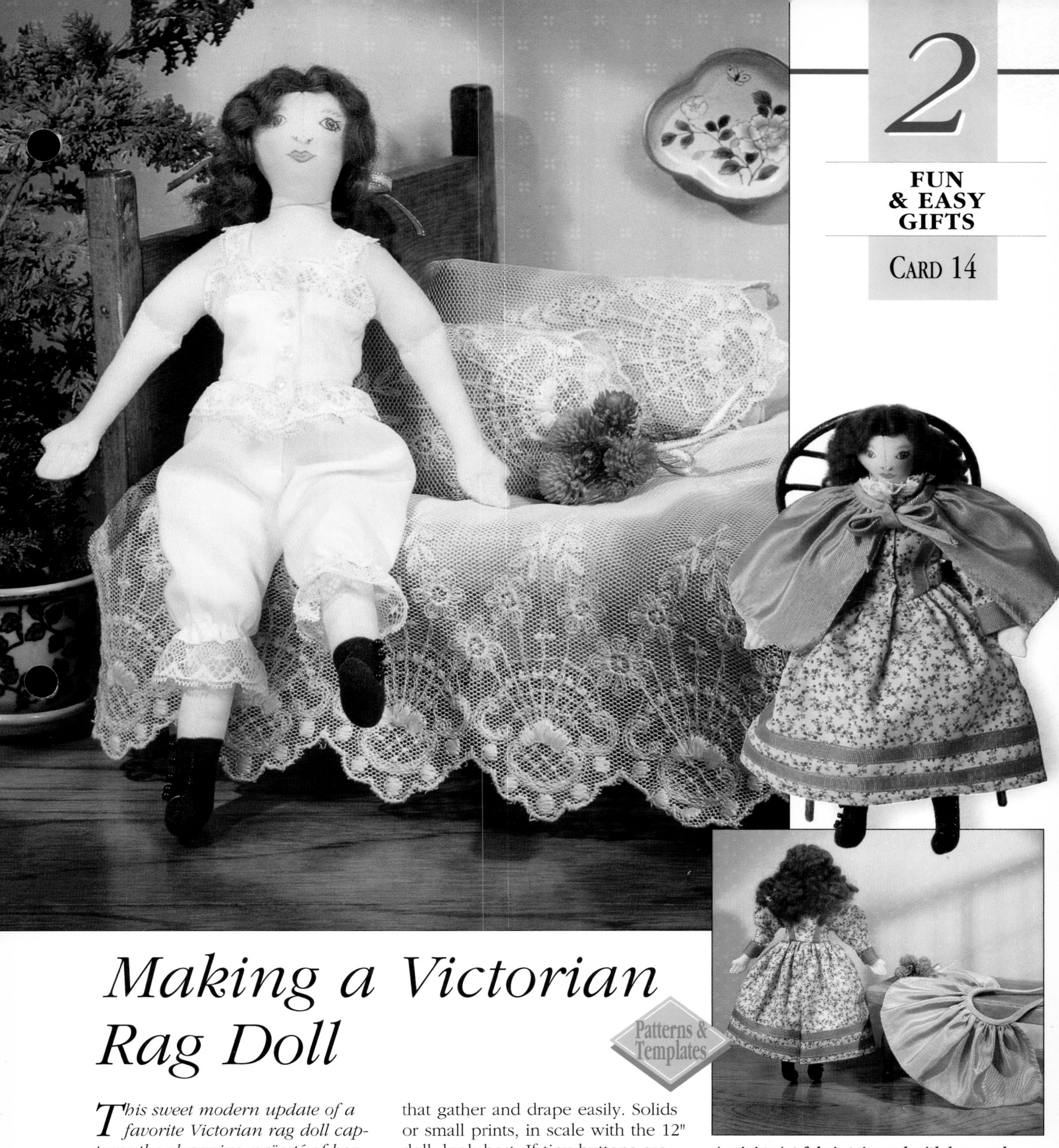

2

FUN & EASY GIFTS

CARD 14

Making a Victorian Rag Doll

Patterns & Templates

This sweet modern update of a favorite Victorian rag doll captures the charming naïveté of her predecessors, complete with period clothing and undergarments.

A few easy pattern pieces are all that's needed to create an adorable reproduction doll and wardrobe. For the authentic-looking doll clothes, choose lightweight fabrics that gather and drape easily. Solids or small prints, in scale with the 12" doll, look best. If tiny buttons are hard to find, use beads instead.

Doll hair is available in craft shops and is easy to handle. It is stitched along the center first, then hand sewn or glued to the crown. After styling, it is fastened to the rest of the head.

A mini-print fabric trimmed with lace and ribbons is perfect for Victorian-inspired clothing. The traditional shaped bodice and puffy muttonchop sleeves are accented with tiny pearl buttons. A solid-colored cape completes the doll's outfit.

Patterns & Templates

Use the patterns from Group 12, Card 8 to sew this Victorian beauty.

To make the doll's face, trace the features onto white paper, then place the paper over graphite paper that is laying carbon side down on the fabric. Outline the features to transfer onto the fabric.

Dollmaking Guidelines

Use tiny machine stitches, about 10–12 per inch, to create a tight bond and to sew the tiny curves easily and accurately.

- Use disappearing fabric marking pen to transfer markings to all pattern pieces.
- Use knitting needle to push out points when turning pieces to right side.

You'll Need

- ***100% cotton fabrics: 2 (7"x11") & 2 (4"x6") off-white for body, 6"x18" white for underwear, ¼ yd. print for dress, & 3¾"x14" coordinating solid piece for cape***
- ***Trims: 1¼ yds. ⅜" ribbon, 7" (⅝") ribbon, 1 yd. ¾" lace, 14" double-fold bias tape, & ¾ yd. ⅜" decorative braid***
- ***¼ yd. ⅛" elastic***
- ***Matching threads & sewing machine***
- ***Tape measure, ruler, disappearing marking pen, scissors, needle, & pins***
- ***Doll hair***
- ***Doll buttons or 3mm. beads (11 pearl, 10 black) & 13 small snaps***
- ***Fabric markers or fabric paints***
- ***Polyester fiberfill***
- ***Paper for patterns***
- ***Iron & ironing board***

Sewing Rag Doll

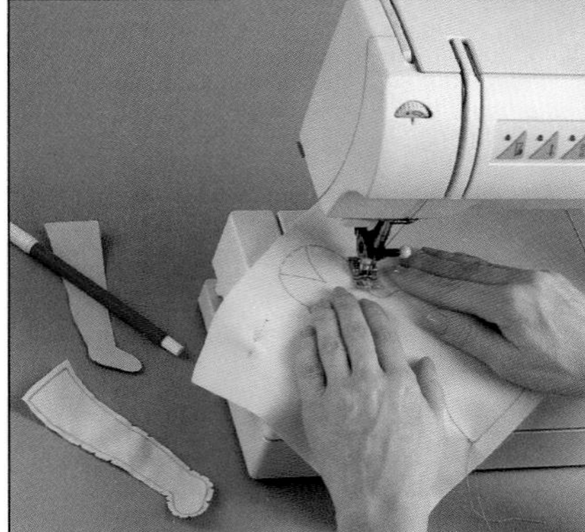

1 Place matching off-white pieces together, right sides facing. Outline body on large piece, legs on small piece; stitch on outlines, leaving bottom of body and leg tops open. Trim, leaving ⅛" seam allowance; clip curves.

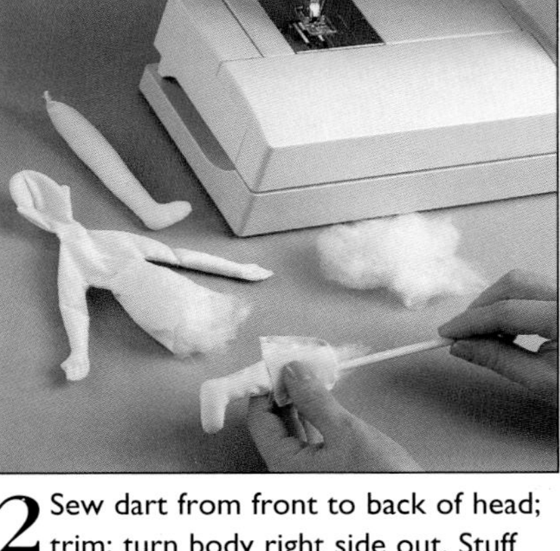

2 Sew dart from front to back of head; trim; turn body right side out. Stuff hands; sew finger lines. Stuff arms to elbows; sew across; complete stuffing. Stuff legs. Insert into body; stitch closed.

3 Paint face and boots. Sew on black boot buttons. Lay 6" length of doll hair on paper; sew across center; remove paper. Hand sew part to center of head; style hair, and fasten to rest of head.

Making Undergarments

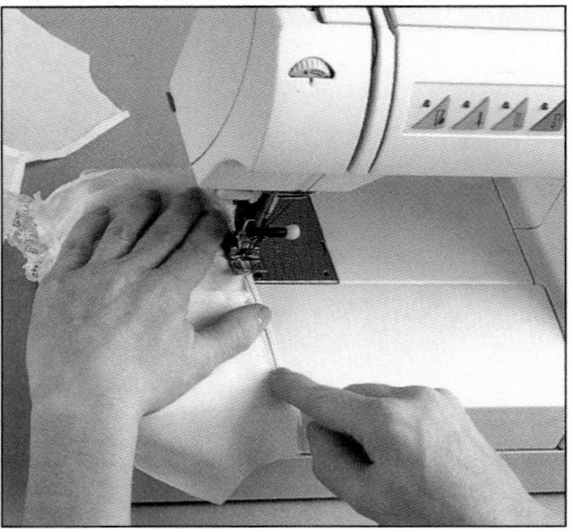

1 Sew centerfront seam of bloomers. Turn seam along waist and leg hems. Sew lace along each leg hem. Zigzag 2¼" of elastic along leg hems; 4½" along waist. Sew center back and inseam; turn.

2 Sew lace to camisole top; tack ends at armholes. Sew fronts to back, and lace to lower edge. Fold 2 (3½") lace pieces in half lengthwise and sew straps. Turn ½" on front. Sew on snaps and pearl buttons.

Making Dress

1 Sew shoulders; press open. Sew ribbon to front and back, crossing over shoulders. Gather lace, sew to neck, then edgestitch seam. Press under ½" on each front edge and topstitch ¼" from fold.

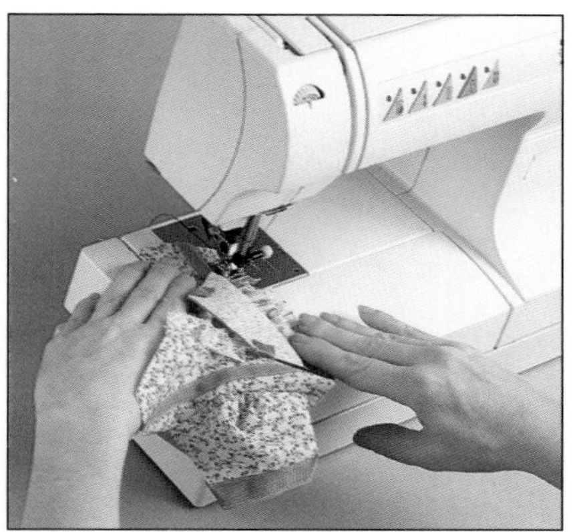

2 Press each wrist seam to right side; align 3¼" piece of wide ribbon to edge, folding ends under; stitch. Gather top of sleeve; sew to armhole, matching marks. Sew continuous seam from top of ribbon cuff to bottom of bodice.

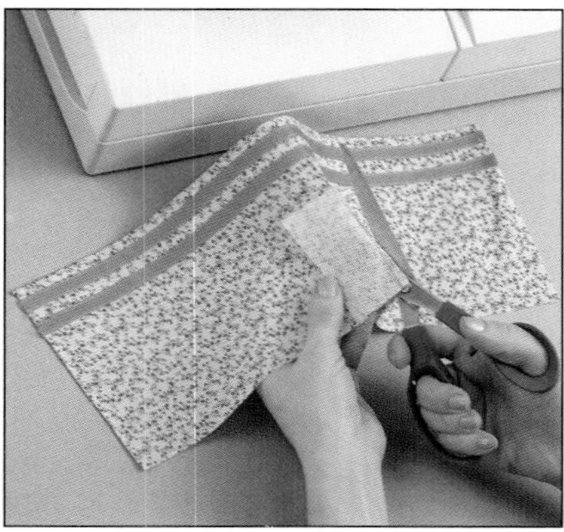

3 Cut 5¾"x16" skirt piece. Sew narrow hem on 1 long edge; sew narrow ribbon ¼" and 1" from hem. Pin 3" fabric square to center top; sew 2¼"-long x ⅜"-wide V in center. Clip into V; turn, press. Sew center back seam.

4 Gather top edge of skirt. Right sides together, pin to fit bodice, placing waist edge of each bodice front ½" below waist edge of skirt. Sew seam; trim excess fabric. Sew snaps to front and cuffs, and buttons along front.

Making Cape

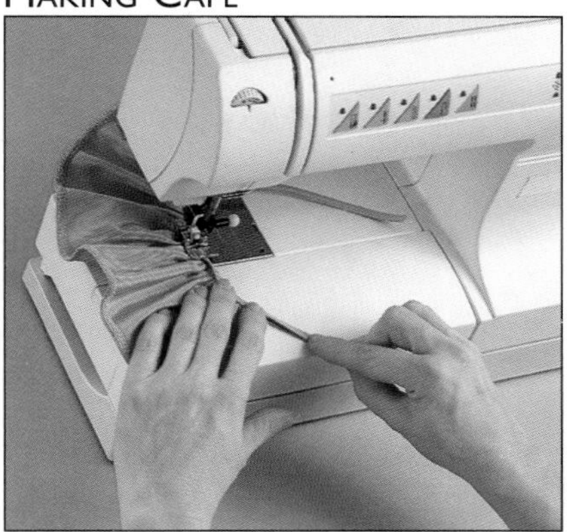

Press cape fabric ⅛" to right side along 1 long edge and both short ends. Topstitch braid over raw edges of fabric. Gather top edge of cape to 4¾". Bind with 14" of bias tape, centered along neck; use ends for ties.

Try This!

To make the full-length cape with openings for arms, shown on the back of this card, cut four rectangles, one 12½"x8", two 3¼"x8", and one 3¾"x14".

1 *Sew smallest rectangles to each end of 12½"x 8" rectangle, leaving 1½" arm opening 3" from top of each seam. Press seams open; edgestitch along each arm opening. Sew ⅛" hem along bottom and along both short ends of cape.*

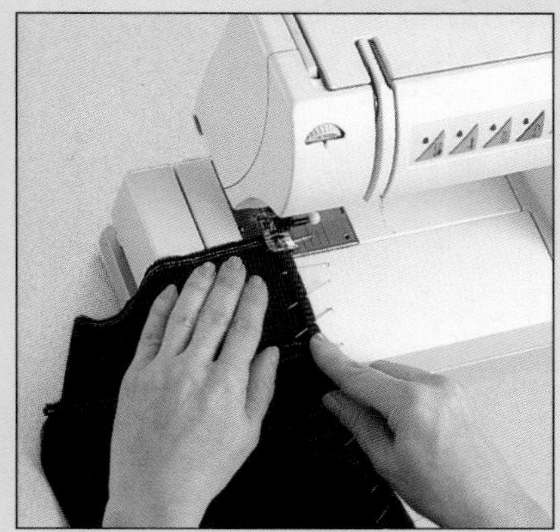

2 *Sew ⅛" hem along 1 long edge and both short sides of remaining rectangle. Pin to right side of lower cape layer, with top raw edges even. Gather tops together to 4¾" long. Bind with 14" of bias tape centered along neck; use both ends for ties.*

Crafter's Secrets

The pretty face of the Victorian doll can be embroidered if desired. Using one strand of tan embroidery thread, stitch her eyebrows and nose with straight stitches. Use satin stitches to create the eyeballs in blue, then outline with black backstitches. Outline stitch her eyes; straight stitch a flutter of lashes in black. Fill lips with pink satin stitches, then outline in rose backstitches; center two straight rose stitches within lips. Rub pink pencil or blush over fabric to make rosy cheeks.

Making a Victorian Bonnet

Using the patterns provided on Group 12, Card 8 and a different fabric, a brand-new outfit can be created for the lady, including a long cape and bonnet.

The bonnet requires fusible interfacing for the brim and a contrasting lining fabric. Use the stitch-and-cut method to sew the main bonnet pieces, and use narrow ribbon for the ties.

The stuffing process used to form the doll is crucial to the success of this project. Work with very small amounts of stuffing at a time, using a stuffing tool or wood skewer to push stuffing from the outside edges to the center of the piece. Make sure the neck is stuffed firmly to hold the head upright and carry the weight of the bonnet. For a smooth face, place a piece of batting, cut to the same size as the face, behind the face fabric before stuffing.

For a change of season, our little Victorian lady is very stylish in her new outfit made of darker, richer colors and heavier fabrics that are just perfect for the colder weather.

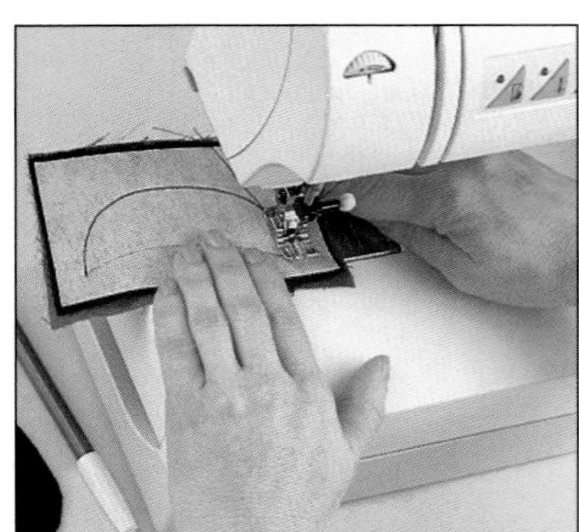

1 Outline brim pattern onto fusible interfacing; fuse to wrong side of bonnet fabric. Sew brim to lining fabric along curved edge. Trim fabric, leaving ¼" seam allowance. Clip curves; turn to right side. Topstitch seam edge.

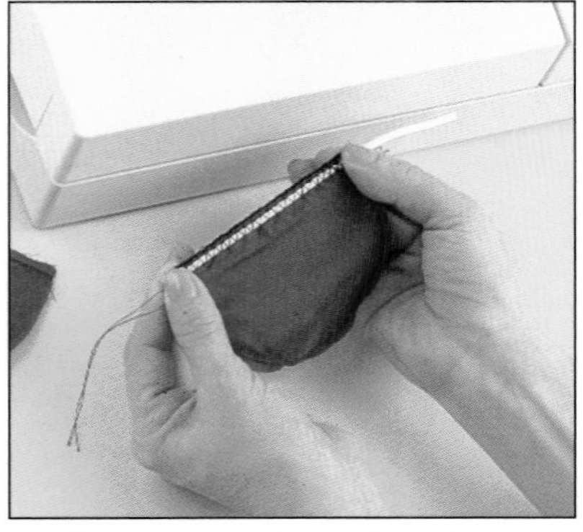

2 Sew crown to lining along bottom straight edge. Trim fabric, leaving ¼" seam allowance. Turn; press. Sew and gather 2 layers between marks. Zigzag 3" piece of elastic on lining side of bottom seam, stretching to fit.

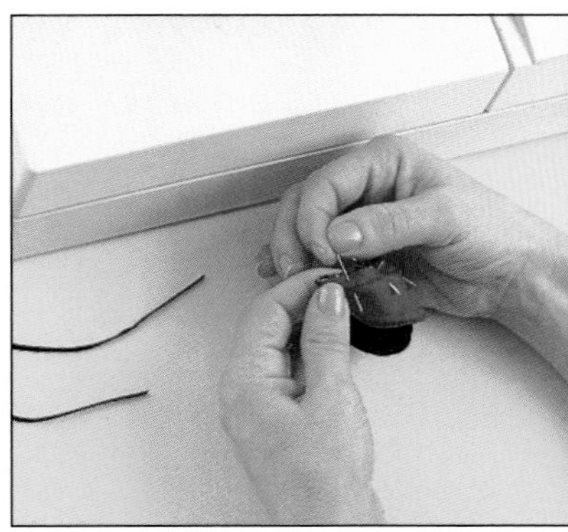

3 With right sides of bonnet fabric together, pin curved edge of crown to inner edge of brim pulling gathers to fit; stitch. Tack 6" piece of 1/16" ribbon to each side of bonnet for ties.

Embroidering on Stenciled Tote Bags

Patterns & Templates

For those trips to the farmer's market or to the beach, make a big, roomy carryall with decorative details embroidered onto colorful stenciled designs.

Tote bags have become indispensable for carrying groceries, gym gear, beachwear—anything needed or collected during the course of a busy day. These cloth bags are sturdy and washable, offering a fashionable and affordable alternative to less environmentally friendly plastic and paper bags.

Bright and colorful stenciled motifs turn an ordinary fabric bag into a handsome accessory. After stenciling, add definition to the design with simple embroidery stitches in colored threads.

The versatile tote bag can be designed for many uses. A stenciled anchor outlined in red gives a jaunty nautical look to a blue bag with long straps to sling over the shoulder. A smiling moon painted on ticking stripe turns a plain cloth bag into a cute tote for carrying baby's things.

Patterns & Templates

Choose from the motifs in Group 12, Card 24 to make stencils for decorating your fabric tote bag. Enlarge or reduce designs on a photocopier if desired.

Make a simple tote bag from sturdy cotton fabric, such as canvas or twill. Prewash fabric to remove sizing so paint will adhere better. Trace motifs onto stencil acetate and cut out with craft knife.

Guidelines for Making Tote Bag

Cut an 18"x40" piece of fabric for bag, then stencil and embroider motifs before constructing the bag.

- Fold stenciled fabric crosswise, right sides together, and stitch side seams. At each bottom corner, mark 2" up on side seams and 2" in from sides at bottom; stitch line connecting points; backstitch to secure. Turn bag right side out.
- Press top edge under 1/2", then 1" for hem and pin.
- Cut 2 (16"x3 1/2") strips for handles. Press long edges under 1/2"; fold in half lengthwise, wrong sides facing. Edgestitch together on both edges.
- Center and pin handles 6" apart at bag top. Edgestitch along top and along edge of hem, catching handles in stitching.

- ***3/4 yd. fabric***
- ***Acrylic fabric paints: red, green, & orange***
- ***Stencil acetate & stencil brush***
- ***Pen & fabric pencil***
- ***Waxed paper & masking tape***
- ***Perle embroidery thread: green, orange, light brown, red, & yellow***
- ***Embroidery needle***
- ***Scissors & craft knife***
- ***Sewing machine & thread***

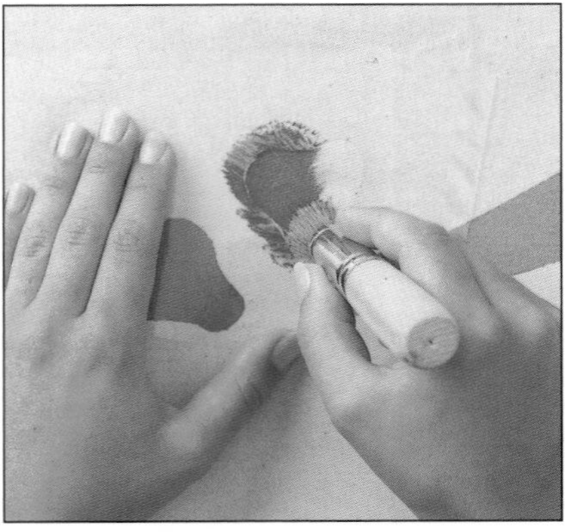

1 For placement, lightly outline strawberry, cherry, and carrot motifs within upper half of fabric. Tape fabric to waxed paper. Working 1 shape at a time, tape stencil to fabric; dab on paint with stencil brush; let dry.

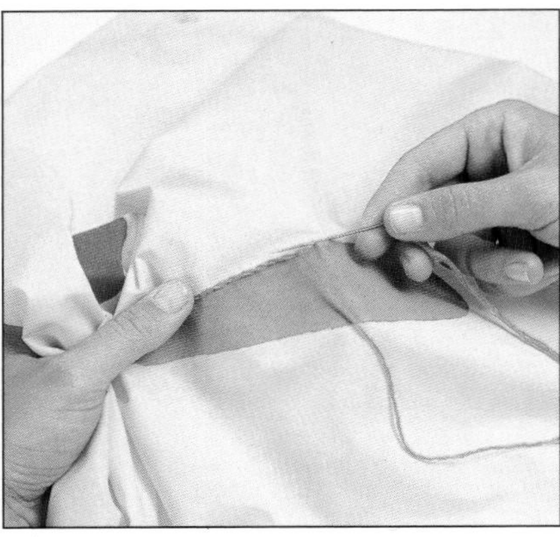

2 Stem-stitch around carrot with orange thread: Working from left to right, make slightly slanting 1/4"-long stitches, bringing needle up midway along stitch with thread below needle.

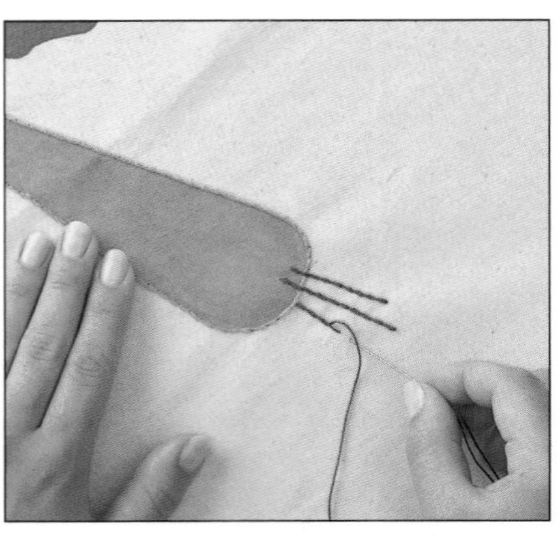

3 Stem-stitch carrot greens with green thread. To add realism, begin some strands inside carrot edge and some precisely on carrot edge.

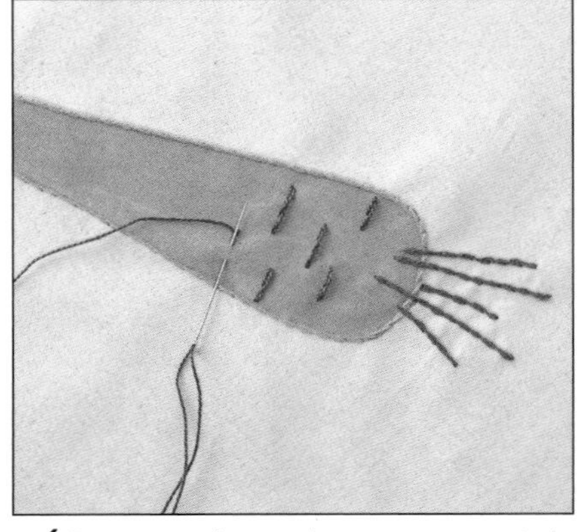

4 Sew carrot's streaks using stem stitch and light brown thread, making 2–3 stitches per streak. Secure thread on wrong side by weaving ends through some stitches. Stem-stitch around each strawberry with red thread.

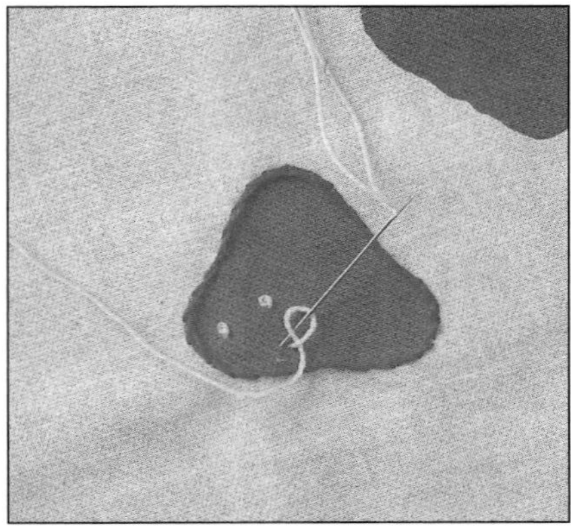

5 Use yellow thread to make French knots for strawberry seeds: Bring needle out at desired position. Holding needle close to fabric, wrap thread once around needle point, and insert needle close to starting point.

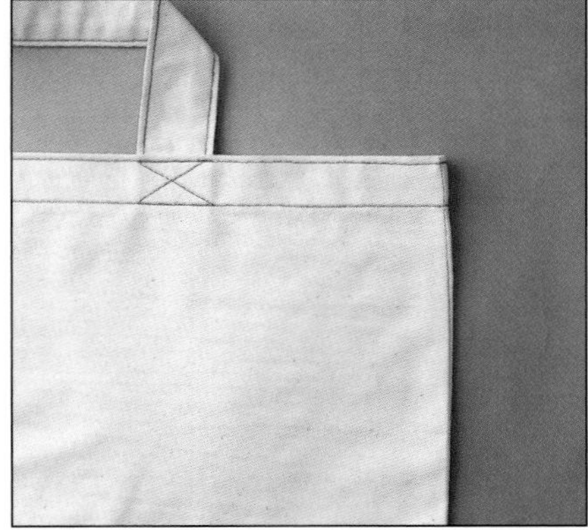

6 Use red and green threads to stem-stitch around cherries and leaves. Sew bag and handles following guidelines. For added reinforcement, topstitch crossing lines over each end of handle.

Try This!

Make these summery beach accessories by stenciling a purchased deck bag and cap with a collection of interesting seashells and tiny stars. Instead of outlining the motifs with embroidery thread, use three-dimensional fabric paint pens in contrasting and complementary colors to give definition to the shapes. The small squeeze bottles of paint are available in art, craft, and hobby shops in dozens of colors and many finishes, including shiny, iridescent, glitter, and matte. Follow the manufacturer's instructions for use.

Crafter's Secrets

If you want to stencil onto a printed fabric, here's a trick to prevent the print fabric from showing through the paint: Stencil the motif onto the fabric in white paint first. Let the paint dry, then restencil over the white in your color of choice.

Sewing a Sturdy Cloth Bag

Large, sturdily constructed cloth bags are great for grocery shopping and especially useful around the home for storing sewing and craft supplies, children's toys, and carrying laundry. You'll find at least a dozen uses for these commodious sacks.

For a bag that will be used to tote heavy loads, such as groceries, stitch the bag with French seams to give it additional stability and to provide a clean finish on the inside without any visible raw edges. Use a medium-weight natural fabric, such as cotton or linen, and add a separate band across the top edge to give extra support.

For a finished 17"x20" bag, cut out a piece of fabric measuring 18"x40" for the body, 2 (5½"x16") strips for the handles, and a 4"x36" strip for the border. Stencil and embroider designs to the front if desired.

A large linen bag will accommodate a generous amount of groceries. The fabric is reliable enough so that you won't have to worry about the handles breaking, even after a big shopping spree.

1 Press long edges of 1 handle strip in toward center. Press strip in half lengthwise and pin together. Edge-stitch along both long edges. Repeat to make second handle. Sew ends of border strip together.

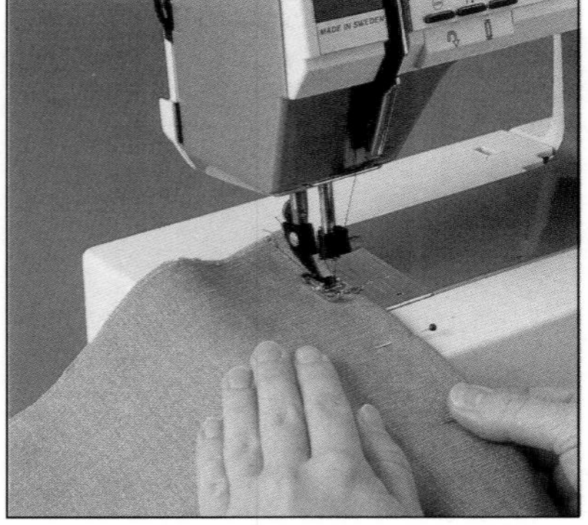

2 Fold bag fabric in half crosswise, wrong sides facing. To form French seam, stitch ⅛" from edges. Turn bag wrong side out and stitch ¼" from finished seams. Stitch across 2" at lower corners to make broad bottom.

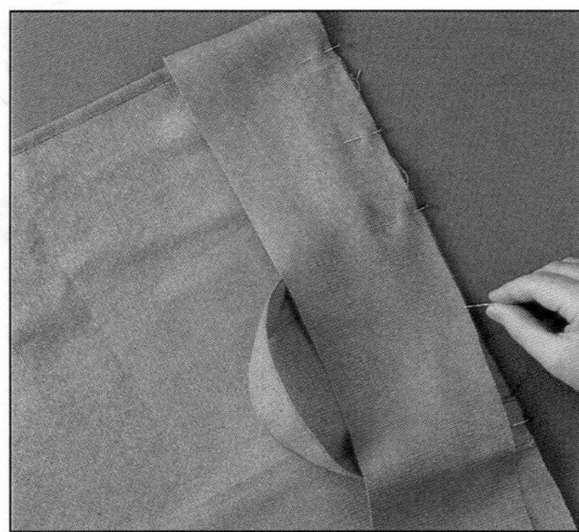

3 Pin handles to wrong side, raw edges even at top; pin right side of border to wrong side of bag and stitch. Turn bag right side out. Press border to right side and raw edge under ¼". Sew border to bag along pressed edge.

Decorating Baskets with Flowers

Trim a basket with a profusion of fresh or silk flowers and fill it with a selection of treats to make a pretty and personal hostess gift.

Decorated with nosegays and garlands of flowers from your own garden or local florist's shop, the baskets are a lovely way to present homemade delicacies, fresh-picked fruit, or other thoughtful items.

Select flowers to suit the season or personal taste and let the basket's shape determine how they are displayed. For a springtime gift of flavored oils and vinegars, as shown above, attach a bouquet of pansies, lilacs, and Queen Anne's lace to the front of a large, deep square basket and a cascade of the same flowers along the handle.

The blue of a square painted basket is an ideal backdrop for a summer nosegay made up of wheat, daisies, pansies, sprigs of Queen Anne's lace, and a rose, and attached with raffia. A garland of cornflowers, lilacs, daisies, and statice festoon the rim of a deep oval basket filled with fruit; a mini wreath bedecks the bottle of sparking cider inside.

Floral arrangements can be made to decorate the rim, handle, front, or side of baskets of any shape or size. The size, shape, and position of the arrangement should complement the basket chosen.

Floral Basket Guidelines

If you are filling a basket with treats, make sure the basket is large enough to accommodate the items to be placed inside.

- Cut flower stems 3"–5" below heads or clusters.
- Attach decorations to basket with "hairpins" made by folding 10" lengths of floral wire in half. Insert wire ends through basket and twist to fasten. Cut off excess wire and tuck ends into basket.
- To form ribbon rosette, fold ribbon back and forth over itself to make 6 loops. Twist 10" length of wire around center of loops to secure. Separate loops into rosette.

You'll Need

- ***Scissors & knife***
- ***Spooled floral wire***
- ***Floral tape***

For handle cascade:

- ***Large square basket***
- ***Flowers: pansies, lilacs, & Queen Anne's lace***
- ***1 2/3 yds. of 1"-wide ribbon***

For raffia-tied bouquet:

- ***Small square basket***
- ***Flowers: 1 rose, 3 wheat stalks, 2 daisies, 3 pansies, & Queen Anne's lace***
- ***Piece of cotton***
- ***Raffia***

For basket garland:

- ***Oval basket***
- ***Flowers: cornflowers, daisies, lilacs, & statice***
- ***Woven cord***

Making a Basket Handle Floral Cascade

1 Secure spooled wire to bottom of basket handle. Wire flowers to handle with stems up: first lilacs with leaves, then Queen Anne's lace and pansies. Continue alternating flowers up 1 side of handle.

2 Make small bouquet with lilacs, pansies, and Queen Anne's lace. Use "hairpins" to wire bouquet to basket, stems pointing up. Make 2 ribbon rosettes; wire above bouquet and to handle.

Attaching a Basket Bouquet

1 Make small bouquet of wheat, rose, daisies, pansies, and sprigs of Queen Anne's lace; wrap stems with floral tape. If desired, wrap small piece of wet cotton around stems before covering with tape.

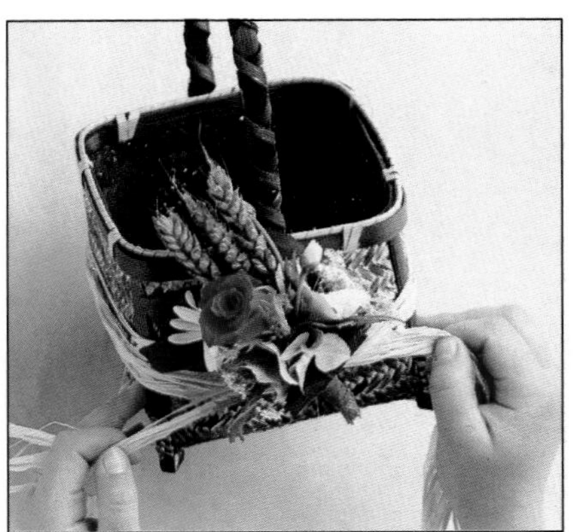

2 Tie raffia strand around basket. Center bouquet on handle side of basket, angling slightly. Knot raffia stems to secure. Tie more raffia around basket; knot and tuck ends into basket.

Making a Basket Flower Garland

1 Knot cord, securing end of wire under knot. Wire 2 cornflowers and lilac sprig to cord. Wire on 2 daisies and statice. Continue until garland fits around basket. Cut cord and knot end.

2 To attach garland, insert ends of "hairpins" around flowers and through basket just below rim. Twist wires to secure; trim ends. Fasten garland at 3 or 4 more points in same manner.

Original Wraps & Cards

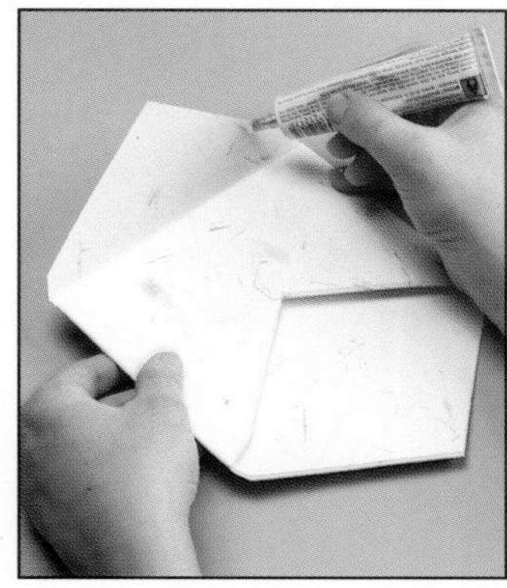

Papers, boxes, notes, and cards for all gift-giving occasions

3

ORIGINAL WRAPS & CARDS

CARD 1

Creating Romantic Valentine's Day Cards

Making specially fashioned Valentine cards is a labor of the heart as well as of the hands. Trimmed with lace, ribbons, foil hearts, and charms, the cards are one-of-a-kind keepsakes.

Whether the object of your affection is a spouse, a parent, a child, or a special friend, creating one of these romantic cards is a thoughtful way to express your love.

Check stationery, art supply, and craft stores for blank, folded card stock and for some with decorative colored deckled edges. Mix together laces, ribbons, shiny papers and trims, paper cherubs and flowers—any pretty little things you can find. Then snip and paste until you have created a shining token of love.

Offering fond memories and lovingly adorned with lace doilies and decorative Valentine motifs, these romantic photo-frame cards are reminders of the sentimental Valentines of a bygone era.

Whether elaborate or simple, making personalized greeting cards is a caring way to show your affection.

Card Decorating Guidelines

Art supply stores are a great source for decorative papers. Look also in card, craft, and stationery stores.

- Découpage papers, called "scraps," are very useful for illustrations. Also look for pictures and images in magazines, catalogs, and gift wraps.
- Metallic wrapping paper glued to heavier paper adds sparkle and shine, while paper and lace doilies and trims add a romantic look.
- Use a glue made specially for paper, and lay down a thin, even coat. Place a heavy object, such as a book, over glued card so piece does not curl.
- Place a piece of waxed paper between card and weight to keep anything from sticking while glue is drying.

To make the floral-print card shown on the front, glue a floral cutout onto red foil paper and center under a gold foil frame with gold foil corners. Glue framed floral piece to a rectangular lace doily pasted onto folded card stock and border with string pearls and ribbons.

You'll Need

- ***Papers: card stock, gold or colored foil paper, doilies***
- ***Decorative frames, heart cutouts, romantic prints, & decorative corners***
- ***Trimmings: ruffled laces, narrow lace trims, picot-edged ribbons, ribbon roses, fabric doilies, & string pearls***
- ***Double-sided tape***
- ***Paper & craft glues***
- ***Decorative edging scissors or pinking shears***

Angel Card

1 Cut card stock ¼" larger than twice finished size. On right side, mark ¼" from edges. Fold in half, taping edges together with double-sided tape placed outside marked lines. Trim away edges.

2 Trim foil background and glue to center. Glue ruffled lace around foil, then glue narrow trim to cover edge of lace. Glue angel print in center and bows, roses, and hearts in corners.

Photo Card

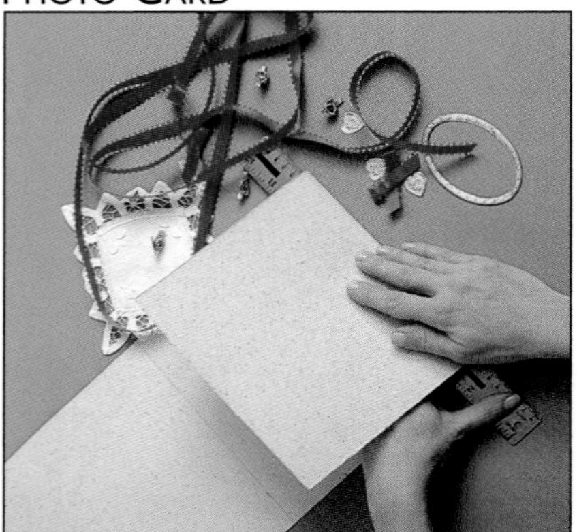

1 Fold card stock into 3 equal sections. To ease folding, use blunt-pointed instrument to score foldline on inside of stock. Place ruler along line and fold up against it to obtain sharp, crisp fold.

2 For card front, center and glue red foil to center section. Cut picot-edged ribbon lengths to match foil edges. Glue ribbon over foil edges, mitering at corners. Glue foil hearts to card corners.

3 Glue frame to center of doily; glue doily to center of red foil. Cut away doily from center of frame. Affix photo; fold and glue right section of stock to back of photo. Glue ribbon bows and roses.

Rose Card

Glue red foil to center of foil doily. Cut gold foil ⅛" smaller than red. Glue pearls along red edges. Glue lace behind doily edges and doily to card front. Glue gold foil in center. Glue prints and bows.

3

ORIGINAL WRAPS & CARDS

CARD 2

Making Cardboard Gift Packages

Patterns & Templates

Whatever the occasion, these unusual cardboard gift containers will delight their receivers and add importance to even the simplest presents.

The attractive paper boxes may appear difficult to make by hand, but these unique gift packages can easily be created out of corrugated paper or lightweight cardboard.

Select the tubular or envelope-shaped package to hold your gift, and wrap the completed present with raffia or an interesting piece of twine. Attach a decorative fastener made from stones, shells, or beads. If desired, decorate the outside with cutout shapes of hearts and stars, or cinnamon sticks, buttons, dried flowers, and twigs.

Handmade packages crafted from corrugated paper are an unusual way to present a gift. If you wish to cover plain cardboard with wrapping paper before making the package, use a glue stick to adhere the paper to a piece of lightweight cardboard.

Patterns & Templates

Use the templates from Group 12, Card 1 to create unusual gift containers. Enlarge or reduce the template so the package fits your gift perfectly.

When making these gift packages, use an appropriate weight of paper that is thick enough to hold its shape, yet flexible enough to bend smoothly. Look in art supply or craft stores for a variety of corrugated papers and lightweight cardboards.

Using Gift-Wrapping Paper

If desired, you may cover smooth cardboard with decorative gift-wrapping paper.

- Follow steps 1 and 2, then cut a piece of wrapping paper slightly larger than cardboard.
- Using glue stick, glue paper to front of cardboard. Press around cardboard edges so paper is tightly bonded.
- Carefully trim excess paper away from cardboard, then follow steps 3 through 5 to finish.

You'll Need

- ***Corrugated paper or lightweight cardboard***
- ***Tracing paper***
- ***Pencil***
- ***Scissors***
- ***Craft knife***
- ***Glue stick***
- ***Raffia or twine***
- ***Fastener: shell, stone, or bead***
- ***Wrapping paper (optional)***

Tubular Gift Package

1 Trace package shape and all lines onto tracing paper. Place on wrong side of cardboard and cut out package shape. With tracing paper in place, mark curved foldlines by pricking tiny holes through cardboard with knife point.

2 Use tip of knife handle to make a deep score along pricked curved line and to score a line through center of package. Crease package inward along center scored line.

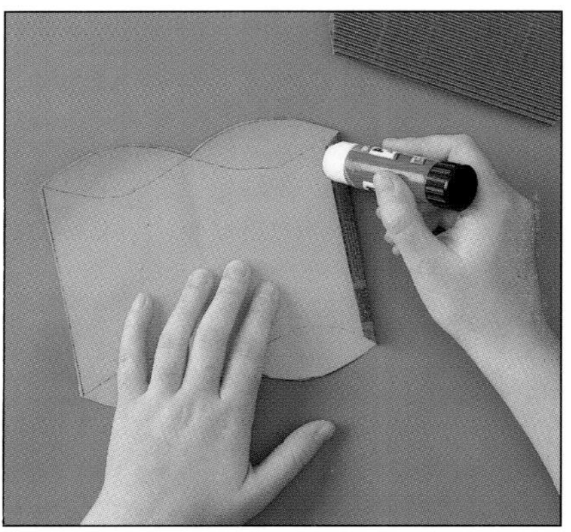

3 Fold long edge inward on markings and apply glue to flap. Bring opposite long edge over flap. Place a weight on top and allow glue to dry.

4 Gently squeeze sides of package to open slightly. At 1 end, fold in curved flaps along scored lines, 1 on top of the other; press in place. Insert gift. Close other end in same manner.

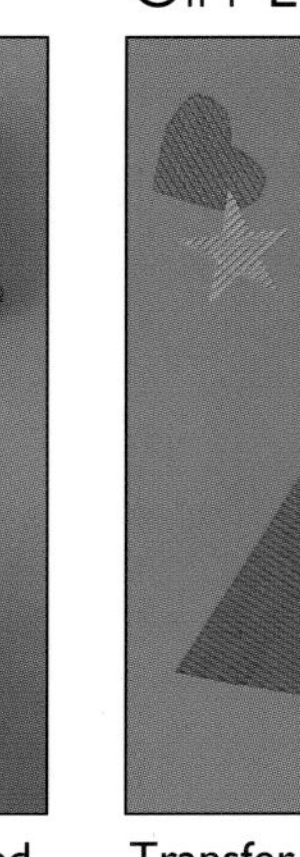

5 Tie raffia or twine around completed package, making sure ends are secure to keep them from opening. Knot raffia to hold in place. Attach selected decoration and fasten in place.

Gift Envelope

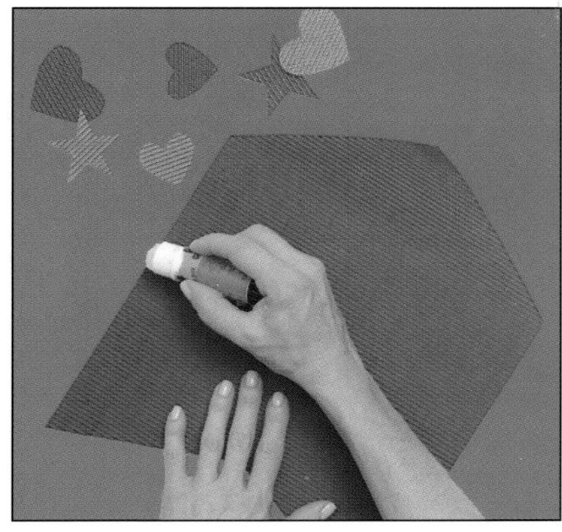

Transfer and cut out envelope pattern. Score on foldline. Glue upper side edges. Fold bottom up. Glue on hearts, stars, and fastener. Weight down and let glue dry. Fold flap down; tie as shown.

For further information: Crafting & Decorating Made Simple™ International Masters Publishers, 444 Liberty Ave., Pittsburgh, PA 15222-1207 1-800-527-5576

3

ORIGINAL WRAPS & CARDS

CARD 5

Stenciling Your Own Decorative Paper

Patterns & Templates

Even simple gifts can make a great impact when wrapped in hand-stenciled paper. Design your own wrapping paper to add just the right touch to any gift.

Handprinted wrapping paper can be used in many ways. Personalize a wedding or family photo album or revitalize an heirloom recipe book with a crisp new cover. A plain old gift box can become a gift in itself as well as a reusable decorative accent when you cover it with your own stenciled paper.

Use one of the motifs shown here, or create your own stencil designs from contemporary folk-art patterns. For an extra-special touch, stencil a motif that reflects the actual gift inside.

Stencil the same gift-wrapping design onto colored card stock to make a matching set of gift tags. With a little hand painting and stenciled designs, a band box becomes an updated version of a Victorian hat box. Add a cord or pretty ribbon for a handle .

Use the templates from Group 12, Card 2 to make hand-stenciled designs.

It is both fun and easy to personalize wrapping paper in different designs and colors.

Types of Paper

Start with paper that is porous and flexible, so it absorbs paint easily and folds gracefully around the object you are wrapping.

- Shelf paper or craft paper can be found in hardware stores.
- Look in art stores for rice paper, tracing paper, or papers used for rubbings.
- Colored tissue papers also work well, but may tend to ripple with wet paint.

Sponges and Brushes

Different types of sponges and brushes will give slightly different effects to your stenciling.

- Flat stencil brushes, found in craft stores, come in different widths to accommodate different-sized stencils.
- For best results, get a "dry-brush" effect by tapping brush or sponge on scrap paper after brush or sponge has been dipped into paint.

You'll Need

- ***Waxed stencil paper, acetate, or cardboard***
- ***Craft knife***
- ***Sponge or brush***
- ***Acrylic stencil paint***
- ***Foil pan***
- ***Shelf paper***
- ***Pencil***
- ***Scissors***

Stenciling Decorative Paper

1 To make stencil, trace design motif onto waxed stencil paper, acetate, or cardboard. Leave at least 1" margin around design. The areas to be cut away will become actual painted motifs.

2 Using a craft knife, retractable utility knife, or scalpel, start cutting out individual shapes of each motif. Some motifs may require small "bridges" of paper to separate the different shapes of each motif.

3 Cut smallest areas of a design first, such as sun rays in example shown above. Cut lines should overlap slightly at corners and points so that small pieces of paper will lift out cleanly.

4 If you are using a sponge to apply paint, cut sponge into long sections so each cut piece is easier to hold and dip into paint.

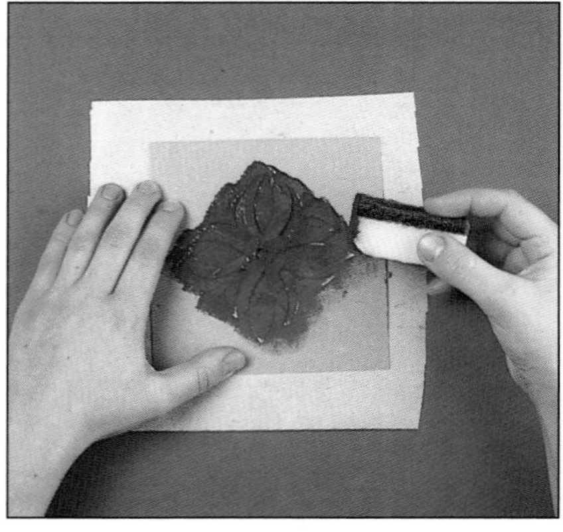

5 Practice on a scrap of paper first to determine amount of paint required. Put some paint in a pan, dip sponge into paint, and dab off excess. Gently dab sponge over cutaway areas of stencil.

6 Lift stencil and check motif. If stenciled shapes are not clean, as in top portion of this pattern, use less paint on your sponge or brush. If design is too light, apply a little bit more paint.

7 Once you have practiced on scrap paper, stencil over shelf paper. Use a different brush for each color, allowing each print to dry before moving on. Experiment with different shapes, colors, and combinations.

Using a Stencil Brush

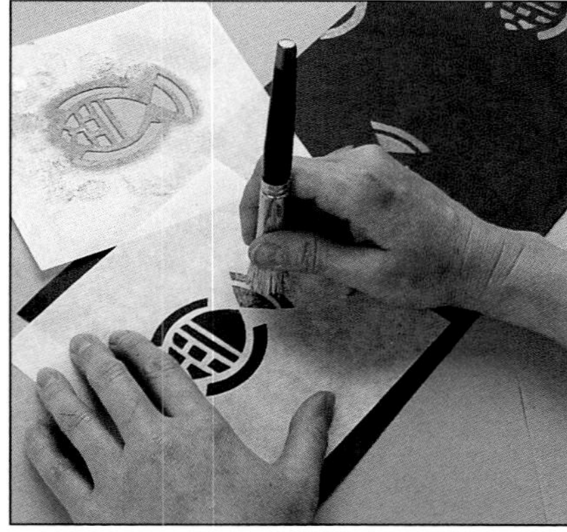

Dip brush in paint, then brush off excess paint. Hold stencil brush perpendicular to paper and gently tap brush up and down over cutaway areas of stencil.

Crafter's Secrets

Use a photo copier to reduce or enlarge a design before tracing it onto the stencil paper.

To make different star shapes, stencil any star motif first; rotate the template so the points of the star are staggered, then stencil over the star again. For a variety of looks, change the colors each time you rotate the template.

Try This!

Waxed stencil paper, which is easy to cut, can be found in craft stores. Acetate makes a more durable stencil, but is slippery and can be difficult to cut. If cutting two stencil papers at once, hold the two layers together with masking tape as you cut.

To clean any acrylic paints off the stencils, use a cloth dipped in rubbing alcohol and gently wipe the stencils clean. Never use water on waxed paper stencils.

Look in craft stores for a utility knife with a snap-off retractable blade. Not only is this knife safer to use, but a fresh sharp blade, which is preferable for best cutting results, is always available.

When you want to add a second color to a design, such as the orange tips on the sun motifs, cut a second stencil, rather than reusing the first one, and be sure to use a different brush for the new color.

Making a Stenciled Book Cover

Renew the outside of a badly worn book, diary, or journal by covering it with pretty stenciled paper. When you select a paper to cover the old surface, be sure the paper will fold and crease easily without cracking or becoming too bulky.

If the paper is at all transparent, glue plain white paper over the old cover first. Use a glue, such as rubber cement, that will allow you to slide the cover paper into perfect alignment and smooth away wrinkles or air pockets. You can also rub off the rubber cement easily without marking the cover paper.

For a more professional look, cut and glue a separate piece of matching or contrasting paper to the inside of each cover to hide the folded corners and edges of the cover paper. The well-finished result on the inside will be worth the extra effort.

A notebook, diary, or well-worn book can easily be dressed up with custom-designed paper. Choose a pattern that reflects the nature of the book or the person to whom it belongs. This is the perfect way to unify a series of personal journals for yourself or a friend.

1 Wrap white paper around book so paper extends slightly beyond edges of covers when book is closed. Glue paper to covers. Trim paper even with book edges.

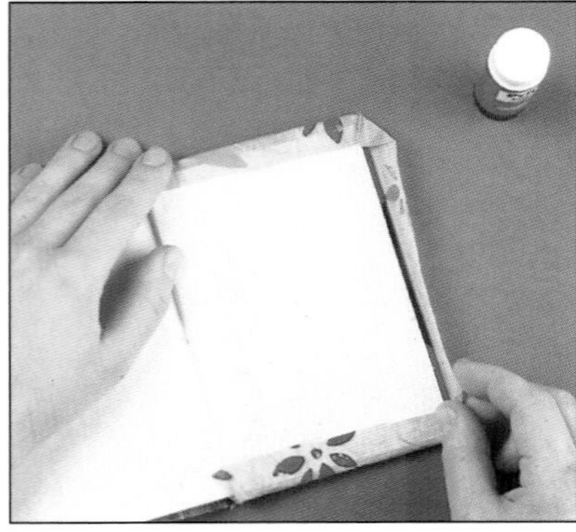

2 Cut stenciled paper, leaving a margin larger than book cover. Close book while covering it. Fold excess paper inside cover, mitering corners. Glue edges in place.

3 Cut 2 pieces of paper that are slightly smaller than inside covers. Glue 1 piece inside each cover to hide glued edges of cover paper.

Making Pressed-Flower Note Cards

Brighten someone's day by sending best wishes on note cards decorated with colorful flowers, leaves, and grasses you pressed and arranged yourself.

Making note cards with pressed flowers is so simple and quick, and the results so pleasing, you'll want to make a box full of them.

When planning the arrangement for note cards, think of using the pressed flowers in groupings that re-create bouquets or feature a particular type of flower. You can even arrange the pressed materials in an abstract composition.

Bear in mind that, with the exception of bright yellow and some orange flowers, pressing softens a flower's original color.

Flowers, herbs, leaves, grasses, ferns, mosses, and weeds make up this lovely pressed floral composition of a straw wreath. A basket made from the flattened half of a peat pot and weed stems holds a bouquet of geraniums, mums, and other pressed flowers.

The classic method of pressing flowers between the pages of a big book is still effective. Or layer plant material between sheets of absorbent paper and weight with a heavy object. If desired, purchase a simple flower press at a craft store.

Handling Pressed Flowers

If pressing your own flowers, pick plant materials just before their prime, when weather is dry and not too hot.

- Handle all dry floral materials carefully with tweezers, as they are very fragile.
- Store pressed materials between sheets of waxed paper in an airtight box or a warm, dry place.
- Plan placement of pressed materials before starting composition. Begin with background pieces and build design in layers.

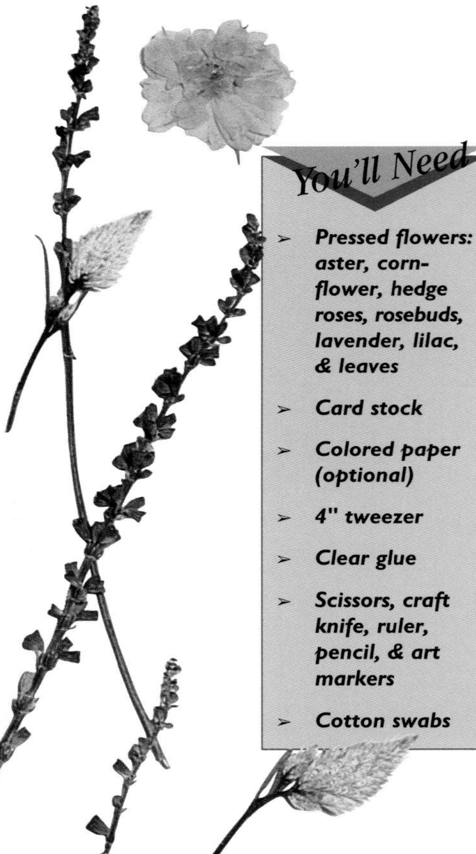

You'll Need

- ***Pressed flowers:** aster, cornflower, hedge roses, rosebuds, lavender, lilac, & leaves*
- ***Card stock***
- ***Colored paper (optional)***
- ***4" tweezer***
- ***Clear glue***
- ***Scissors, craft knife, ruler, pencil, & art markers***
- ***Cotton swabs***

1 Cut and fold card stock to finished size, creasing fold with ruler edge. If using paper overlay as background, cut and fold to fit card stock and glue in place. Draw ruled border ½" from edges of card front with marker.

2 Decide on placement of botanicals. Carefully position onto front of card using tweezers to avoid damaging delicate materials. Handle pressed floral materials as little as possible; use tweezers whenever possible.

3 Using tip of cotton swab, lightly dab glue onto back of hedge roses, leaves, and lavender selected to create background, positioning them carefully with tweezers. Replace swab as needed.

4 Position and glue cornflower, rosebuds, lilac, and aster, as shown, using clean swab to gently press pieces onto card; carefully glue on overlapping pieces. Glue on smallest floral pieces to finish display.

Crafter's Secrets

Here are a few suggestions to help you make and send professional-looking pressed-flower cards:

- *Use neutral-colored card stock, such as white, cream, beige, or tan, to contrast with plant materials.*
- *To achieve a crisp folded edge, fold card then score fold with blunt side of a dinner knife by running it along foldline.*
- *Dab a bit of glue on back of petals that have broken off, and position them in place on card.*
- *To mail a card decorated with pressed flowers, wrap in tissue or lay a piece of rice paper over the card to protect it. A small flat box lined with tissue is a more protective mailer than an envelope.*

Trimming Wrap with Tissue Paper

Ordinary brown paper becomes one-of-a-kind gift wrap when embellished with colorful tissue paper pieces. Natural twine and torn-paper tags complete the look.

Strips and small irregular shapes torn from two or three colors of tissue paper enliven plain-paper packages. Tissue paper is semi-transparent and creates unusual, beautiful effects when layered.

Strips torn by hand are attractive in their varying widths. Apply stripes around the package, or form a lattice by crossing contrasting-color strips on an angle. Accent with randomly placed irregular shapes. To finish, tear a gift tag from plain white paper and attach to twine wrapped around the box.

Crumpled balls of green and blue tissue paper are glued to a wrapped box to create abstract patterns or relief shapes. Red and orange torn circles create a stunning look on a small package. Overlap the circles and add yellow to expand the color effect.

Choose from a wide assortment of colorful tissue papers, available in art supply and stationery stores. Save your scraps from other craft projects; even a little piece of a special color can have a big visual impact.

Decorating Guidelines

Select tissues in different colors that blend nicely together. For example, layer cool blues and greens, or warm reds and oranges.

- Cut ordinary brown or other solid-colored wrapping paper to size for your package, then decorate paper. You can even use brown paper bag as base for decorated wrapping paper.
- Tear tissue paper, rather than cut it, to give decorations lively, handmade look.
- When attaching tissue paper, use glue sparingly on edges to avoid unsightly lumps.
- To position decorative crumpled balls in a specified area, glue balls onto base paper after gift is wrapped.
- To finish, tear off piece of white paper for gift tag. Hole-punch tag, then thread onto piece of household twine; tie twine around package.

You'll Need

- ***Plain brown paper or brown paper bag***
- ***Tissue paper in assorted colors***
- ***White paper***
- ***White craft glue***
- ***String***
- ***Scissors***

Decorating with Tissue-Paper Stripes and Squares

1 Cut brown wrapping paper to size needed. Choose 2 complementary colors of tissue paper. Tear long strips of varying widths from 1 color. Tear several square pieces from other color.

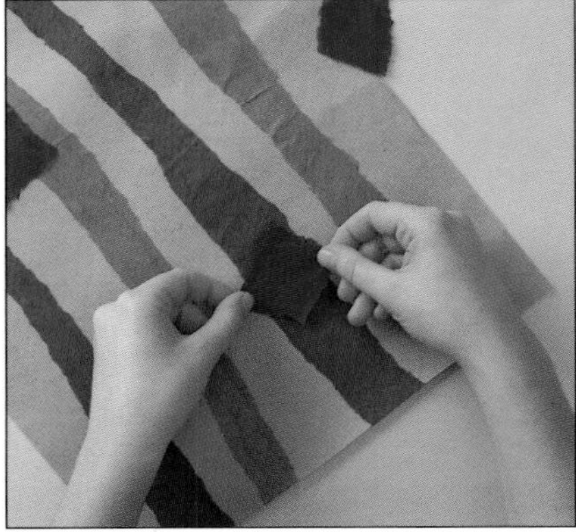

2 Applying glue only to edges, attach strips in stripe pattern across surface of paper. Glue squares in random but balanced pattern over stripes. Wrap gift after glue has dried completely.

Decorating with Crumpled Tissue-Paper Balls

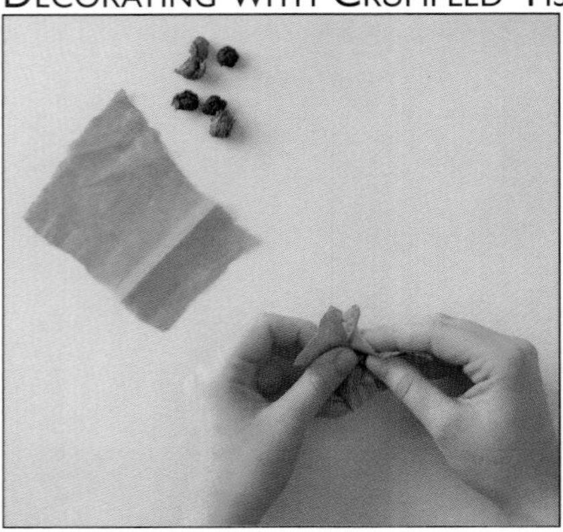

1 Tear small pieces of colored tissue paper. Crumple pieces up and roll in your hand to make little balls.

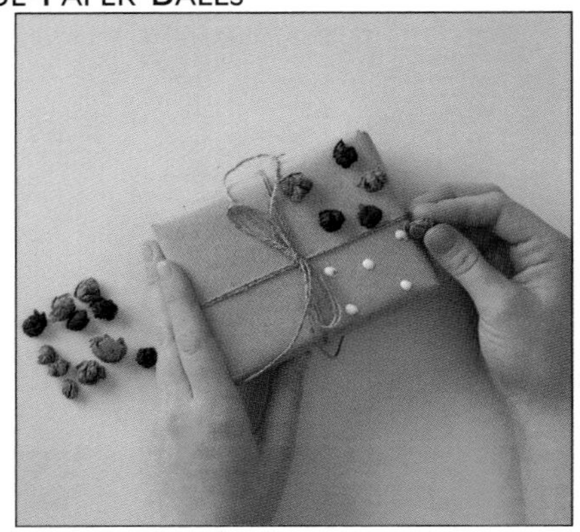

2 Wrap gift in wrapping paper and tie with string. Apply glue in small dots to wrapping and attach tissue balls. Make abstract pattern or outline specific shape, such as heart or star.

Decorating with Tissue-Paper Circles

1 Choose 2 complementary colors of tissue paper. Tear them into circular shapes of roughly same size.

2 Gluing only edges, attach shapes in tight, overlapping pattern over surface of paper. Wrap gift after glue has dried completely.

ORIGINAL WRAPS & CARDS

CARD 11

Stamping Tags for Bottles and Jars

Everyone loves receiving homemade or hand-decorated goodies. Give both by tying a handmade gift tag colorfully stamped with cut pieces of fruits or vegetables to a jar of treats from your own kitchen.

Holiday visits, housewarmings, or simply a friendly invitation to dinner are fitting occasions to bring a little something that says "love from our house to yours."

Pack mason jars with your special homemade preserves or condiments, or fill pretty bottles with fresh herbs and vinegars. Present them with gift tags stamped with one of the fruits or veggies used in the recipe for another personal touch. The reusable containers will be a reminder of your thoughtfulness.

The classic glass mason jar is both attractive and practical. Dress up the contents with a pretty ribbon tied around its neck and put your personal stamp on a tag that tells at a glance what is inside.

Accompany bottles and jars filled with homemade goodness from your kitchen with fun-to-make tags and labels printed with stamps made from fruits, vegetables, and herbs. Turn a plain container into a charming, resuable gift package by covering the lid or cork with fabric scraps and tying ribbon and twine around the neck of the container.

Stamping Guidelines

Select produce for stamping that is firm and not too watery. Apples, radishes, and mushrooms are good examples.

- Choose a motif that identifies contents of container, such as a pepper for a jar of salsa.
- If desired, use half a potato to carve out motifs that represent other varieties of fruits and vegetables.
- If desired, use an inked stamp pad instead of paints as stamping medium.
- Practice stamping on scrap paper until satisfied with results.
- Punch holes in lightweight cardboard for gift tags or use spray adhesive to affix labels.

1 Cut each mushroom or other vegetable or fruit in half, leaving a smooth cut surface to create a well-defined shape when stamped.

2 Place sheet of watercolor paper flat on work surface. Brush thick layer of acrylic paint directly onto paper to serve as paint pad. Tape fabric, craft paper, or cardboard to waxed paper to protect work surface from paint seepage.

3 Press cut side of mushroom into paint on paint pad, making sure paint completely covers cut surface. Or, if desired, use brush to carefully apply paint directly onto cut surface of stamp.

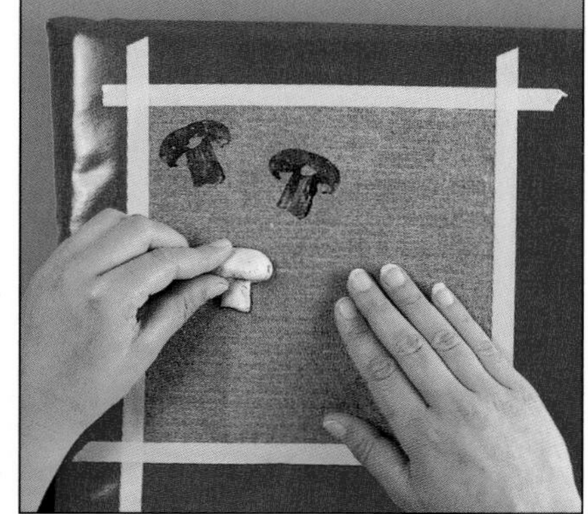

4 Press mushroom, paint-side down, firmly onto piece. Let paint dry. Cut out stamped motifs; attach to bottles or jars with ribbon or twine.

You'll Need

- ***Mushrooms or other vegetables & fruits***
- ***Self-adhesive labels, fabric, craft paper, or cardboard***
- ***Ribbon or twine***
- ***Acrylic paint & brush***
- ***Watercolor paper & waxed paper***
- ***Masking tape***
- ***Sharp knife & scissors***

Images that reflect the tastes or interests of a special someone can be fashioned into one-of-a-kind cards. Use sheet music, for example, for a musician friend; flowers for someone with a green thumb. Trim with ribbons, doilies, and foil tape.

Making Colorful Greeting Cards

Cutting, pasting, and a little imagination is all it takes to create these cheerful and colorful postcards and greeting cards. They're fast and fun to do, and you'll always have the right card for every occasion.

No more hunting from store to store to find the perfect card. When you make your own greeting cards, you can tailor them to fit the individual and the event. It's a thoughtful, personal way to send your best wishes.

Use the same cut-and-paste technique to create original postcards, invitations, thank-you notes, and gift bookmarks with pictures from magazines and catalogs, as well as old greeting cards.

To achieve the best results when making your own greeting and postcards, use good quality paper or card stock, which can be found in stationery, art supply, and craft stores.

Decorative papers, such as sheet music, gift wrapping, foil, and paper doilies, make attractive backgrounds and trims.

If you plan on mailing your card, use any envelope that fits or make a custom one. Decorate the envelope with bits of paper and trim used on the card inside. You can also decorate the back of the postcard, but do not obscure the message or mailing address.

Cutting Guidelines

Measure carefully and mark with a pencil before cutting.

- To cut straight, clean lines, use a craft knife.
- To cut out intricate patterns, use small, sharp, pointed embroidery scissors.
- Always protect work surface with a piece of cardboard or a self-sealing cutting pad.
- Always cut with the blade moving away from your body.

You'll Need

- ***Card stocks: colored & white or standard postcard***
- ***Paper: colored or glossy, colored foil, & sheet music***
- ***Trim: colored, glossy tape; paper doily; cutout of printed motif; ribbon***
- ***Craft knife, ruler, & pencil***
- ***Spray adhesive & craft glue***

Decorative Postcard

1 Mark a piece of colored card stock about ½" larger all around than postcard or white stock. Affix postcard to center of colored card with spray adhesive; smooth surface. Using ruler and craft knife, cut colored card on marked edges.

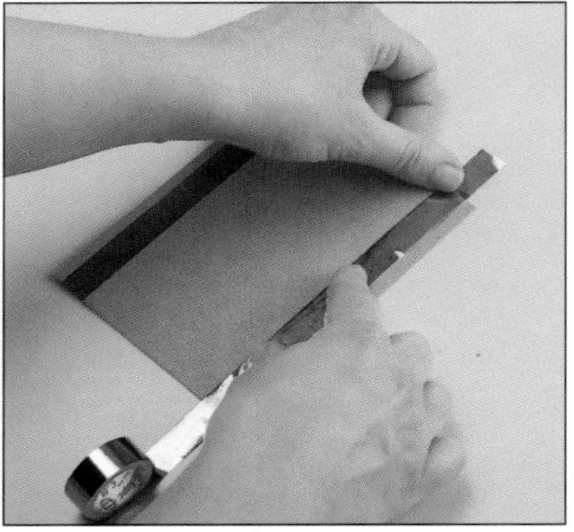

2 With card colored side up, apply strip of colored glossy tape ¼" from and along both long edges, extending about 1" beyond card. Smooth with fingertips. Turn card over and trim excess tape even with card edges.

3 Cut a square of contrasting colored card stock larger than print motif. Using spray adhesive, glue diagonally to center of card front. Using craft glue, glue motif to center of colored square.

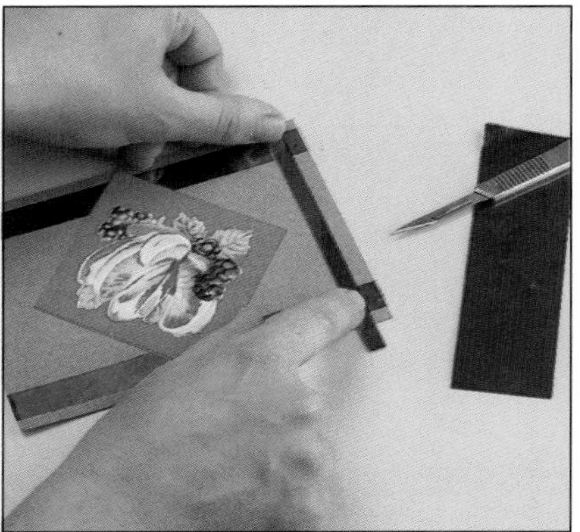

4 Cut 2 (½") strips of glossy paper to fit across short ends, with edges extending about 1". Glue strips about ½" from and along short edges of card. Turn over and trim excess paper even with card edges.

Paper Doily Postcard

Glue glossy or foil paper to front of card. Turn card over and, using craft knife and ruler, trim paper even with card edges. Cut paper doily into decorative pieces. Spray-glue doily and press in place.

Sheet Music Card

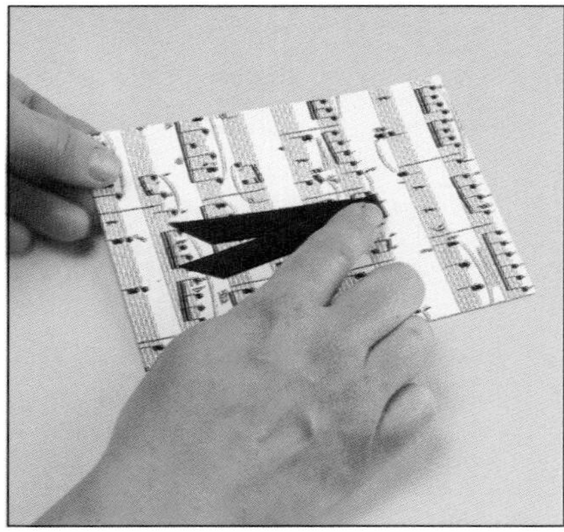

Glue sheet music to front and back of scored and folded card; trim edges even. Fold 6" length of ribbon in half, trim ends to points, and glue on card front. Glue motif over folded ribbon end.

Stenciling Holiday Wrapping Papers

Patterns & Templates

Add an artistic touch to your Christmas presents this year by wrapping them with papers you have designed and stenciled with easy decorative motifs.

Friends and family will be delighted with their holiday gifts dressed in handmade stenciled gift wraps with matching gift tags. Golden angels and polka dots, shimmering Christmas trees, and bright starbursts and hearts are easy motifs to stencil.

Using a stippling sponge applicator or household sponge to apply the acrylic paint onto solid-colored heavy paper results in a well-defined, textured shape. The same technique can be used with other theme-specific motifs.

Make coordinated gift tags for your Christmas packages. Simply transfer a simple motif, such as the star or angel, onto a sturdy piece of decoratively textured paper or lightweight cardboard. Cut out the shape, punch a hole in the top, and tie it to the package with a piece of twine or ribbon.

Patterns & Templates *Use the motifs from Group 12, Card 23 to make stencils for your holiday gift-wrapping paper and accompanying gift tags.*

Stencils for the painted designs can be easily made from cardboard. For a textured look, apply the paint with a stippling sponge, available at any art or craft store. For opaque shapes, use matte acrylic paints. To achieve a more translucent look, use watercolors, but do not water them down too much or the image will run.

Paper-Stenciling Tips

Select an attractive solid-colored recycled paper, plain white, or a subtle tone-on-tone color. Remember that paint adheres best to paper with a matte finish rather than a shiny, slick surface.

- As an alternative to using stippling sponge, paint can be applied with stencil brush or pieces of household sponge. If using sponge, have several pieces handy and change to new piece when used sponge becomes saturated.
- Do not overload stippler with too much paint or stenciled motif outlines will blur.

You'll Need

- ***Papers: solid-colored matte wrapping paper; white paper for template***
- ***Pencil & graphite paper***
- ***Cardboard***
- ***Scissors, craft knife, & cutting mat***
- ***Stippling sponge***
- ***Acrylic paints***
- ***Newspapers or paper towels***

Stenciling Hearts onto Wrapping Paper

1 Transfer stenciling shape to white paper using graphite paper; cut out shape with scissors to make template. Outline template onto piece of smooth cardboard.

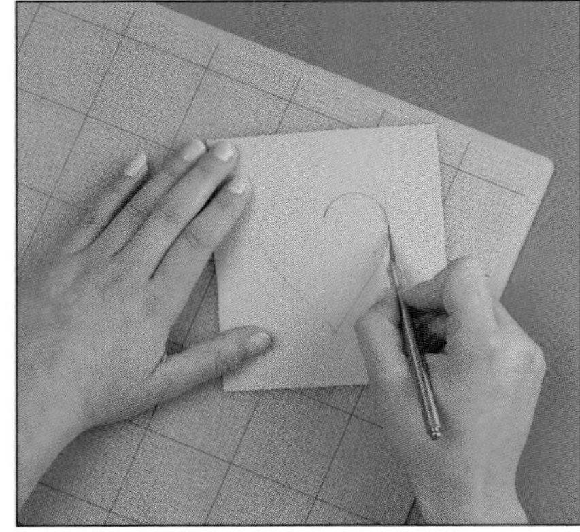

2 Working on cutting mat or other protective surface, cut out stencil using craft knife; turn cardboard instead of knife to cut curves.

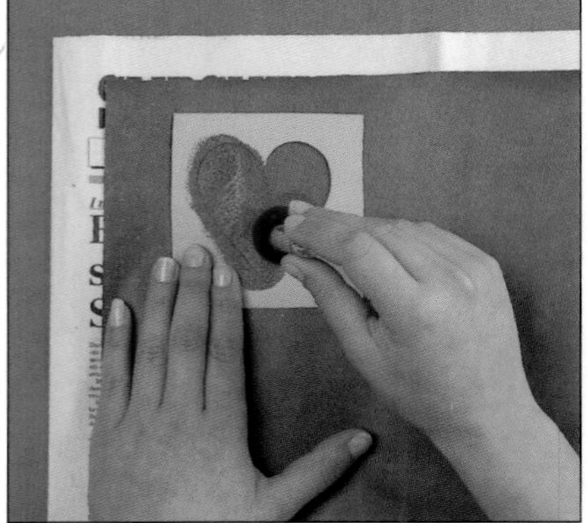

3 Place wrapping paper over several layers of newspaper or paper towels. Position stencil. Dip stippler into paint and dab paint onto paper, working from edge of stencil in toward center.

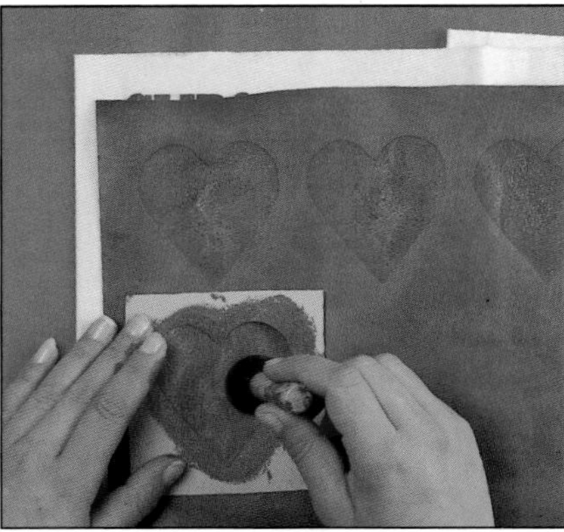

4 Continue stenciling in this manner, making as many rows of motifs as desired. Avoid touching wet paint. When all rows are completed, allow paint to dry completely.

Stenciling Bright Stars

Make star stencils, as described above, in various sizes. Using bright-colored paint against dark paper, stencil stars in random, yet balanced design across paper.

Stenciling Decorative Dots

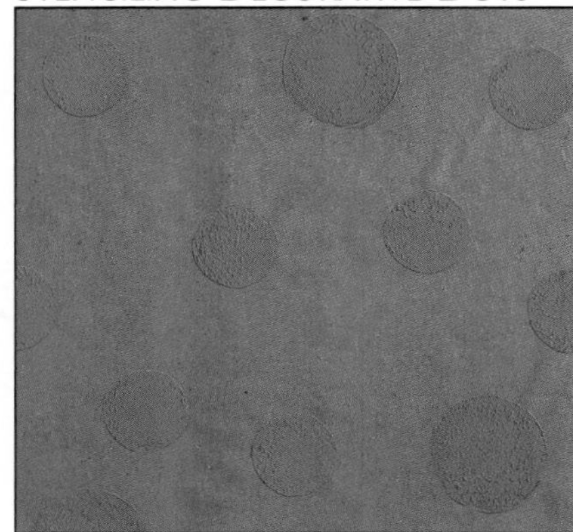

Make circle stencils, as described above, in various sizes and stencil them with green paint in random pattern across bright-colored paper.

Decorative Home Furnishings

Interior decorations that reflect your personal style

Painting Fun Theme Chairs for Children

Patterns & Templates

It takes so little to delight a child and ignite a young imagination. Painted chairs and stools transport a child to the garden, baseball diamond, or pond!

A child's room is much more than a place to sleep; it is the safe haven that inspires elaborate imaginings. A bright flowered garden chair complete with lattice trellis and climbing green vines is a cheerful addition to a bedroom or playroom.

Regardless of your room's decor, a painted furnishing adds color, interest, and life. Use acrylics to paint personalized designs on any freshly painted piece of furniture and transform a room into an enchanted play area.

A vibrant red, white, and blue chair is just right for a baseball enthusiast, especially when it comes with hooks to hold a glove and hat and a place for a real baseball. The bright colors of this jolly frog sitting on a flowering lily pad will make this stool, with each leg painted a different color, a favorite with any youngster.

Use the patterns provided on Group 12, Card 32 for the motifs used on all the featured chairs. Patterns fit a standard child's chair with a seat measurement that is about 12" deep by 14½" wide. Enlarge or reduce the size of the motifs to fit your chair.

Whether using new or previously painted furniture, prepare surfaces for the best results.

Preparing the Surface

Wash prepainted wood with soapy water. If existing finish is not cracking or peeling, just sand and prime.

- If necessary, remove old coats of paint or varnish, then sand with fine-grade sandpaper. Remove dust with tack cloth.
- Once piece has been stripped and/or lightly sanded, apply two coats of primer.

You'll Need

- **Wooden child's chair**
- **Graphite paper, tracing paper & pencil**
- **Paintbrushes: flat foam & small tapered**
- **Polyurethane varnish**

For garden chair:

- **Acrylic paints: dark pink, bright green, lavender, medium blue, medium orange, brown, & yellow; white primer**
- **Jumbo craft sticks; thick tacky glue**
- **Artificial ivy**
- **Hammer & finishing nails**

For baseball chair:

- **High-gloss latex paint: red, white, & blue**
- **Plastic J-hooks**
- **Shallow wooden or plastic cup, 2½"– 3" diameter**
- **Screwdriver & screws; drill & drill bit**

Creating a Garden Chair

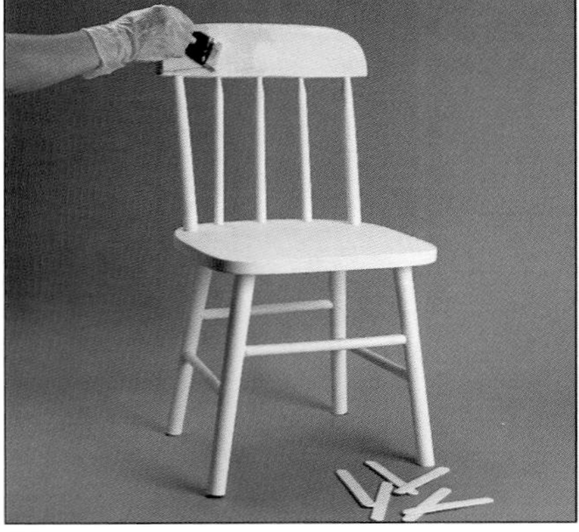

1 Apply 2 coats of white primer to both sides of jumbo craft sticks. Paint all sections of clean and sanded chair in same manner. Allow coats to dry between applications.

2 Transfer flower motifs to chair: Trace motifs onto tracing paper; tape to chair and insert graphite paper, carbon side down, between tracing paper and chair. Draw over design lines.

3 With small tapered brush, work from back of seat to front to avoid smudging paint. Paint 1 color at a time, beginning with green foliage, followed by pink tulips and large center flower. Use clean brush for each color; let dry between coats.

4 Paint remaining flowers and let dry; then paint center with small tapered brush. Repeat for chair back. Touch up all motifs as needed once paint has dried completely. Apply several coats of polyurethane varnish.

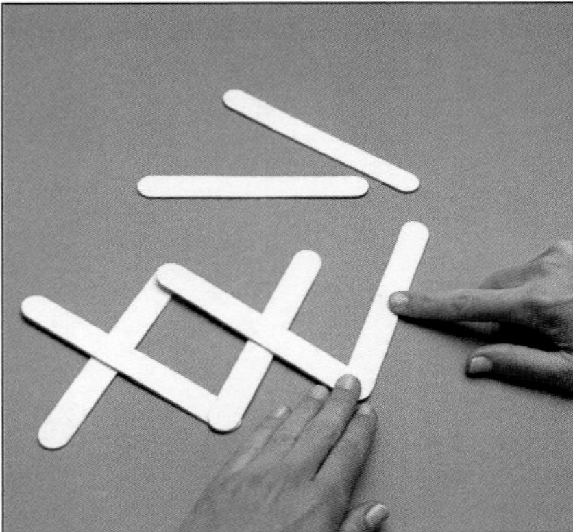

5 To determine trellis length, measure distance between front and back chair legs just under chair seat and between side chair legs just above floor. Lay out painted craft sticks in touching X's, angling them to obtain exact trellis lengths.

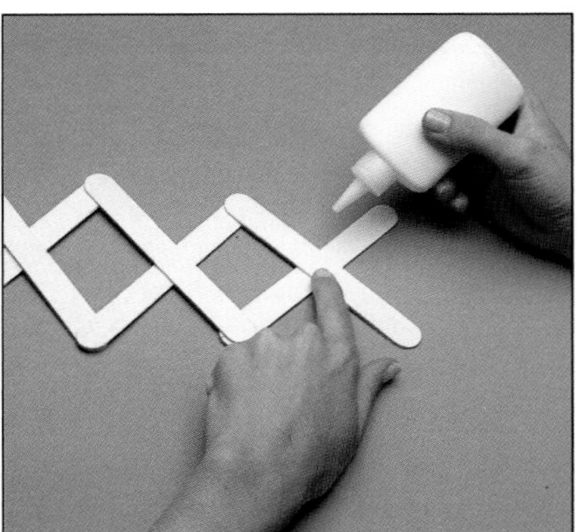

6 Carefully apply thick tacky glue to top, middle, and bottom of craft sticks as arranged in previous step. Put pressure on glued spots until pieces hold together. Let glue dry completely.

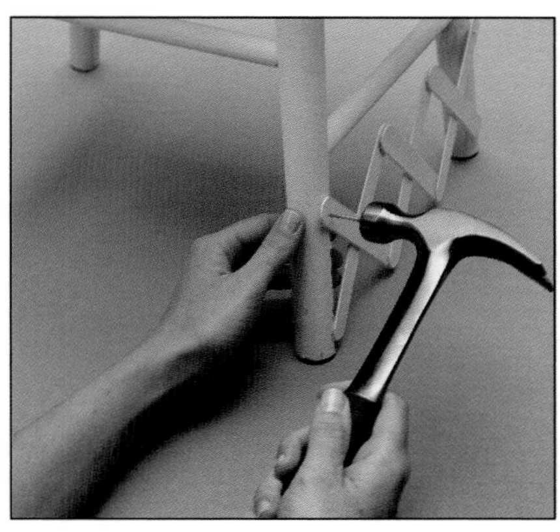

7 Pencil-mark trellis locations on chair legs. Glue or use small finishing nails to attach trellises all around legs. Make sure sticks do not extend beyond chair seat where they may be bumped.

8 Wind vines of artificial ivy through latticework and up and around chair legs. If necessary, glue in strategic spots to secure. Arrange vines so that leaves face out and have a full appearance.

Try This!

For guaranteed sweet dreams, paint a wooden rocking chair with primer tinted a soft blue. Cut compressed sponges into various cloud shapes, then dip them in water, squeeze them out, and stamp white acrylic paint clouds on the seat and back. Protect the paint job with several coats of non-yellowing polyurethane varnish. For extra impact, cut sun, moon, and star motifs from colored craft foam using the patterns provided on Group 12, Card 32. Attach them around the chair with glue. The foam is soft and thin and will not disturb an occasional adult nap!

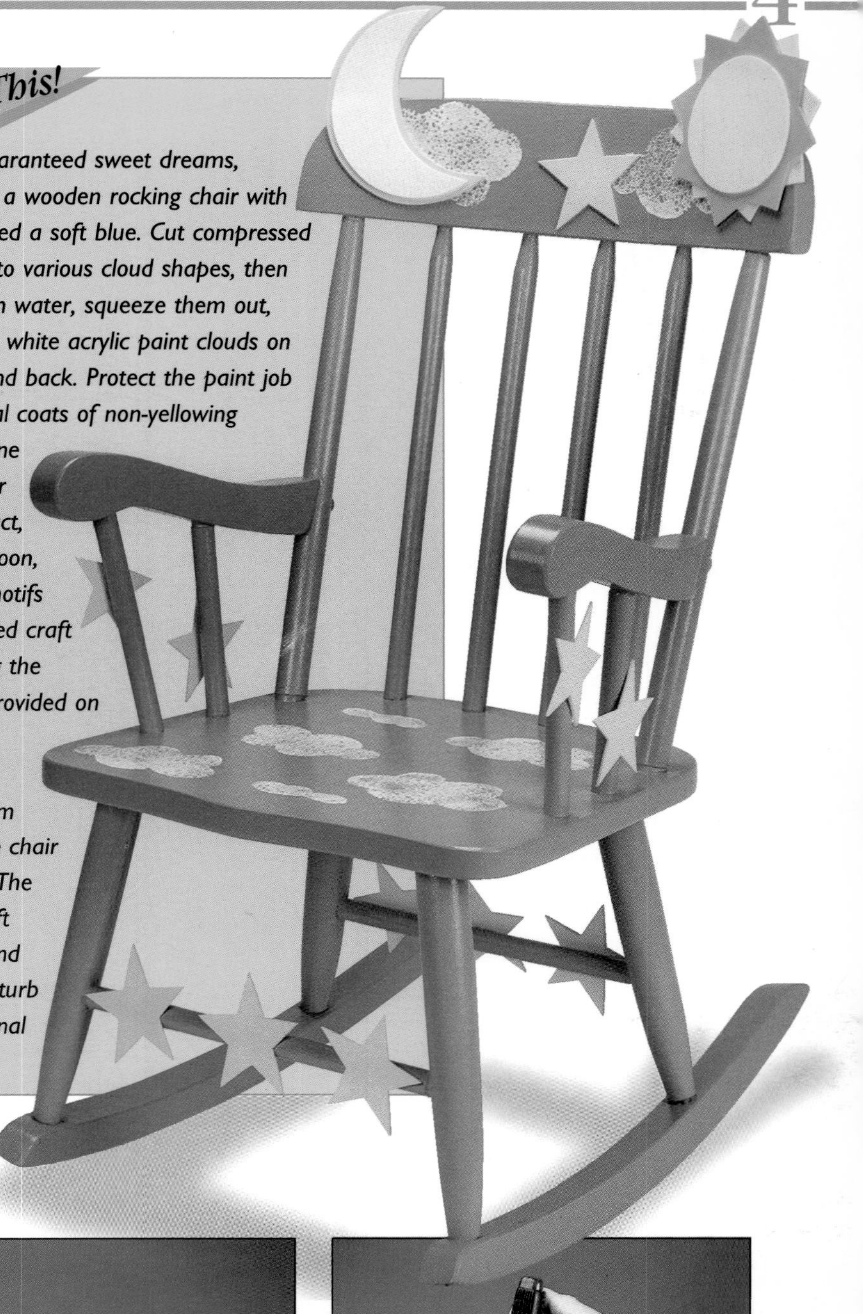

Painting a Baseball Chair

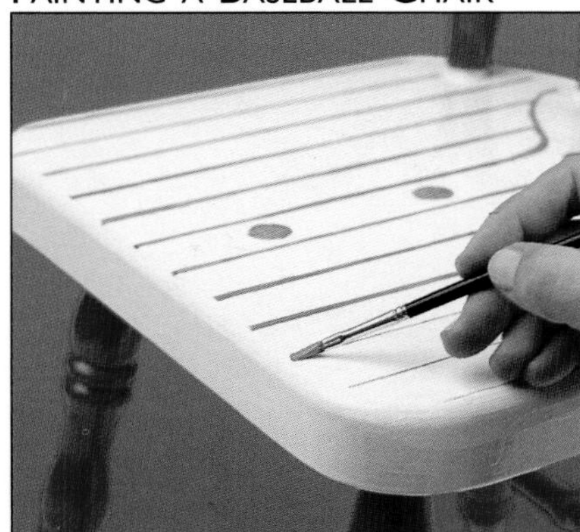

1 Paint chair seat white; legs, back, and slats red. If desired, paint any decorative slat knobs blue. When dry, transfer shirt front pattern from Group 12, Card 32 to seat and paint blue.

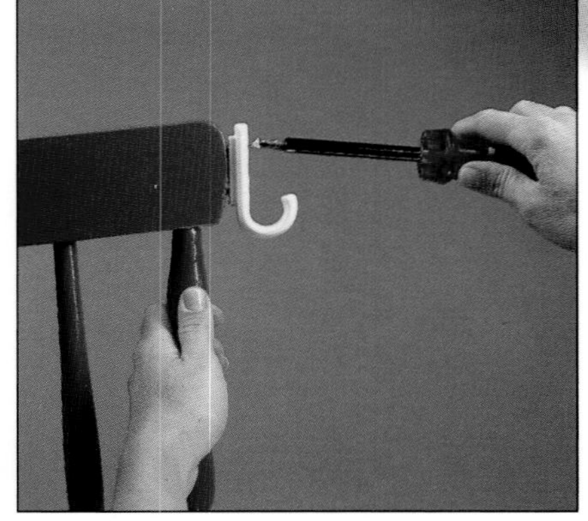

2 Using drill or hammer and nail to start pilot holes, screw plastic hook to each side of chair back. Hang baseball cap or glove from hooks. If desired, attach looped piece of rope around bat, so bat can also be hung from hook.

3 To make baseball holder, drill hole in center of colorful shallow wooden or plastic cup. Screw to top of chair. If desired, glue a decorative baseball to opposite end of chair top.

Just a little imagination, paint, and adhesive letters and numbers turn a plain table and chair set into an exciting and informative addition to a child's room, perfect for all sorts of hands-on activities.

Creating a Colorful Furniture Set

A child-size table and chair set is a delightful precursor to a desk and is infinitely useful. Sets are often sold at unfinished furniture stores at reasonable prices and are easy to work with since they require very little surface preparation. Hand-me-down or used furniture is even less expensive and often needs only a good cleaning and a light sanding before painting. Wipe away the dust after sanding, and apply two coats of primer.

For a cheerful set like this, use acrylic or latex paints in bright colors. The letters and numbers are 2" black self-adhesive vinyl.

To paint the black stripe around the rim of the table and chair, cut several strips of 1"-wide low-tack masking tape and apply them side by side across the rim; remove every other piece and paint across the tapes with black paint. The tape can be repositioned as you work.

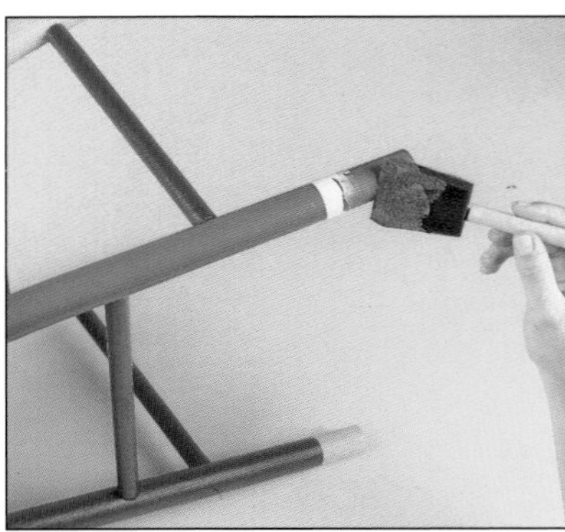

1 Paint furniture 1 color at a time, leaving tabletop and chair seat rims unpainted; let dry. Paint rims white; when dry, paint black stripes. To paint different colors on legs, wrap low-tack tape around adjacent painted sections.

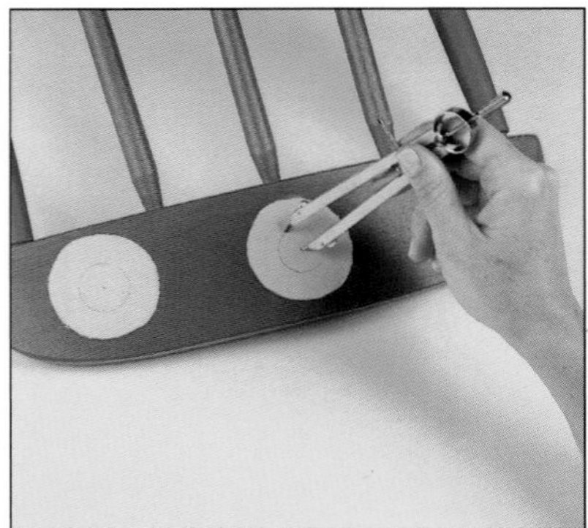

2 For decorative circles, determine diameter of outer and inner circles based on width of chair sections. Use compass to draw outer circles, then paint. Once paint is dry, use compass to draw inner circles and paint.

3 Cut around each vinyl letter and number; do not remove from backing. Position them on table and chair seat as desired. Remove backing, 1 letter/number at a time, and smooth onto surfaces. Apply 2 coats of varnish.

DECORATIVE HOME FURNISHINGS

CARD 11

Painting Floors with Colorful Designs

Patterns & Templates

Add color and interest to a room by painting the floor with colorful geometric patterns. Then seal your handiwork with clear polyurethane to protect it from wear.

Like quilt blocks assembled to form a larger design, these squares, rectangles, and diamonds team up to create an attractive colorful pattern that covers the entire floor surface and anchors the room's decorative scheme.

Parallel and intersecting straight lines are marked and then edged with tape to provide a temporary frame for painting. With the pattern outlines masked this way, the painting itself can be less painstaking but still yield sharp, straight, clean edges when the tape is removed.

Use the same block pattern, but in a smaller scale, to paint the edges of a white floor, adding soft color without dominating the room. A stenciled floral border frames a golden finished wood floor.

Patterns & Templates

Follow the block diagram on Group 12, Card 25 to paint your floor design.

Measure the floor's outer dimensions, then plan the layout of the design on paper, dividing the floor into individual whole blocks that fit fully into the space. For floors with irregular edges, adjust design as necessary. Color in the paper design plan to use as a guide.

General Guidelines

Prepare a wooden floor by sanding in the direction of the wood grain. If the floor originally had a laminate finish, apply a primer coat and let dry before painting. Mark the center of the floor with intersecting perpendicular lines.

- Mark areas of block pattern with painter's tape before painting. Burnish tape edges with thumb to prevent paint from seeping underneath.
- Use second coat of paint for more opaque color. Let each coat dry before applying next.
- If stenciling, apply repositionable adhesive to back of stencil. Press all edges of stencil securely onto floor surface.

- ***Latex paints: eggshell (base coat), violet, teal, pea green, & pale yellow***
- ***Clear polyurethane sealer in satin finish***
- ***Wide foam brushes & small & large paint rollers with extra covers***
- ***Painter's tape***
- ***Craft knife***
- ***Sandpaper & tack cloth***
- ***Gloves & paper towels***
- ***T-square, yardstick, & pencil, or chalk line***
- ***Vacuum cleaner***

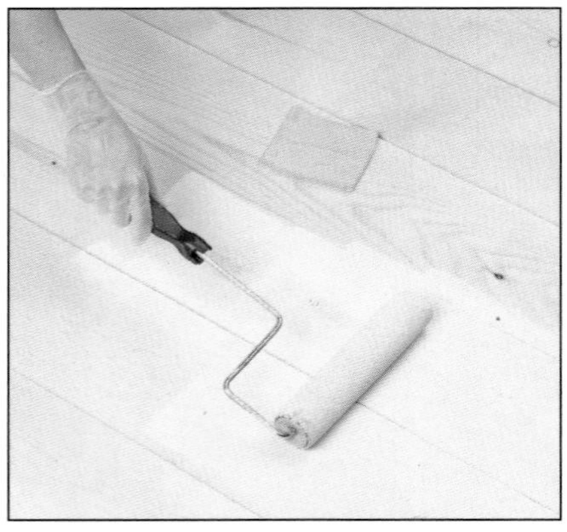

1 Vacuum, then use tack cloth to remove any dust. Cover baseboards with wide painter's tape. Apply eggshell base coat with large paint roller. Touch up with brush as necessary; let dry. Apply second coat for opaque color.

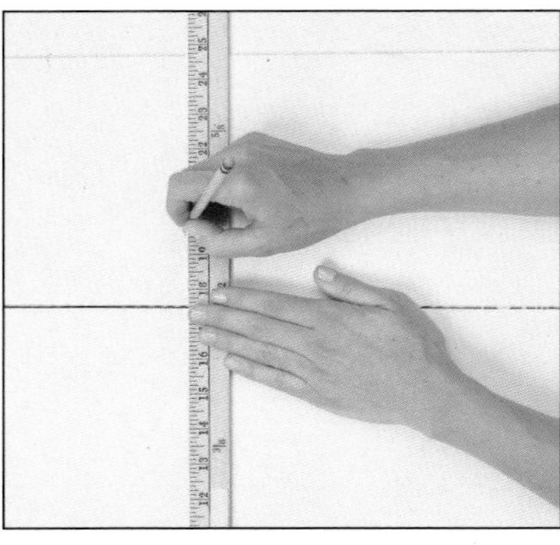

2 Beginning at center of floor, use yardstick and pencil to mark all horizontal and vertical lines of pattern grid. Refer to your paper plan for placement of squares and rectangles. Use T-square to check accuracy of right angles.

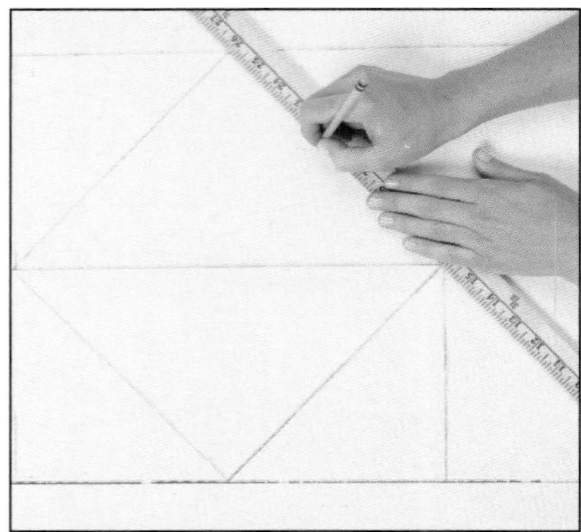

3 Draw diamond inside each large square: Mark midpoint of each eggshell-colored square. Draw diamond connecting midpoints.

4 Place tape along edges of rectangles that will be painted pea green. Position tape just outside pencil line so that each rectangle is completely framed and paint will cover lines. Use craft knife to trim tape at corners for clean angle.

5 Use wide foam brush to apply coat of green paint to framed rectangles. Let paint dry completely, then apply second coat of color. Remove tape carefully after second coat is completely dry.

6 Use tape to frame small squares at intersections of painted rectangles to prepare them for painting. Use small roller to apply 2 coats of violet paint. Remove tape carefully when paint is completely dry.

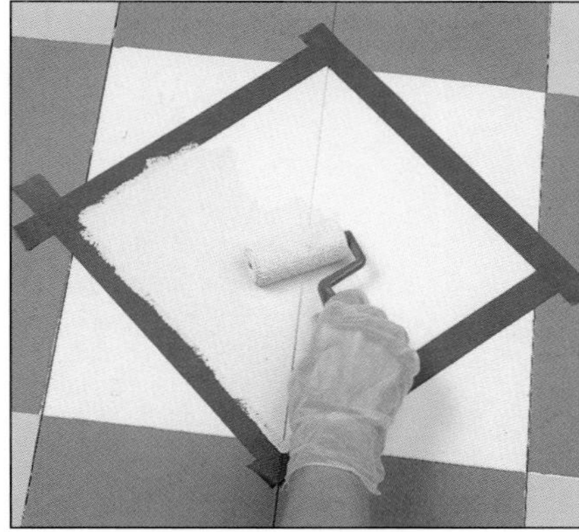

7 Place tape along edges of diamonds, overlapping at corners for sharp points. Consult paper plan, then apply 2 coats of pale yellow or teal within diamond. Let paint dry completely, then carefully remove tape.

8 Following plan, finish painting entire floor. Use foam brush or large paint roller to apply several coats of clear polyurethane sealer over floor. Let each coat dry completely before applying next. Dry completely before replacing furniture.

Crafter's Secrets

Speed the process of marking diamonds within large squares by creating a template. Trace the dimensions of your diamond onto firm cardboard or clear acetate and cut it out with a craft knife. Position this template within each square, matching the diamond points to the marked midpoints of the square's sides, and then outline quickly.

Try This!

Apply two coats of pale blue base paint to the entire floor, then use fleur-de-lis stencil on Group 12, Card 25 to paint motifs over the floor. Measure and mark the placement of each motif before beginning to paint. For a rich, dramatic effect, use metallic gold paint to stencil the designs. Finish the floor with several coats of clear sealer to protect your work from wear.

Stenciling Tiles for a Play Room

Stencil solid-colored interlocking foam tiles, available at tile stores and home supply centers, with fun motifs of your child's favorite animals; then connect them into a full room-floor covering. If you prefer, cover just part of the floor for a play area, or even make a play mat that gets disassembled and stored in a closet when not needed.

Select one or all of the animal motifs given on Group 12, Card 25. If desired, make your own stencil designs by tracing simple shapes from a favorite coloring book onto clear acetate, then cut out with a craft knife. Use bright acrylic paints to stencil a one-color silhouette in the center of each tile. Placing the animals on the diagonal of the tiles adds another dimension to the finished floor design.

To install as a full-floor covering, cut down the tiles that go along the walls as necessary. Either leave them as is or add a simple painted border to coordinate with the animal design.

Create a four-color checked floor pattern by alternating two different-colored tiles in two adjoining rows. If you stencil the same animal on the same colored tiles, the animals will be alternating as well.

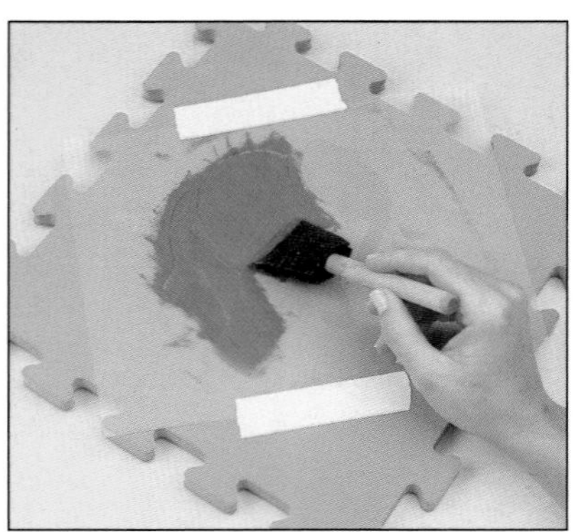

1 Center stencil on diagonal of tile and tape down edges. Use wide foam brush to paint cutout areas of stencil, applying paint with smooth strokes in 1 direction. When paint is completely dry, remove stencil.

2 Apply 2 or 3 coats of clear acrylic sealer to entire top surface of tile to protect painted motif from wear. Let sealer dry completely between coats and before putting tiles in place. Assemble tiles in alternating pattern.

4

DECORATIVE HOME FURNISHINGS

CARD 9

Making Button-Back Fitted Slipcovers

Use beautiful decorator fabrics to create a slipcover for a unique and personal design statement. These slipcovers have a softly tailored look that is complemented by the distinctive button-back closure.

Make a single stunning cover for a living room chair, or make covers for a set of chairs to coordinate a dining set. Fabric and trim will determine the finished look. Use piped trim and buttons that match, or make a statement with a contrasting color to enhance the look.

These covers are easy to remove for cleaning. When made for the change of season or holidays, redecorating is a breeze. Use these slipcovers as a way to add color and style to any room setting.

Slipcovers can be designed to suit individual chair variations. Make the seat gusset narrow or wide as desired. Solid-colored fabrics tend to have a formal look. Fabrics with an even stripe, while making cutting easy, create a more casual ambiance.

When selecting fabrics for your slipcovers, choose a closely woven fabric with enough weight to withstand daily wear and tear. Medium-weight linen, cotton, or chintz are good choices as they are easy to sew and have a smooth finish. If you select a lightweight fabric, back it with an inner lining or fusible interfacing to add body.

Slipcover Guidelines

Preshrink fabric before cutting and always check to ensure fabric is colorfast and soil resistant.

- When cutting out, cut each section on straight lengthwise grain of fabric. Mark center front and back on all pieces.
- After pieces are cut, pin them together on chair, wrong side out, and adjust fit.
- Center large motifs on front and back sections as well as on seat of chair.
- If desired, cushion seat with foam. Use foam that has high durability and won't slide. Cut foam using seat pattern. Place foam on seat under slipcover.
- If desired, make contrasting colored piping from continuous bias strips and medium cording, and sew piping around seat.

You'll Need

- ***Slipcover fabric***
- ***Contrasting fabric & cotton cord for piping***
- ***Butcher's paper & marker; fabric marker***
- ***Fusible fleece***
- ***Tape measure & straight ruler***
- ***Scissors: paper & fabric***
- ***Sewing machine & matching thread***
- ***6 buttons***

Measuring and Cutting

You will need to measure and make patterns for the following pieces:

(a) Front of chair back
(b) Back of chair back (including overlap and facing)
(c) Chair back gusset
(d) Seat (Cut from fabric and fusible fleece.)
(e) Seat gusset
(f) Skirt (Cut out along lengthwise fold of fabric; piece if necessary.)

Trace patterns onto fabric and add 1" seam allowances to all edges to allow for fit. For gussets (c) and (e), add extra length. It is easier to trim excess if gusset is too long. Cut 1 of each piece unless otherwise stated.

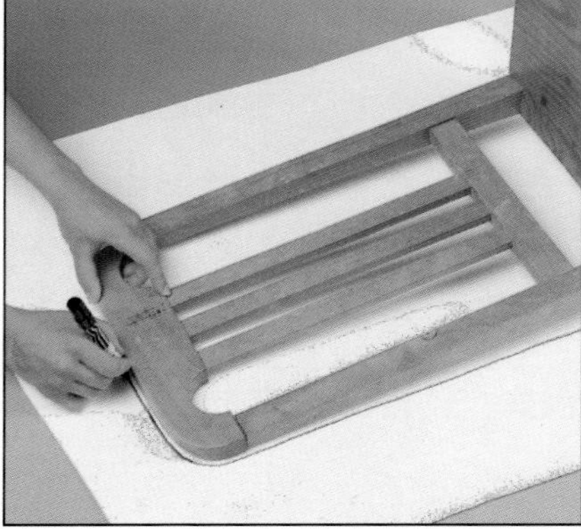

1 Lay chair on piece of paper and trace around chair back. Mark dotted line to indicate lengthwise center and straight line 1" to right for overlap and foldline. Measure sides and top of chair back for length of chair-back gusset **(c)**.

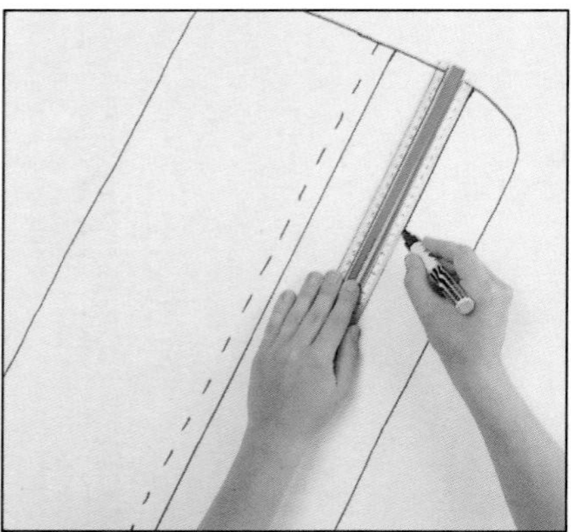

2 Draw parallel line 3" to right of foldline for back facing. Cut piece **(a)** from entire pattern. Use 1 side + overlap and facing of pattern to cut 2 pieces of **(b)**. Cut 4"-wide chair-back gusset **(c)**.

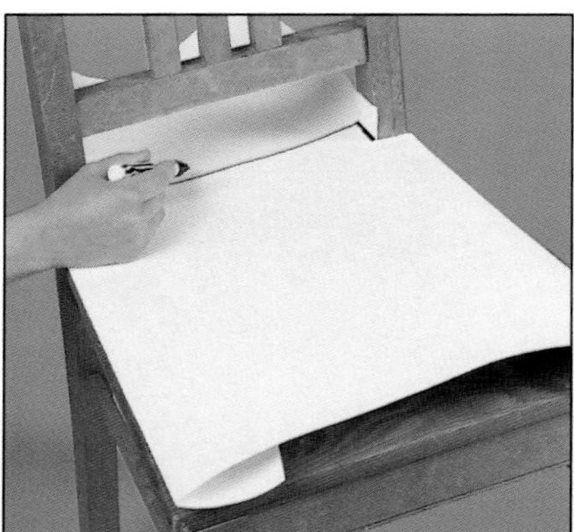

3 Place piece of paper on seat and crease to follow seat shape. Fold sides under to mark. Clip into paper at back seat corners and mark. Cut out seat pattern **(d)** and check for fit.

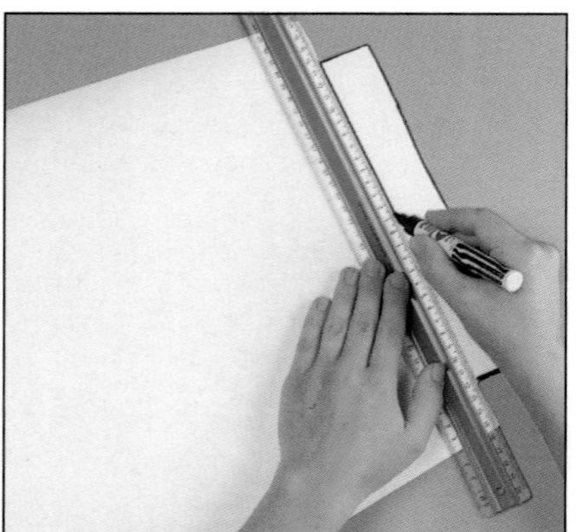

4 Draw line on seat pattern across back rest; trim away. Use seat pattern to cut fusible fleece. Following manufacturer's instructions, fuse fleece to wrong side of fabric. Mark seam allowances around fleece and cut out fabric.

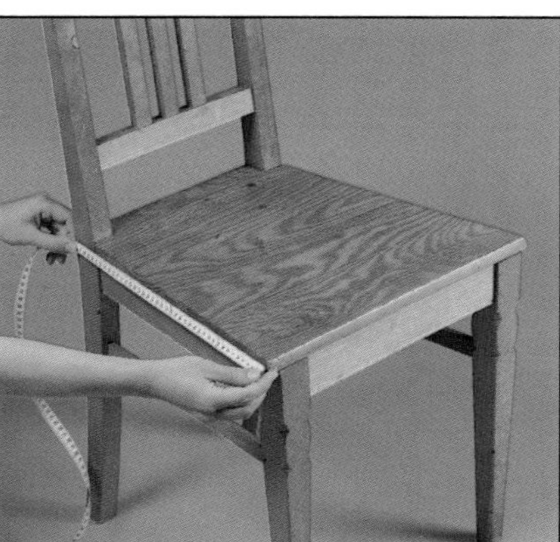

5 Cut seat gusset **(e)** to equal 4" x measured circumference + 3" for overlap and facing. Cut skirt **(f)** to equal measured seat circumference + 6" overlap and seam allowances + 60" for corner pleats x desired skirt length, doubled.

6 Press all facings to wrong side along back and gusset foldlines. Right sides facing, pin all pieces together to make inside-out cover to check for fit and make adjustments: Begin by pinning front **(a)** and chair back gusset **(c)** together along upper and side edges. Lap backs **(b)** at center and pin to remaining edge of back gusset **(c)**. Place pinned cover over chair back and make fit adjustments. Trim away excess fabric, leaving ½" seam allowances. Place seat **(d)** on chair and pin to front of chair back **(a)**. Pin seat gusset **(e)** around seat, matching center fronts. Clip into seam allowances at top and bottom corners for better shaping. Press skirt piece **(f)** in half lengthwise with right sides together and stitch along short edges. Turn right side out; press. Matching center fronts and center backs, pin raw edge of skirt **(f)** to seat gusset **(e)**. Mark and pin 15" box pleats at each corner of seat, with each side of pleat 3¾" deep. Make fit adjustments; trim seam allowances. Remove slipcover; detach seat gusset **(e)** and skirt **(f)**. Narrow hem overlap edges. Stitch pieces together in order of pinning, attaching any piping to each side of seat gusset **(e)** if desired.

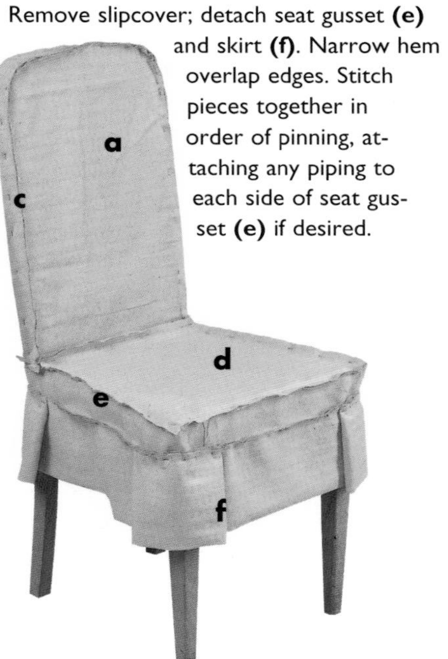

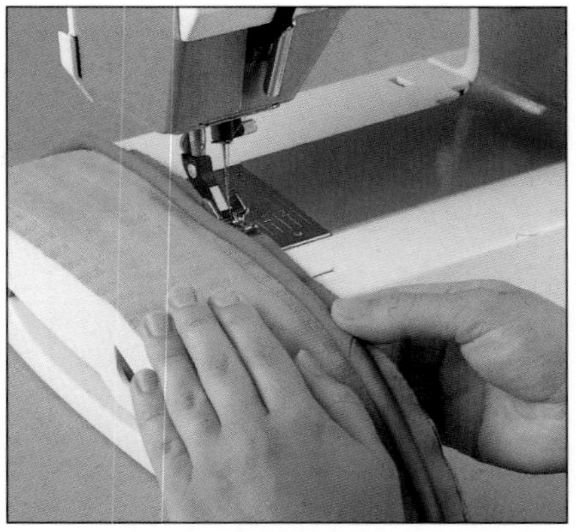

7 To make piping, cut 1½"-wide bias strips and join together at right angles. Center cord on wrong side of strip, and fold over cord. With zipper foot, stitch fabric close to cord to encase. Sew piping to each side of seat gusset **(e)**.

8 Press all seams flat after stitching and again after completing slipcover. Finish all raw edges on inside with zigzag or serger. Mark for 6 evenly spaced buttonholes on back. Sew buttonholes, then sew buttons to match on opposite side.

Try This!

Slipcovers can be made to fit most styles of chair. For a chair with a padded seat and partial seat back, sew a separate cover for the seat, then make a cover for the chair top with matching fabric. Try forming box pleats all around the chair seat.

Making Slipcovers for Seats

A slipcover looks attractive even when covering just the chair seat. You can sew the skirt either fully pleated as described below, or with just an inverted box pleat in the corners following the basic instructions. If you are making the fully pleated skirt, it is best made with a single thickness of decorator fabric and a lightweight backing, so the skirt won't appear too heavy. Narrow hem the lower edge.

Measure the chair for the seat, gusset, and skirt measurements, making patterns as necessary. Add a ½" seam allowance to all seams. Make the skirt for the front and sides in one piece, and make a separate back skirt. Plan for overlapping openings that are held securely with hook-and-loop fastener tape. A fully pleated skirt requires three times the length around the chair plus seam allowances and facings. The cover shown has 6" long and 4"-wide box pleats.

Create a harmonious effect in a room by making a fully pleated slipcover for the seat of the chair out of leftover curtain fabric. The coordinated styling brings a sense of composure to a setting.

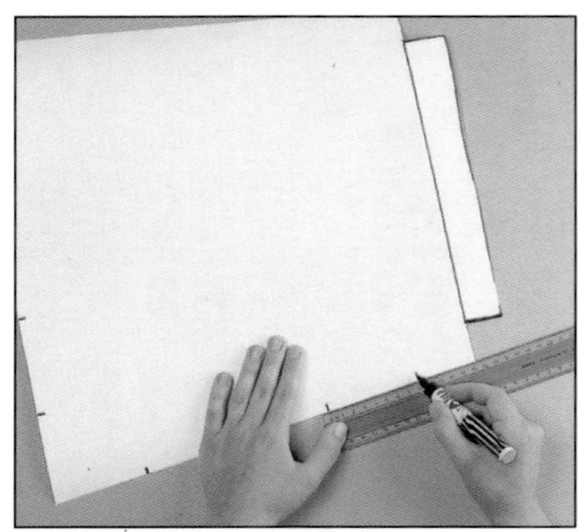

1 Make pattern for chair seat as previously directed, but do not cut off back extension. Mark pleat placements at regular intervals, beginning pleats at each front corner and evenly dividing area between corners.

2 Cut out fabric and backing. Put together and treat as 1 piece. Measure front, sides, and across back of seat; cut out gussets adding extra for overlaps. Sew gussets to seat. Pin-mark, press, then baste pleats on skirt.

3 Place slipcover over chair and check for fit. Mark placement for hook-and-loop fasteners and stitch in place. Press pleats and all seams. Place cover on chair and fasten.

Creative Wall Accents

Hand-crafted pieces to highlight your walls

5

CREATIVE WALL ACCENTS

CARD 1

Creating a Wreath with Dried Oats

A wreath made of dried oats is an imaginative way to accent a room. The oats are easy to work with and their rustic country image looks great on a door or wall.

A basic wreath like this one, made out of sheaves of dried oats and dotted with dried roses, berries, and bits of bark, is a perfect example of an effective decorative touch that costs very little to create. It can be trimmed in any number of ways. By adding different types of bows and dried materials, you can totally change the final result, giving it a country look, Victorian charm, or contemporary style. With seasonal trims, it could become a Christmas or other holiday wall decoration.

While the oats are beautiful by themselves, a cluster of dried red roses provides an accent of rich color. The heart-shaped wreath suggests a gift for Valentine's or Mother's Day or just to tell someone that you are thinking of them fondly.

To achieve thick, professional-looking results in the finished wreath, you will need at least two or three bunches of oats for a wall wreath, and twice that amount for a full two-sided wreath to hang in a window.

Wreath-Making Guidelines

Before beginning to make the wreath, estimate the number of small bunches of oats you'll need and make enough bunches so you won't have to interrupt your work flow once the construction of the wreath is under way.

- Trim stems of oats and other plant materials to about 3" before forming small bunches.
- If using purchased dried rosebuds without stems, insert a 6"–8" piece of spooled wire halfway through base of dried rosebud, then fold it in half to form a stem.
- You can make your own wreath form by bending heavy-gauge floral wire or a wire hanger into desired shape and wrapping it with floral tape. You can also purchase ready-made wire wreath forms in flower and craft shops.
- Choose a shade of floral tape that blends with color of oats. Floral tape both helps produce a finished look and holds plant materials in place, preventing them from sliding around on slippery metal of wreath base.

- **Plant materials: dried oat stems, rosebuds, pieces of bark, & artificial berries**
- **Heavy floral wire, spooled floral wire, & wire cutters**
- **Floral tape**
- **Lace or ribbon (for bow)**

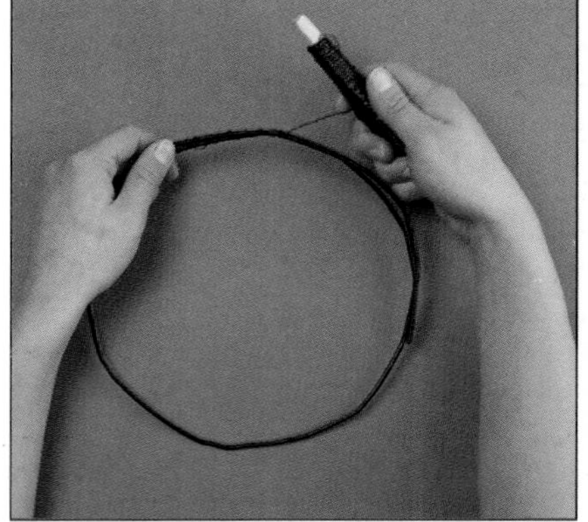

1 Bend heavy floral wire into circle of desired size. For a large wreath, strengthen shape by forming several overlapping circles of wire. Wrap circles with spooled wire to hold them securely together.

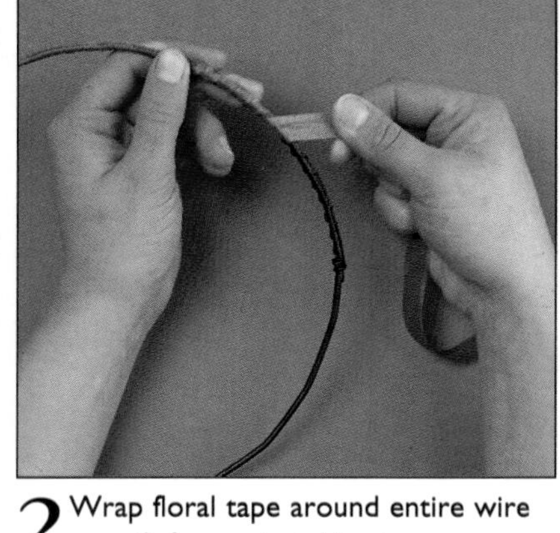

2 Wrap floral tape around entire wire wreath form, stretching tape as you wrap and overlapping tape slightly to completely cover ring. Tape will give added strength to wire and help keep plant materials in place.

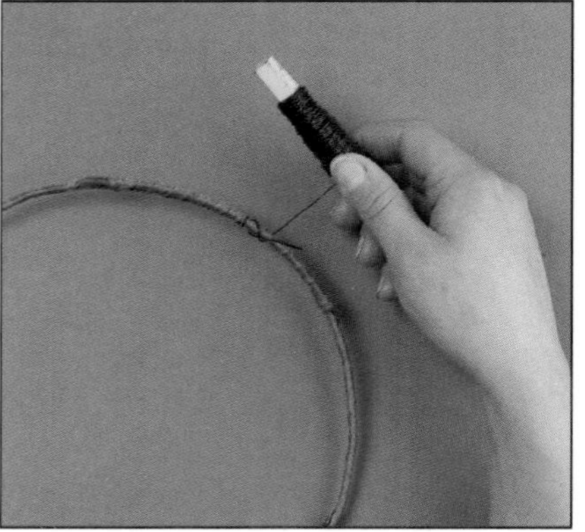

3 Beginning at point where taped ends of wire base overlap, wrap spooled wire around ring a few times to secure end of wire.

4 Place a small bunch of wired oat stems on base, heads pointing upward, and continue to wrap spooled wire tightly around base and over stems, securing oats to ring.

5 Add rosebud to wreath base, placing it so it overlaps oat stems at bottom of bunch; continue wrapping wire, catching rose stem under it.

6 Make a cluster with another bunch of oat stems, a piece of bark, and some artificial berries. Place it on wreath base, overlapping stems of last bunch and covering base. Tightly wrap wire around new stems to keep them in place.

7 Continue adding oat stems, rosebuds, bark, and berries around entire ring, placing bunches close together and wrapping each addition tightly in place with wire. Clip wire, leaving a 2" tail, and wrap around ring to secure.

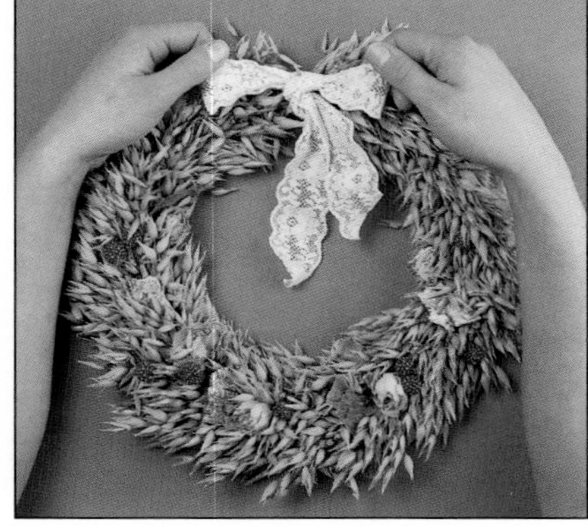

8 Tie a piece of lace into a soft bow, trimming ends into points. Slide a 6" piece of spooled wire through back of bow knot; twist, then wrap ends around wreath to attach bow.

Try This!

Spruce up the basic oat wreath by adding dried flowers and citrus slices, nuts, cinnamon sticks, and any other ornamental details that strike your fancy. Experiment with the bits and pieces you have on hand or work around a theme, such as a season or a holiday.

For a shimmery, opulent look, spray the wreath with a metallic paint before adding the decorative trims, or spray the finished wreath with all its trims in place.

9 Fold a 10" piece of spooled wire in half, then wrap with floral tape. Fold taped wire in half to form a loop. Wrap ends of loop around back of wreath base for a hanger.

Crafter's Secrets

If you are having difficulty getting the wire for the wreath form shaped into a perfect circle, bend it around a large round shape, such as a stock pot. A Dutch oven will provide a perfect oval for your wreath. Look around your home for items that will lend their shapes to a wreath.

Using Colored Oats

Oats not only are available in their natural state, but they can also be purchased already treated and colored in a number of interesting shades. The store-bought deep blue oats used in this striking oval wreath provide an appropriate background for the decorative seaside motif.

Shaping the wreath into an oval rather than a circle adds another degree of interest. To make the wreath freestanding, the wire ends are wrapped round the oval several times when the shape is formed, then bent down and "planted" into a clay pot filled with floral clay or plaster of paris to form a stable base. A wreath of this sort forms a unique backdrop for a collection of small treasures and found objects.

Even the shape of this shell-trimmed blue wreath suggests the flow of the ocean. With the addition of colored seed pods or artificial fruit and gilt wood shavings, it makes a very strong decorative statement.

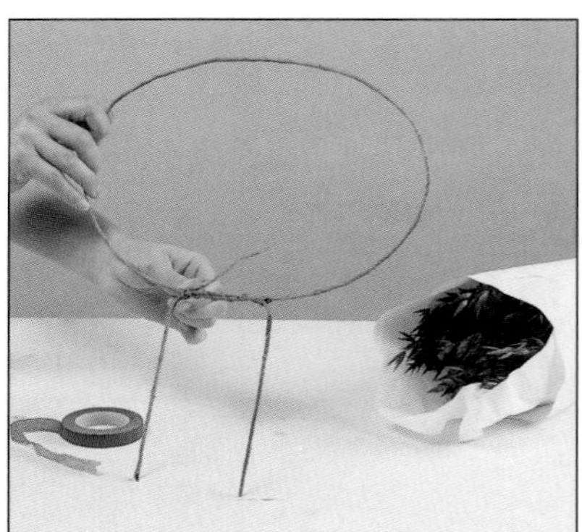

1 Bend floral wire into an oval ring base. Overlap and twist wire together for about 2" at bottom of oval, then bend wire ends down, perpendicular to ring. Wrap floral tape around oval portion of wreath base.

2 Wire blue oat stems around entire oval section of wreath base, covering both front and back of oval with oat stems. Fill a container with floral clay and insert wire "legs" into clay.

3 Glue or wire shells, seed pods or artificial berries and fruit, and gilt wood shavings to front of wreath. Cover floral clay with colored stones or sand, or top with gilt shavings. Use gloves if working with gilt shavings.

Creating Beautiful Seasonal Garlands

As each season arrives, nature provides an abundance of new plants in a range of colors, scents, and textures. A garland made from this bounty is a beautiful way to invite the outdoors inside.

A stroll in the garden, a walk in the woods, or an amble along the shore will yield a treasure trove of plant materials and seasonal bits and pieces to use as accents for the garland. Look for shells, seed pods, and colorful flowers to dry in the summer, and dried leaves, nuts, and grains in the fall. Holly and pinecones are perfect for a winter garland, while lavender and other delicate blooms herald in spring. What you can't find, you'll be able to locate at flower or craft shops.

Trim a horseshoe-shaped straw form with sprigs of rye for summer, then add seashells and coral, dried roses, cornflowers, seed pods, and leaves. Emphasize the breezy, fresh look with cascading bows of double-faced deep pink satin ribbon.

To create a seasonal garland, gather dried plant materials, such as dried roses, strawflowers, sunflowers, rose hips, tansies, and assorted nuts and green leaves.

General Guidelines
Divide each plant material into two piles so it can be used equally on each side of the garland.

- Wire together small bunches of plants, some with small and some with large blossoms.
- Group smallest plant materials, such as rose hips, into tiny bundles, then add them to other bunches. Keep all bunches about the same size.

Wiring Guidelines
Use spooled wire to hold plant materials in bunches and to attach bunches to straw form.

- To wire plant materials together, leave a tail of wire about 1" longer than stems, and run wire up stems to base of flower heads. Wind wire around once, then spiral it down stems; twist ends together and clip.
- To wire bunches to form, start from center of form and work toward one end. Work one side of garland at a time.
- Wire bunches close together so all stems and stalks are hidden.
- When adding heavy materials, such as nuts or heavy flower heads, push 16-gauge wire into them, then push wires into form and bend to hold.

You'll Need

- ***Straw garland form***
- ***Dried grasses & flowers***
- ***Nuts & leaves***
- ***16-gauge & regular spooled floral wire***
- ***Floral tape***
- ***Sharp knife, clippers, & scissors***
- ***Glue gun & sticks***
- ***Raffia***

1 Gather 4–5 stems of rye grass together. Wire stems up to heads and angle stems at 90°. Wire together 5–6 stems of plant material, such as rose hips, in same manner, but do not bend.

2 To make looped hangers, cover 2 (16"-long) pieces of 16-gauge wire with floral tape. Form a 1"-long loop around finger and twist 2–3 times. Force ends of each looped hanger into ends of form so only loop protrudes.

3 Using spooled wire, fasten a wired bunch of rye grass along lower edge of garland form with heads hanging down and stems pointing toward 1 end of form; wind spooled wire around form, catching bent end of stem.

4 Wire a rounded shiny green leaf behind each bunch of rye grass to force rye forward, setting it off and helping to fill out garland.

5 Position a row of mixed flower bunches above rye and across form with stems of bunches pointing toward end of form. Wrap wire tightly across stems and around form to hold each bunch in place.

6 Prepare nuts with wire stems. Insert wire stems of each nut into form, pushing them in at an angle or straight down.

For further information: Crafting & Decorating Made Simple™
International Masters Publishers, 444 Liberty Ave., Pittsburgh, PA 15222-1207 1-800-527-5576

7 As you work toward 1 end, use bunches of smaller flowers and leaves. Continue to attach bunches of rye grass, each with a leaf behind it, along lower edge. Fill in any thin spots with small bunches of alfalfa, clover, or dock.

8 Continue adding bunches of dried material up to 1" from end of form. Wrap wire tightly several times and cut, leaving a 4"–5" piece. Force wire end into form. Hot-glue a few leaves in place to cover end of form and hanging loop.

Try This!

Make a rustic-looking three-quarter harvest wreath using the bounty of nuts, grains, mosses, and dried fruits of the season. Wire and hot-glue the natural materials onto a straw form and finish with wire loops as for the garland. Trim with autumn-bright wired ribbons fashioned into bows and suspend from a length of jute or twine.

9 Begin covering second half of form by securing spooled wire about 1½"–2" from center. Working in same manner as first half, point plant material toward unfinished end and cover space in center with a few bunches of interesting flowers.

Crafter's Secrets

Look for attractive ways to hide the hanger loops. Ribbon bows are an obvious choice. Another way is to make fluffy bows from raffia: Wrap the raffia around the palm of your hand, slide it off and wrap it tightly in the center using a second piece of raffia. Leave the ends long enough to tie the finished bow over the hanger loops. Fluff the finished raffia bow for added fullness.

Create a Floral Garland with Lavender Swags

To give your garland a more dramatic look, hang small nosegays from its ends to act as decorative swags. The nosegays are fastened to the garland with spooled wire, which is hidden under luxurious bows. Add dried lavender to the nosegays to fill the room with a delightful floral scent. Consider using other scented herbs, such as sage, artemisia, rosemary, and mint, which have wonderful fragrances when dried and are suitable to use as decorative accents.

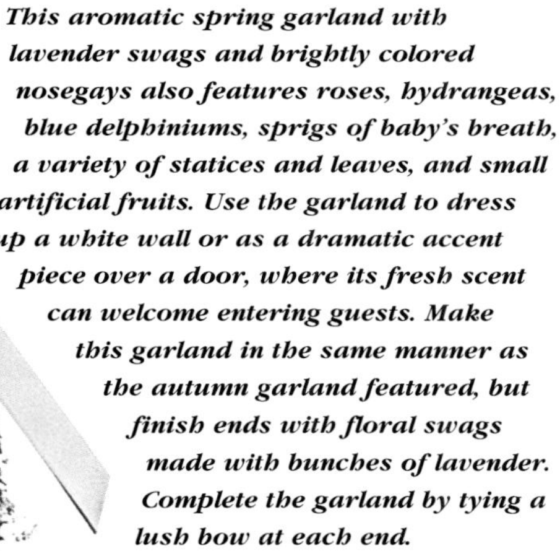

This aromatic spring garland with lavender swags and brightly colored nosegays also features roses, hydrangeas, blue delphiniums, sprigs of baby's breath, a variety of statices and leaves, and small artificial fruits. Use the garland to dress up a white wall or as a dramatic accent piece over a door, where its fresh scent can welcome entering guests. Make this garland in the same manner as the autumn garland featured, but finish ends with floral swags made with bunches of lavender. Complete the garland by tying a lush bow at each end.

1 Arrange flowers and plant materials, excluding lavender, into a nosegay. Add leaves to base. Wrap spooled wire around base to hold stems together. Trim stems to desired length of finished swag.

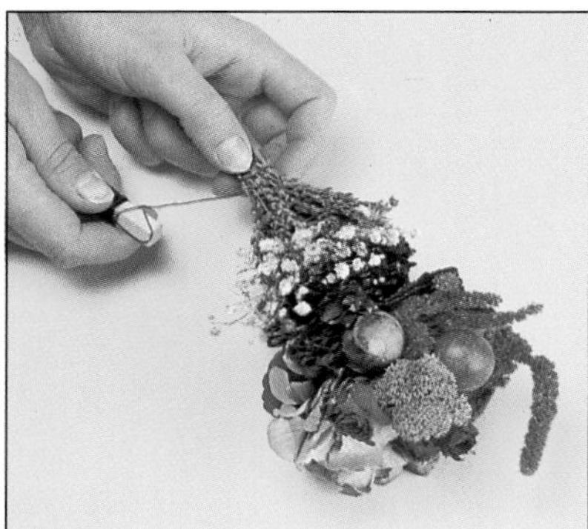

2 Tie a bunch of baby's breath below nosegay, then cover stems with lavender, wrapping with wire as necessary. Use fewer and shorter pieces of lavender as you get closer to end, but cover all bare stems.

3 Trim lavender stalks. Fasten off wire, leaving a short length to attach swag to garland. Wrap wire securely around looped hanger of garland. Cover hanger with a full satin bow made with long streamers.

For further information: Crafting & Decorating Made Simple™ International Masters Publishers, 444 Liberty Ave., Pittsburgh, PA 15222-1207 1-800-527-5576

Creating Colorful Hanging Baskets

Hanging baskets filled with flowers and vines accent the outside and inside walls of your home with cheery splashes of color.

For an eye-catching display, combine colorful sun-loving plants, such as purple and hot-pink petunias with hot-pink ivy geraniums and vincas. Hang the baskets in a place where the walls can provide a framing backdrop for the plants as they are admired from all sides.

Plan to make your outdoor baskets in the spring, when flowering plants are small and inexpensive. To keep the flowers looking bright and luxuriant all summer long, water them regularly and prune any dead flowers that may accumulate in the basket.

Gold and yellow hardy mums look perfect in a natural wicker basket when hung against the background of a garden trellis. Peace impatiens and "non-stop" begonias in a hanging wicker basket provide long-lasting splashes of color in front of an outside brick wall.

The most beautiful hanging arrangements contain plants that grow out through the sides as well as tops of the baskets. In the basket shown at right, two rows of petunias and vincas are planted around the sides of the basket, while the top is filled in with ivy geraniums and a little Spanish moss to cover the soil.

As the plants grow around the sides and top, their leaves and blossoms will fill in all the spaces so that very little moss is showing except at the bottom. Soon the basket will become a beautiful ball of color that will last all summer.

Wire Basket Frames

Plants in a hanging basket are usually built upon a ready-made wire frame that is lined with moss.

- Moss lining holds soil inside frame, but is porous enough for good drainage.
- Traditionally, sphagnum moss was used, but today sheet moss, which is readily available, is most often used.
- Wide openings all around frame allow clumps of plants to be pushed through moss from outside, so roots can be covered with soil on inside.

You'll Need

- ***Plants: purple & hot-pink petunias, hot-pink ivy geraniums, vincas***
- ***Wire or wicker baskets***
- ***Sphagnum or sheet moss***
- ***Spanish moss***
- ***Plastic liner dish***
- ***Knife or scissors***
- ***Potting soil***

Planting a Hanging Basket

1 To plant a wire basket for use outdoors, first line bottom and lower sides with sphagnum moss or with sheet moss, which is easier to find.

2 To conserve water and retard drips, insert a plastic liner dish on top of bottom layer of moss. If desired, use a plastic pot for maximum drip control.

3 Build bottom row of 4 petunias and vincas by pushing their roots through wire openings and moss from outside. Fill in large spaces of wire openings all around bottom of basket.

4 Using potting soil, cover roots of first row of plants. Place soil around edges, then in center to make a bed for next row of plants to be inserted through wire.

5 Add another row of 4 petunias in same manner, but stagger them so they are not placed directly over petunias in first row. Cover their roots with soil.

6 Fill in top with 3 or 4 ivy geraniums. Scatter soil all around their roots and press down firmly. Fill in noticeable holes with moss. Water basket and hang in a sunny location.

Planting a Pocket Basket

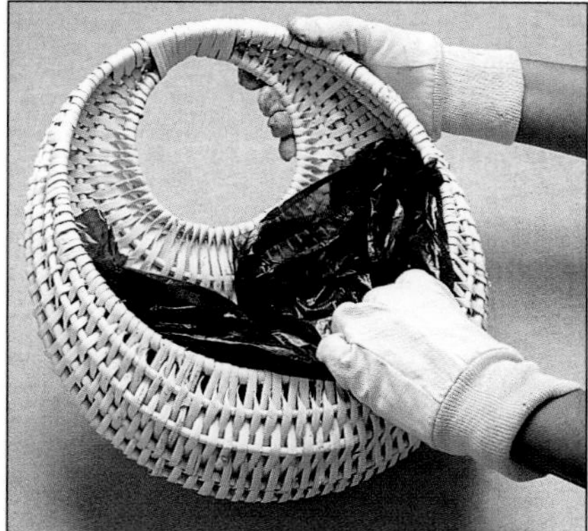

1 Line a wicker basket with plastic sheeting. Remove pink petunias and white wax begonias from enough 4" pots and fill basket as shown. Fill basket with potting soil around roots.

2 Cover all traces of plastic by weaving Spanish moss through openings between plant stems. Tuck moss around rim between plastic and lip of basket.

Try This!

To add a decorative touch to your basket, fashion a nest out of a branch of curly willow lined with Spanish moss; nestle a feather or mushroom bird inside. To make a bow, form a series of 3" loops from 1½ yds. of ribbon and pinch together in the center. Twist wire around the center and fasten the bow to the basket.

3 If you wish, finish arrangement by adding decorations, such as ribbon, curly willow, berries, bittersweet, and even a bird in a homemade nest made out of moss.

Crafter's Secrets

Consider the following when making a floral basket:

- *Be sure basket is well lined so water does not drip through when watered.*
- *Cover top of potting soil with Spanish moss to give basket a finished look.*
- *To make a quick floral basket, place small plants in their pots into a basket and cover tops of pots with Spanish moss.*

Decorate an outside shingled wall with a flowery sconce made from a white wicker pocket basket filled with pink petunias and white wax begonias..

Planning Baskets for Indoor Use

Fill a cheerful wicker basket with fresh, fragrant herbs and hang it outdoors all summer long. When cooler weather arrives, bring your brimming basket indoors and hang it in a sunny area where the scent of fresh herbs can fill your kitchen all winter long. The herb-filled basket shown above contains creeping rosemary, silver and common thyme, burnet, anise hyssop, and purple basil.

Indoor baskets made of natural materials must be lined with a plastic pot or liner to prevent drips. Some plastic baskets come with their own drip tray. Because water evaporates rapidly, potted plants must be watered regularly. Test for moisture by poking a fingertip into the soil.

Plants for indoor use require lots of sunlight. Those on the "indoor" list at right grow best near a window, with some, such as geraniums, preferring a southern exposure.

Crafter's Secrets

The best plants to use for outdoor and indoor baskets are listed below.

Outdoors	Indoors
Ivy geranium	Reiger begonia
Impatiens	Gloxinia
New Guinea impatiens	Cyclamen
Browallia	African violet
Verbena	Kalanchoe
Petunia	Hibiscus
Primrose	Azalea
Non-stop tuberous begonia	Persian violet
Fuchsia	Geranium

Making a Classic Grapevine Wreath

A rustic grapevine wreath is the ideal background for seasonal embellishments, such as autumn's bounty of dried wheat, seed pods, and bright red pomegranates.

Free-form grapevines are easily shaped into a simple wreath. Natural objects enhance the wreath's woodlike appearance best. Ribbons and dried materials that reflect the season create a classic look.

Much of the real fun of wreath-making comes from taking pruning shears to a nearby thicket, cutting the vines, stripping their leaves, and fashioning them into a wreath yourself. However, ready-made grapevine wreaths are available in a variety of shapes in craft and florists' shops.

Clusters of dried white baby's breath, millet, dusty miller, and purple statice give a wintery feel to a round wreath. The heart-shaped wreath is dressed for spring with pink and blue delphiniums, green wheat flax, and yellow strawflowers.

The materials for decorating your wreath may vary, depending on what is available in your area. Be open to substitutions. If pomegranates can't be found, pinecones or dried artichokes, which are similiar in both size and shape, would be suitable replacements.

Making a Grapevine Wreath

If you are gathering grapevines from an arbor or thicket, harvest only small amounts from each plant, so that plants may continue to grow and reproduce.

- To make wreath with interesting texture, look for vines with curly tendrils, peeling bark, and leaves.
- To freshen dried vines and make them easier to bend into shape, wrap them in loose circle and soak them in bucket of water until they become pliable.
- Use wide variety of natural materials of different textures to add interest and position them attractively to wreath base.
- Use glue gun to attach decorative materials, such as shells, nuts, and pieces of wood.

You'll Need

- ***Bunch of grapevines***
- ***Dried materials: seed pods, pomegranates, wheat flax, woodland mushrooms, yarrow***
- ***Preserved holly branches***
- ***Spooled floral wire***
- ***Hot-glue gun & glue sticks***

1 Bend several long vines several times into a circle of desired circumference. Wrap vines with floral wire at several points on circle to secure shape; tuck in free ends of vines.

2 Continue adding vines to base circle, overlapping and weaving them in and out of first round of grapevines, until wreath is thick and full. Wire wreath vines at ends and wherever more stability is needed.

3 Cut 5–7 stems of wheat about 4" long. Wrap stems together with floral wire about 2" below wheat heads to end of stems. Make 5 more bunches.

4 Cut 5–7 small branches of preserved holly to 4"; wire stems together in same manner as wheat. Make a total of 6 holly bunches.

5 Position 2 wheat bunches diagonally end to end on wreath, with heads facing outward. Hot-glue ends of bunches to wreath base. Repeat with 2 more pairs of wheat, spacing them evenly around surface of wreath.

6 Position holly bunches end to end on an alternate diagonal from wheat; place next to, but not on top of, wheat bunches; ends of wheat and holly bunches may overlap. Hot-glue holly to wreath.

7 Attach pomegranates to wreath with glue gun, arranging them so they cover stems of wheat and holly bunches. Hold pomegranates in place until glue hardens, about 2–3 minutes. Glue seed pods to face outward.

8 Using glue gun, attach dried mushrooms to wreath with tops of mushrooms facing outward. Hold mushrooms firmly in place while glue dries, about 2–3 minutes.

Crafter's Secrets

To preserve the wreath and keep the flower colors brighter longer, spray lightly with a clear matte fixative, which is available in hardware and art and craft stores. If desired, use a clear polyurethane sealer, which will give the wreath a slight sheen. Hang the wreath out of direct sunlight and where the humidity is low.

9 To make hook for hanging, insert an 8" length of floral wire through back of wreath and twist ends to secure it to vine. Twist a small loop at end of wire to hang wreath on wall.

Try This!

Create an unusual dimensional grapevine wreath by attaching dried materials vertically to the inner edge of the wreath. Vary the height of the objects for additional visual interest. Use floral wire to secure tall items, such as stalks of grain, seed pods, and holly branches. Add volume and depth by gluing materials such as lotus pods and dried mushrooms to the front of the wreath.

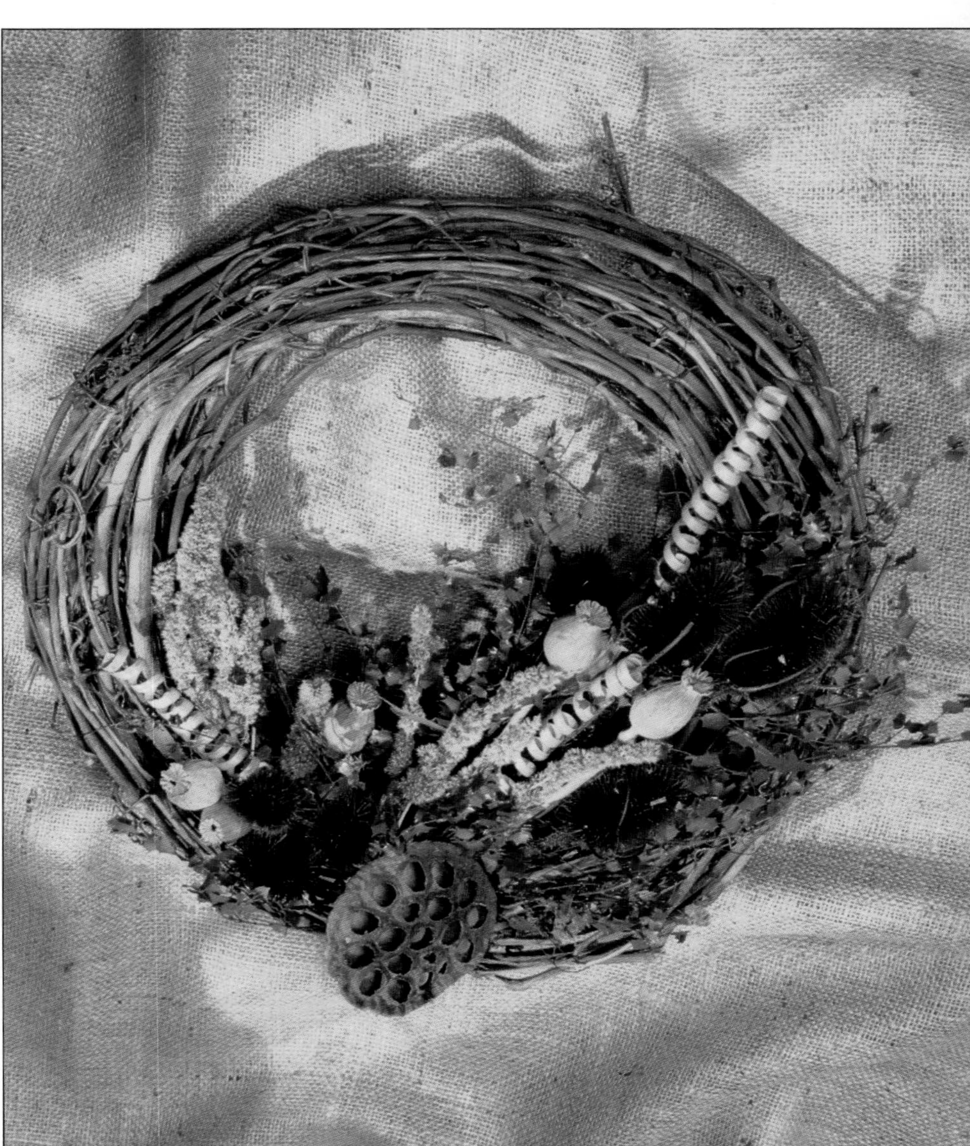

Hang a grapevine swag of herbs in the kitchen and you can break off the seasonings as you need them. Change the look of the arch by adding pink roses and delphiniums as the herbs are used, then add a lace bow to the base.

Making a Dried Herbal Arch

Fashion a pretty grapevine swag arch especially for the kitchen from vines twisted and tied with wire and decorated with dried cooking herbs.

Aromatic thyme, the purple flowers of oregano and lavender, the silvery foliage of sage, and the pale green leaves of bay are wired in small groupings to cover the arch. The arch is tied at the bottom with a deep rose raffia bow that brilliantly coordinates with the purple and green shades of the herbs. A wire, twisted around the center of the grapevine form, is made into a loop on the back for hanging.

If you prefer, decorate the arch with herbs you use most. Parsley, dill, majoram, basil, and tarragon are others to consider. Then select raffia to complement the colors in your kitchen.

1 Gather several grapevines and bend them to form an arch. Secure vines at ends of arch and at several points in between by wrapping several times with floral wire.

2 Wire together small bunches of mixed herbs at stem ends. Position bunches of herbs on arch, and secure in place with spooled floral wire.

3 Continue adding bunches of herbs until arch is covered. Gather about 12 strands of raffia and tie them into a bow. Attach bow with floral wire to end of arch; fluff out bow.

Making a Wreath of Dried Leaves

As the weather turns cooler, hang a simple wreath of dried leaves in spicy autumn colors on your front door to offer a warm welcome to all who enter.

Stroll in the park or in the woods when the trees are ablaze in their autumn finery and you'll see leaves of every firey shade. Take a big plastic bag with you to collect a bundle of leaves that have fallen to the ground and bring them home to make a glorious wreath.

The leaves are fastened to one side of a straw wreath form in overlapping bunches separated by loops of gossamer ribbons.

Hung on a door or wall or given as a gift, this autumn wreath is as warming as its rich, earthy colors.

Fall supplies a bounty of dried plant materials that can be used to make or embellish a seasonal wreath. Glue opened seed pods to a dried leaf wreath for visual and textural interest, or make a pale, shimmery wreath from dried grasses and strawflowers.

Select similar leaves of a particular size and color, or mix different colors or shades for various tonal effects. Pick the leaves a few days before you begin making the wreath to allow them more time to dry. Pick twice the amount of leaves you think you'll need, as they will shrink as they dry. The straw wreath base is available at florists' and crafts shops.

General Guidelines

Place selected leaves to dry between layers of newspaper for two days to keep them from curling.

- Spray leaves with bit of water before beginning wreath to make them more pliable.
- Prepare small clusters of leaves to wire to wreath form: Gather bunch of 8–10 leaves firmly by stems and wind floral wire tightly around stems.
- Working from outside to inside of wreath, wire bunches of leaves close together for full appearance.
- Use stiff, sheer ribbon, such as organza, in subtle color that doesn't dominate leaves.
- To protect finished wreath and prolong its life, spray with clear acrylic sealer, available in craft and hardware stores.

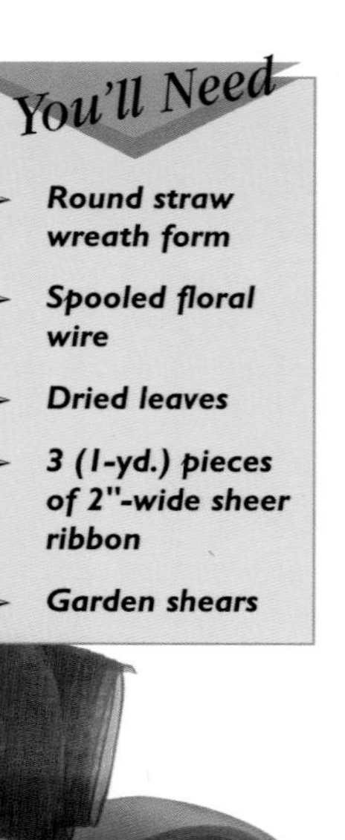

You'll Need

- ***Round straw wreath form***
- ***Spooled floral wire***
- ***Dried leaves***
- ***3 (1-yd.) pieces of 2"-wide sheer ribbon***
- ***Garden shears***

1 With rounded front of straw wreath base facing upward, wind floral wire around base several times to secure.

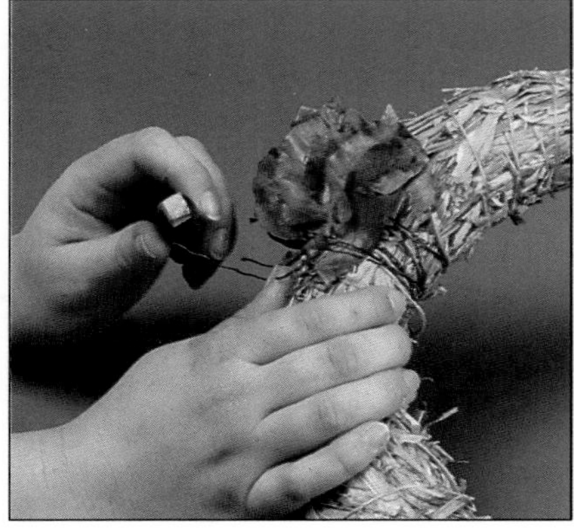

2 Place small cluster of leaves on outer edge of straw base. Wrap wire around stems and base several times; wire another cluster tightly beside first, toward inside edge. Wire additional rows overlapping stems. Continue for about 6".

3 Place 1 end of 1 ribbon piece centered over stems of last leaf cluster, letting long tail of ribbon trail over leaves. Wrap ribbon's short end with wire.

4 Fold long ribbon tail over wired end to form small loop. Holding loop in place with fingers, wrap with wire to secure. Wire on leaf clusters beside ribbon on inner and outer edges of base.

5 Make 3 or 4 even loops surrounded by tightly placed leaf clusters. Check that base is covered and wreath is uniform. Cut excess ribbon.

6 Cover end of ribbon by wiring 2 leaf clusters over end. Continue attaching leaf clusters for about 6", then attach another piece of ribbon and form loops as before.

7 Turn wreath over periodically as you work to check that back is free of leaf clusters, ensuring that wreath will hang flat against wall or door.

8 Continue wiring leaves and ribbons, spacing them evenly around wreath. As last clusters are attached, hold back first cluster. Wire last cluster; release first cluster, allowing leaves to cover wire.

9 Turn wreath to back; twist wire to form loop. Cut wire and tuck end into straw base. Hang wreath from loop on nail or hook.

Crafter's Secrets

When the wreath is completed, check it from all angles to see if there is any straw or wire showing. If there is, carefully glue a few leaves over these spots to hide the unfilled spaces. Use a glue gun and glue sticks for a secure hold. Finish by spraying with acrylic sealer to keep the wreath from becoming brittle.

Try This!

Make a spectacular wreath in rich, warm burgundy tones. Collect the exquisite ruby-red autumn leaves of the beech or other tree and overlap the leaves one at a time, as you wire them to create a full, tightly compact wreath. When wreath is completed, hot-glue on a bow made from several strands of heavy twine.

Making an Aromatic Tree

The earthy colors of fall's leaves are reflected in the warm tones of dried fruits and spices, which can be used to make distinctive seasonal decorations.

The base is a 10" cone of floral foam or polystyrene onto which dried orange, lemon, or lime slices and the unusual star-shaped pods of aniseed are glued. Several cinnamon sticks glued together form a thick "trunk," and the entire tree is supported in a 4" pottery pot filled with clay.

To dry the citrus slices, space them evenly apart on a cookie sheet covered with newspaper or paper towels to absorb the juice and place them on a radiator to air-dry for several days, turning them every day. Or place them, without the paper, in a 160° F oven for about two hours. Use a glue gun to attach all materials securely to the foam.

Experiment with a variety of spices to create aromatic combinations for a spice tree. Here, cinnamon sticks and dried red peppers are used with slices of orange and star anise. Cover the clay with wood shavings or dried grasses.

1 Using glue gun, put dot of glue on back of an orange slice and press slice onto bottom edge of foam. Continue adding more orange slices, overlapping them around and up to cover half of cone.

2 Glue star anise to cone, beginning around bottom edge and working up, placing pods point to point until foam is covered.

3 Insert 3 cinnamon sticks into center of pot filled with modeling clay. Push cone onto "trunk." Cover clay with wood shavings, dried grass, or moss, then add star anise, citrus slices, and cinnamon for additional decoration.

Creating a Fabric-Scrap Collage

Turn to your scrap bag to make a charming no-sew picture collage of your home. Working from a photo, cut and fuse fabric pieces for a unique "portrait."

Select fabric pieces that closely resemble elements that make up the photo. For example, in the collage shown above, a cloudy blue fabric was used as the sky background, while appropriate print scraps were used for the striped awnings and textured fabric roof. Feel free to enhance your collage with details that are not in the photo, such as the picket fence, flower garden, and pebbled walk.

Matted and framed, a house collage makes a very personal wall decoration.

To make a fabric collage of your house, take a color photo of it from the front, including the surroundings, such as the lawn, trees, etc. Note the areas of detail, such as the wood trimming, awnings, and dormers, then select fabrics accordingly to add architectural realism to the collage.

Take the photo of your house to a photo shop and have it enlarged to 11"x14". Or have an enlarged color copy of the photo made at a copy shop.

Because everyone's collage will differ, depending on the various features of the house, use your photo and the steps as guides, adding your own details as you build your collage. Begin with the largest single piece of fabric—the house shape—and fuse on increasingly smaller details, "building" the house layer by fabric layer.

Fusing Guidelines

Break your photo into the small elements to be represented in the collage and select scrap fabrics for each. Be sure the fabric scrap is larger than the corresponding element to allow for slight shrinkage when fusing.

- Set iron to manufacturers specified temperature to ensure perfect bond. If set too high fusible will wrinkle, causing unwanted creases in fabric. Test on scrap fabric before beginning.
- Fusing may cause fabrics to shrink a bit, so cut out final shapes after fusible web has been bonded to fabric scrap.

You'll Need

- ***Photo of house, enlarged to 11"x14"***
- ***Tracing paper, pencil, & ruler or straightedge***
- ***Masking tape***
- ***Scissors***
- ***1½ yds. paper-backed fusible web***
- ***Fabric scraps & 12"x15" piece of backgound fabric***
- ***Iron & ironing board***
- ***11"x14" picture mat***
- ***16"x20" frame***

1 Make simple tracing of each element of house and surrounding landscape. Outline each element onto paper side of fusible web with wrong side of element facing up.

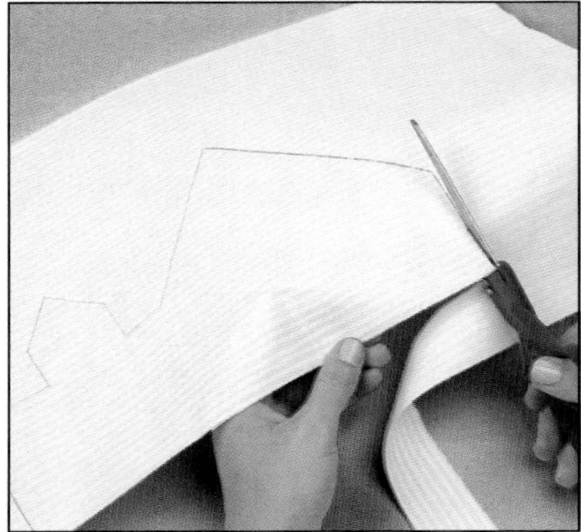

2 Using iron, fuse largest element (house) to wrong side of selected scrap fabric. Cut out shape from fused fabric along marked line.

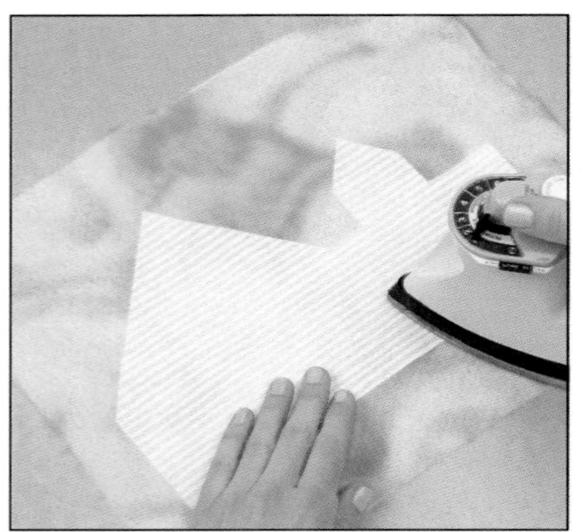

3 Press any wrinkles from background fabric. Peel paper backing from fusible cutout of house. Center house right side up on background and fuse house to background.

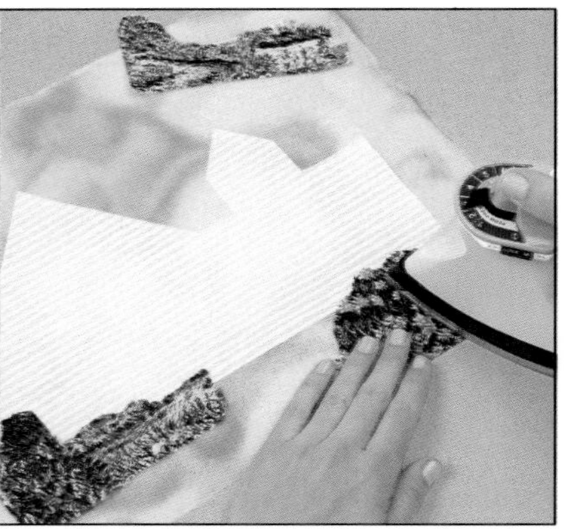

4 Using same outlining and fusing technique, position next largest elements (garden pieces) on background fabric, overlapping house slightly; fuse.

5 Fuse other large elements of house, such as roof and walk, to background. Fuse smaller collage elements, such as fence, windows, doors, curtains, window boxes, and beams, to fused house pieces; keep details level.

6 Continue fusing details over elements already in place. When collage is completed, position mat over finished collage; glue edges. Let dry. Assemble into frame.

Try This!

Create a still-life fabric collage: Make a simple line drawing of a pleasing interior scene in your own home or one enlarged from a magazine photo. Choose fabric scraps that blend nicely with the setting. Fabrics in the same color tones, such as the blues in the foyer scene, are soothing when used together. The darker tones of the brown frame and bright red apples add balance to the collage. To give dimension and sparkle, a special charm was glued on to represent a drawer knob.

Crafter's Secrets

Large fabric stores and sewing centers often have remnants or scrap pieces for sale at a very inexpensive price. Always look through these piles whenever you shop for fabric. You never know what will turn up that can be used in a collage. Try to find textured fabrics that look like brick, clapboard, or tiles for a house collage; also look for fabrics with garden scenes that have cutable flowers and tree motifs to add a bit of whimsy to your collage.

Making a Landmark Collage

Snapshots and videos of a memorable vacation ultimately wind up in the back of the closet. But here's a way to create a tangible reminder of that fun time: Make an 8"x10" color enlargement of a postcard or photographed landmark you would like to capture, and use it as a guide for a fabric and fusible web creation.

The process is the same as that for making a collage of a house on Group 5, Card 16. In the Manhattan-skyline-by-night collage, for example, the starry night background fabric sets the scene perfectly. By mixing gray, black and navy fabrics in striped, checked, and blocked patterns, an eye-catching cityscape is formed. Tiny golden yellow fabric squares for windows remind one and all that "the city never sleeps."

New York City by night, a classic picture postcard scene, is rendered in a fabric collage using nighttime colors of gray, black, and navy. The touches of yellow in the stars and lit windows illuminate a darkened city.

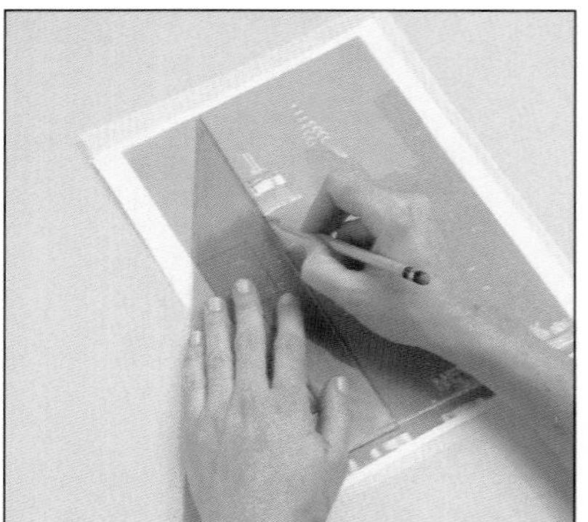

1 Place sheet of tracing paper over 8"x10" color copy of photograph or postcard; using pencil, trace outlines of buildings and other elements that you wish to represent in collage. Draw small squares for windows.

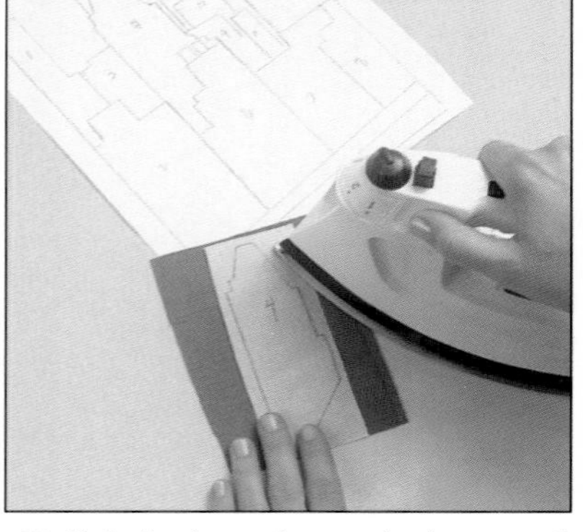

2 If desired, number each element of collage to indicate order in which they are to be fused. Transfer each element to paper side of fusible web; fuse to wrong side of selected fabric scrap. Cut out each element on outline.

3 Using color copy and numbering as guide, remove paper backing from each fused piece and begin "building" collage layers on background fabric. Fuse all details, such as windows and pointed towers in place.

5

CREATIVE WALL ACCENTS

CARD 18

Making a Romantic Ruffled Lace Wreath

Gathered tiers of lace and luxurious silk roses mingle with cascades of ribbons and pearls to form a romantic wreath.

So easy to make, this frilly and very feminine wreath is composed of delicate silk roses nestled among billows of ruffled lace and surrounded by swirls of ribbons and strings of pearls.

A perfect accent for a woman's dressing room or bath, the wreath can be made with lace and flowers in colors that match her decor or personal preference.

Use silk roses with this wreath; they tend to hold their color and shape over time. However, to protect the wreath from premature fading, keep it out of direct sunlight.

Different fabrics, flowers, or wreath shapes produce lovely variations. A 6" width of soft floral print and a nosegay of matching roses and ribbons create a perky country-style wreath. A heart-shaped base adds to the romantic impression made by roses and lace.

The secret to making a ruffled wreath is to choose fabrics that are easy to gather and attach to a foam base with floral pins. For a sheer ruffled wreath, lace, organdy, organza, chiffon, and voile are good lightweight fabrics to use. Taffeta, silk, moiré, and linen are heavier fabrics that create a more formal-looking wreath.

General Guidelines

To ensure the ruffle will retain its shape, choose a fabric or lace trim, preferably with at least one finished edge, that is no more than 6" wide.

- Coordinate fabric, roses, and ribbons in complementary colors and patterns.
- For a touch of added color, run narrow ribbon through lace openings along edges of ruffle.
- To make a balanced, even ruffle, keep even spacing between each gathered section.

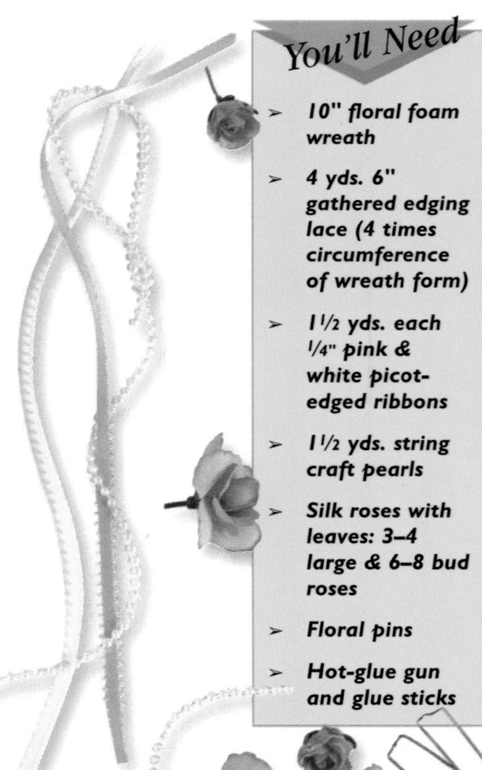

You'll Need

- ***10" floral foam wreath***
- ***4 yds. 6" gathered edging lace (4 times circumference of wreath form)***
- ***1 1/2 yds. each 1/4" pink & white picot-edged ribbons***
- ***1 1/2 yds. string craft pearls***
- ***Silk roses with leaves: 3–4 large & 6–8 bud roses***
- ***Floral pins***
- ***Hot-glue gun and glue sticks***

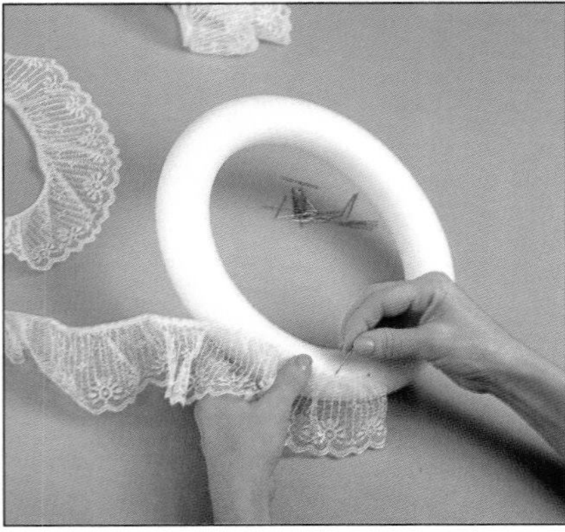

1 Holding wreath form securely, attach about 3" of 1 end of lace to center of wreath width using floral pins. Be sure right side of lace is facing upward and pins are inserted into finished edge of lace.

2 To form ruffle, pleat lace approximately 1/4" every 3" and secure gathered pleats with floral pins. Continue attaching lace clockwise until lace circles wreath once and ruffle is even.

3 Form another tier of ruffles, gathering and pinning finished edge of lace about 1/4"–1/2" above previous tier. Continue making 4–5 tiers of ruffles. Pin end of lace to secure. Wreath should be full and ruffles fluffy.

4 Spread apart last 1 or 2 tiers of lace with fingers, so scalloped edges fall toward opening in wreath and form a ruffled center. Be sure that foam base is not visible in any spots.

5 Group together 1 yd. each of ribbons and pearls. Holding them in center, form into a bow and place onto wreath at top, where inner and outer tiers separate. Fasten bow with pin, allowing ends to fall freely over lace.

6 Arrange ends of bow in a cascade of waves on both sides of wreath. Pin at 3–4 evenly spaced points around wreath, between inner and outer tiers; loosely drape ribbons and pearls between each point to create a flowing effect.

7 Group together 1 large rose and 2 bud roses and place them at point where ribbon is pinned to wreath. Hot-glue them in place. Make 3 other groups and glue in place.

8 Make a bow with remaining ribbons and string pearls. Pin bow to wreath below center on 1 side, between inner and outer tiers. Allow excess ribbon to hang decoratively from bow.

Crafter's Secrets

When choosing silk roses for a fabric wreath, select blossoms of varying sizes, with leaves if possible, to add visual dimension, texture, and interest. If roses chosen are of different colors, they should complement each other and the fabric used for the ruffle.

Try This!

Make a ruffled wreath to hang in a window. Because the wreath will be viewed from both outside and inside the house, ruffles must be added to both sides. Follow steps 1–4 from Group 5, Card 18 to create the ruffle on one side of the wreath form, then repeat on the other side. Pin or glue individual roses evenly around the wreath on both sides, with a silk leaf on each side of the blossoms. Create a hanging loop with spooled wire, and insert it into the form on the back of the wreath.

Making a Ruffled Sunflower Wreath

A variety of different decorator looks, such as country, Victorian, and contemporary, can be achieved with a fabric wreath, depending on the fabric and artificial flowers chosen. Decide where in the house the wreath is to hang, and make your choices accordingly.

This bright sunflower wreath, for example, is sure to bring a touch of summer sunshine to a cozy kitchen all year long. It is made from 6"-wide edging lace that has been folded back along its straight edge and sewn to form a casing to fit around the wreath. Purchase enough lace to equal twice the circumference of the wreath, and gather a bouquet of silk sunflowers to pin or glue to the bottom of the wreath. For that extra sunny touch, weave yellow silk ribbon through the lacy openings along the edge of the lace ruffle.

Many sunflowers of varying sizes are clustered along the wreath's inner rim, giving the single-ruffle wreath a simple but striking look. When using a fabric with a large pattern, select flowers in one of the lesser-used colors to create a unifying effect.

1 Using a serrated knife, slice foam base completely through to create an opening for the fabric sleeve. Be careful not to crack the foam while cutting through it.

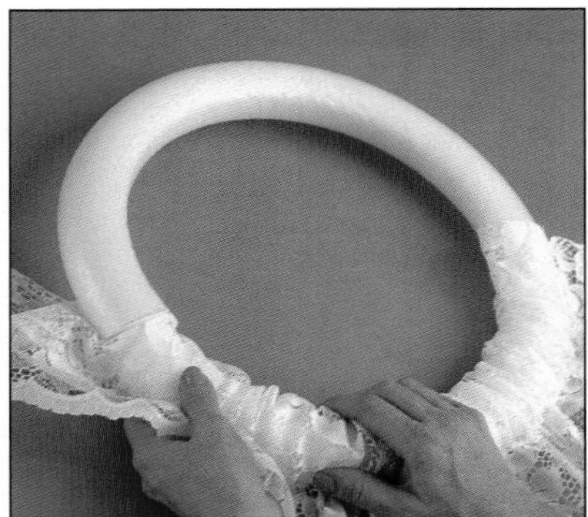

2 Slide sleeve onto foam base, pushing fabric together to gather it evenly around entire base and create a ruffle. Tuck under ends of fabric to hide raw edges and using floral pins, pin close together to base.

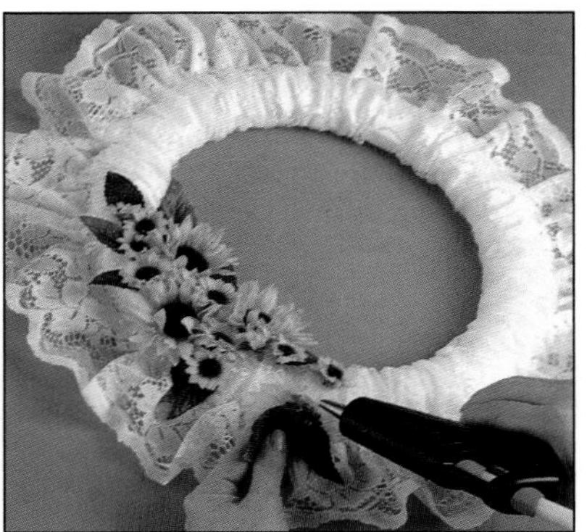

3 Thread tapestry needle with 1/8"-wide yellow ribbon and weave through outer edge of lace. Using glue gun, attach sunflowers to inner rim of wreath in an attractively arranged elongated cluster as shown.

Finishing Touches for the Home

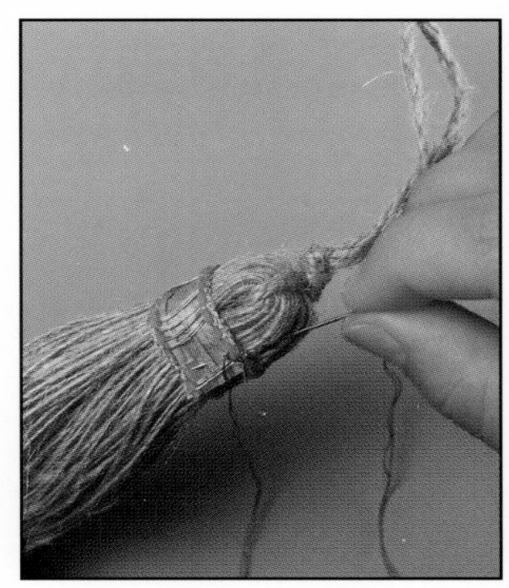

One-of-a-kind accessories to brighten your home

FINISHING TOUCHES FOR THE HOME

CARD 1

Cross-stitching Geometric Motifs

Patterns & Templates

The clean geometric designs of these decorative, yet functional, projects are worked with counted cross-stitch on natural linen.

Unlike cross-stitching over motifs printed directly onto the fabric, counted cross-stitch is worked from pattern charts. One shaded square of a charted design represents one cross-stitch. By varying the number of fabric threads represented by each square, you control the size of the stitch, and ultimately the finished motif size. Experiment with different yarns and fabrics to obtain a pleasing combination. Choose from the motifs supplied in Group 12, Card 2 and style a towel, tie-back, or sachet in colors that coordinate with your decor.

Even-weave fabrics are used as the ground for counted cross-stitch embroidery and are always woven with an even number of threads in both the vertical and horizontal directions. Combine multiple geometric motifs for larger projects, or feature a single motif as shown in napkin ring above.

Patterns & Templates *Select one of the motifs in Group 12, Card 2 to decorate your next cross-stitched project.*

The "count" of an even-weave fabric refers to the number of threads woven, lengthwise and crosswise, within a 1" square. A high fabric count means there are many threads within an inch.

Even-weave fabrics are available in many fashionable looks and colors. For a decorative kitchen towel, select a washable cotton or linen fabric. Cut the towel to your desired size and thread-baste the center lines at the motif position.

Embroidery Floss and Needle

Select cotton or linen embroidery threads for washable projects. For nonwashable projects, silk can be used if desired.

- Both cotton and silk floss are sold in skeins having six strands; use strands singly or in multiples to achieve proper fabric coverage.
- Use linen embroidery thread as a single strand. Just be sure fabric threads are of a comparable size to linen embroidery thread.
- Use a tapestry needle in a size that easily pulls through fabric. The needle's blunt point automatically separates rather than pierces fabric's threads.

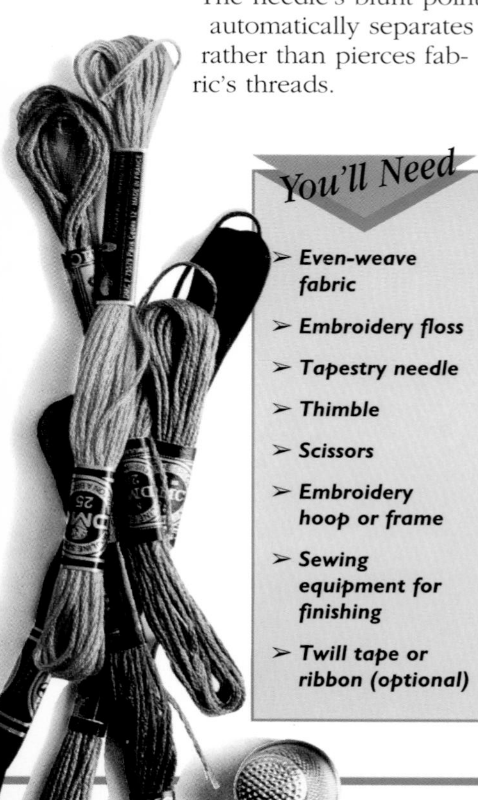

You'll Need

- ***Even-weave fabric***
- ***Embroidery floss***
- ***Tapestry needle***
- ***Thimble***
- ***Scissors***
- ***Embroidery hoop or frame***
- ***Sewing equipment for finishing***
- ***Twill tape or ribbon (optional)***

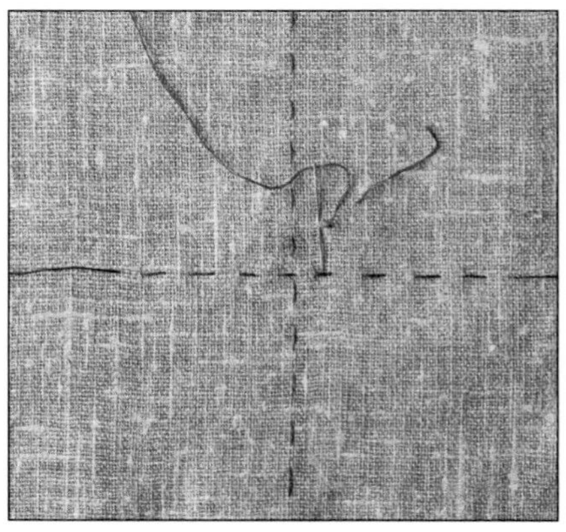

1 Starting at top right quadrant of thread-marked lines on towel, insert needle; leave long unknotted end. Bring needle up at lower right of first charted stitch. Work first half of stitch from lower right to upper left over 2 threads.

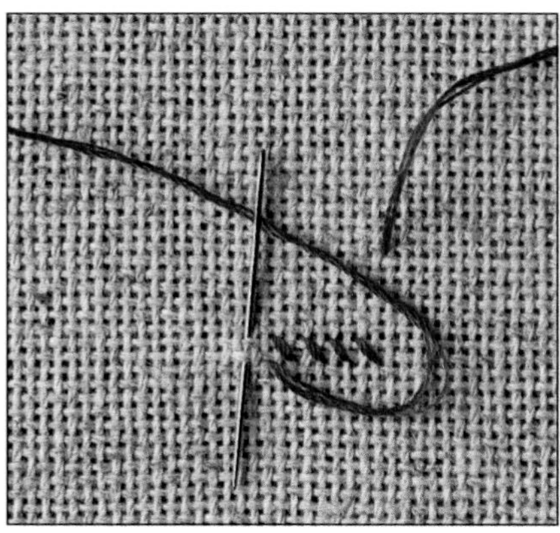

2 Continue working in same manner to end of first row, always forming first half of each stitch from lower right to upper left over 2 threads.

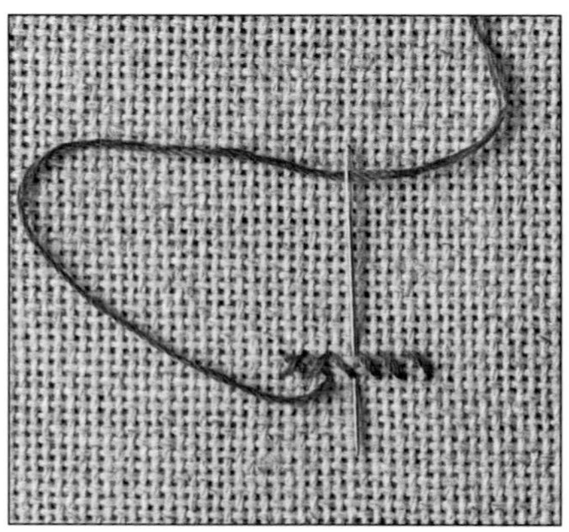

3 To complete first row, cross second half of Xs from lower left to upper right, inserting needle each time in same holes made for first half of Xs. As you work, catch and cover starting length of floss on back side.

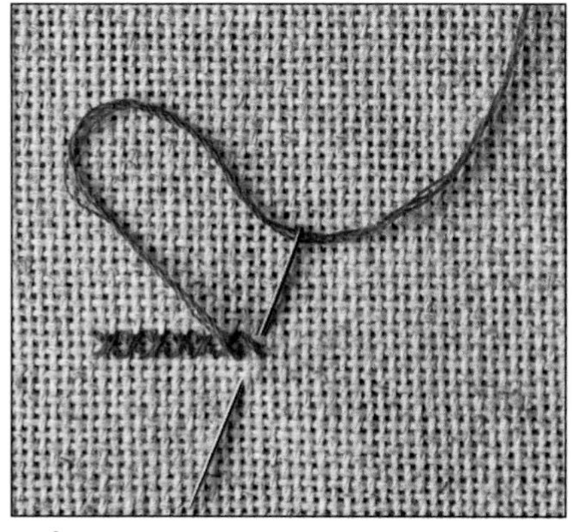

4 When row is complete, angle needle downward 4 threads instead of 2 to start first stitch of next row. Continue forming cross-stitches in same manner as before. Follow charted motif to work additional rows.

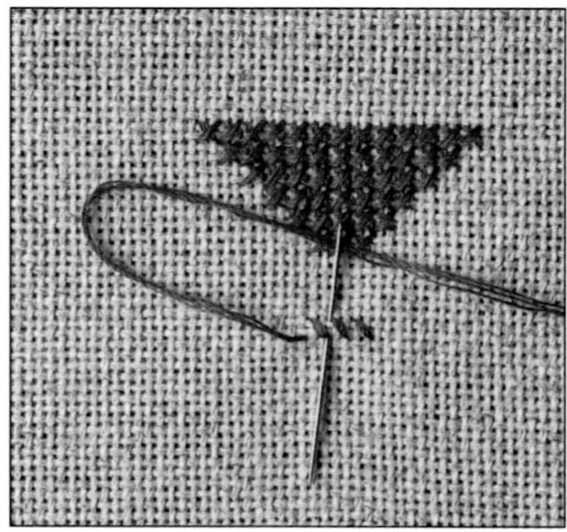

5 Count charted squares to work any other single-color area of design on fabric. Finish off each piece of floss following step 6, then start and secure each new length of floss as needed, following steps 1–3.

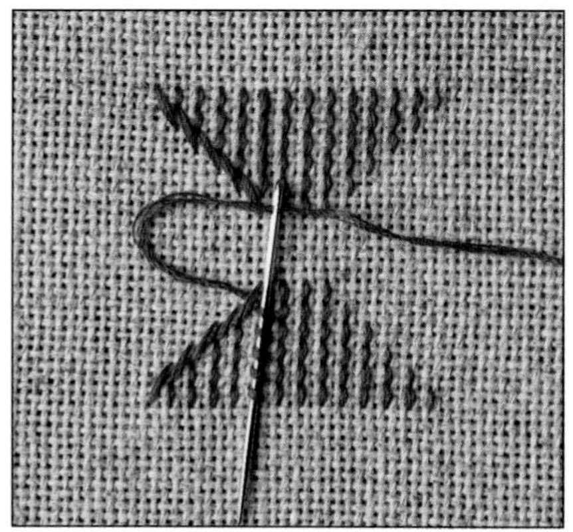

6 To finish 1 colored area (or when you run out of floss), insert needle under back side of cross-stitches for about 1/2" without catching fabric. Pull floss through; cut floss off close to needle's exit position.

7 Finish cross-stitching other areas in towel motif that call for same color of floss. Following charted pattern, fill in remaining area of motif with new floss color.

8 Continue following charted pattern and complete all cross-stitched motifs, changing floss colors as indicated. Sew a narrow double hem around towel edges, mitering at corners and catching a twill-tape loop at center of top edge.

Crafter's Secrets

When caring for washable embroidered items such as a towel, press or iron them with care: Place a terry towel on the ironing board with the damp embroidered towel right side down on top. Press the entire towel from the wrong side until it is dry. This method keeps the embroidery stitches raised and looking like new, and avoids a shine on the embroidered fabric.

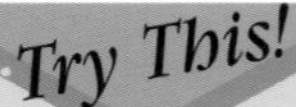

Try This!

Any long border motif will make handsome cross-stitched tiebacks for draperies. Determine the finished length of the tieback by wrapping a tape measure around the pulled-back draperies. Embroider the border, allowing the even-weave fabric to "frame" your stitches. Fold the tieback along the top, and sew the center back and ends, using ½" seam allowances. Include loops or utility rings at the ends to hold tiebacks in place on cup hooks attached to the wall.

Creating a Geometric Sachet

The natural sweet scent of dried herbs, spices, and flower petals can make closets and dresser drawers fresh-smelling for a long time. It's an ancient practice that is still popular today. As a gift for yourself or a friend, decorate a small linen pouch with a geometric cross-stitched border and fill it with your favorite potpourri. The motif can be stitched directly on the pouch or on a separate even-weave fabric that is appliquéd onto a pouch made from any fashion or decorator fabric. Use non-oiled fillers so your handiwork will not become oil-stained.

Depending on the motif shape you select, the sachet can be rectangular or square. Form a top loop from three inches of twill tape or ribbon, so you can hang the sachet on a hook or hanger in the closet. As an alternative, leave two long ribbon ends and tie into a bow.

Follow instructions given on Group 6, Card 1 to embroider the motif, then appliqué the embroidery to the front of the pouch (see below). Remove herbs and petals from branches and crush them before stuffing into the sachet.

1 Cut 2 pouch pieces 1½" wider and longer than cross-stitched motif. Pin right sides together and stitch ¼" from sides and bottom. Turn right side out. Press ¼" to inside along top edge. Form twill tape loop as shown.

2 Press under edges of cross-stitched motif leaving a ¼"-wide "frame" of fabric around cross-stitches. Center appliqué on 1 side of pouch; pin; slipstitch to pouch with sharp needle and sewing thread.

3 Fill pouch with spices, herbs, or flower petals (crushed, if necessary) to within ½" of top. Pin top opening together with loop tucked ½" inside. Slipstitch opening closed.

6

FINISHING TOUCHES FOR THE HOME

CARD 3

Arranging a Small Dried-Flower Basket

A small basket is the perfect setting for a dainty floral arrangement of delicate flowers. Its diminutive size permits it to be a grace note on a dresser, desk, or shelf.

The sweet innocence of this delightful little arrangement calls to mind a flower girl's basket. The design of the arrangement and the sizes of the dried flowers and plant materials are tailored to complement the basket's shape.

Select the basket first, then choose the dried materials. For a well-balanced arrangement, the height of the tallest materials should be about twice the height of the basket base. Add shells, pinecones, nuts, and berries to personalize your arrangement.

An eye-popping way to vary a floral basket is to group each type of flower and plant in a cluster, so each is prominently displayed in the arrangement. Use strong contrasting floral colors to increase visual impact.

Arranging dried plant materials in a basket is an easy way to make a floral decoration. You can use almost any flower or plant and any type of basket. In these basic instructions, the arrangement is made in a small, shallow, round basket. The plants follow the shape of the basket, so the finished arrangement is balanced and pleasing to the eye. The base is easily made from floral foam, which is dry and porous and easy to work with. It can be purchased from florists or craft shops.

General Guidelines

The arrangement is symmetrically built and falls in a soft arch toward the lower basket edges.

- Use a single rose as starting point. To maintain arch shape, cut additional rose stems to different lengths.
- Measure tallest flower against basket and cut stem to an appropriate length. Trim balance of flowers to fit as they are added to arrangement.
- Pack plants close together so none of the floral foam is visible. Continually check arrangement to make sure shape remains uniform.

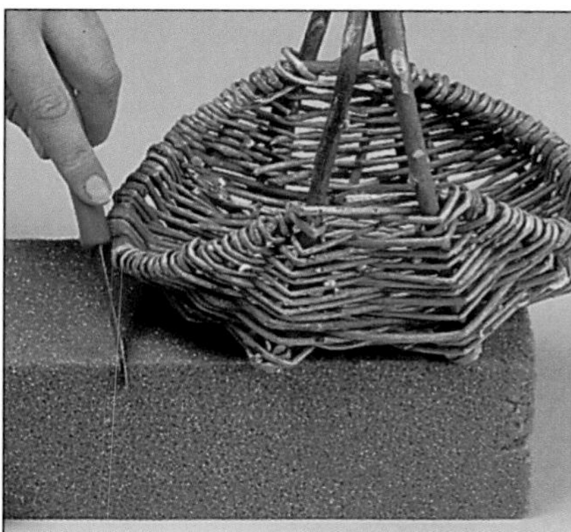

1 Cut a piece of floral foam slightly taller than height of basket base. Set basket on top of foam piece and cut foam to match length and width of basket. Trim lower edges as necessary so foam can fit inside basket.

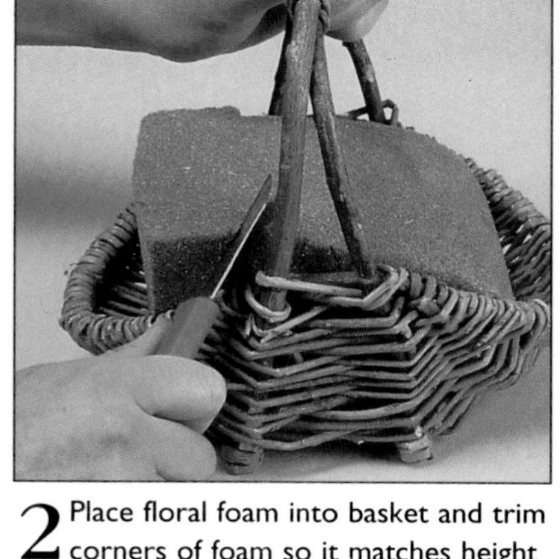

2 Place floral foam into basket and trim corners of foam so it matches height of basket sides and center is slightly mounded. Cut a length of spooled wire equal to 4 times length of basket base.

3 Thread wire through bottom of basket base so wire ends come up on either side of floral foam at handle sides. Twist ends of wire together over floral foam and tuck in any excess.

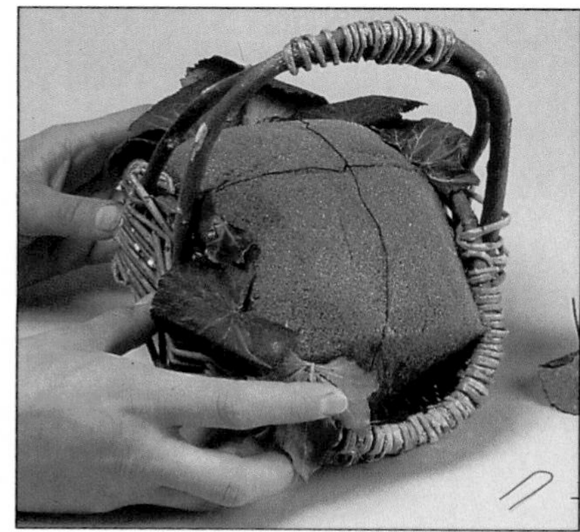

4 Cut spooled wire into several 2" lengths and bend into hairpin shapes. Fasten leaves along edges of floral foam by pushing wire pins through leaves. Be sure leaves cover spaces between foam and basket.

5 Place a rose in center of foam so top of bloom is about 1" below handle. Insert 3 roses slightly lower around first rose. Angle and center a rose at each end of basket's shallow sides and at either side of handle ends.

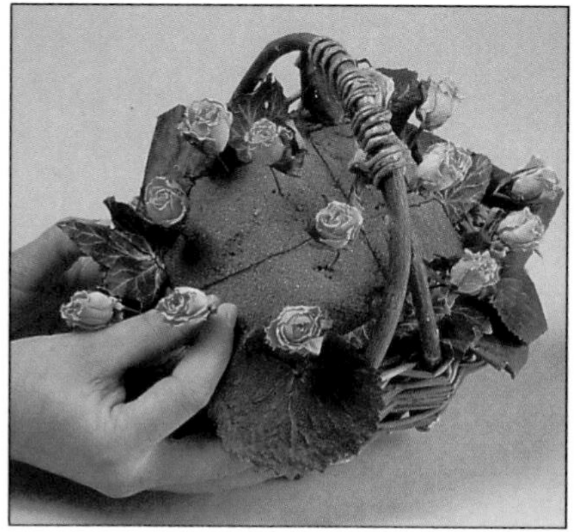

6 Position additional flowers between roses flanking handle ends and roses at shallow sides; be sure flowers are arranged at similar heights above foam. There should now be 4 center roses and 10 roses around basket rim.

For further information: Crafting & Decorating Made Simple™
International Masters Publishers, 444 Liberty Ave., Pittsburgh, PA 15222-1207 1-800-527-5576

Try This!

The choice of plant materials is limitless. You can dry plants you have grown in your own garden or purchase already-dried materials, including some exotic varieties.

The arrangement shown at right was created in the same type of basket used in the previous arrangement. To achieve a colorful fall-like look, consider using strawflowers, roses, and carnations in autumnal colors, along with grass fillers, such as briza, and horse chestnuts for added interest.

7 Insert strawflowers and seed pods between roses, keeping all flowers and pods at an even height. Angle stems of plants along sloping sides to maintain rounded shape of arrangement.

8 Fill open spaces with oats and seed pods, keeping smaller seed pods taller than larger ones to create a lacy effect. Make sure all open spaces are filled in and no floral foam is visible.

Crafter's Secrets

Because small bunches of oats, rye, and other grains easily cover the open spaces in a floral arrangement, they make great fillers when creating a dried-flower basket. These grains complement the look of the dried flowers and add a variety of textures to the arrangement.

Arranging Plants in Clusters

Another method of arranging plants in a basket is to use them in clusters, so that each plant is prominently displayed within the basket and its colors more forcefully enhanced.

If clusters are to be used, gather a few stems of like plants into a bunch and secure them together with a short length of spooled floral wire. Be sure to leave a short length of wire that can be pushed into the floral foam to secure the cluster. Prepare the desired number of floral bunches before starting.

Crafter's Secrets

To create textural interest, add other materials to the dried-flower arrangement.

- *Moss provides a pleasing plant surface that easily covers the floral foam.*
- *Pinecones add a rustic touch to any basket arrangement. Wind a length of wire along lower ridges of pinecone, tucking wire into ridges. Twist wire ends together to form a stem.*
- *Heavy pieces, such as lotus seed pods, horse chestnuts, and shells add points of interest. Use heavy 16-gauge wire to poke a small hole in object, then insert wire and use ends as a stem.*

Ears of wheat and clusters of cockscomb, amaranths, red roses, white delphiniums, seed pods, and Spanish moss make up this rustic arrangement.

1 Follow steps 1–3 of basic instructions to fit foam into basket. Twist wire around a bunch of wheat, then push wire ends into floral foam, angling and laying wheat bunch diagonally.

2 Push clusters of other plants into floral foam, then place groups of flowers diagonally against each other for harmony and balance. Make sure all wires are completely covered. Fill empty spaces with seed pods.

3 Poke or drill a tiny hole in decorative shell. Loop a piece of floral wire through hole and twist ends. Push wire into foam. Wire lotus pod and push into arrangement, placing it across from shell.

088-055-000 Printed in U.S.A.

Packet 0
For further information: Crafting & Decorating Made Simple™
International Masters Publishers, 444 Liberty Ave., Pittsburgh, PA 15222-1207 1-800-527-5576

FINISHING TOUCHES FOR THE HOME

CARD 6

Arranging an Elegant Bouquet of Lilies

Lilies are among the most joyful of flowers, trumpeting their beautiful colors and bold forms. A bouquet of these gorgeous blossoms makes a regal display.

To fill any lackluster area in the home with a profusion of color and warmth, turn to lilies. They are both easy to work with and last for days.

Lilies are available in a wide array of colors, such as the pink Uchida, yellow Destiny, and white spotted *speciosum*, so you are bound to find shades that complement your decor.

Their range of sizes—from small, colorful Peruvian lilies (also called alstroemeria) to large white Easter and calla lilies—allows them to be used in floral arrangements of varying proportions.

In a short or tall arrangement, lilies create a dramatic display. With stems cut short, lilies and tulips make a colorful low arrangement. Using a tall, clear container makes arranging easy because the lily and mimosa stems support one another without the need of floral foam or pebbles.

The many varieties, colors, and sizes of lilies open up endless possibilities in floral arrangements. The featured display is a classic triangle arrangement.

Using Lilies in Arrangements

The showy trumpet-shaped flowers and strong stems make lilies easy to work with when creating an arrangement.

- To show lilies to their fullest advantage, keep arrangement as simple as possible.
- Pinch off tall pollen-laden ends of stamens, as their pollen can stain anything it touches. It is also believed that blossoms will last longer if pollen is removed.
- Always recut stems of purchased flowers at least 2", cutting on an angle with a sharp knife or flower cutters.
- Take care not to crush stems when cutting or inserting them into floral foam. Damaged stems inhibit a flower's ability to absorb water, causing heads to quickly droop.
- Don't use daylilies from your garden or roadside, because they wilt after a few hours.

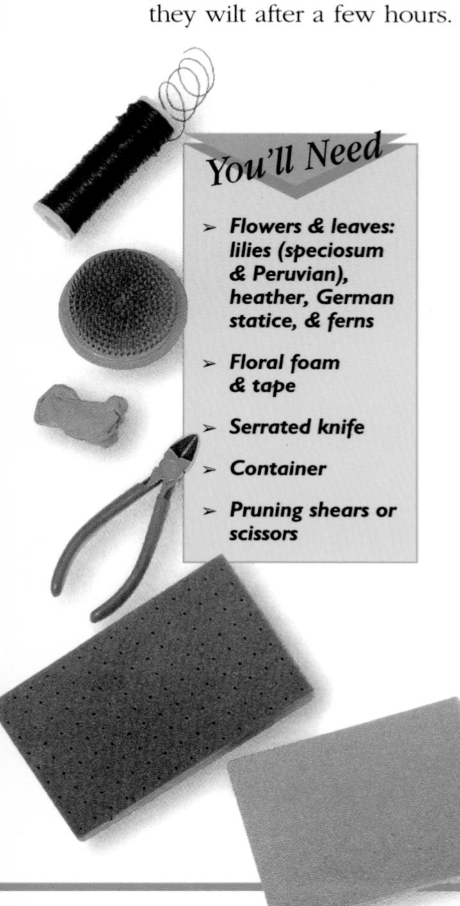

1 Using serrated knife, trim floral foam to fit snugly inside container of choice; allow about 2" of foam to extend above top of container. Saturate foam with water, then insert it firmly into container.

2 Place piece of floral tape across top of foam to provide additional stability, attaching ends of tape to rim of container. Repeat with another piece of tape across center of first piece.

3 Cut first lily stem about twice height of container and insert about ½" forward from center of foam. This stem establishes tallest point of arrangement and determines finished height.

4 To begin rounding front of arrangement, cut second lily stem about three-fourths height of first and insert in foam diagonally, slightly forward and left of center, with flower heads positioned just below first blossom.

5 To finish rounded front shape of triangle arrangement, cut third lily stem about half height of first and insert in foam almost horizontally, just right of center and above container rim.

6 To thin heather stems so they can drape gracefully in arrangement, remove lower sprigs of 3 heather stems with serrated knife or sharp paring knife.

7 Insert 1 stripped heather stem behind each lily stem, matching angle of lily, with heather tips extending several inches between and beyond flowers on lily stem; maintain rounded shape.

8 Insert tips of fern fronds almost horizontally to cover exposed front surfaces of foam, allowing ends of tips to drape over front rim of container.

9 Insert additional lily stems at varying heights within triangle shape formed by first 3 stems. Fill in with Peruvian lilies and German statice stems to complete arrangement, maintaining both triangle form and rounded shape.

Try This!

Create a classic mounded arrangement using small lilies. These delicate Peruvian lilies, sometimes called alstroemeria, have a cluster of flower heads on each stem and are available in a number of colors, such as the pink ones used here. They combine well with other flowers and keep fresh for about a week. Mixed with roses, heather, and sea lavender, they make a lovely arrangement for a bedroom.

Crafter's Secrets

The trick to successful flower arranging is to maintain the proper proportion between flowers and container. The mistake most often made is not trimming the stems to fit the size of the container. A good rule of thumb to follow is that the tallest flowers in the arrangement should be twice the height of the container. Once the height is established, the other flower stems should be trimmed to varying heights to fill the space between the tallest flower and the container.

Using Lilies in Japanese Style

With just a whisp of background color to set them off, large-size lilies can be arranged by themselves, following the simple, clean lines established in the classical art of Japanese flower arranging called *ikebana.*

With this type of flower arrangement the individual stems of blossoms are formally set in three heights: tall flowers representing the sky, low flowers symbolizing the earth, and medium-height flowers representing mankind. Because the large, stately flowers of many species of lily are very impressive at any stem height, and because their stems provide a strong support, they are ideal to use in this type of arrangement.

To maintain balance and to keep the eyes moving from level to level, the container should be as shallow as possible, yet still permit floral clay or pebbles to hold the stems securely.

From a round, shallow bowl, stems of day lilies rise to three different heights, drawing the viewer's attention to the brilliance of the blooms, which are offset against a yellow shower of mimosa.

1 Hand knead a small ball of floral clay, softening and warming it for better adhesion. Press clay onto bottom of floral frog; place frog inside bottom of clean and dry container.

2 Place first stem of mimosa in center back of frog to set height of arrangement. Add another stem in front of first stem. Place first lily in front of mimosa, with flower just below top of arrangement. Clip off excess leaves.

3 Insert second lily with tallest flower at half height of arrangement and angled forward. Insert third lily stem with flower close to and horizontal with container. Add mimosa to fill out shape. Cover frog with polished pebbles.

6

FINISHING TOUCHES FOR THE HOME

CARD 8

Mixing tall, spiky flowers and other plant materials with round flower heads and seed pods adds interest as well as texture to the arrangement. Stay within one color range or add accent flowers of contrasting colors.

Making a Floral Fan Arrangement

The fan is a classic shape used in flower arranging. It produces a dramatic sweep of glorious color and, with its flat back, fits snugly against a wall either in a standing vase or a hanging wall container.

Very popular during colonial times, the fan form is most often used for large, opulent displays, but can also turn out striking smaller arrangements. By using dried flowers in the arrangement rather than fresh ones, you can enjoy and share its beauty with friends and family for many months. Look for flowers that complement your decor and have rich, deep color. Just be sure all the plant materials used in the arrangement are in proper scale with the container.

It isn't difficult to produce magnificent fan-shaped arrangements. Here are a few tips to help you achieve success.

General Guidelines

The container should have clean lines that will not detract from floral materials and should be heavy and stable enough to support the weight of the flowers.

- To steady a wobbly container, fill it half-full with small pebbles or marbles before inserting floral foam.
- If using a tall, narrow vase, highest flowers at back of fan should be at least as tall as vase.
- If container is short and squat, highest flowers should be twice the height of container.
- Choose plant materials with long, straight stems or add length and strength by twisting a length of spooled floral wire around them, extending it beyond stem ends.
- Try to work on a surface that is of similar height to surface on which finished arrangement will be placed. If that isn't possible, place arrangement in its final location and step back to view it frequently as you work.

- ***Dried flowers & grains: millet, oats, roses, strawflowers, tansies, thistles***
- ***Floral foam***
- ***Container***
- ***Cutting tools: serrated knife, pruning shears or scissors, wire cutters***
- ***Spooled floral wire***
- ***Clear polyurethane spray***

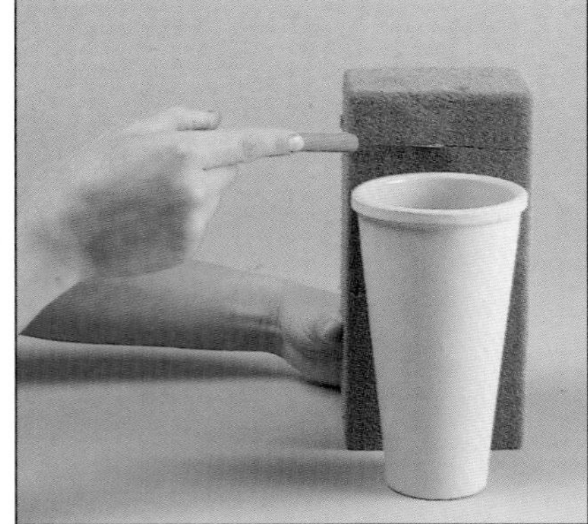

1 With serrated knife, trim floral foam to fit snugly inside container or vase. Allow about 1" of foam to extend above container top. Insert foam, pressing it firmly into container.

2 Begin with millet and oat stems. Place first stem about ½" in from center back of foam to establish tallest point of arrangement. Continue to add mix of oat and millet stems in open fan shape across back of foam.

3 Place row of roses about ½" in front of millet and oat stems (uneven number of roses works best). Begin at center and position flower heads about 2" lower than tops of stems along back of fan, spacing flowers evenly.

4 Insert tansies between roses just under base of blooms. Insert strawflowers and thistles between tansies and in front of roses beneath blooms. When placing thistles, insert them angled slightly forward to begin rounding front of arrangement.

5 Place more dried flowers in rows of decreasing height, filling in front. Continue inserting stems diagonally to keep front rounded. As stems get closer to front rim of container, angle them more horizontally to maintain shape.

6 Insert last row of roses and other plant stems horizontally close to rim of container to hide foam. Center 1 rose in last row as focal point. If desired, add large green leaves along bottom, as shown in photo on card front.

7 After all plant materials are in place, turn arrangement and view it from side. Flowers should form evenly rounded front; adjust stems if needed. Back of arrangement should be flat and against back rim of container.

8 Apply light coat of clear polyurethane spray to finished arrangement to seal flowers, give them a slight luster, and make them easier to keep clean. Use matte spray to avoid a shiny, artificial look.

Try This!

An interesting fan-shaped arrangement can be made in a wall container with the flowers placed in clustered groups instead of evenly spaced rows. Here, bunches of poppy seed pods, lavender, red amaranthus, German statice, larkspur, and hydrangea blooms are set off by a frame of cut twigs and a base of leaves and moss.

Crafter's Secrets

Dried flowers lose their colors easily. To keep them looking bright longer, place the arrangement out of direct sunlight and where the humidity is low. If you do want an arrangement for a sunny window, choose naturally pale flowers that have interesting shapes and textures, such as delphiniums, globe amaranths, nigella, and artemisia.

Making a Round Fan Arrangement

This full, round fan arrangement is made so that the finished piece can be viewed from all sides. Featuring the contrasting colors and textures of oats and roses, it is constructed almost the same way as the flat fan-shaped display, except that the completed half is turned around and repeated at the back.

Begin by dividing the plant materials into two equal piles so that you will have the same amount for each of the two sides.

Remove the lower leaves from the stems and wire them with spooled floral wire, so a greater number of stems can be pushed into the floral foam and placed closer together. Take advantage of the graceful heads of the oat stems and let them droop over the edge of the container.

As with the flat fan-shaped arrangement, the floral foam should rise about 1" above the top of the container. This is necessary so that the final stems can be inserted horizontally to keep the rounded shape of the arrangement and to completely cover the foam.

The rustic earthiness of matured oats and the cultivated elegance of red roses form a display that is both striking and abundantly lush. Arranged in an ornate silver vase, it would be a fitting centerpiece in a formal room.

1 Wrap each floral stem with a length of spooled wire to strengthen stem and hold it upright. Fill container with floral foam as for previous arrangement and place 1 rose stem in center of foam.

2 Add roses along each side of center bloom to form odd-numbered row of roses in fan shape across center of foam. Insert clusters of oat stems between roses.

3 Continue adding roses and oats, following basic method to form fan-shaped arrangement on 1 side of container. Turn container and repeat arrangement on other side, to complete full, round shape.

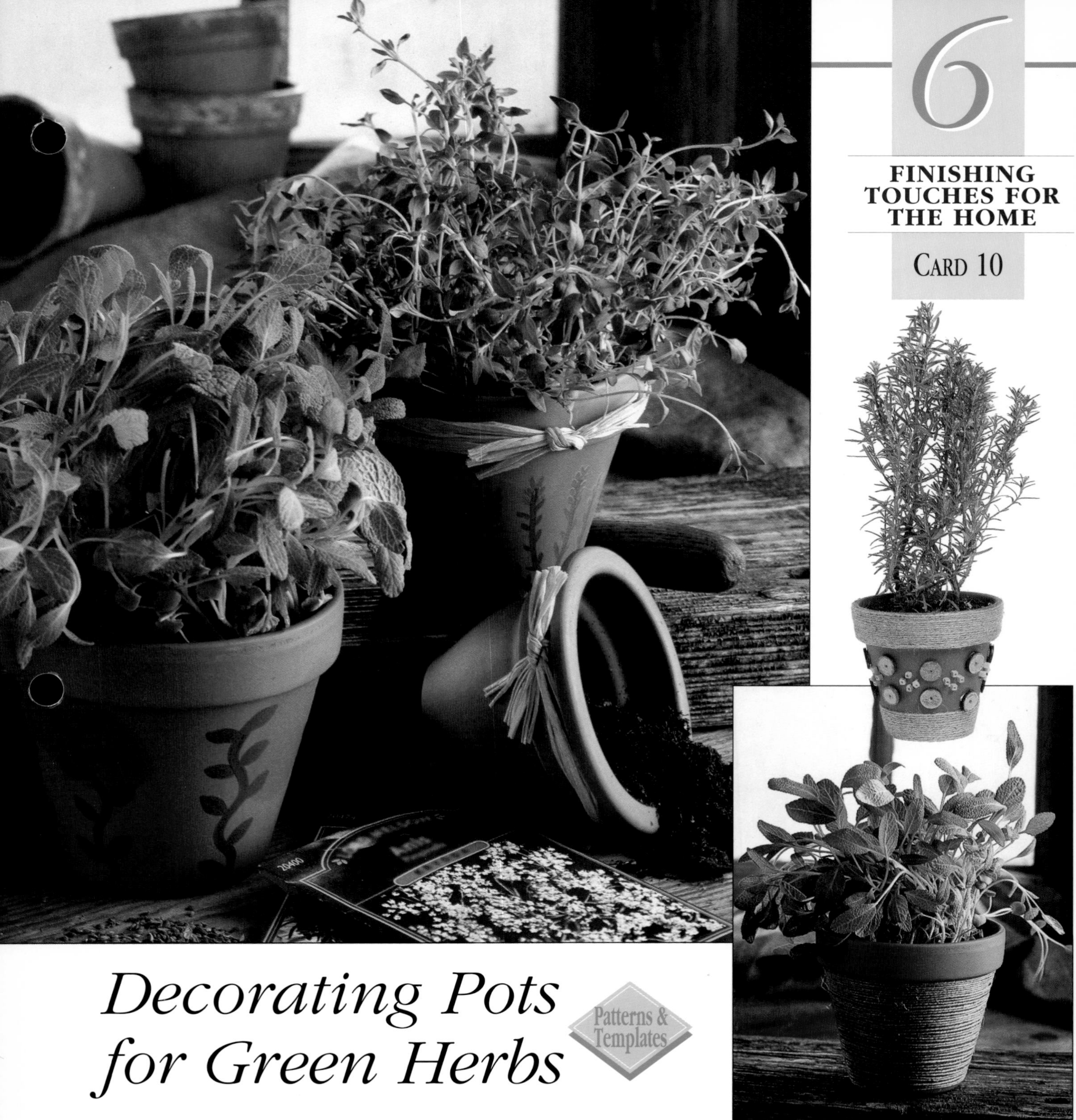

Pretty up the pots even more by wrapping with twine or gluing on beads, shells, buttons, or other trims. When arranging pots of herbs on a windowsill or a counter, alternate those with long pointed leaves, such as rosemary or tarragon, with those having rounded or lacy leaves, such as basil or parsley.

Decorating Pots for Green Herbs

Patterns & Templates

Parsley, sage, rosemary, and thyme, all adorned with raffia, paint, and twine, turn small, ordinary clay pots into a charming windowsill garden.

Fresh herbs add color and fragrance to the kitchen as well as flavor and spice to the cooking. By lining a sunny windowsill with decorated pots of herbs, you'll be able to snip off a couple of leaves as you need them to toss into a simmering stew, a soothing soup, or a favorite casserole. Choose simple painted designs from the templates in Group 12, Card 3, or paint your own freehand. For added texture, wind pots with twine or raffia. These pots are quick to do and make delightful last-minute gifts.

Patterns & Templates

Use the templates from Group 12, Card 3 for the clay pots. Enlarge or reduce the templates as needed.

Decorating clay pots is a simple and fun way to add a personal grace note to your kitchen.

Always use clean pots; old ones may contain plant bacteria that will react with the glue or paint. Never use a pot that is mossy or moldy. To clean used pots, scrub them thoroughly and then run them through the dishwasher. The heat will kill any remaining bacteria.

Tips for Decorating Clay Pots

Pick a motif that complements the herb to be planted.

- Try dipping a leaf from the herb into craft paint, then remove excess onto a paper towel; use the leaf to stamp shape directly onto pot. Stamp shapes randomly, or make leaves look as though they are attached to a painted stem.
- Choose designs that suit kitchen's decor. Craft paint comes in a variety of colors, or mix several colors together to get exact shade needed.
- Look in home-supply, craft, and hardware stores for interesting cords and twines, and in catalogs and gift shops for additional decorating ideas.
- Add interesting twigs and other bits and pieces when tying a bow or knot.

You'll Need

- **4"–6" terra-cotta pots**
- **Acrylic craft paint**
- **Paintbrush**
- **Raffia or twine**
- **Household cement**
- **Scissors**
- **Pencil**

Hand Painting Pots

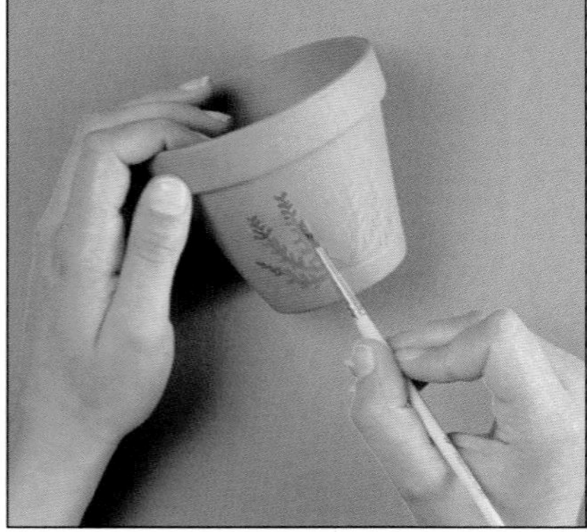

1 Lightly pencil design or pattern, either traced, outlined, or drawn freehand, on outside of pot. Paint over penciled design, applying 1 paint color at a time; allow each to dry completely before applying next.

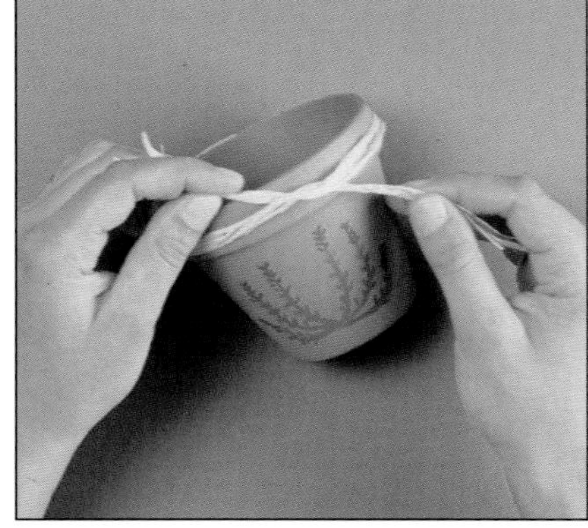

2 When painted design is completed and dried, use length of raffia to decorate pot rim: Wrap raffia several times around outside of rim. Tie ends of raffia together in large knot and then trim ends even.

Wrapping Pots with Twine

1 Apply cement to outside of pot and just below rim, covering desired twine-wrapped area. Work with 1" of cement at a time to keep it sticky; apply thick coat, smoothing out any lumps.

2 Press 1 end of twine firmly onto top of cemented area. Carefully and tightly wrap twine around pot, placing rows of twine close together to cover entire band of cement so pot doesn't show through.

Making a Pillow with Fused Appliqués

Inspired by the traditional Baltimore quilt designs of yesteryear, colorful fabric tulips are appliquéd to make lovely pillows that become inviting additions to your home.

Simple fusing techniques, using paper-backed fusible web, make this an easy appliqué project. The flowers, cut from strong solid-colored or printed cotton fabrics, can be arranged into a traditional basket design or formed into a wreath. The stems are cut on the bias from fabric backed with fusible web, enabling them to be shaped into position.

Complete the pillow by sewing the front and back together, then stuff with a purchased pillow form or polyester filling.

Floral motifs cut from cotton fabrics and fused in place make a beautiful pillow front. Delicate prints and an added ruffle result in a country-fresh look. The interesting basket bursting with solid red tulips is simply lengths of bias tape woven over and under each other and fused in place.

Patterns & Templates *Use the templates from Group 12, Card 7 to make patterns for the tulip pillow appliqués.*

The success of this project depends on perfect fusing. Follow the manufacturer's instructions for the proper amount of heat and pressure needed for a secure bond.

Guidlines for Fusing

A heavyweight paper-backed fusible web will provide strong adhesion and prevent fraying of fabric edges, so appliqués do not need any finishing.

- Choose 100% cotton fabrics. Wash and iron fabrics to remove sizing before cutting.
- Transfer templates to paper side of fusible web with pencil, placing like motifs together to save fabric.
- Use sharp scissors to avoid fraying at edges of motifs. Use embroidery scissors to make cutting small motifs easier.
- Protect ironing board with pressing paper, brown paper, or an old sheet.
- Always use a presscloth between iron and fabric when ironing fusibles. Place iron on top of presscloth and hold for several seconds. Lift, then replace on another spot. Do not slide iron over work.

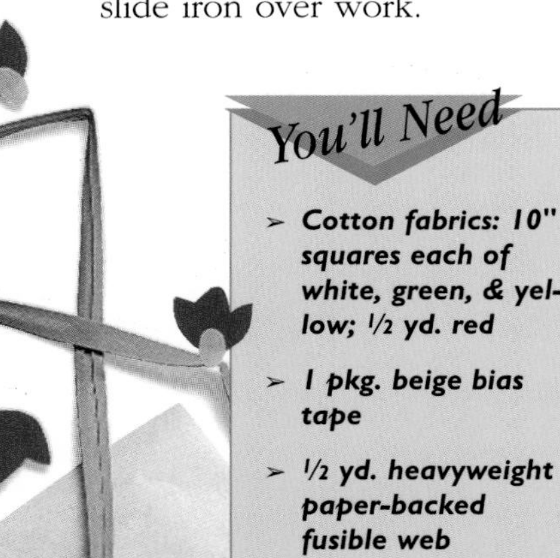

You'll Need

- **Cotton fabrics: 10" squares each of white, green, & yellow; 1/2 yd. red**
- **1 pkg. beige bias tape**
- **1/2 yd. heavyweight paper-backed fusible web**
- **14" pillow form**
- **Ruler, rotary cutter, pencil, pins, & sharp pointed scissors**
- **Iron & ironing board**
- **Brown paper**

1 Transfer 10 tulips and 6 buds onto paper side of fusible web. Transfer 10 oval and 6 bud bases and 22 leaves onto 2 more web pieces. Transfer design outline to white fabric, 1¼" from lower edge.

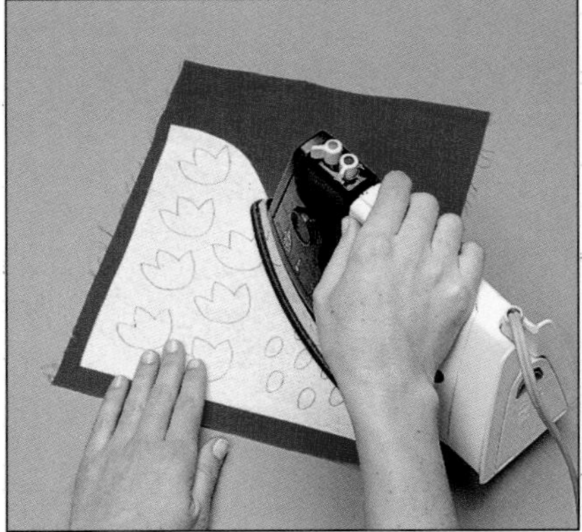

2 Place traced tulips and buds on wrong side of 10" red fabric square, textured side of web down. Fuse web and fabric together. Fuse oval and bud bases to yellow fabric, and leaves to green fabric.

3 Using scissors, carefully cut out individual red shapes for fusing. Cut out shapes from green and yellow fabrics. Keep paper backing on each piece until ready to fuse.

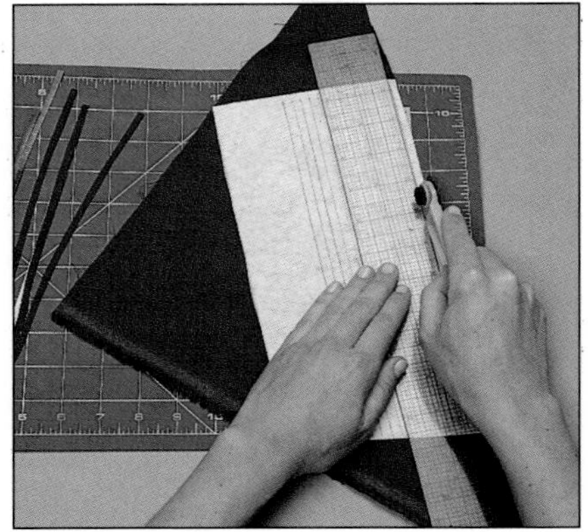

4 Fuse piece of web to wrong side of remainder of green fabric. Using ruler and rotary cutter, cut 13 (¼"-wide) bias strips for stems. Trim strips to lengths that are slightly longer than stems on design outline.

5 Working 1 stem at a time, remove paper backing. Using flowers as a guide, position and pin longest stems on white fabric, curving stems as needed; position ends slightly inside basket outline. Fuse long stems in place.

6 Fuse shorter stems to long stems. Remove paper backing and fuse red tulips and red buds in place. Next, layer and fuse yellow oval bases over red flowers and yellow bud bases over red buds; fuse leaves along stems last.

7 Place brown paper on ironing surface. Lay 12 (6") lengths of bias tape wrong side up on paper. Cover tapes with piece of fusible web; fuse. Peel away paper and trim off any excess fusing adhesive.

8 Cut lengths of fused bias tape to fit diagonally across basket outline in 2 directions. Pin 1 end of each tape, with fusible side down, along basket edges. Weave tapes over and under to fill basket outline; pin close to basket edges.

9 Trim ends of woven tapes to fit basket outline. Remove pins and fuse entire woven basket to white fabric. Work slowly, taking care that all sections of weave are fused in place.

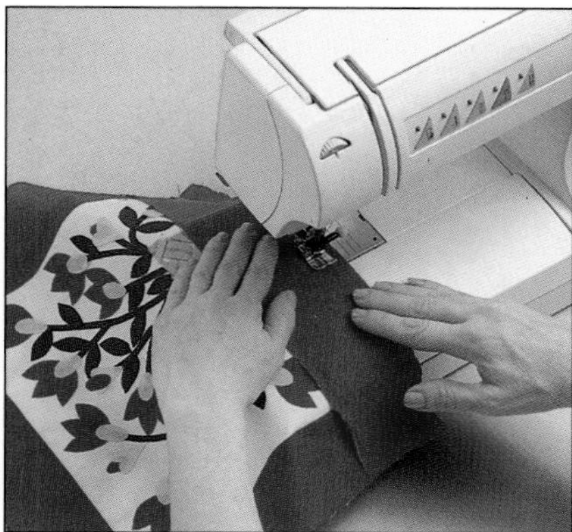

10 Cut 2 (10½") strips and 2 (14½") strips from red fabric. Right sides together, sew short strips to sides of square with ¼" seams; sew long strips to top and bottom. Cut backing to same size as front. Sew front to back and stuff.

Try This!

By using the same fusing technique and motifs in the featured project, you can turn a plain, purchased, covered throw pillow into a handmade treasure. For best results, undo the closure on the pillow cover and remove the pillow form. Cut a selection of flowers and leaves and place them in a pleasing arrangement. Follow the steps for fusing them in place.

Fusing Printed Flowers

There are many printed floral fabrics available that have large, beautiful flower-and-leaf motifs. These can be fused to decorate a pillow in much the same way as pencil-outlined appliqués. Choose a fabric that has definite design motifs that are easy to follow when cutting.

After the design has been fused in place on the pillow front, cut a backing the same size as the front. With right sides together, sew the front to the back with a ¼" seam, leaving an opening in the center of the bottom edge that is large enough to insert a pillow form. Turn the cover right side out, insert the pillow form, and slipstitch the opening closed.

To finish the pillow, slipstitch rayon twisted cord around the edges, making small loops at each corner. Apply fray prevention liquid to the cord ends.

Bold beautiful blooms cut from a printed decorator fabric and fused in place create a unique design that is quick and easy to make. Simply cut out flowers carefully and fuse them onto a piece of fabric cut to fit a pillow form.

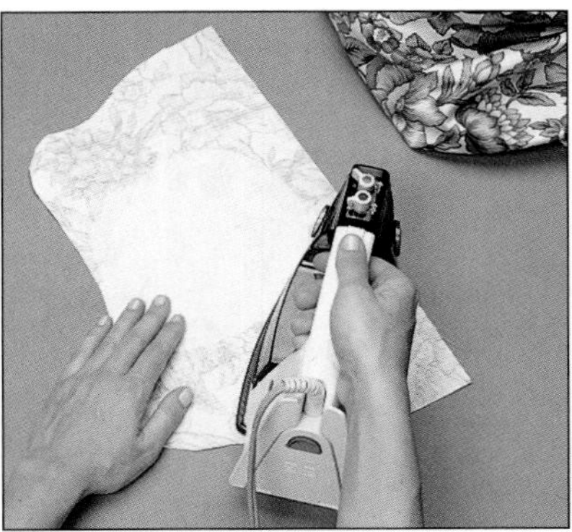

1 Fuse piece of paper-backed web to wrong side of floral print fabric, covering back of fully formed flowers and leaves planned for use.

2 With sharp, pointed scissors, carefully cut out individual floral elements, including leaves that are either part of single flowers or are separate pieces. Cut groups of flowers as well.

3 Remove paper from back of shapes. Place shapes on right side of pillow front in pleasing arrangement, then fuse flowers in place.

Creating a Country Floral Arrangement

A country-style flower arrangement looks as fresh and carefree as a country field, brimming with stems of common blooms abundantly displayed in an old earthen-ware pitcher or some other humble container.

Put away the formal silver and porcelains and look instead for simple household receptacles, such as watering cans, kettles, baskets, or even a teapot that has lost its lid.

The key to creating a convincing country aragement is to mix bunches of casual, unpretentious blooms, such as daisies, asters, mums, and sunflowers, with lots of greens and filler stems to form a round, lush display that doesn't look "arranged."

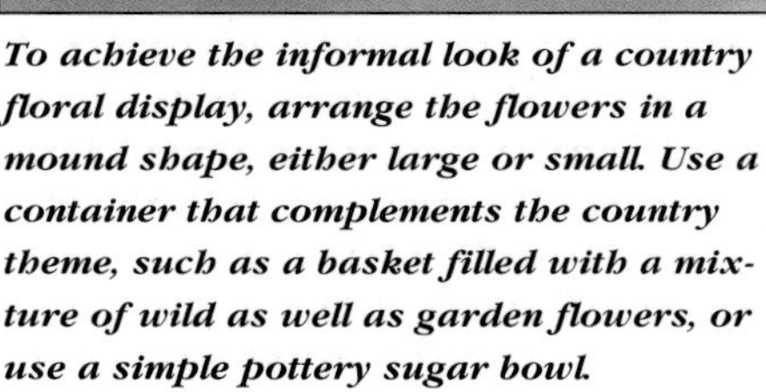

To achieve the informal look of a country floral display, arrange the flowers in a mound shape, either large or small. Use a container that complements the country theme, such as a basket filled with a mixture of wild as well as garden flowers, or use a simple pottery sugar bowl.

It is an art to create something that looks effortless, like these lovely, casual country-style floral arrangements. The secret is simplicity, both in choice of flowers and container. Use generous bunches of three or four different types of flowers and fill in with stems of greenery.

Select a container that suits a country motif. Opt for neutral colors, clean shapes, and interesting textures. Glazed or unglazed pottery, baskets, and wooden bowls and boxes are good choices.

Conditioning Fresh Flowers

Flowers picked from the garden or gathered from the roadside must be conditioned before they are used in an arrangement.

- Always cut flower stems on an angle to avoid pinching stems closed so flowers are unable to take in water.
- Keep stems as long as possible, even if you think you won't need length. You can always cut a stem shorter if necessary.
- Strip stems of all leaves that might be under water. Place stripped stems in a bucket and fill with cool water up to last leaf on stem. Allow them to rest there two or three hours before starting arrangement.

You'll Need

- ***Flowers & leaves: spider & cushion mums, alstroemeria, Queen Anne's lace; lemon leaves or other greens***
- ***Floral foam & tape***
- ***Floral frog***
- ***Serrated knife & pruning shears or scissors***
- ***Container***
- ***Aluminum foil***

1 Using knife, trim off bottom leaves from floral stems. Holding each stem under water, cut off several inches from bottom to help absorbtion of water and keep blooms longer. Keep flowers in water until needed.

2 Press container top into floral foam to imprint shape. Using knife, trim foam to fit, allowing about 1" to extend above top of container. Roll foil into ball and place in bottom of container. Saturate foam with water then press firmly into container.

3 Place piece of floral tape across top of foam, attaching ends of tape to rim of container to provide stability. Place another piece of tape across foam and first tape, securing to container rim.

4 Insert first stem of lemon leaves into foam about ½" from center back to establish tallest point of arrangement. Add more stems of lemon leaves in decreasing height, angled at sides and in front to establish basic shape.

5 Insert first stem of spider mums about ½" in front of tallest leaf stem, with tallest flower about 1" lower than topmost leaves. Insert more spider mums in decreasing height at sides and in center front, angling them to begin rounding.

6 Insert alstroemeria stems, angled at varying heights, between spider mums. Insert cushion mums at an angle to fill in arrangement, placing stems closer to front rim of container and more horizontally to maintain rounded shape.

7 Place stems of Queen Anne's lace to fill spaces between mums, nestling these flower heads below others to set off other flowers and to give completed arrangement a full and lush appearance.

Try This!

To make a country-style arrangement for a mantel or window, where height is necessary, combine flowers of similar shapes but of different size blossoms, such as sunflowers and daisies. Mix buds and fully opened flowers to prolong the life of the arrangement, and fill in between the flowers with bright clusters of feathery goldenrod.

If your container is a basket, there are several ways to turn it into a watertight container. You can purchase a clear plastic liner from flower shops and craft stores, which is flexible yet strong enough to hold water. However, if your basket is large or an odd size, look through your kitchen for containers that will hold water and fit within the shape of your basket. Lasagna pans or tempered-glass baking dishes make great liners for large, shallow baskets.

A lovely fireside bouquet, just perfect for autumn, glows with the warm golds and russets of fall leaves, sunflowers, and a variety of chrysanthemums. The low-to-the-ground arrangement resembles a footstool of flowers. If the fireplace is used often, mist the arrangement every day to keep the flowers and leaves moist and fresh looking.

Arranging a Fireside Bouquet

A bouquet that is arranged to be viewed from below eye level, such as one placed beside a fireplace, requires a slightly different approach to arranging than one at eye level.

Here, you are not looking for dramatic lines and sweeps of stems, but for a mass of color and bloom. When finished, the arrangement sits low and wide, rather like a floral floor cushion.

Use an abundance of plant materials, such as colorful autumn leaves, to cover the floral foam and any tape or wire that is used. Keep all stems trimmed to 8" or less. If they are too long, flowers will poke out at odd, unattractive angles.

Use hardy flowers that are known to last long, such as mums, asters, sunflowers, and daisies. Fragile blossoms will not be able to withstand the drafty conditions found near the floor. When completed, the arrangement should last for several weeks without fussing over it.

1 Place several blocks of floral foam into a large, shallow container, such as a lasagna or tempered-glass baking pan, pressing firmly to secure. Place this container inside a long, low basket. Saturate foam with water.

2 Insert stems of fall foliage lengthwise along center of foam container to establish height of arrangement. Insert other stems almost horizontally into foam to cover edges of container and to form background for flowers.

3 Beginning with largest flower heads, insert stems at varying heights, placing tallest stems in center to establish height and angling others, with those closest to rim placed more horizontally to maintain rounded shape.

Balancing the height of the stems with the vase is important to creating harmony in the arrangement. Tall stems of calla lilies, grasses, and ferns create a statuesque arrangement in a tall, narrow vase.

Arranging Flowers in the Japanese Style

Bring a touch of color and a feeling of serenity to a room with the grace and delicacy of flowers arranged in the simple style developed by the Japanese.

The "less is more" principle behind Japanese flower arranging emphasizes the beauty of a few individual blooms and the clean, classic lines of their placement. In this art form, called *ikebana*, flowers are arranged in the rough shape of a triangle, the three points symbolizing heaven, earth, and man.

As shown in the shallow bowl of irises and stars of Bethlehem, each flower is a different height and positioned with leaves, vines, and grasses to create a flowing line for the eyes to follow.

The emphasis of Japanese flower arranging is in the beauty of the lines and angles formed by the arrangement rather than in the profusion of colors of various blooms. To achieve this, use one to three flower types with no more than two to five single-flowered stems each. Some stems of grass or leaves, and an interestingly shaped branch or twig can also be used within an arrangement.

General Guidelines

Trim the leaves from the flower stems so they don't detract from the overall shape formed by the stems.

- For low arrangements, use flowers with thick, fleshy stems, such as lilies, irises, gladioli, tulips, and orchids. Their stems absorb water easily even in very shallow bowls.
- For tall arrangements, use tall vases to support long-stemmed flowers that tend to droop, such as tulips, daffodils, and anemones.
- Use spiked flower holder to position stems. If desired, cover holder with pebbles when arrangement is complete.

You'll Need

- ***Spiked flower holder***
- ***Sharp knife & garden shears***

For low arrangement:

- ***1"–1½"-deep bowl***
- ***Plant materials: 5 irises, 3 stems stars of Bethlehem, 2 dried willow branches, eucalyptus sprigs***
- ***Floral clay***

For tall arrangement:

- ***Tall glass vase***
- ***Plant materials: 3 calla lilies, 3 stems bear grass, 1 asparagus fern stem, several grass stalks***
- ***Pebbles***

Making a Low Japanese-Style Arrangement

1 Adhere piece of floral clay to bottom of spiked flower holder. Press firmly to secure flower holder to bottom of bowl at front edge.

2 Insert curving willow branches into holder, placing them to left side, 1 behind other and about ¾" apart.

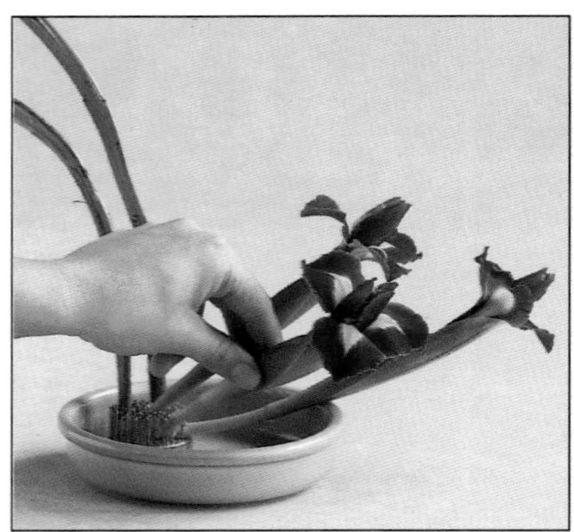

3 Cut 3 irises 5", 6", and 7" below flower. Insert into spiked flower holder to form triangle: Place longest almost horizontal at right, resting on rim; angle mid-sized iris toward right from center; and insert shortest at side front.

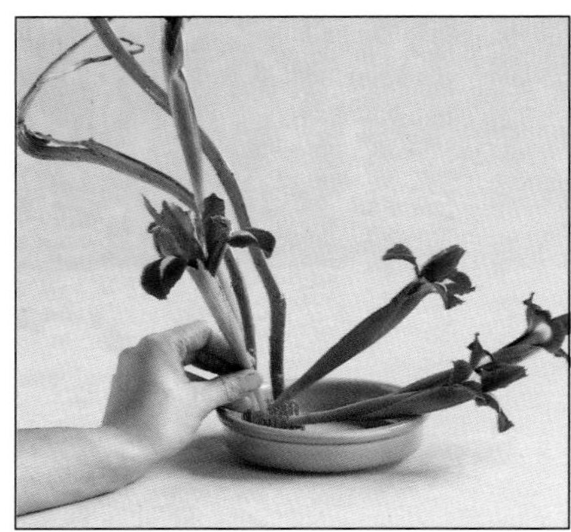

4 Insert 12" iris stem in front of willow branches. Cut remaining iris 6"–7" below bloom; insert it in front of tall iris, following line of willow, and angled left and to front, to form larger triangle in combination with 5" and 6" irises.

5 Place 1 star of Bethlehem stem to left and slightly in front of tall iris; cut stem of second star of Bethlehem to about 4" and insert in front of arrangement, angled right.

6 Insert sprigs of eucalyptus around flower stems to give volume to bottom of arrangement and to balance angle created by flowers and willow. Add water to bowl.

Making a Tall Japanese-Style Arrangement

1 Place flower holder in bottom of tall glass vase. Add pebbles to hide sides of holder from view. Add bear grass and grass stalks toward back of vase, securing between spikes in holder.

2 Cut callas into 3 lengths, with tallest just below heads of bear grass; mid-sized lily just below head of tall lily; and smallest lily about 2" below mid-sized flower. Insert lilies in front of bear grass.

3 Insert stem of asparagus fern into vase at front and wind it around arrangement. Twine grass stalks around flowers; add more pebbles to hold shape of arrangement. Add water to vase.

Try This!

Use a broad-bottomed vase as a pedestal and construct an arrangement on top of it. Select an interesting branch and bind it to the vase with raffia. Fill the vase with water to stabilize it. Using the branch as the base on which to create the arrangement, place a large flower, such as a dahlia, into the vase, with blossom resting on branch. Insert a few long-stemmed calla lilies, or other flowers with a graceful sway, into the vase, along with a few long, thorny fruit-bearing twigs; use the branch to support them in position.

Crafter's Secrets

Before using dried or brittle twigs in a Japanese-style arrangement, refresh them and make them more pliable and easy to shape by letting them soak in a pan of water for about 10 hours.

Making a Multilevel Display

The art of *ikebana,* or Japanese flower arranging, is inspired by the shapes and forms of our natural environment. The arrangement at right is built around the reed-straight bamboo or cane, which is cut to varying heights to set the shape of the arrangement. If bamboo is not available, substitute ordinary hollow reeds.

Use a heavy ceramic pot for stability and to securely hold the cane upright. The cane is cut to size after it is arranged in the pot. For color and as a complement to the straight lines of the cane, a few stems of stars of Bethlehem and veronica are added, along with a spill of amaranthus to bring the eye below the pot as a way of elongating the form of the arrangement.

Bamboo, cane, and reed are very hearty and will last several months. Clean the inside of canes with a skewer if necessary to insert flowers. When the flowers perish, just replace them with new ones.

The simplicity and clean lines of Japanese floral displays are complemented by modern settings. In the arrangement above, the blue and white conical-shaped flowers soften the linear precision of the potful of cane.

1 Snugly fill 4" pot with 14"–16" stalks of cane. Using garden clippers, cut front stalks 1"–1½" above rim. Leaving 6 stalks uncut at back, cut remaining stalks to varying heights, none more than half that of tall stalks.

2 Cut 4 stars of Bethlehem at different heights. Insert 3 tallest into hollow of canes, in size order; insert smallest into 1 center front cane. Cut 3 veronica stems 3"–4" below last flower head. Insert into canes at front left.

3 Insert 1 tall veronica stem to left of tallest canes and 2 stems of cascading amaranthus at front and side. Fill pot with water to 1" below rim.

6

FINISHING TOUCHES FOR THE HOME

CARD 21

Sewing Ruffled Throw Pillows

Toss on lots of light and airy ruffled throw pillows to add plushness and comfort to a chaise lounge or a made-up bed. Make the pillows from scratch or sew ruffled covers for ready-made forms.

Ruffles add interest to a pillow and can enhance needlework designs by acting as a frame for the hand work. Ruffled pillows made from embroidered fabrics and eyelet lace are a lovely addition to rooms with a romantic point of view. In bold colors and prints they blend into more contemporary settings.

Coordinate fabrics with curtains and spreads to tie the space together in an attractive, understated way. Make pillows square, round, or heart-shaped, as desired.

Sew on ribbons, a double ruffle, or make a patchwork front to give pillows more handcrafted details. Make many pillows and arrange them in an eye-catching group to create a soft, luxurious corner for lounging.

Pillow tops framed by ruffles make attractive showcases for embroidered eyelet fabrics. For a striking effect, use a colored fabric to make the pillow form.

Pillow-Making Guidelines

Choose pretty fabrics that fit the design of the pillow, then embellish with rows of lace and bows if desired.

- Enlarge the diagram below onto graph paper and make two pattern pieces for heart-shaped pillow. Use half of heart shape for pattern 1 and full pattern shape for pattern 2.
- Use pattern 1 to cut one pillow front and pattern 2 to cut two pillow-back pieces.
- Use purchased ruffle or make enough ruffle to encircle pillow. See Crafter's Secrets, Group 6, Card 22 for technique.

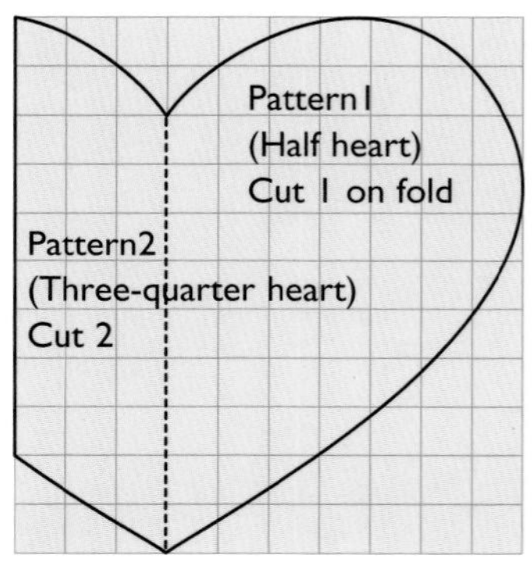

I square = I"

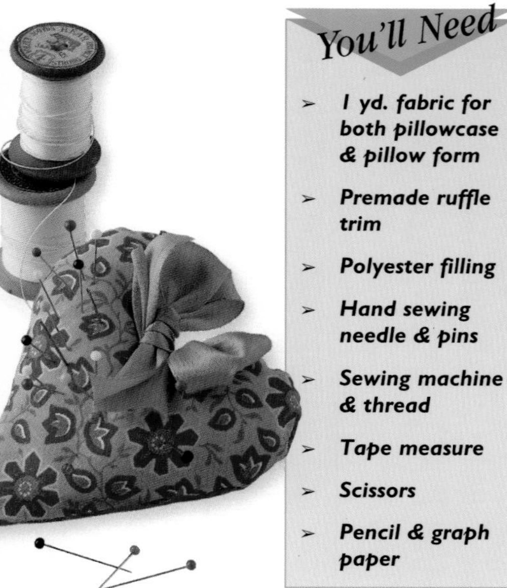

You'll Need

- ***I yd. fabric for both pillowcase & pillow form***
- ***Premade ruffle trim***
- ***Polyester filling***
- ***Hand sewing needle & pins***
- ***Sewing machine & thread***
- ***Tape measure***
- ***Scissors***
- ***Pencil & graph paper***

1 Fold pillowcase fabric in half, right sides together. Place pattern I on foldline for I pillow front and pattern 2 beside it for 2 pillow backs. Cut with ½" seam allowances all around.

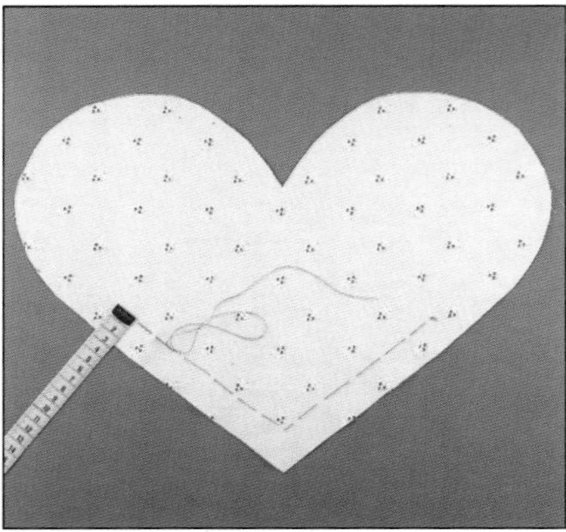

2 Hand baste around pillow front I" from edge, using contrasting colored thread.

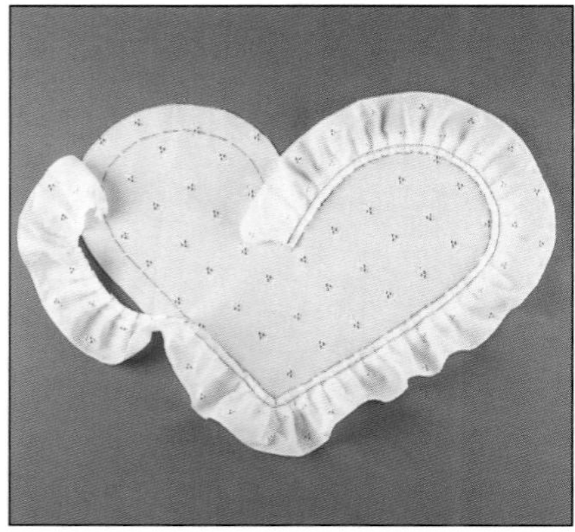

3 Place finished gathered edge of ruffle along basting line on right side of pillow front. Sew ruffle to pillow following ruffle's gathering line and overlapping ends to make seam look crisp and tidy.

4 Turn under a ¼" double hem along straight edge of pillow back; topstitch. Repeat with second back piece.

5 Right sides facing up, align back pieces to form heart shape, overlapping about 3" in center to create opening for inserting pillow form. Sew a seam along overlapping top and bottom edges of heart to hold firmly in place.

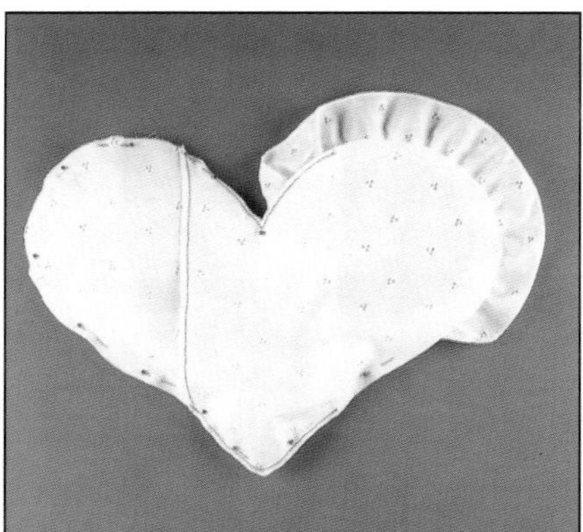

6 Right sides together, place pillow back on pillow front, matching edges and sandwiching ruffle in between. Pin, tucking ruffle inside to avoid catching it in seam. Topstitch around edge; clip at V.

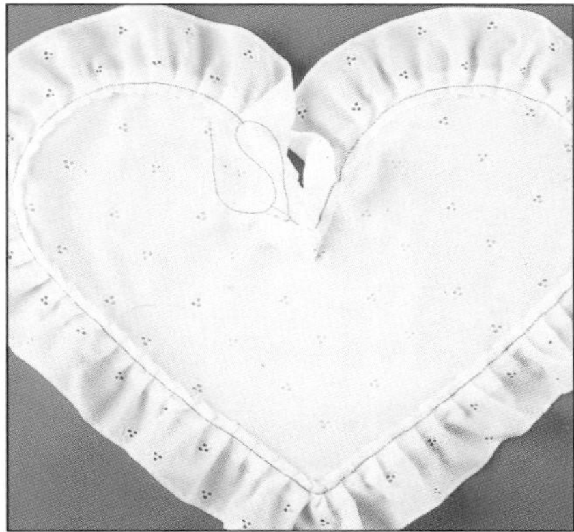

7 Turn right side out. Fold ruffle to back where 2 halves of heart meet and tuck under excess fabric. Hand sew along seam to hold excess fabric down; use small stitches to keep seam neat.

8 To make pillow form, cut 2 pillow front pieces with ½" seam allowances all around. Right sides facing, sew together along edge, leaving about 4" opening on 1 side of heart.

Try This!

Customize your pillows with pretty lace ribbons. Fabric stores have a large selection of fine lace yard goods and trims from which to choose. Select your favorite to create a romantic pillow to dream on or to use as a ring bearer's pillow at an upcoming wedding. For a truly romantic pillow, make a pillow front from cotton lace, then sew a double ruffle of lace onto the pillow front before sewing the front to the pillow back.

9 Turn right side out. Fill pillow with stuffing and slipstitch opening closed by hand. Insert pillow form into heart-shaped pillowcase.

Crafter's Secrets

To make ruffles long enough to go around the pillowcase, measure very accurately. Ruffles are usually about 3" wide, but choose a larger or smaller width if desired. If you are using a ready-made ruffle trim, purchase a length equal to the pillow's perimeter plus 4"–6".

If you are making ruffles, cut and join a length of fabric to equal twice the pillow's perimeter plus 4"–6". Fold edges under ⅛" twice and hem. Make 2 rows of gathering stitches about ¼" apart along 1 long edge; pull thread ends to form uniform gathers.

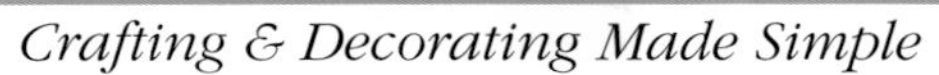

Making a Log Cabin Lace Pillow

Here is a pillow so appealing, with the inviting warmth of country patchwork and the softness of ruffles, that it is destined to become a family heirloom.

Use embroidered eyelet or combine different laces to piece the classic yet simple log cabin pattern, which evolves from a center square to which fabric strips are stitched, then cut to progressively longer lengths.

Plan ahead for the positions of special or favorite fabric scraps in the log cabin motif, such as a piece from a wedding dress or from a particular curtain or bedspread. Consider making a number of pillows with varied designs to create an exciting bedtop arrangement.

Wash and press all fabrics before sewing to avoid shrinking the pillow when it is washed. Press seams after each strip addition.

This pretty embroidered pillow, with its front pieced in a log cabin quilt pattern, has the look of an inherited keepsake. Because this technique is based on a very simple system of sewing strip to strip counterclockwise around a center square, it is not difficult to make.

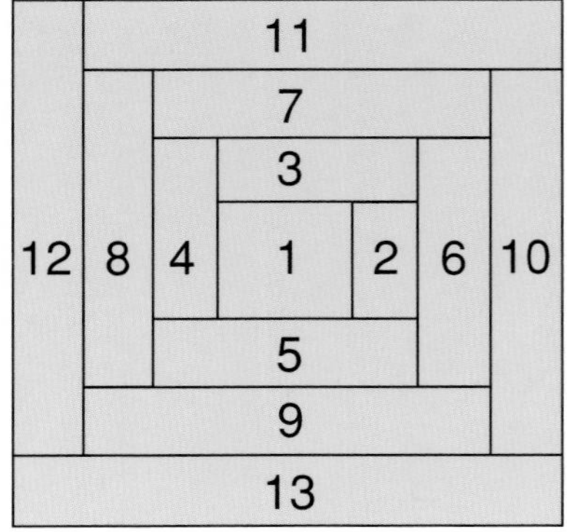

The log cabin pattern begins with a center square (1). A long fabric strip is stitched to the square, then cut to size (2); each successive strip is then stitched and cut to its length (3–13) in the numbered progression shown.

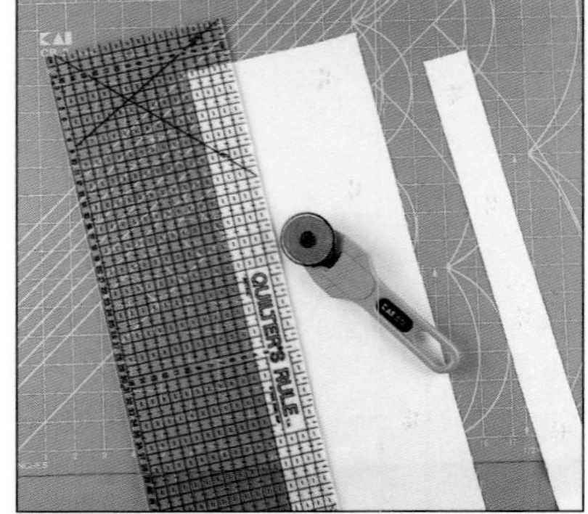

1 Cut out a 3" center square. Cut long 2"-wide strips of chosen fabrics to stitch and cut. For neatest results, use rotary cutter and cutting grid to cut strips accurately.

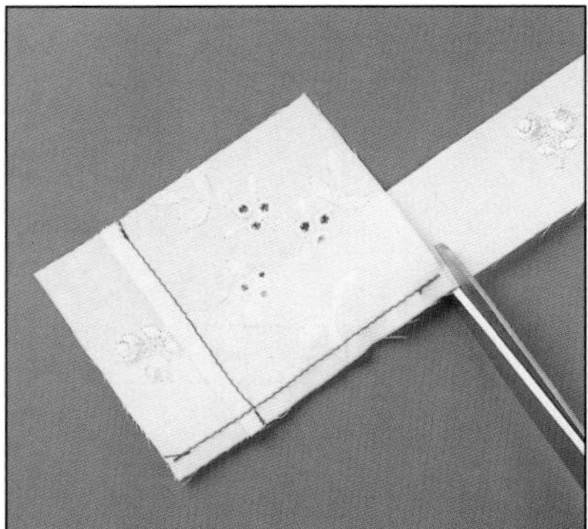

2 Right sides together, align and sew strip 2 to side of square. Cut off excess so strip and square are even. Turn counterclockwise; sew on strip 3; cut off excess. Continue adding strips until square is of desired size.

Quilting Fancy Designs on Pillows

Join generations of quilters who have elevated practical sewing skills to an art while creating heirloom pieces, such as this lovely pillow, with a shell motif quilted at center and around the borders.

No piecing or appliqué is used to turn a plain light blue fabric into an intricately quilted pillow cover. The entire design is made with simple running stitches that follow the outlines of the shell patterns and the crosshatched background.

Choose washable fabrics with a firm, even weave, such as 100% cotton or a cotton-polyester blend. Stitch the lines of the pattern in a matching color for a tone-on-tone dimensional effect or in a contrasting color for artistic impact.

Show your quilted handwork in a variety of ways. Make a tiny corded pillow quilted with a traditional Celtic design to use as a tiny tasseled pincushion, or stitch a simpler version of the shell motif and frame it to hang on a wall.

Patterns & Templates *Use the templates from Group 12, Card 15 to reproduce the quilting patterns used to embellish the pillow and pincushion.*

Follow the steps to create the quilted piece, then transform it into a 14" pillow cover edged with contrasting piping.

Making Quilted Pillow Cover

After completing the quilted design, remove the quilted square from the frame and trim it to a 15" square.

- Baste cording to right side of front. Cross ends of cording at center of bottom edge so ends will be caught in seam.
- Fold 11¼"x15" back cover pieces under 1½" twice along one 15" edge; press; sew or fuse hems in place.
- Mark and sew three buttonholes on top hem of back cover. With buttonhole piece on top, overlap hemmed edges of both pieces to form 15" square. Baste or pin overlapped edges together.
- With right sides together, pin and sew pillow cover front and back, catching cording within seam. Clip corners and turn to right side.

- ***Fabrics: 1 yd. fabric for pillow front & back & 22" square lining***
- ***22" square batting***
- ***18" quilt frame***
- ***Basting & matching sewing threads***
- ***Hand-sewing & quilting needles***
- ***Thimble, scissors, pencil, tracing paper, masking tape***
- ***Sewing machine***
- ***14" square pillow form***
- ***1¾ yds. covered contrast cording***
- ***3 (¾") buttons***

1 Cut 22" square for pillow front. Transfer design motifs from Group 12, Card 15 onto fabric as directed in Crafter's Secrets, Group 6, Card 26.

2 Tape lining flat, wrong side up. Layer batting on lining, then fashion fabric on batting; pin layers together. Using darning needle and basting thread, baste layers together in large grid pattern. Secure basted square in quilt frame.

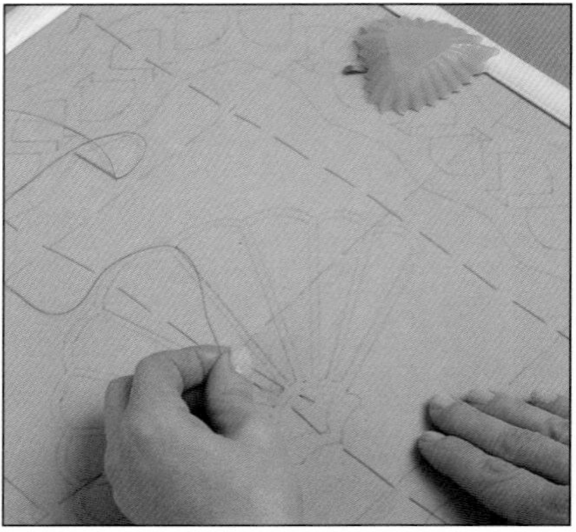

3 Thread quilting needle and tie knot in 1 end. Insert needle into top fabric only about ½" from start of stitching and bring out at stitching point. Pull thread until knot pops through to underside of top fabric.

4 To quilt, place 1 hand under layered fabrics and insert needle until point touches finger of hand under quilt. Bring needle up at next point, pressing thumb down on top of quilt where needle point comes up. Pull needle through. Repeat.

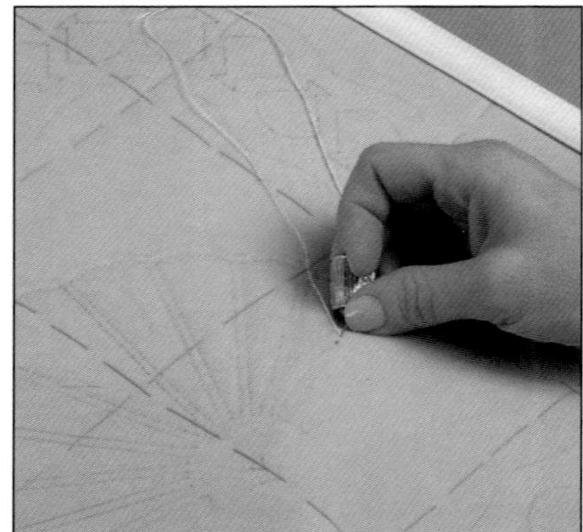

5 Continue making small, even running stitches through all layers along design lines. Quilt shell first, then border and ground. At end of stitching, tie knot on top of fabric, take a stitch in top fabric only, and pull knot through. Cut thread.

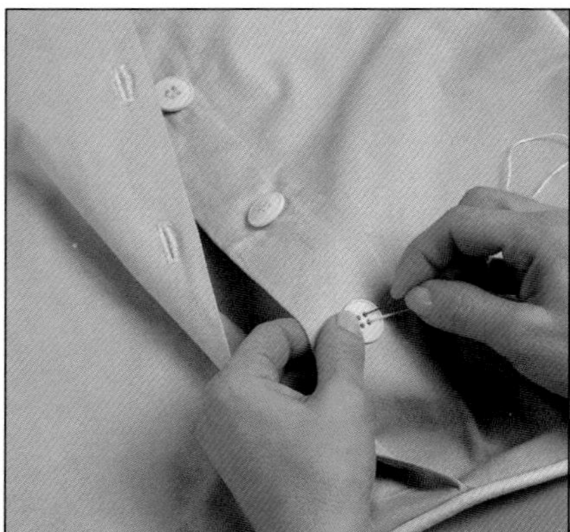

6 Make pillow cover as instructed at far left. Sew buttons to bottom hem to match buttonholes on back of cover. Insert pillow form, fitting corners of form into cover; button back of cover closed.

Try This!

For an elegant white-on-white neck roll, use purchased templates for quilting designs and cover a 6"x15" neck roll with a Victorian-inspired repeat clamshell pattern and a braided border.

- *Trace border design along lengthwise edges of an 18"x22" piece of fabric to make 15"x19" quilting area. Trace standard shell template to fill in between borders.*
- *Layer lining, batting, and fashion fabric. Pin and baste, then quilt design lines; trim piece to 16"x20". Baste covered cording to long edges of quilt top.*
- *For each pillow end, fold 6"x20" piece of fabric in half lengthwise, wrong sides together. Sew 1/2" from fold to form casing. With right sides together, sew one pillow end to each long edge of quilt, catching cording in 1/2" seam.*
- *With right sides together, sew remaining edges, including pillow ends, leaving casing ends open. Turn to right side; lace ribbon or decorative cord through casings. Slip cover over pillow form, pull cords to close ends, and tie ends of cords into bows.*

Crafter's Secrets

To transfer the quilting shell and border motifs to the top of the pillow featured on the front of Group 6, Card 25, make a tracing of the pillow motifs first: Tape sheets of tracing paper together to accommodate a 14" square, then trace the border motif to form a square with the large shell pattern in the center. Tape the tracing to a work surface, center fabric right side up over the shell, and, with a pencil, lightly trace the full design onto the fabric. Add quilting lines for background grid after main motif is quilted: Mark diagonal lines 1" apart in both directions. Quilt as instructed.

Echo-Quilting Pillows

Use the templates from Group 12, Card 15 to quilt charming farm animal shapes that echo across these pillow tops with concentric outlines. Space echoing lines evenly apart to fill the background quickly with strands of quilting thread that match either the background fabric or the borders.

Border the quilted square with a homespun fabric that complements the country motifs: Sew 3" strips across the top and bottom edges with ½" seams. Cut these strips on the straight grain, or as shown on the bias for visual interest. Sew another strip to each side and across the ends of the top and bottom strips. Trim the pillow top to 13" square.

To make the pillow back, cut two 9"x13" pieces; turn under 1½" hem along one long edge of each, and fuse. Overlap hemmed edges to make back the same size as pillow front; pin in place. Sew hook-and-loop dots to close overlapped edges. Sew pillow front and back along all edges with ½" seam. Turn cover right side out and insert pillow form.

Quilted barnyard animals form the centers of these 12" square pillows, framed in country colors. Each corner is punctuated with a fabric-covered button.

1 Using soluble marker, outline shapes onto center of 12" fabric square. Layer fabric, batting, and lining; baste across center lengthwise, crosswise, and diagonally. Secure in frame. Quilt along outline.

2 Mark next line ⅜" from first outline of shape, smoothing line where curves of original are too intricate. Quilt along this marked line around entire animal. Mark next echo line ⅜" from last.

3 Quilt each subsequent echo line 1 at a time, spacing each ⅜" apart until fabric top is entirely quilted. As quilting lines radiate outward, soften curves as needed. When done, remove piece from frame and complete pillow.

FINISHING TOUCHES FOR THE HOME

CARD 31

Etching Stenciled Designs on Glassware

Patterns & Templates

Transform everyday glassware into beautiful table accessories or decorative objects with a simple technique that lets you simulate the skilled artisanship of Old World etched glass.

Glass etching is an elegant way to personalize and decorate almost any glass item, from drinking glasses and pitchers to mirrors and crystal bowls. The technique is easy and requires very few tools.

Motif stencils are cut from vinyl shelf lining, which is adhered to the glass. Then *etching cream* is applied to the glass within the stenciled shape and left on for a few minutes. When the cream is washed off, a beautiful "frosted" design is etched into the glass forever.

Etched glassware is suitable for every room. Individual plain glasses and a pitcher become a matched set when etched with frosted cherries. For the bathroom or dressing table, etched bows and roses make a pretty accent on decorative bottles.

Patterns & Templates

Use the templates from Group 12, Card 8 to create the etched glass motifs on the front of this card. Or design your own, using motifs from magazines, catalogs, and books as inspiration.

Etching glass is quite simple with etching cream, which oxidizes on contact with the glass, leaving a frosted impression of the design. Etching cream is available in jars at craft and hardware stores.

Guidelines for Etching

Work slowly and carefully, following the manufacturer's directions for using the etching cream.

- Wear rubber or plastic gloves and glasses or goggles to protect yourself when working with the cream.
- Be sure there is good ventilation in work area and surfaces are covered with newspaper. Keep all tools close by.
- Work near running water for quick cleanups.
- As you cut out stenciled shape, hold craft knife firmly and pull slowly toward you, keeping fingers away from path of knife.
- Rinse off etching cream in aluminum sink, not porcelain or enamel, which chemicals can damage. Remove all traces of cream before wiping dry.

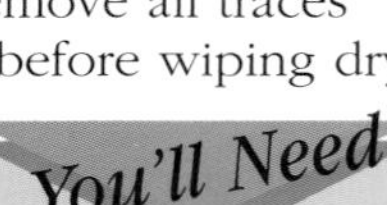

- ***Glass for etching***
- ***Etching cream***
- ***Adhesive-backed vinyl shelf lining***
- ***Tracing paper, carbon or graphite paper, & pencil***
- ***Tape, scissors, & craft knife***
- ***Cotton swabs, steel wool, paper towels, & newspapers***
- ***Protective goggles, & latex gloves***
- ***Pot for warm water***

1 Trace selected template. Lightly rub right side of vinyl with steel wool to roughen surface for transfer of design. Tape traced design to graphite paper; tape graphite paper, carbon side down, to vinyl. Outline design onto vinyl.

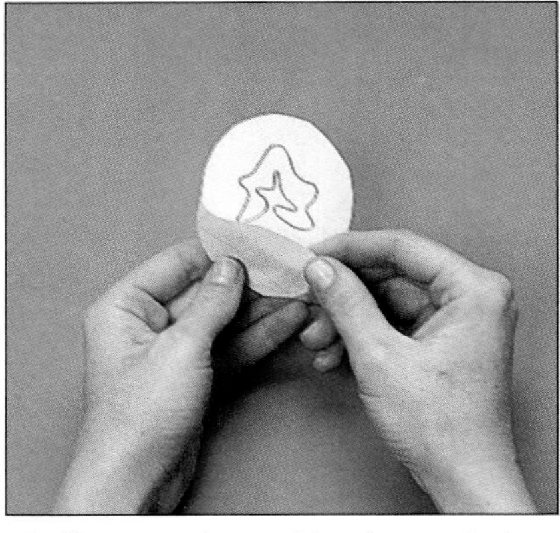

2 Cut around traced border on vinyl, leaving about ¾"–1" around design, which will protect surrounding glass surface from etching cream. Peel away paper backing from vinyl patch.

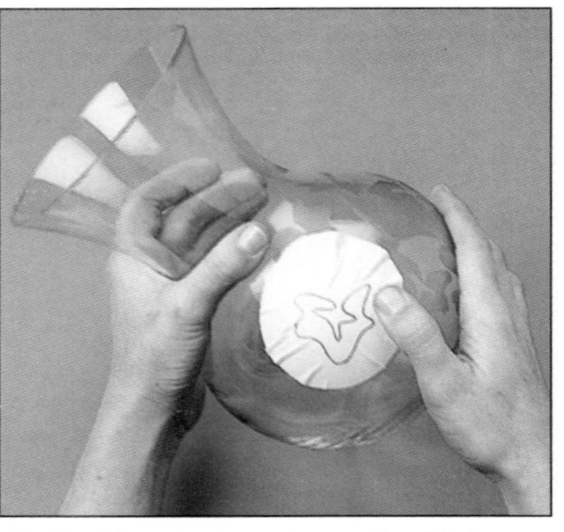

3 Position vinyl on glass; rub with fingertips to adhere, pressing out any air bubbles trapped beneath outlined design. To fit patch over rounded objects, clip edges of vinyl and pleat excess so patch can lie flat against glass.

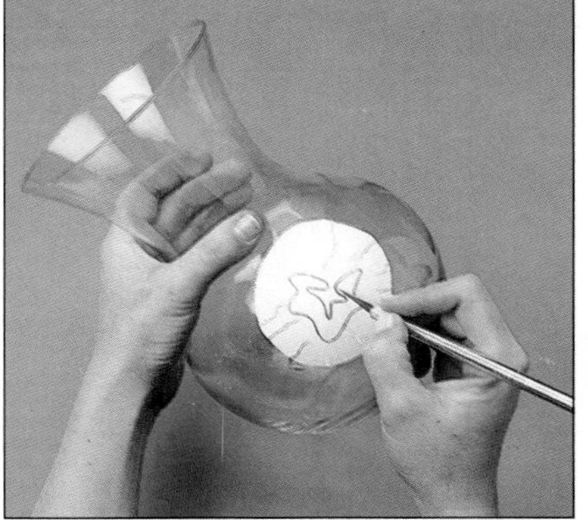

4 To cut out stenciled motif, pull sharp pointed blade of knife slowly and smoothly along motif outline. With tip of blade, carefully lift out cut vinyl to expose shaped area to be etched. Press down cut edges of vinyl to ensure adhesion to glass.

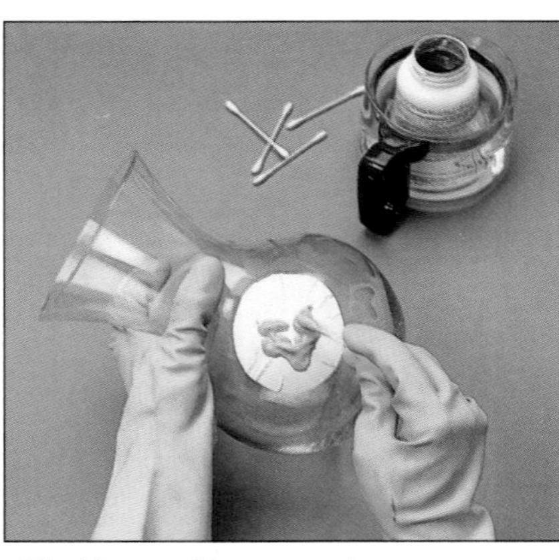

5 Heat etching cream in warm water bath. Wearing protective goggles and gloves, apply thick layer of cream with cotton swab to cover only exposed design. Use swab to gently burst any air bubbles in cream.

6 Leave cream on glass 5–6 minutes to complete etching action. Using low water pressure to prevent splashing, completely rinse cream from glass, working from top of design down. Dry with paper towels. Peel off vinyl stencil.

Lush topiaries can be made from one or more types of flowers in one or more colors. Tie a rich ribbon around the trunk of a pale arrangement made with dried strawflowers and heads of canary grass for added distinction. Create a striking topiary of classic red roses and boxwood.

Making Potted Dried Flower Topiaries

The simple yet irresistible display of delicate dried flowers crowning a potted topiary tree evokes the romance of a gentle, bygone era.

Elegant topiary trees made of dried flowers look wonderful decorating a sunroom or welcoming guests in a front hall. These dainty little trees are easily made by spiking a floral foam ball onto a twig stem that is supported in a clay-filled, moss-covered pot. Decorate the ball with dried flowers, leaves, seed pods, nuts, and other plant materials.

You can change the flowers seasonally. For spring, follow the example above and use lots of yellow strawflowers and pearly everlastings offset with glossy boxwood.

Decide how you would like the finished tree to look: Do you want to it to be predominantly one color or several? Will the crown be smooth and even or spiky? Consider the type, form, and color of various dried plants before purchasing them. As you work, distribute the different plants evenly across the surface of the floral foam to create a harmonious appearance.

Although a round head is the traditional shape for a topiary, floral foam in other shapes, such as a cone, oval, block, or heart, can be used to create some interesting results. Or cut floral foam to any shape you desire.

Topiary Guidelines

Before you begin, be sure you have enough plant materials on hand. Cut stems to no more than 2".

- Finished size of floral foam ball, exposed trunk length, and container should be about equal in height. Remember that finished head of topiary will be larger than foam ball.
- Container plays major role in unifying arrangement, so select pot that enhances color scheme of tree but is simple enough not to distract from it.
- Use floral clay to stabilize tree in pot. Pack clay firmly into pot, keeping in mind that clay shrinks when drying.
- Use straight twigs, branches, reeds, bamboo, dowels, or other sticks for trunk.

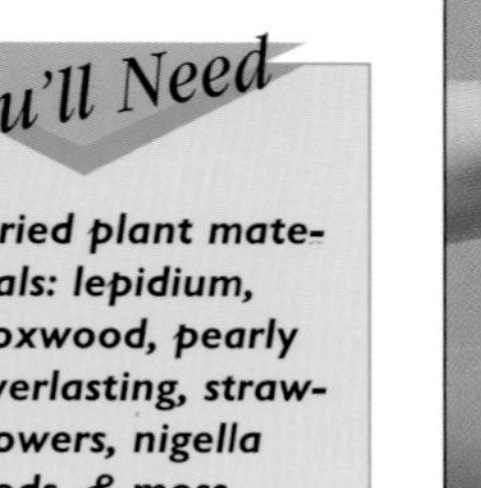

You'll Need

- ***Dried plant materials: lepidium, boxwood, pearly everlasting, strawflowers, nigella pods, & moss***
- ***Floral foam ball, 4" in diameter***
- ***Straight twigs***
- ***Raffia***
- ***Floral wire & clay***
- ***Clay pot***

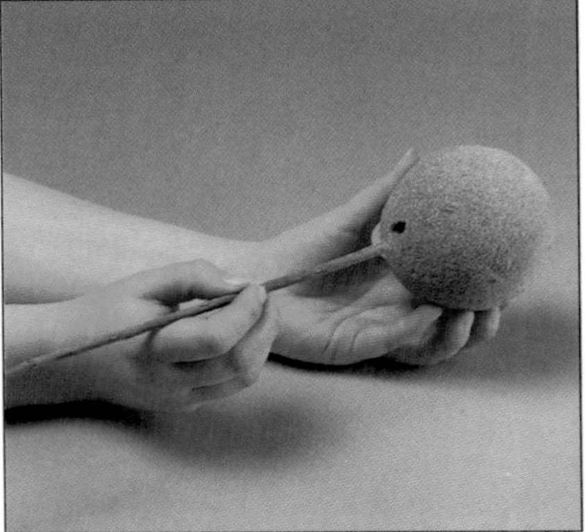

1 Using straight twig, make hole for trunk in foam ball that is wide enough for trunk but tight enough so foam ball sits securely on top.

2 Begin by covering lower half of topiary crown: Insert short stems of lepidium and boxwood into ball around hole, keeping plants close together, but not too tight.

3 Insert strawflowers, nigella pods, and pearly everlasting between boxwood and lepidium. Distributing larger flowers evenly between filler plants, continue adding flowers and leaves in rings until lower half is covered.

4 Tightly pack pot with floral clay to within ½" of rim; smooth surface. Using raffia, wrap several twigs together 2" from each end to make trunk.

5 Push trunk straight down into middle of clay until lower wrapping of raffia touches surface of clay. Check that trunk is straight and stable in pot.

6 Push half-dressed ball down over trunk, widening original hole as needed, until upper wrapping of raffia is flush with ball. Be careful stem does not go entirely through ball.

7 Continue to add plant material as before to complete upper half of ball. Turn tree as you work to ensure even distribution of each plant and to maintain regular round shape.

8 As crown nears completion, check for any bare spaces and fill in with pearly everlasting or lepidium. Check to make sure that dried materials are well placed for shape and balance.

9 Cover clay with moss. Bend 3"– 4" pieces of floral wire in half to make small "hairpins" to secure moss in place.

Try This!

Change the look of your topiary tree by using different stems and dried materials. For an exotic look, use twisting or other interestingly shaped or textured branches for the trunk and a variety of nuts, seed pods, and pinecones to decorate the crown along with dried roses, orange slices, and canary grass. Pottery fragments from old terra-cotta flowerpots cover the clay base and add to the topiary's unique appearance.

Crafter's Secrets

Topiary trees make an original and pretty alternative to ordinary floral centerpieces for decorating small tables at a garden party or luncheon. Or make one to coordinate with your bedroom decor and display it on a dresser or windowsill. In the living room, use two topiaries as end pieces on a shelf or mantel.

Making a Bilevel Topiary

This bilevel tree has a lovely sculptural beauty and finely tuned color scheme. To create the arrangement in subtle variations of pale green, use nigella orientalis for the lower ball and thistle pods for the upper ball.

You can use straight branches or other sticks for the trunk (actually two trunks—an upper and lower), but you'll achieve the best results with branches that are a little gnarled and knotty. The upper ball should be smaller than the lower ball for a well-balanced look. Keep only a small portion of the upper trunk visible—about 2"—to maintain the visual symmetry of the two levels.

Use a clear container and fill it with floral clay rolled in sand so the topiary looks as if it has been grounded in a pot of sand. Cover the clay with more sand and marbles for a glittering effect. For a decorative holiday piece, spray-paint the topiary with metallic gold paint.

This bilevel topiary gives the impression of a bonsai tree or a small shaped bush. In actuality, it is two floral foam balls dressed up with thistle and nigella seed pods and set atop individual branch trunks.

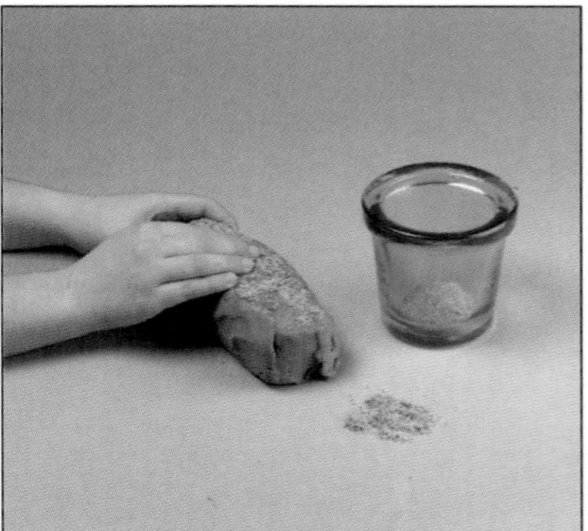

1 Pour some sand into bottom of pot. Using hands, pat sand onto sides of clay to cover. Shape clay to fit into pot; push clay into pot to fill, leaving about ½" space below rim.

2 Make hole for trunk in large ball; dress lower half with nigella. Make 6" and 8" trunks. Push large trunk into center of clay; press large ball onto trunk. Make hole in ball top and insert small trunk.

3 Dress top of larger ball. Make hole in smaller ball and dress lower half of it with thistle pods. Push ball down on top of upper trunk. Finish dressing top ball.

FINISHING TOUCHES FOR THE HOME

CARD 45

Stenciling Bathroom Accessories

Patterns & Templates

The sea is a natural source of inspiration for decorating your bathroom. Give your accessories a fun seaside look with stenciled marine-life motifs.

Images from the shore, such as sea horses, shells, and flowing algae, are especially appropriate for a bathroom. Decorated brushes and bowls add interest to a dressing table or powder room.

Many bath necessities are made of wood. You can make these items as handsome as they are handy by stenciling them with fresh seascape designs. Coordinate the shoreline look by painting a variety of motifs on bowls, brushes, and towel racks. Complete the beachfront illusion with sun-washed colors.

Make your bath time feel like a holiday at the shore: Decorate a towel holder with an ageless snail shell, and a brush with a blooming marine plant. You can use the motifs to help identify personal items such as towels and brushes.

Patterns & Templates

Use the patterns on Group 12, Card 32 for all the sea motifs shown. Mix them to create your own marine environment.

Wooden bath items suitable for painting are found in department stores, craft stores, and gift shops.

Stenciling Guidelines

Use acrylic paints for stenciling bath items.

- Apply base color with damp natural sponge. If you want wood grain to show through, apply thin layer of color. For opaque surface, apply several base coats. Allow each coat to dry before applying next.
- To shade and highlight motif, make three separate stencils. On first stencil, cut out sea horse following solid line on pattern sheet. On second stencil, cut out only gray shadows, and on third, only small blue fields. Each stencil should include entire sea horse outline so it can be properly aligned.
- For precise outlines, paint with tapered artist's brush rather than blunt-cut stencil brush.

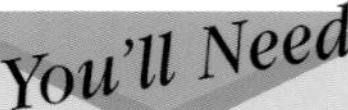

You'll Need

- ***Wooden brush & towel rack***
- ***Acrylic paint: sage green, yellow, light yellow, light brown, white, black, light gray***
- ***Small natural sponge***
- ***Medium and thin, tapered paint-brushes***
- ***Acetate, tracing paper, graphite paper, fine-tip permanent marker, & pencil***
- ***Craft knife***
- ***Repositionable adhesive***
- ***Matte-finish varnish***

Stenciling Sea Horse Motif on a Brush

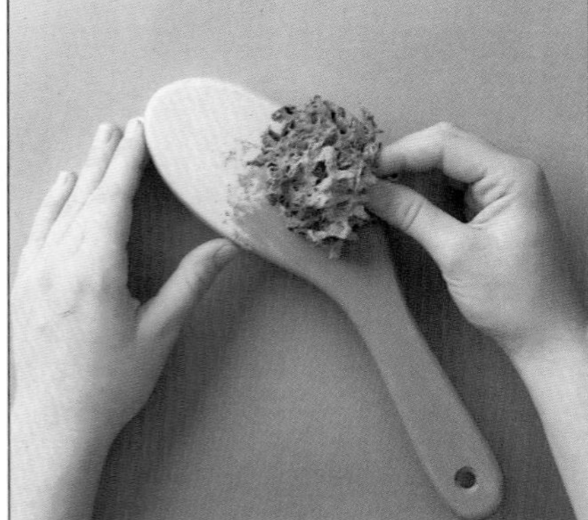

1 Use small natural sponge to apply light, uneven coat of sage green over brush surface so that woodgrain shows through paint.

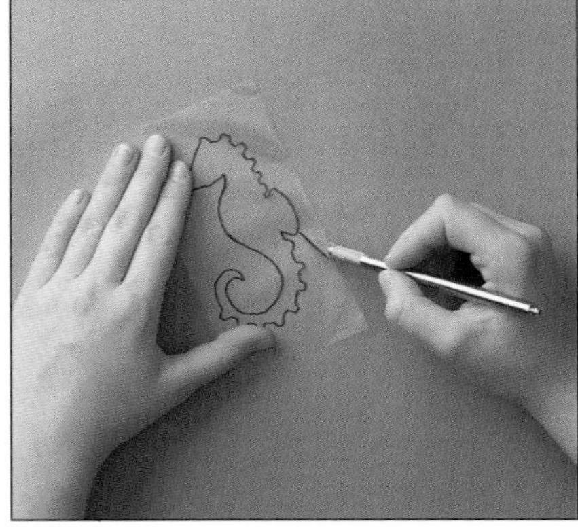

2 With fine-tip permanent marker, trace sea horse outline from pattern sheet onto stencil acetate. Use craft knife to carefully cut out motif. When cutting curves, turn acetate rather than knife.

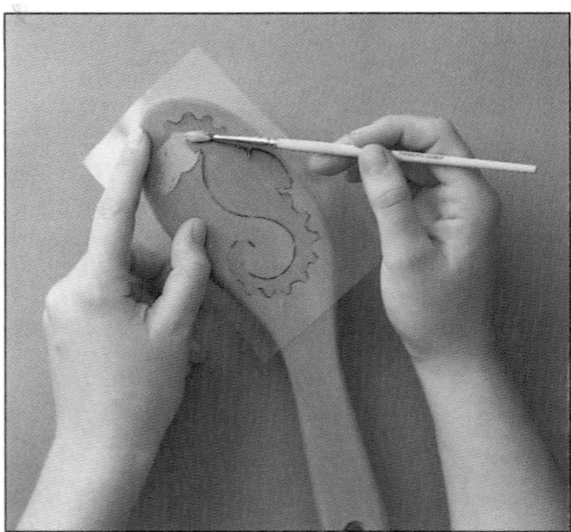

3 Secure stencil onto back of brush with repositionable adhesive. With medium paintbrush, fill in motif with yellow paint. Be sure paint does not run under stencil edges. Let dry completely, then remove stencil.

4 Make second stencil, this time transferring gray shadows. Holding acetate firmly and carefully, cut out only small shadow pieces.

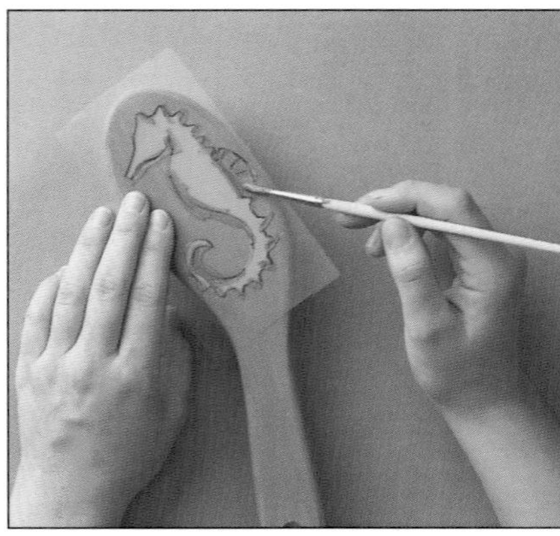

5 Place stencil over painted sea horse, aligning outlines carefully. Paint shadows light brown. Let dry, then remove stencil.

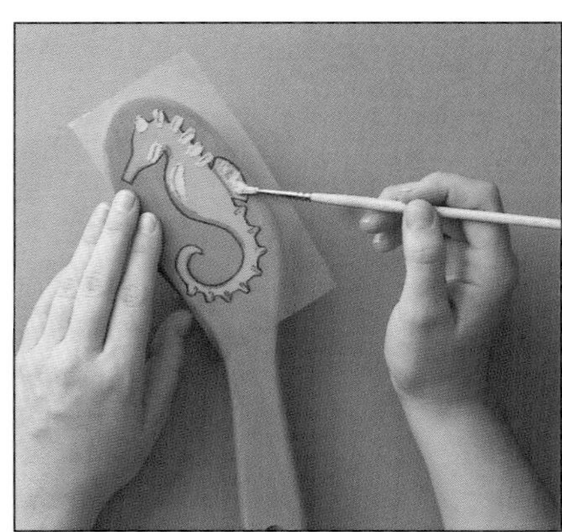

6 Make third stencil, this time tracing small blue fields; cut out. Position stencil over motif. Paint cutout sections light yellow. When dry, remove stencil. When all paint is completely dry, apply 2 coats of matte-finish varnish.

Painting Shell Motif on a Towel Rack

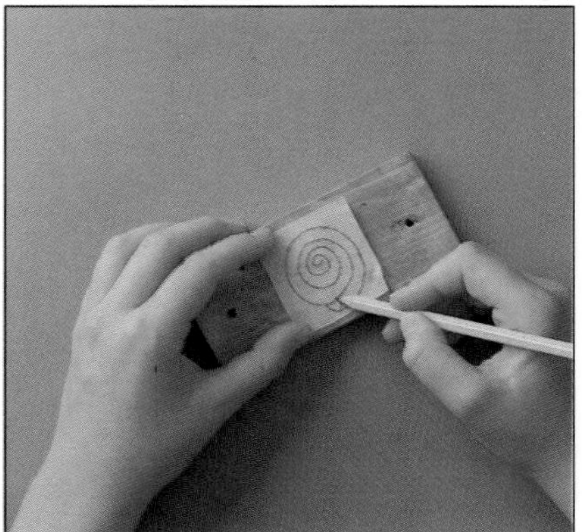

1 Remove hooks. Lightly sponge sage green paint over base. Trace pattern onto tracing paper and place over wood; slip graphite paper, carbon side down, between tracing and wood; retrace lines.

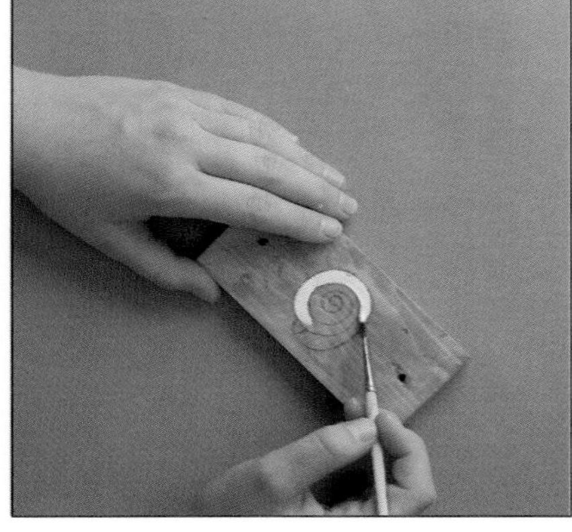

2 Using thin tapered paintbrush, paint shell white. By painting outermost spiral first and working inward, brush marks will follow concentric-circle outline. Let dry.

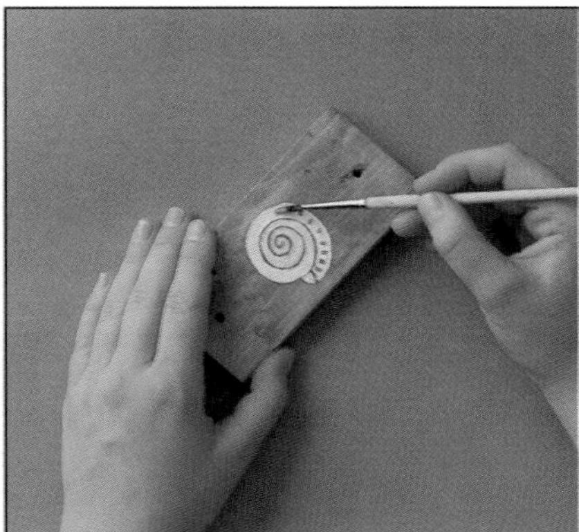

3 With thin tapered brush, outline shell and spirals with black paint. Highlight shell with small light gray shadows across spirals. Seal hanger with a matte-finish varnish. Let dry. Replace hooks and hang on wall.

Crafter's Secrets

Bathroom tile work is costly to replace, but ceramic tiles can be painted individually to accent one area, or as a border to enliven the whole room. Choose a simple motif that fits the tile size. Details highlighted in a contrasting color are bright and attractive.

Before painting, clean tiles with grease-removing detergent. Paint with oil-based gloss enamel and seal with two coats of alcohol-based shellac.

Try This!

It's also fun to stencil nonwooden bath accessories. Try stenciling on frosted glass or plastic bath items.

Transfer patterns and cut stencils as described in the guidelines. Use acrylic gloss enamels or other paints suitable for glass surfaces.

Be careful when painting nonporous surfaces. First clean the surface with a glass cleaner. Don't overwork the paint or it will lift back up into the brush. Paint one or two thin coats rather than one heavy coat. Let each coat dry thoroughly. Work with a fairly dry brush. To hasten drying, apply a specially designed topcoat spray.

Never apply any paint or sealer to the rim of a bathroom glass or cup, where it would come in contact with the user's mouth.

Painting a Shower Curtain

Turn a practical shower curtain into a decorative accent for the bath. Because a shower curtain is so big, it's important that it complement your bathroom style. Instead of purchasing a patterned curtain, paint your own custom design. All you need is an ordinary white polyester curtain, a paintbrush, and some fabric paint. Moisture-resistant fabric paints are available in arts and crafts stores.

Decide on your pattern ahead of time. Use the seaweed motif given on Group 12, Card 32, or adapt a motif from wallpaper, tiles, or fabric used elsewhere in the bathroom.

If the curtain is somewhat translucent, you can paint, rather than stencil, the design onto the curtain. Tape the pattern to the back of the curtain and trace the design outlines with paint directly onto the curtain, then carefully fill them in with a tapered paintbrush. Stretch the curtain taut and use the paintbrush to work the paint into the fabric's weave.

A hand-painted shower curtain is a fun alternative to a store-bought one. Repeat one motif, as shown in the curtain above, or transfer several different sea-life motifs and paint them in different colors

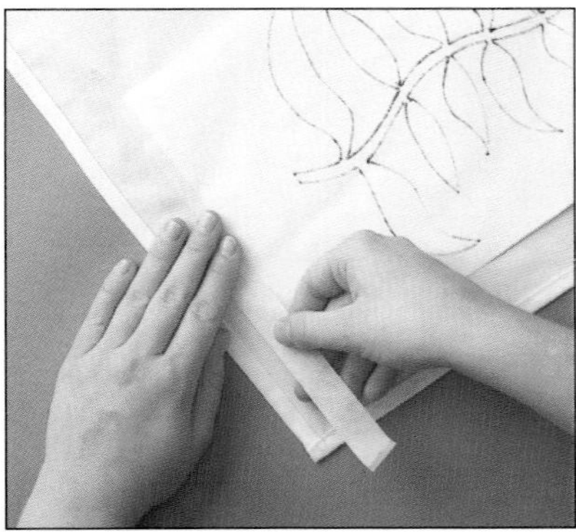

1 Measure curtain and plan layout so motifs are repeated with ample spacing. Transfer motif onto sheet of paper and darken lines so they are visible through curtain. Position first motif and tape to back of curtain.

2 Working on right side of curtain, stretch it out and carefully outline shape with thin tapered paintbrush and green paint. Paint slowly because curtain is not very absorbent.

3 Remove pattern paper and fill in leaves with same green color. Be sure that paint does not bleed out of shape. Follow manufacturer's guidelines for setting paint and laundering curtain. Repeat for each motif.

Wonderful Walls & Windows

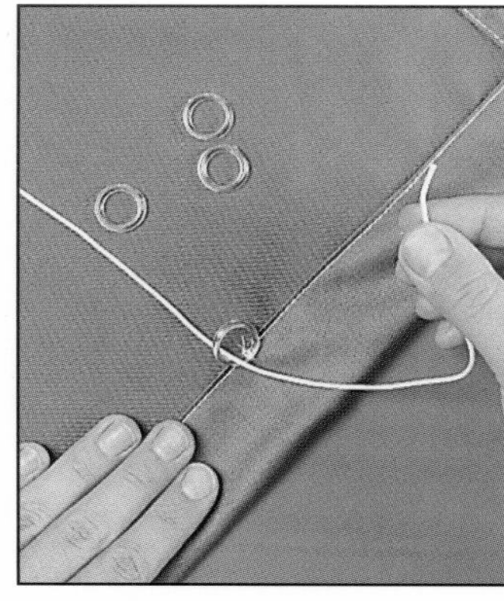

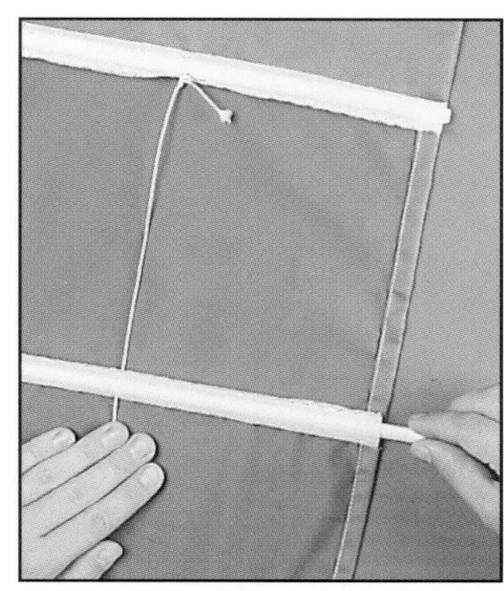

Fresh colors, textures, patterns, and styles for every room

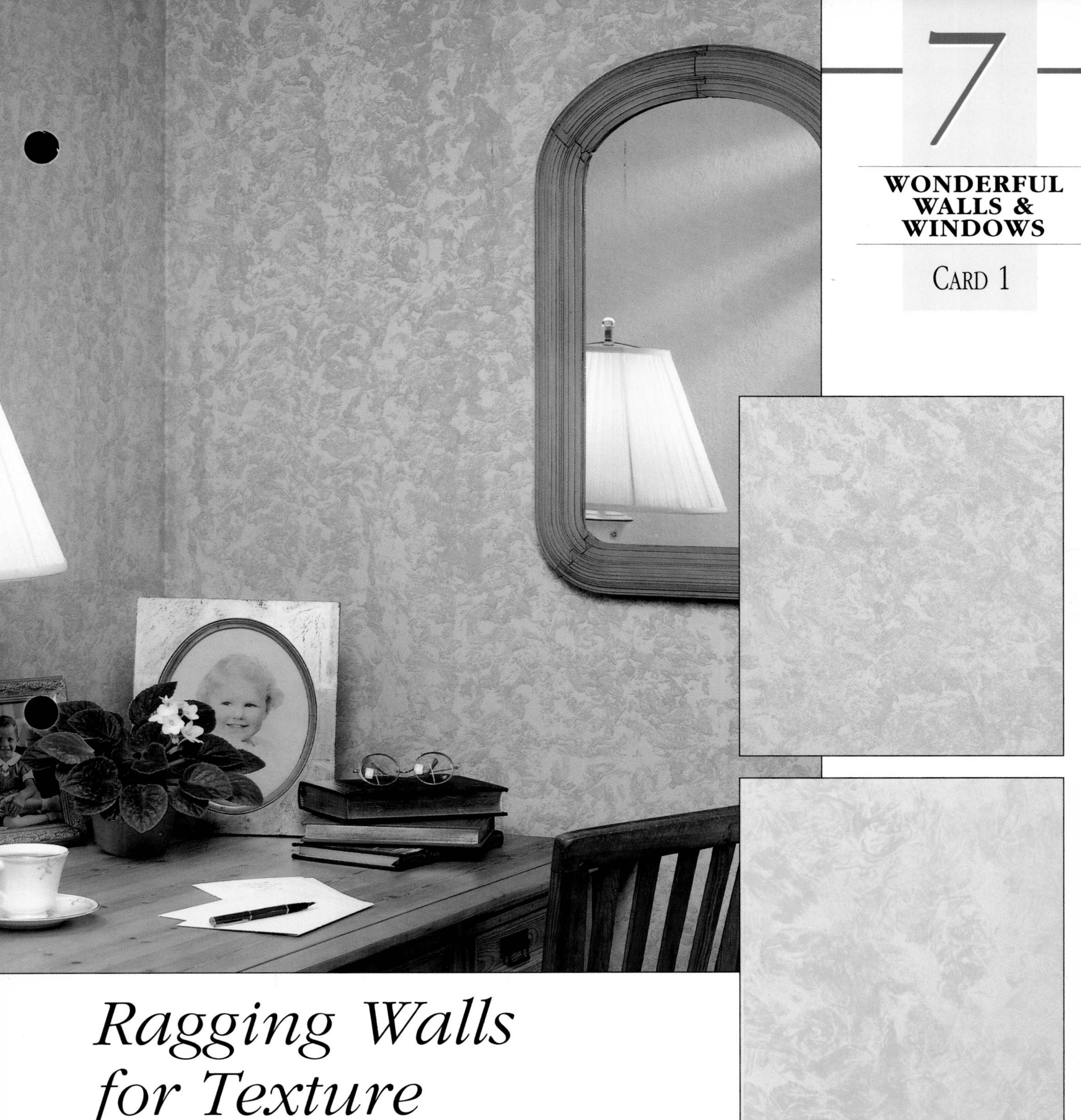

Two of the most basic variations of ragging are shown in the samples above. The pink swatch was rag-rolled with 2 additional colors, while in the yellow swatch, only 1 color in a darker shade of the base coat was used for dabbing.

Ragging Walls for Texture

Transform any room from blah to beautiful with two simple ragging techniques that can give walls a decorator-quality finish.

Painting walls by ragging requires at least two paint colors, either shades of the same color or complementary colors. The lighter color is most often used for the base coat, while the deeper second color adds contrast and texture.

The first ragging technique called *rag-rolling* uses a rag or other soft, lint-free material to roll a second color of paint over a wall painted with the first color. A simpler method called *rag-dabbing* uses a bunched up piece of cloth to dab the second color over the base-colored wall.

Interesting paint patterns can be made by using household paper towels to roll on a second color of paint. For best pattern results, experiment with ragging technique on a small area of a wall first.

Paint Information

Use a water-based interior paint for easy cleanup.

- When estimating paint amount, remember that ragged or rolled coat calls for half as much paint as base coat.
- Select base color from light end of paint chip. Generally second color is about two shades darker.
- If third color is desired, use one that is two shades deeper than second color, or use a complementary color in same hue.

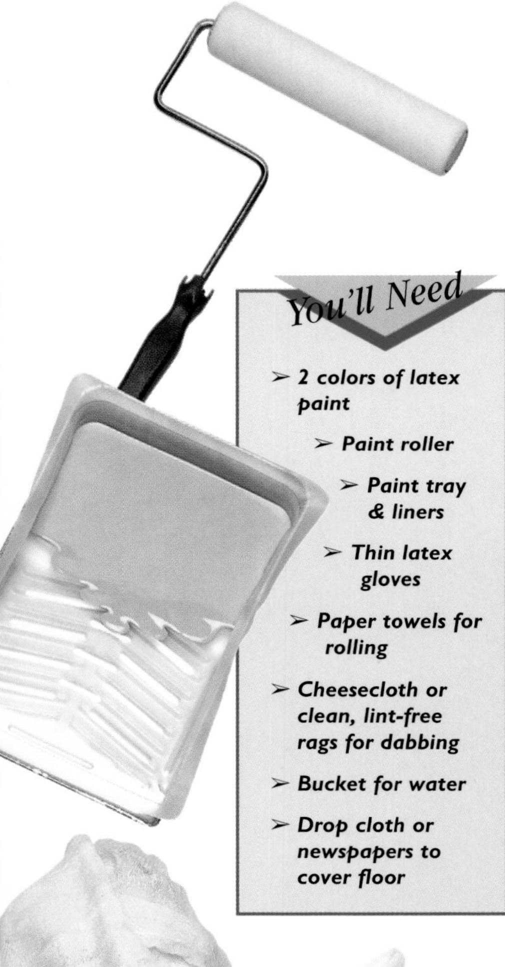

You'll Need

- ➢ ***2 colors of latex paint***
- ➢ ***Paint roller***
- ➢ ***Paint tray & liners***
- ➢ ***Thin latex gloves***
- ➢ ***Paper towels for rolling***
- ➢ ***Cheesecloth or clean, lint-free rags for dabbing***
- ➢ ***Bucket for water***
- ➢ ***Drop cloth or newspapers to cover floor***

RAG-ROLLING

1 Wearing thin latex gloves to protect your hands, paint walls with base color using a paint roller. Apply paint with an irregular "N" stroke to avoid streaks. Allow paint to dry.

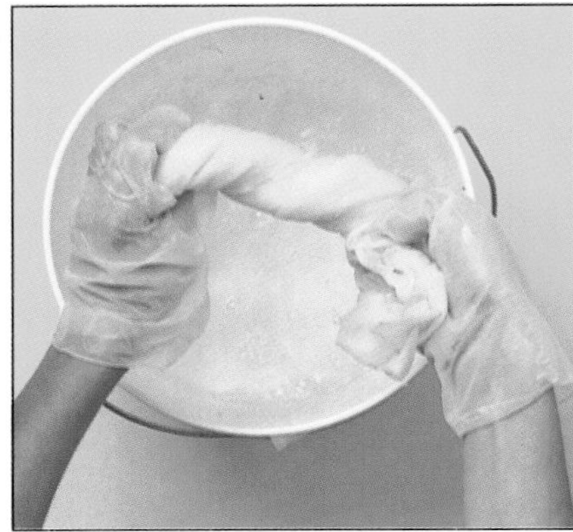

2 Gather 2 lengths of paper towels, each length about 3 or 4 squares long; layer both lengths, fold in half lengthwise and twist. Dip into clear water to saturate; wring out completely.

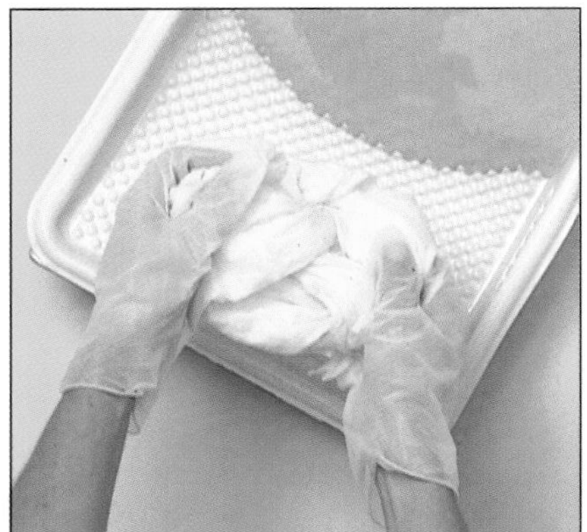

3 Form twisted paper towels into a pretzel shape. Pull ends of toweling loosely through hole created in center.

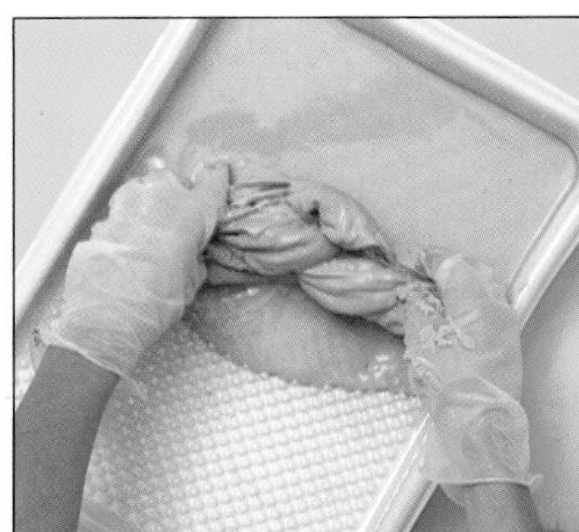

4 Roll pretzel-shaped toweling into second paint color. Gently squeeze and press out excess paint over flat area of paint tray.

5 Beginning at top of wall, roll toweling down in a straight line, reforming it as needed to maintain twisted shape for pattern interest.

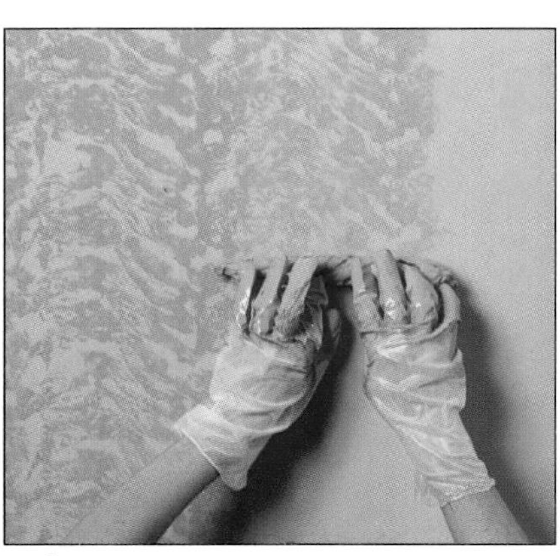

6 Continue rolling paint over wall in vertical rows, adding paint to toweling as necessary. When toweling begins to shred, replace it with fresh twisted paper towels.

For further information: Crafting & Decorating Made Simple™ International Masters Publishers, 444 Liberty Ave., Pittsburgh, PA 15222-1207 1-800-527-5576

Try This!

For a richer and more detailed effect, apply an unexpected accent color over the rag-rolled wall. Roll it on very sparingly to show just a hint of the third color. In the photo at right, a robin's egg blue was added over a wall that was rag-rolled in a deep rosy pink. You might also try using three entirely different colors or three contrasting shades of the same color.

Rag-rolling can also be used to finish small pieces of furniture, such as an end table or a snack tray as shown below. For a decorator look, update various room accessories; try rag-rolling wooden boxes, picture frames, candlesticks, trays, or any of your favorite items that can be painted.

Crafter's Secrets

Diverse textural effects can be created by rolling or dabbing on the second paint color with other household materials. In addition to adding beautiful textural finishes, ragging can disguise uneven and cracked walls.

- Try ragging with plastic wrap, terrycloth, or chamois.
- After painting base color, lightly pencil plumb lines spaced about 2' apart; use guides to roll paint in straight rows.
- Should a blob of excess paint occur when applying second color, quickly dab a clean paper towel over spot until sufficient paint has been removed.
- Apply a coat of clear polyurethane after paint dries to protect wall and give it a tough finish that can be wiped clean.

Rag-Dabbing Walls

Rag-dabbing is a very easy painting technique that creates a textural look similar to stucco. It's done by using a bunched up rag and the flat of your hand to press a second color onto a painted wall.

Apply the base color following the instructions in step 1 for rag-rolling. When applying the second color, keep reshaping the rag to maintain the creases that form the pattern.

The final look is determined by the selection of the second color. Selecting a lighter color than the base will create a frosty look that will make the room seem larger and airier. A darker second color will perk up a neutral base coat, adding interest and drama to the room.

Ragging on a third color increases the decorating options. The most common arrangement is to apply a lighter and a darker color over a middle-tone base. Other options include combining a light base color with two darker accent colors, or accenting a dark base tone with two lighter tones.

Rag-dab your kitchen walls in shades of yellow to create the cheerful glow of sunshine even on the dreariest of days.

1 Paint wall as in step 1 of rag-rolling. Cut off about 2' of cheesecloth; dip in clear water to saturate and wring out completely. Scrunch cheesecloth into a compact shape to fit into palm of hand.

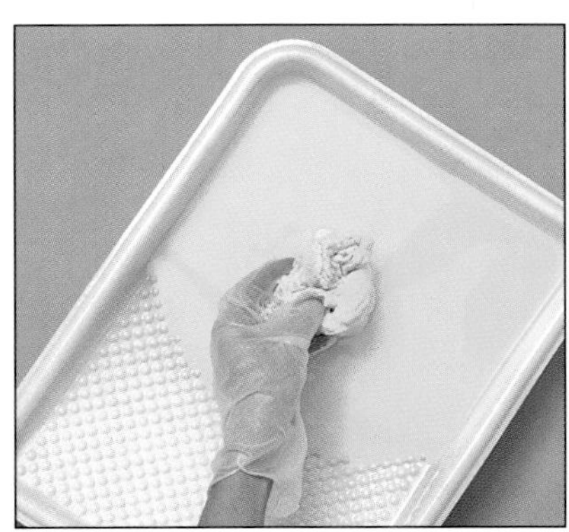

2 Lightly dip scrunched-up cheesecloth in second paint color, but do not saturate cloth. Dab out any excess paint over tray.

3 Position cloth against palm of hand and, keeping hand flat, press paint onto wall. Continue dabbing and reshaping rag periodically, adding more paint as needed.

For further information: Crafting & Decorating Made Simple™
International Masters Publishers, 444 Liberty Ave., Pittsburgh, PA 15222-1207 1-800-527-5576

Sewing Tab-Top Curtain Panels

Adding tabs to the top of curtain panels is one of the easiest ways to transform a simple window dressing into something special. It's no trouble to do, and requires only a small amount of extra fabric.

Easy-to-sew tab tops create a cozy, informal, decorative finish for plain curtain panels. Finishing the top of unlined gingham curtain panels with loops or ties of fabric, rather than with the more conventional rod casing, gives the window a pleasant, airy look.

The wide loops of the tabs also make the curtain panels easier to hang and to draw. Allow the curtain panels to hang free or sweep the panels to one side and use a tieback to hold them open.

Give a fresh appearance to tab curtain panels with little effort by tying fabric strips into perky bows across the length of the curtain rod. For a refined, contemporary look, use a linen trim, rather than self fabric, for the tabs and for a matching decorative border.

Tabs made from the same fabric as the panels give a crisp, polished look to the curtains.

Measuring for Curtains

Measure accurately and follow these guidelines to determine how much fabric you'll need to make the curtains and tabs.

- Measure from top of curtain rod to desired finished length. Use this as a base measurement.
- Before cutting, add 1/2" for top hem allowance and 2" for hem allowance at bottom; add 3" for width of tab strip and 2" for heading strip. For example, for a 40"-wide curtain with a finished length of 50", you will need 57 1/2" of 45"-wide fabric (50"+1/2"+2"+3"+2").
- Bows for tabs will require an additional 1/2 yd. of fabric.

Preliminary Sewing

Cut strips of fabric for the curtain tabs and complete hems for the curtain panels.

- Using a ruler and tailor's chalk, carefully draw a line across full width of fabric 2" up from bottom and another line 3" above first line. Cut fabric along these lines to make two separate strips. On long edge of 2"-wide strip, press under 1/2" to wrong side; set strip aside.
- On bottom edge of curtain piece, turn under 1" to wrong side and press. Turn under 1" again and press. Open out turned-under edges.

All the seams for the curtain are sewn with 1/2" seam allowances unless otherwise noted.

You'll Need

- ***Curtain fabric & matching sewing thread***
- ***Tape measure & ruler***
- ***Scissors***
- ***Straight & safety pins***
- ***Sewing machine***
- ***Tailor's chalk***

SEWING TAB-TOP CURTAINS

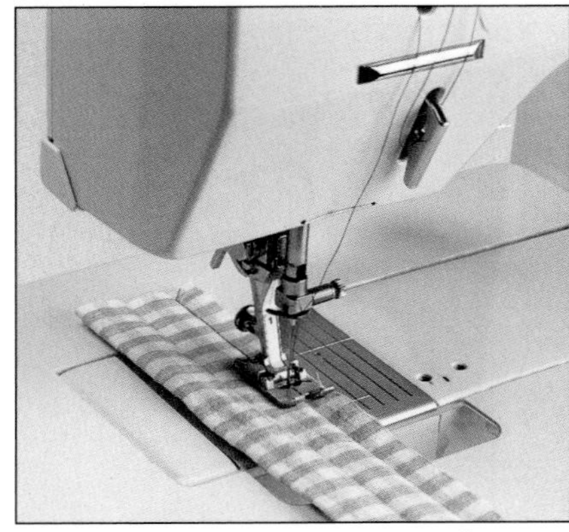

1 Begin making tabs by folding 3"-wide strip in half lengthwise, right sides facing. Sew long edges of strip together. Trim seam to 1/4".

2 Attach a safety pin through both layers of fabric at 1 end of seam allowance. Push pin through opening of fabric tube and work it through to other end; pull pin and fabric to turn tube right side out.

3 Press fabric tube flat, centering seam along back of tube. Cut tube into 11 tabs, each 4" long. Fold each tab in half crosswise with seam inside. Pin raw edges together.

4 Fold under and press 1" along each side edge of curtain panel, then fold under and press 1" again. Topstitch each side hem in place, then refold bottom hem and sew it in place.

5 Pin a tab at each upper corner of curtain panel, raw edges even and right sides facing. Pin remaining tabs along top edge of panel, spacing them evenly between both end tabs.

6 With right sides facing, pin unfolded edge of 2"-wide fabric strip to top of curtain panel, sandwiching tabs between panel and 2" strip. The strip extends 1/2" beyond panel at each end.

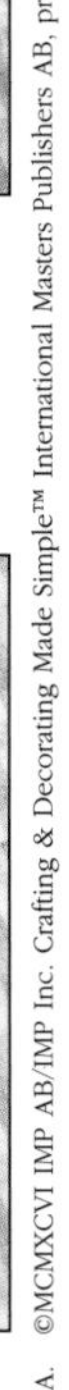

7 Sew heading strip to top of curtain panel, catching ends of tabs in seam. Press seam toward curtain, and press under ½" extensions at each end of strip.

8 Fold heading strip to wrong side of curtain; press, then topstitch folded bottom edge in place.

Try This!

When sewing fabric strips for the tab bows, make two extra strips to embellish the matching tiebacks. Make a buttonhole at the center of one end of each tieback. Sew a button to the opposite end. Make a buttonhole in the center of each bow strip. Button each strip to a tieback, then tie a bow to match the bows on the rod.

Making Bows for Tabs

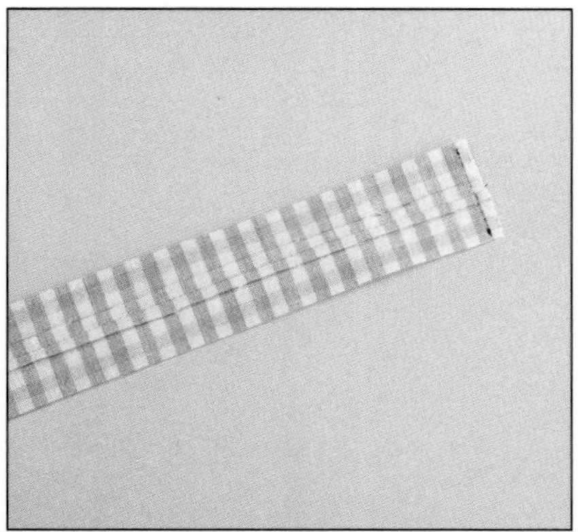

1 Cut 11 (3"x20") strips of fabric. Fold each strip in half lengthwise, right sides facing. Sew long edges together, leaving an opening in center. Press seam open. Refold strip so seam runs along center, and sew across short ends.

2 Trim seams, clip corners, and turn right side out through opening in seam. Press bow piece flat. Install curtain onto rod and tie bows around base of each tab top.

Crafter's Secrets

Tab-top curtains call for decorative curtain rods, but these specialty items can be expensive. Consider instead adding purchased curtain rod tips, such as the cast-iron arrowhead and stylized iris design shown, to the ends of bamboo pieces. Or buy simple wooden knobs or finials and attach them to lengths of wooden closet poles. Paint, stain, or cover with paper or fabric as desired.

Look for interesting window treatments in home decorating magazines, catalogs, and stores, then search hardware, drapery, and houseware shops for inexpensive alternatives to duplicate them.

Making Tabs from Trim

Fabric stores sell an incredible array of decorative trims that can be used in place of matching fabric tabs. Because their edges are finished, your job is even easier. Use trim about 1" wide. Consider adding tabs of eyelet or lace on sheer curtains; ribbon or braid will add pizzazz to solid-colored curtains. When working on lightweight fabrics, sew matching trim along the top of the curtain so that the edges of the tabs don't show through to the right side.

Linen is a natural fiber that ranges from a lightweight silklike fabric to heavier grades with coarse textures. It is available in a wide range of colors, but looks best in its natural shade. Linen works with almost any decor and can be dressed up or down with trims. This linen curtain's soft look is accentuated by a simple tieback of braided jute with a decorative tassel.

1 Fold under and press 1" twice along side edges of panel. Sew side hems. Cut 9 pieces of ribbon, each 4" long. Fold each in half and pin to wrong side of curtain, placing a tab at each end and spacing remaining tabs evenly across.

2 Cut a piece of ribbon to fit across top of curtain with ½" extensions at each end. Pin edge of ribbon along seam with wrong side of ribbon overlapping seam allowance and sandwiching ends of ribbon tabs between.

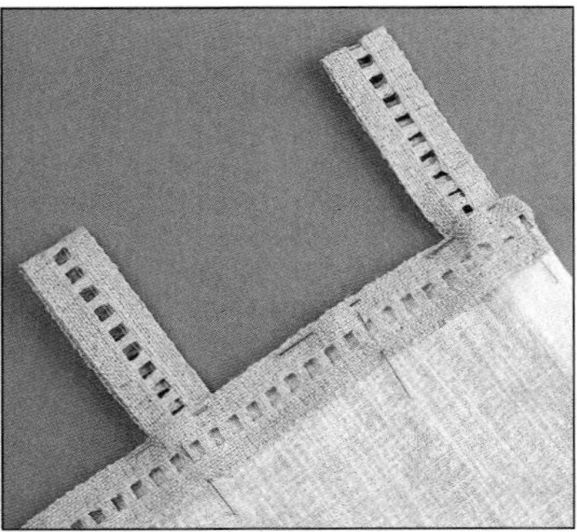

3 Fold long ribbon to right side of curtain, tucking under ½" extensions at each end. Press and pin ribbon in place. Sew ribbon along each edge, catching ends of tabs in stitching.

WONDERFUL WALLS & WINDOWS

CARD 7

Creating Elegantly Bound Curtains

Make a personal style statement in the decorating of your windows. Choose a mix of colors and fabrics to sew curtains that feature bias-bound edges.

Be your own designer in making any of the curtain designs shown here. Combine favorite styles of large and small prints, contrasting solids, or mix prints with plaids and stripes. Then, to complete your design, select a fabric for the bias binding that matches or contrasts with the curtains' fabrics. For a time-saving way to bind the curtains and tiebacks, purchase a ready-made ¼" double-fold bias binding in a complementary color. Prepackaged bindings are sold in 4-yd. packages in fabric stores.

Begin your creative experience by selecting fabrics for the curtains, including popular prints with romantic flowers, boughs of fruit, ethnic geometric shapes, and classic country looks. For all the designs shown, select soft to crisp fabrics in medium to light weights.

Before purchasing fabrics for curtains, select a curtain rod that is appropriate for a curtain with a casing. Install the rod, then decide on the length of the curtain (from the bottom of the rod to the sill or to the floor), the depth of the heading which extends above the rod, and the number of panels (widths of fabric) that will be needed.

For opaque fabrics, the full combined curtain widths (including the contrasting center bands) should equal at least twice the window's width. For sheer or lace fabrics, it should be three times the window's width.

Determining Yardage

Use the following formula to determine the cut lengths of the panels and center bands. The cut panels may have to be stitched together.

- Cut length = heading depth (1"–3") x 2 + ½" seam allowance + casing depth (depth of rod + ¼" ease) x 2 + length from rod to hem + 8" for a double hem.
- To determine yardage, multiply cut lengths with number of panels needed.

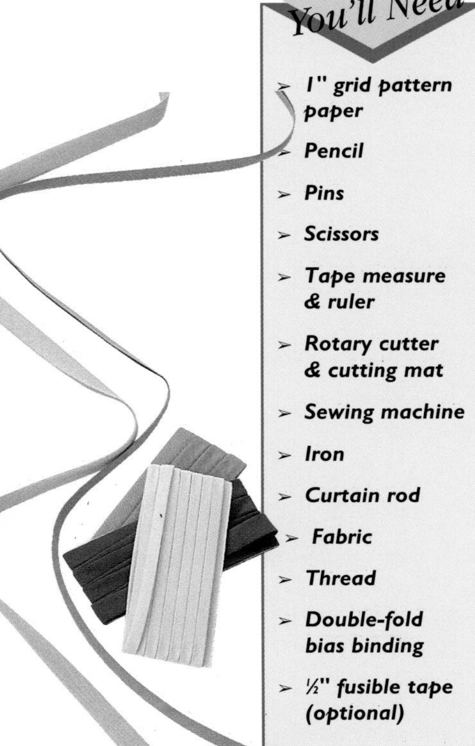

You'll Need

- ***1" grid pattern paper***
- ***Pencil***
- ***Pins***
- ***Scissors***
- ***Tape measure & ruler***
- ***Rotary cutter & cutting mat***
- ***Sewing machine***
- ***Iron***
- ***Curtain rod***
- ***Fabric***
- ***Thread***
- ***Double-fold bias binding***
- ***½" fusible tape (optional)***

Long Curtains with Contrasting Center Bands

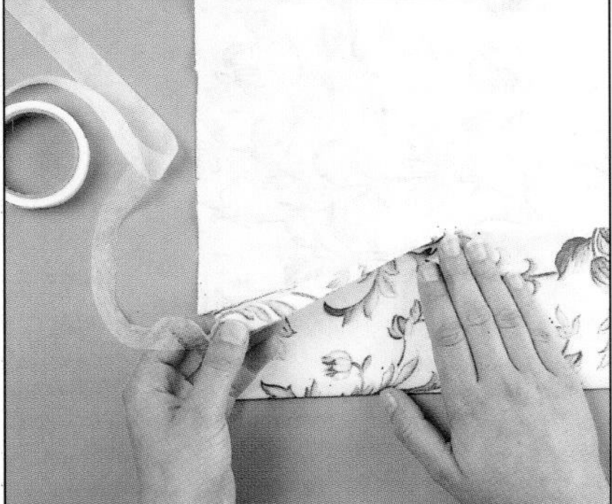

1 If multiple outer panels are needed for width, sew together with ½" seams. Form a double hem by pressing 4" to wrong side twice. Fuse top of hem in place with fusible tape. If curtain is sheer, edgestitch top of hem in place.

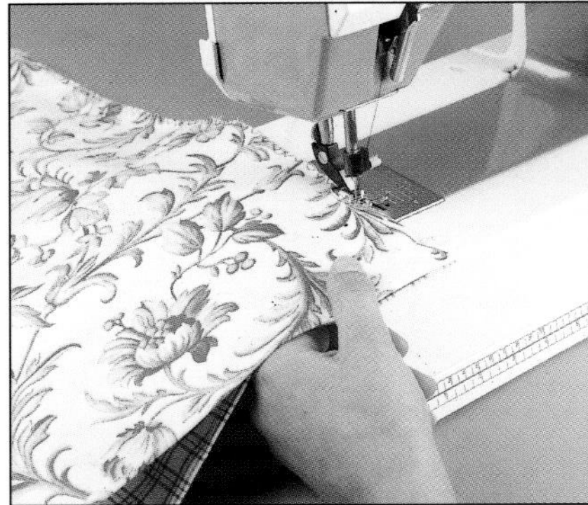

2 Cut center bands to desired widths. Hem in same way as panels. Wrong sides together, and hemlines aligned, zigzag 1 center band to 1 outer panel along long edges.

3 Open out bias binding. Right sides together, pin narrower seam allowance of binding over 1 side of zigzag stitches; leave 1" of binding beyond hem. Stitch binding to curtain along crease line; be sure stitching covers zigzag stitches.

4 Fold end of binding to opposite side of curtain. Refold binding to encase zigzagged edges, then edgestitch along inner edge. Sew a 1" double hem along outer long edges of outer panels. Encase inner curtain edges with bias binding.

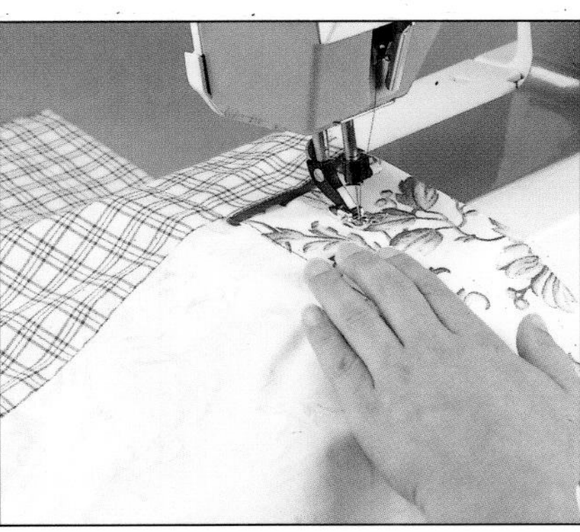

5 At curtain top press ½" to wrong side. Measure down to a length equal to desired height of finished casing + heading + ¼" ease and crease fabric. Edgestitch along lower casing seam, then topstitch upper casing seam.

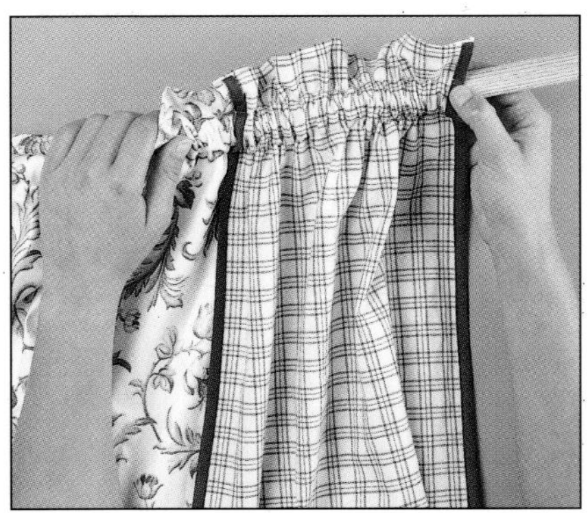

6 Press finished curtain panels. Remove rod from window and insert rod through curtain casings so contrasting bands hang together in center.

Making Your Own Double-fold Bias Binding

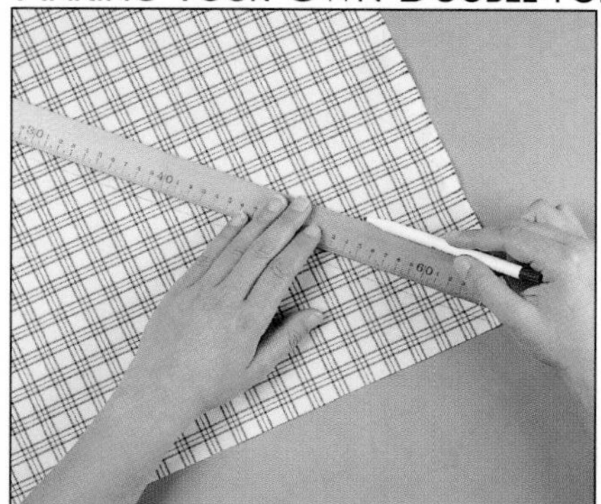

1 Decide on finished width of binding (¼"–1"). Place fabric on top of table or cutting board. Determine true bias (45° angle) across fabric and draw bias lines that are spaced at a distance equal to 4 times finished binding width.

2 Cut enough bias strips to equal length of edges to be bound. Right sides together, stitch strip ends together with ¼" seam allowances to form desired length; press seams open. Press strip in half, wrong sides together.

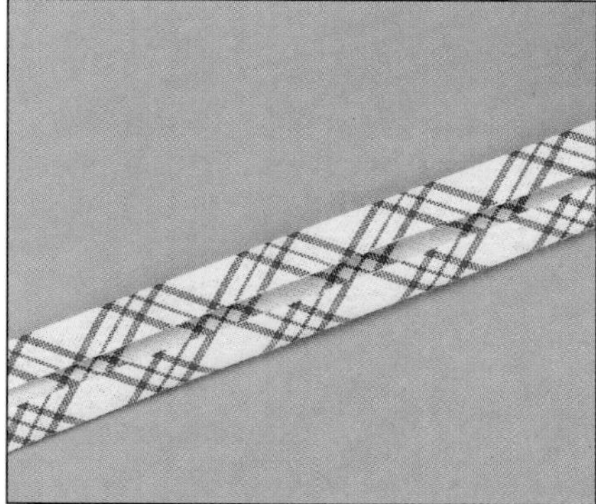

3 Open out strip. Press 1 cut edge to meet at center crease, wrong sides inside. Press opposite edge toward first cut edge, leaving a ⅛" gap between cut edges. Refold binding and press. Folded edges should be offset by ⅛".

When all bias-binding strips are cut across the fabric in the same bias direction, the stripes will angle identically on curtain halves. When half the strips are cut in the opposite diagonal direction, the stripes on both halves will form chevrons.

The muslin curtains above have a valance that is cut all-in-one with the body of the curtain. The valance portion is then pressed toward the front of the curtain. For this style, select fabrics that are identical on both sides, such as woven stripes and plaids in muslin and broadcloth. To cut, use the formula given on the back of Group 7, Card 7, but omit the hem allowance and seam allowance that finishes the normal casing, and add 8"–15" to the cut length for the depth of the valance below the casing. Proportion the valance depth to about one fourth to one third the finished curtain length. Finish the edges of the curtain with a 1"-wide bias binding. To form straight tiebacks, stitch the same binding width with a 1"-wide seam allowance.

Making Contoured Tiebacks

Shaped tiebacks bound around the edges can enhance any curtain. To determine the correct length of the tieback for your curtains, wrap a tape measure around the hanging curtains and loosen or tighten the tape for the desired appearance. Use the grid art below to make a half-pattern piece, lengthening or shortening the pattern from the foldline to match your measurement. Place the pattern on the fold of fabric to cut a whole tieback piece.

To make a set of tiebacks, you will need to purchase ¼"–⅜"-wide double-fold bias binding, two pairs of ½" hook-and-loop fastener circles or squares with adhesive backings, two ½"-diameter plastic rings, and two cup or shoulder hooks for the wall.

Two colors of ¼" gingham check were used to create these sill-length kitchen curtains, which were bound with a 1"-wide yellow binding. For a dramatic effect, try combining different check sizes. Just be sure the sizes are noticeably different, such as a 1" versus a ¼" check or a ½" versus a ⅛" check. The same guideline can be used when combining two coordinating fabric prints.

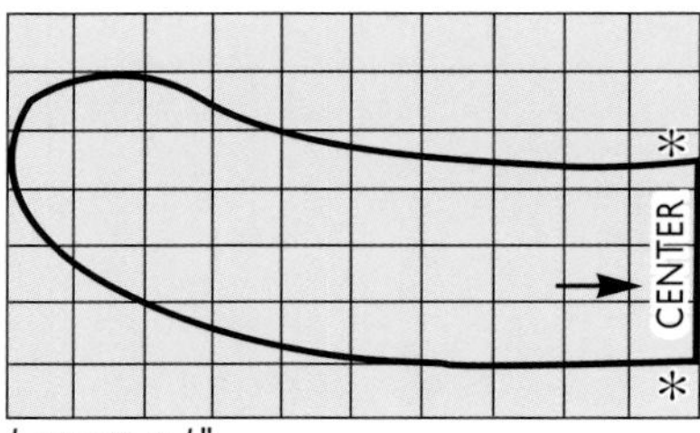

1 square = 1"
** Lengthen or shorten here*
For 1 pair of tiebacks, cut 4 from fabric and 4 from interfacing.

1 Fuse interfacing to wrong side of tieback pieces. Pin wrong sides together and zigzag around cut edges. Open out binding; fold 1 end ½" to wrong side; pin.

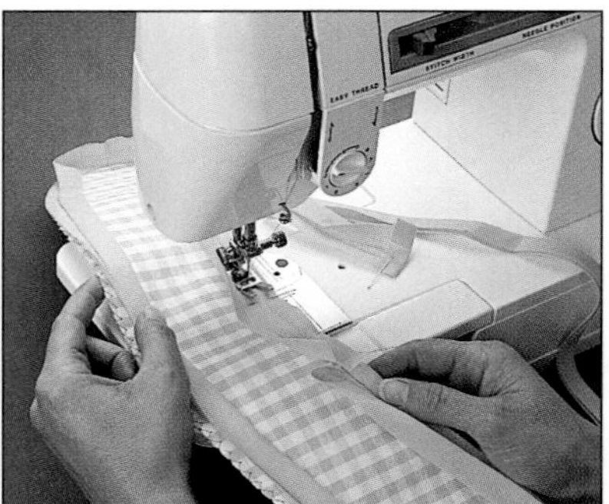

2 Right sides together, pin narrow seam allowance of binding over tieback edges; stitch along crease line; overlap binding ends. Refold bias binding to encase zigzagged edges.

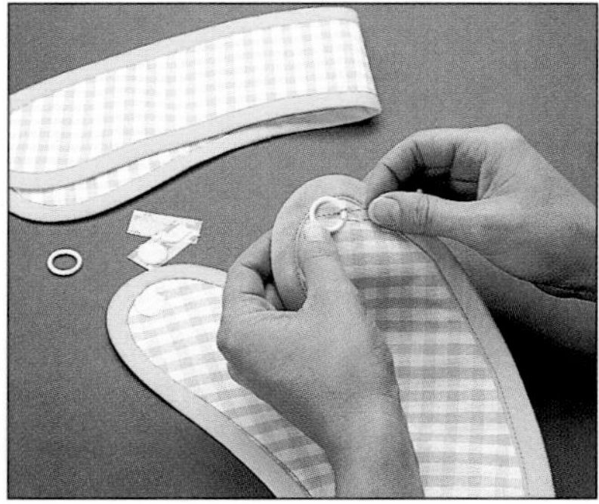

3 Edgestitch inner edge of binding. Attach each half of fastener tape to insides of curved ends. At 1 curved end of each tieback, sew 1 ring to back side. Attach hooks to wall.

Patterns & Templates

Painting a Plain Roller Shade

Paint, a versatile decorating tool, is used to transform a plain roller shade into an exciting customized window treatment, adding style to a room.

A solid-color vinyl or fabric roller shade is like an empty canvas waiting to be painted. Painted roller shades offer an inexpensive way to add design interest to a window as well as to provide privacy or block an unpleasant view.

Paint simple graphic stripes or checks, or embellish with a pattern to match the curtain fabric or wallpaper used in the room. If you prefer, turn to the templates in Group 12, Card 16 to paint on a border of cheery spirit-lifting pansies as shown above.

A painted border is ideal for a shade whose lower half is always visible. Create an inviting window treatment for your kitchen by hand-painting a border of teapots and teacups in soothing blue and white that matches a striped valance.

Patterns & Templates

Use the templates from Group 12, Card 16 as patterns for roller shade border designs.

Most stock shades are vinyl, but to make a shade with your own fabric, purchase roller-shade kits and notions at home centers and hardware stores.

Choose a firmly woven cotton or linen cloth. Medium-weight fabric is best. If the fabric is too thin, it will crease when rolled; if it is too heavy, it will not roll evenly. You can buy ready-made roller-shade fabric that has been commercially treated to stiffen and prevent fraying. Or use a stiffening agent or fusible backing to adapt a furnishing fabric.

General Guidelines

Acrylics, emulsions, and fabric paints are all suitable materials for painting shades.

- Before painting border on shade, plan placement of design and make full-size placement pattern to fit shade by taping together sheets of tracing paper.
- Trace each leaf and floral motif several times onto white paper and cut out.
- Stripes can be painted freehand for soft look or by masking with painter's tape to ensure exact straight lines.
- Apply as many coats of paint as necessary for even finish.

You'll Need

- ***Plain roller shade***
- ***Papers: white, tracing, & graphite***
- ***Pencil & ruler***
- ***Painter's tape***
- ***3 paintbrushes: 1" & ½" flat; 1 round***
- ***Acrylic paints: rose, green, purple, & pink***

1 Make placement pattern and mark 1"–1½" stripes with ½" spaces in between; mark ½" stripe across bottom. Starting at shade center, mark scallops along bottom of border. Arrange cutout motifs within border.

2 Using taped-together graphite paper, transfer all stripes from tracing onto shade. Using 1" brush, paint alternating rose and green stripes down shade, leaving ½" stripe unpainted. Mask every other stripe with painter's tape if desired.

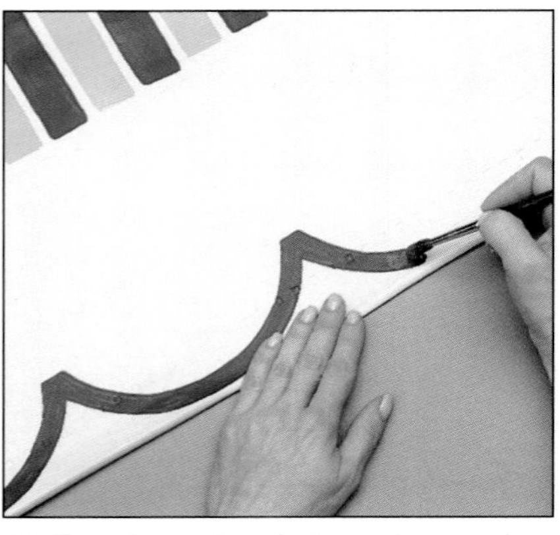

3 Transfer scallop design to lower edge of shade so bottom of scallop is aligned with lower edge of shade. Using ½" brush, paint scallop green; let dry.

4 Apply painter's tape to each side of horizontal border stripe, pressing on tape to prevent paint seepage. Using ½" brush, paint stripe green. Let dry before removing tape.

5 Transfer floral designs to shade 1 at a time, following full-size placement pattern. Using round brush, paint flowers rose, pink, and purple, as shown, applying 1 color at a time; allow first color to dry before adding next.

6 Transfer leaves, stems, and ivy 1 at a time; paint green. Leave small sections unpainted, as shown, to create dimensional highlights. Let dry completely.

7

WONDERFUL WALLS & WINDOWS

CARD 12

Creating a Decorative Kitchen Garland

The kitchen is the heart of your home and should be decorated as carefully as any other room. Perk up kitchen windows with seasonal garlands to give them the attention they deserve.

A plain kitchen window dressed in simple curtains becomes a stunning focal point when festooned with a garland swag. Garlands are easy to construct from silk or dried flowers, fruits, nuts, berries, and leaves. Add ribbons, cookie cutters, seasonal decorations, and other trims to create a unique design.

Don't be limited to decorating windows—these garlands also look attractive hung around doorways or draped around the front of a dresser, mantel, or shelves.

Garlands celebrate the seasons. Deck the windows with holly, poinsettias, pinecones, and Christmas-red bows trimmed with dried apple slices. Or herald autumn with wreaths of dried leaves, flowers, grasses, eucalyptus, and pinecones.

Braided clothesline forms the base for these striking window-framing garlands. Be sure to gather enough of each material to create a visual balance.

Tips for Making Garlands

To calculate the basic length of the garland, measure across the top of the window and three-fourths of the way down on each side. If garland is to drape loosely across top, add another 24". Double this amount for cutting clothesline.

- To hang garland, attach hooks at center and on both sides of top of window frame. Drape garland over hooks.
- If garland slips, twist wire around braid and attach firmly to hook.

To clean garland, tie a piece of gauze or cheesecloth over small vacuum cleaner nozzle and hold slightly away from garland as you vacuum it.

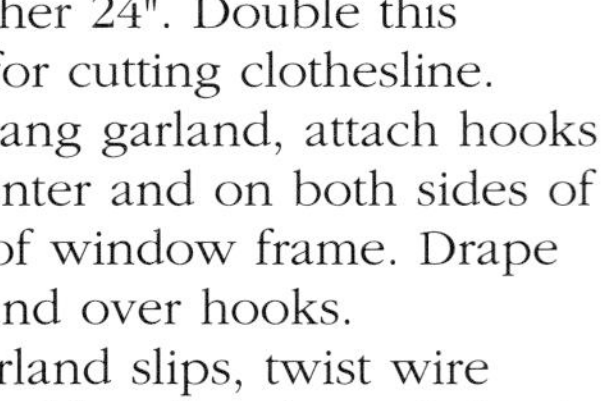

You'll Need

- **4½ yds. clothesline (for 40"-wide window)**
- **Silk floral materials with leaves: white daisies, sunflowers, stems of small blue & white blossoms & yellow cluster blossoms; ivy vines**
- **Pinecones**
- **2 daisy-shaped cookie cutters & 2 small copper kitchen molds**
- **22-gauge spooled floral wire & wire cutters**
- **Floral tape**
- **6 yds. 1½"-wide wire-edged ribbon cut into 2-yd. lengths**
- **Scissors & pliers**
- **White spray paint**
- **Hot-glue gun & glue sticks**

1 Cut 3 lengths of clothesline. Knot together 6" from 1 end. Braid clothesline, testing length on window. Trim if necessary and knot 6" from other end. Separate strands of clothesline below knots to form tassels. Trim ends even.

2 Form floral bunches of varied lengths. Trim ends even; secure with wire. Wrap wire with floral tape. Loop wire around each pinecone; twist ends. Paint pinecones; let dry. Twist together wired stems of 4 pinecones with 1 floral stem.

3 Coil ivy vine into ring with 6" inner diameter. Coil vine 1 or more times around ring until wreath is full. Wrap spooled wire around base stem of vine to hold coils of ring together. Make 2 more ivy wreaths.

4 For each bow, make 1 (10") loop, pinching ribbon at bottom. Make next loop in opposite direction, pinching again in center. Continue folding ribbon back and forth into 6 loops. Wire loops at center; spread out. Glue fruit slice in center.

5 Thread 12" length of wire halfway through hanger loop of 1 copper mold. Twist wire to secure; spread wire ends open. Wrap ends around edge of cookie cutter and twist together on outside so mold hangs in center of cutter. Repeat.

6 Hang braid. Wire wreath with glued bow to center of braid; wire remaining wreaths at window corners. Alternate wiring floral bunches and pinecones, beginning across top. Wire bows just above tassels; add cookie cutters.

Patterns & Templates

Stenciling Chair-Rail Borders

A decorative border hand-stenciled across a wall at chair height is a fresh way to bring color, dimension, and your own sense of personal style to a room.

Chair-rail borders were originally strips of patterned wallpaper intended to prevent chairs from leaving scuff marks on painted walls when they were pushed back.

Creating these borders with stencils and paint is a dramatic new way to enliven a living space.

Using nontraditional colors, such as the blue swirls and black-and-white checks of the border on the sponged coral walls shown in the featured photo, creates an exciting backdrop for simple furniture and decorative accessories.

The same swirl stencil and fresh paint colors can create a different mood. Here, the swirled border painted in softer colors on a solid pale wall makes a soothing choice for a bedroom or bath. The whimsical green starfish swimming in waves is a stencil that would be appropriate for a child's room.

Patterns & Templates

Use the templates from Group 12, Card 16 to make patterns for stenciling chair-rail borders across painted walls.

Carefully consider the wall or walls you want to stencil. There should be a long, exposed area at chair height that is not inhibited by large pieces of furniture, which would block the chair rail from view. The wall should have a smooth, even surface, not textured like stucco, to allow the stencil to lay flat.

General Guidelines

Be sure the walls to be stenciled are clean. Wash them down with a damp sponge and allow them to dry before applying paint.

- Trace swirl and block-border template onto tracing paper, piecing if necessary to form two or more motifs.
- To aid in shaping swirl stencil when cutting motif, turn stencil clockwise.
- Cut away shaded areas around swirl motif, leaving swirls attached to stencil acetate at top and bottom.
- Use acrylic paints and allow each color to dry before removing stencil or before changing colors.
- If stenciling chair rail in child's room, use safe, nontoxic paint.
- Use separate stencils and clean brush for each paint color.

You'll Need

- ***Tracing paper***
- ***3 (11"x14") sheets stencil acetate***
- ***Ruler or straight-edge & pencil***
- ***Craft knife & cutting mat***
- ***Painter's tape***
- ***Acrylic paint: blue, black, & white***
- ***3 stencil brushes***
- ***Paper towels***
- ***Rubber gloves***

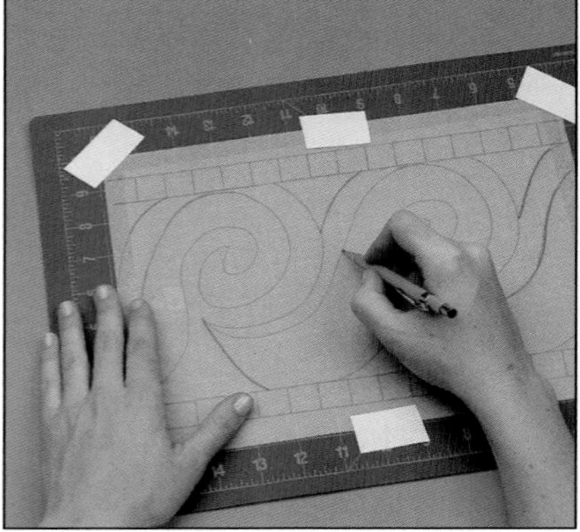

1 Tape 1 sheet of stencil acetate over tracing on cutting mat. Trace only swirl design; to aid in cutting, shade areas to be cut away. Trace top and bottom block-border design on 2 separate acetate sheets.

2 Tape swirl motif to mat. Cut away shaded areas. Tape 1 block-border pattern to mat. Starting with first square at left of each row, cut out every other square. Repeat with other block-border, cutting from second square.

3 Measure and mark distance along prepared wall from floor to desired location of chair-rail border. Tape swirl stencil to align with pencil lines on wall.

4 Dip stencil brush into blue paint; tamp off excess on paper towel. Holding brush perpendicular to wall, gently tap brush up and down over cutaway areas of stencil, starting at edges and working toward center. Let dry.

5 Remove stencil, align with dry painted swirl and pencil line, and tape to wall. Repeat paint-stenciling process across wall until swirl design of chair-rail border is complete. Let dry completely.

6 Tape first block-border stencil over first painted swirl. Paint cutout squares black; let dry. Continue across wall; let dry. Repeat with second border stencil, painting cutout squares white. Continue across; let dry completely.

Try This!

Stencil blooming rose-vine borders along the chair rail and continue it up and around the windows. Purchased stencils save you cutting time and come in an assortment of designs. If stenciling around a window, place lower edge of chair-rail design level with and parallel to bottom of window sill. Keep stencil equal distance from frame all the way around window.

Crafter's Secrets

Use the following tips to help you achieve professional stenciling results:

- *If using more than one stencil, label each with masking tape.*
- *To avoid dripping paint when stenciling on a vertical surface, do not overload brush with paint.*
- *Wipe paint from stencil after every usage to remove buildup of paint in corners and around edges.*
- *Rinse stencil brushes thoroughly and dry completely by blotting on paper towels.*

A stenciled chair-rail border of trailing ivy makes an unusual base for an arrangement of paintings or other wall treatments. While stenciling, the horizontal line can be interrupted at any time to add the charmingly askew vine.

Stenciling a Free-form Ivy Border

Give a chair-rail border an interesting focal point by breaking from the straight horizontal lines of the traditional border with a cascading ivy vine. In addition to bringing a sense of informality to the border, this asymmetrical chair-rail feature provides an ideal place to display artwork or photographs by drawing the viewer's eye to the immediate area.

To make a portion of the border ivy cascade down, simply turn the stencil at an angle, matching it up to the finished portion, and fill in with paint. Then resume stenciling in the usual horizontal manner.

Consider painting a border around the crown moldings and have it cascade down the corners of the walls; or trellis the ivy vine around the windows and doors.

1 Prepare stencil, piecing if necessary to obtain full motif. Measure clean wall from floor to intended position of chair rail; mark along wall with pencil. Using artist's tape, tape stencil. Make sure stencil is straight and level.

2 Dip stencil brush into green paint. Tamp on paper towel to remove excess. Holding brush perpendicular to wall, dab up and down, painting leaves from edges in toward center. Let dry; remove stencil.

3 At cascade area, angle and tape stencil, aligning top leaves with stenciled leaves and lowest leaf about 8" below border. Paint leaves; let dry. Reposition stencil at right, aligning with previous stenciling, and continue.

Glazing Natural Wood Paneling

Bathe a wood wall with translucent glaze, sponging on soft reflections of color and texture. One simple technique results in an infinite variety of decorator looks.

Using traditional staining methods to finish wood surfaces requires much time and effort. But you can obtain a professional-looking finish almost instantly with only a sponge and acrylic glazing paints.

Glazing lets you cover the surface quickly and produces a soft see-through finish. Experiment with color combinations to create subtle tone-on-tone effects or more striking contrasts. Because of the translucent nature of glazes, the beauty of the wood grain can still show through.

Even smooth plywood paneling can benefit from combinations of sheer glaze colors. On top, a coat of blue glaze is brushed rather than sponged onto the wood for a soft glow. Sponging pink over blue creates a gently textured mottled effect.

Purchase acrylic glazing paints in hardware, paint, or craft stores. Choose glazing colors that complement the fabric or furniture already in the room. Select one color to let the background tone of the wood show through or two colors for a blended effect. For two-color treatments, use dark and light shades of the same color for a tone-on-tone look or different colors for dramatic contrast. Add a third color for accent, if desired, perhaps to coordinate with a fabric trim.

Glazing Guidelines

Apply glazes with a natural sea sponge, cellulose kitchen sponge, or a flat paint brush.

- For more open, dappled effect, apply glazing paint with dry sponge or brush to avoid thinning paint.
- If sponging more than one color of glaze, use separate sponge for each color. Let each color dry before applying next to obtain distinct pattern throughout.
- Use large sponges to cover larger areas. Cut sponges into smaller shapes for smaller areas and to apply subtle traces of accent colors.
- For a more open pattern, lightly sponge paint over area. To cover surface more completely, sponge paint on more closely; avoid overworking an area.

You'll Need

- *Acrylic glazing paint*
- *Natural or cellulose sponge or flat brush*
- *Shallow plate*
- *Fine sandpaper & tack cloth*
- *Paper towels*
- *Gloves*
- *Clear acrylic sealer & flat brush*

Preparing Wood Surfaces

1 Use fine sandpaper or sanding block over surface of wood to remove any rough spots. Sand lightly to keep detail or grooved edges sharp; sand in direction of wood grain.

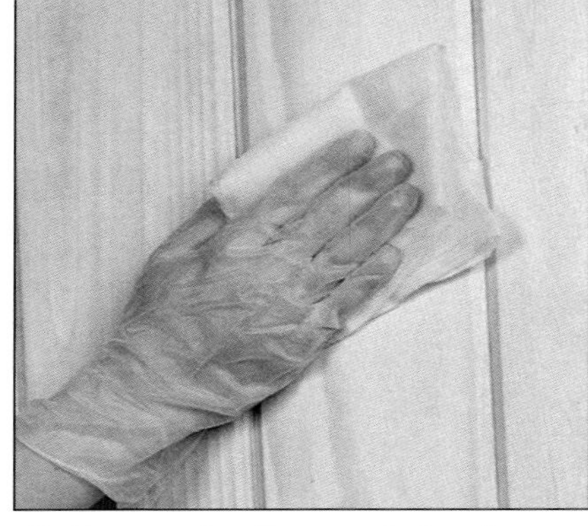

2 Remove dust from sanded surface with tack cloth or soft cloth dampened with mixture of equal parts water and distilled vinegar. Allow wood to dry completely before applying glazing paints.

Glazing with Cellulose Sponge

1 Pour paint onto plate. Dip dry cellulose sponge into paint; tamp excess on paper towel. Press sponge onto wood, dabbing in random pattern until sponge is empty; repeat.

2 After paint has completely dried, use clean brush to apply thin finish coat of clear acrylic sealer over surface. Brush sealer on in direction of wood grain.

Glazing with Natural Sponge

For a more dappled effect, use a natural sponge. Follow same procedure as for cellulose sponge. This is the best method for glazing when using more than 1 color.

Glazing with a Brush

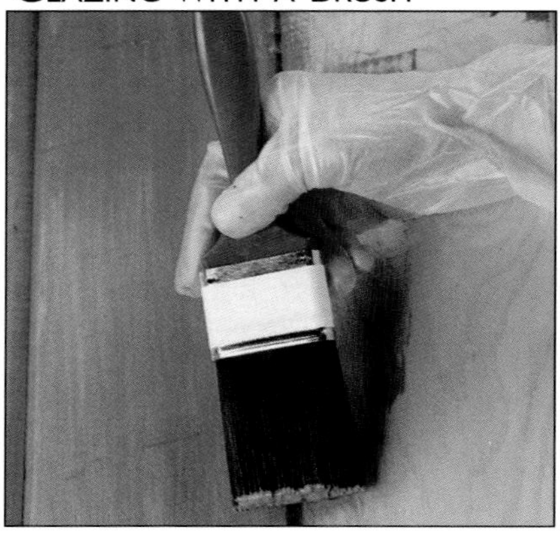

Apply thin coat of glaze, brushing in direction of wood grain. While glaze is still wet, press handfuls of crumpled paper towels against surface to remove some paint to create pattern.

Try This!

Any wood surface can be a candidate for glazing. Consider giving small pieces of furniture an extra lift with glazing colors that complement the room's decor. Try highlighting different sections of a chest of drawers with a selection of three or more colors that work well together. Emphasize each drawer front with a different brushed-on color. Paint knobs with contrasting colors to add more excitement. Cover the chest top with one of the bolder colors. To keep these surfaces the focal point of the piece, use one complementary opaque paint color to cover the sides of the chest. Finish with a clear sealer to protect the surfaces from wear.

Sponge-Glazing Flat Walls

Refresh traditional wallboard or plaster walls with an easy-to-put-on glaze covering. Applying the glaze with a sponge eliminates the need for matching patterns and joining wallpaper seams, because the sponging creates a random allover pattern. Since there are no overlap lines to worry about, you can stop at any time to run an errand or reach for the phone. Adapt the pattern as you work, adding another paint color to achieve a decorator-style finish.

If desired, you can apply the paint by dabbing with the bristle edge of a dry, flat brush. Then remove some color by dabbing the paint while it is still wet with crumpled paper towels, which will form a pattern in the paint remaining on the walls.

Because acrylic glazing paint does not adhere well to oil-based paints, use latex paint as the base coat, then apply the glaze.

Add the drama of bold color to a plain wall by using two distinctly different colors of glaze and separating them with a striking wallpaper border that complements both.

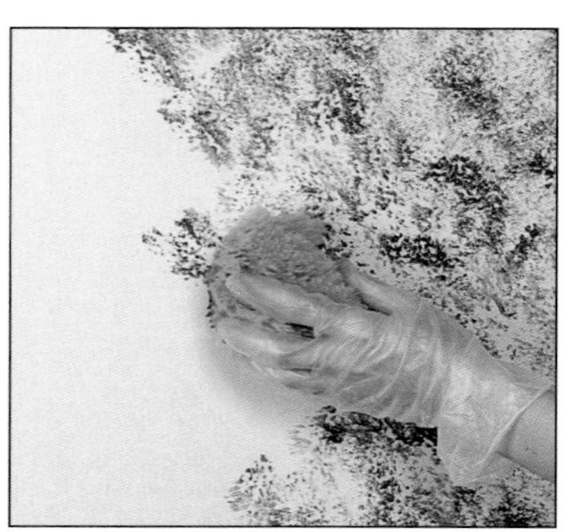

Use natural sponge to press paint onto dry wall that has been painted with base coat of latex paint. When sponging on dark colors, press lightly as you work.

Or use soft, dry, flat brush to lightly dab paint onto surface. Remove excess paint and soften edges by blotting paint off with crumpled paper towels or clean, soft cloth.

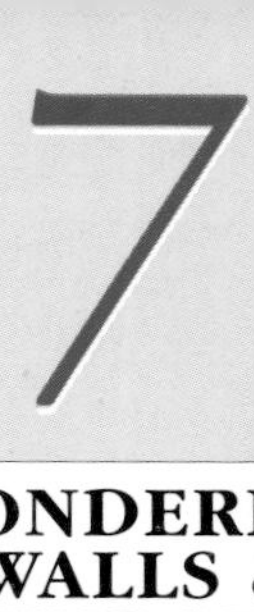

WONDERFUL WALLS & WINDOWS

CARD 21

Making a Fabric-Covered Cornice

Patterns & Templates

For an upscale and uplifting window treatment, top curtains or draperies with a padded cornice that is easily constructed from foam board or plywood and covered with batting, fabric, and trim.

In addition to its elegant appeal, a cornice hides hardware, frames window treatments, protects curtains from dust and saves energy by restricting airflow at the top of the window.

Purchase either a cornice kit, available at most fabric stores, or make your own basic cornice. Simple carpentry skills are all that are needed. Use pieces of 1"-thick foam board and glue them together to form the cornice base, or use ½" pine, which works equally well.

Whether graphically shaped like the tasseled points on this modern cornice, or softly curved and covered with a traditional fabric, these cornices can customize your decor. Sew them from two layers of fabric, then wrap around and staple to a rectangular batting-covered cornice. Add coordinating trims for a true professional look.

Patterns & Templates

Use the templates from Group 12, Card 23 to create a shaped covering for your padded cornice. Templates can be adjusted to fit individual windows.

Foam board (½"-thick polystyrene sheet) is lightweight, and can easily be cut with a craft knife, then glued together.

Measuring & Cutting Guidelines

Before measuring for cornice, install hardware to ensure dimensions of cornice will be correct. Measure the window width from the outside edges of the installed hardware.

- Cornice should measure about 15" high x 6" deep x measured width of window + 4".
- Cut foam board pieces: 1 face board 15" x window width + 4"; 1 dust board (top) 5" x window width + 4"; 2 end boards 5" x 14".
- Cut batting rectangle: 27" x window width + 4" + 16". Batting is 2" larger than cornice.
- Cut fabric rectangle: 6" longer and wider than batting piece; join pieces if necessary.
- Plan placement of dominant fabric motifs or stripes before cutting. While working, check front of face board to ensure fabric pattern is straight before stapling.

- ***Cornice kit or 1"-thick foam board***
- ***Craft knife & straightedge***
- ***Glue: craft & fabric***
- ***Staple gun***
- ***Batting***
- ***Fabric & trim***
- ***Scissors***
- ***Angle irons & screws***

For shaped cornices:

- ***Fabric & lining***
- ***Trim or tassels***
- ***Tracing paper & marking pen***

1 Before cutting face board, confirm width by holding foam board to window and marking outside edges of molding. Add 2" to each side. Cut face board, dust board, and end pieces from foam with sharp craft knife and straightedge.

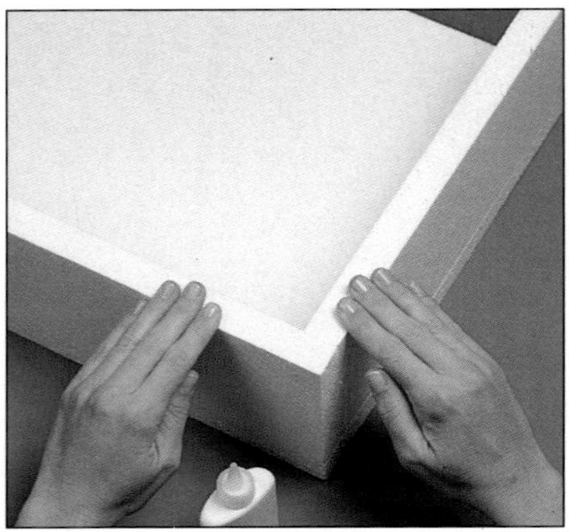

2 To assemble cornice boards, apply craft glue to 1" edge on 1 long side of each end board. Place ends on face board, leaving 1" gap at top. Apply glue to long edge of dust board; position on face board and across end boards.

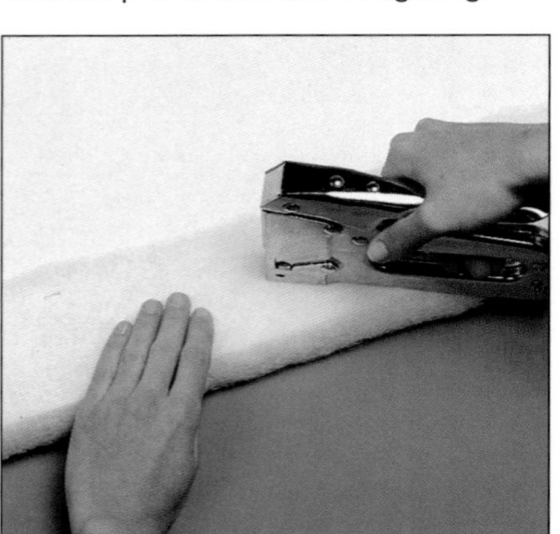

3 When glue is dry, center face board over batting. Wrap batting around edges to wrong side to cover all surfaces smoothly; cut and trim batting where necessary to get round corners, then staple inside cornice to secure.

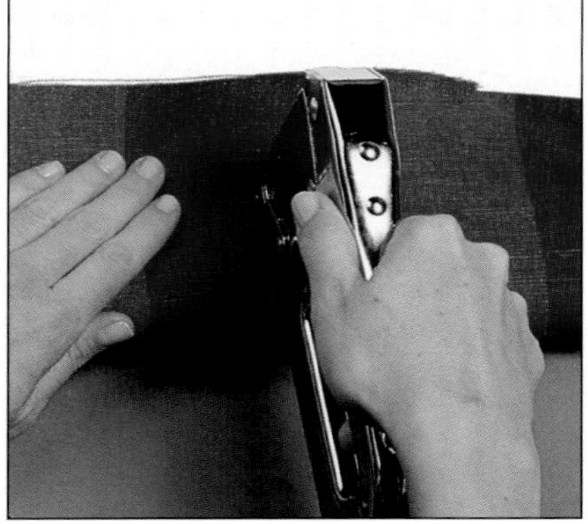

4 Center face board on wrong side of fabric. Beginning at ends, pull fabric taut and wrap to wrong side; staple ends. Trim any excess fabric. Fold top edge of fabric over dust board. Fold and lap corners to miter. Staple in place.

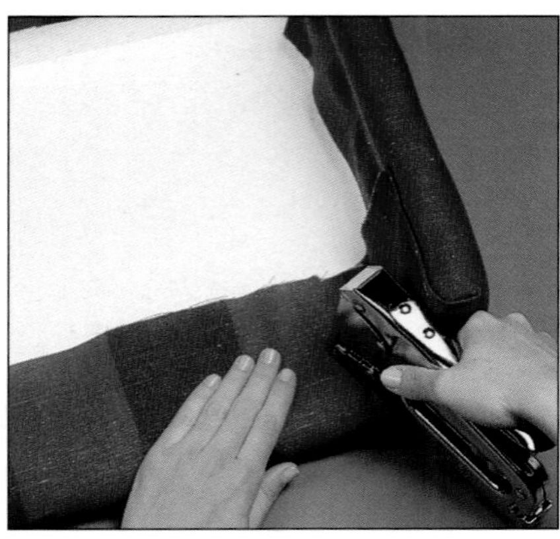

5 Once corners are neatly folded, mitered, and stapled, pull fabric taut across face and staple to back along both long edges.

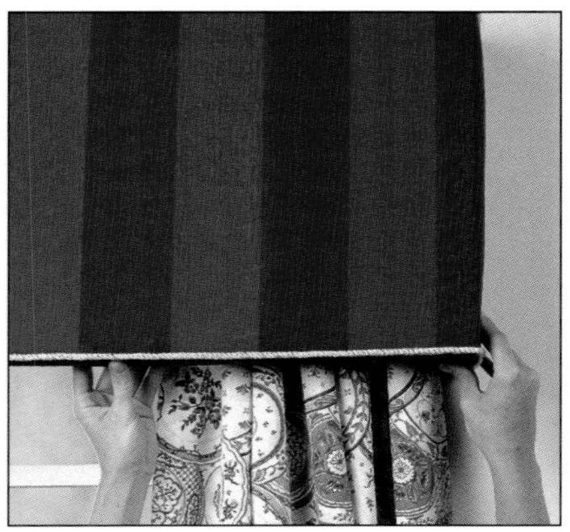

6 With fabric glue, apply decorative trim to lower edge of cornice. When glue is dry, hang cornice from angle irons, covering window hardware. Check that cornice is straight and even.

Making a Shaped Cornice

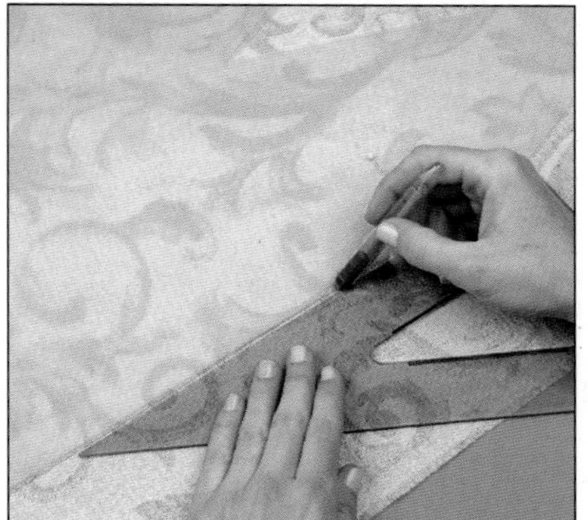

1 Use template and cornice dimensions to make pattern for pointed edge of cornice cover, which extends below board. Mark cornice shape on wrong side of fabric; cut ½" outside marked lines.

2 Cut lining in same manner. Right sides together, pin fabric to lining. Sew along marked lines on sides and lower edges. Notch seam allowances. Turn to right side; press.

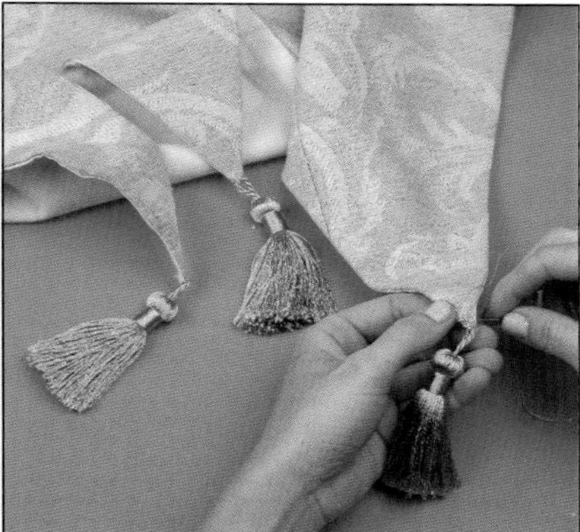

3 Hand sew tassels to end of each point. Wrap cover around batting-covered cornice board and staple at sides and upper edge, with lower edge hanging free. Glue cord along upper edge.

Try This!

A gracefully shirred fabric cornice is made in almost the same way as a flat fabric-covered cornice.

- *Prepare cornice boards and cover with batting, following directions on Group 7, Card 21.*
- *Cut fabric length same as for flat cornice, but cut fabric width to equal twice window width.*
- *Run two rows of gathering stitches along both long edges. Pull thread ends to gather until fabric fits width and around sides of cornice.*
- *Adjust gathers. Wrap and staple fabric over cornice boards, taking care that gathers are straight and evenly distributed.*

Adding Jabots to a Cornice

Add to the natural elegance, grace, and formality of a padded cornice with gracefully cascading jabots on each side. When selecting fabrics, keep in mind that the lining fabric will be visible, so choose a lining that coordinates or contrasts with the chosen decorator fabric.

Cover the cornice following the directions on Group 7, Card 21. To make the jabots, follow the diagram below to cut two pieces each from fabric and lining. Then cut two 4" x 15½" binding strips from fabric to finish top edge. Sew a narrow hem along both short ends of each binding strip.

Jabot Cutting Diagram

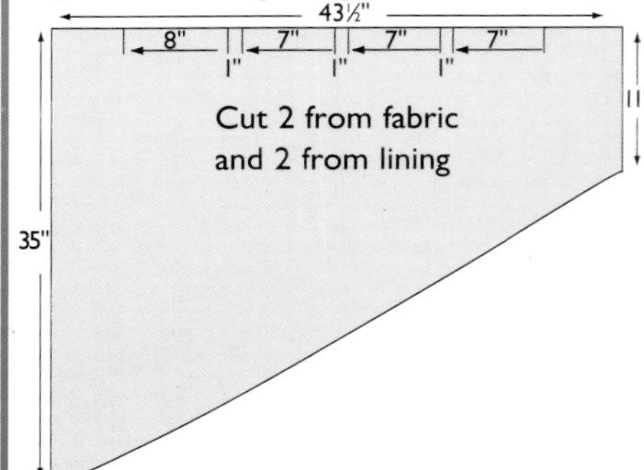
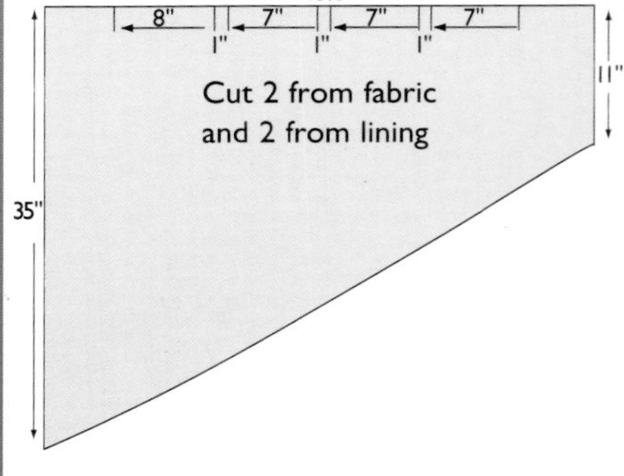

The bold stripes used for this cornice and jabot add both height and drama to the window treatment. Note how the dark blue lining peeking out along the jabot folds provides an ideal contrast to the mulitcolored fabric stripes.

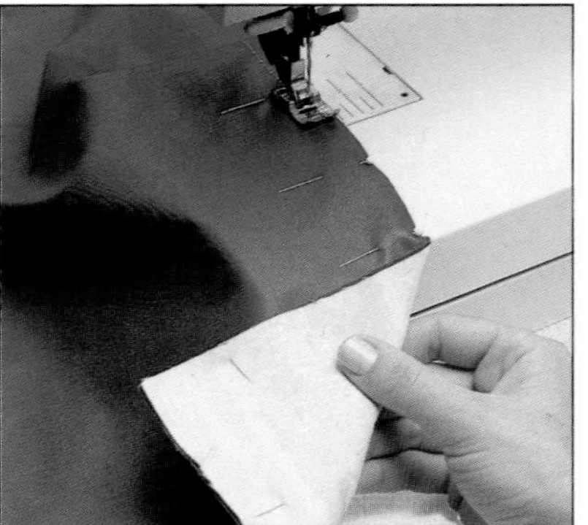

1 With right sides together sew jabot lining to fabric, leaving top edge open. Trim seams across points. Turn right side out; press. Baste top edges together. Use pins to mark pleats as shown in diagram.

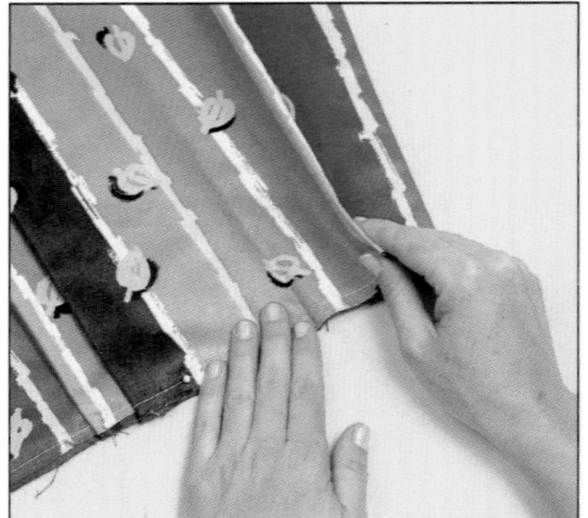

2 Fold pleats toward long sides and pin. Press, then baste top edge. Press binding strips in half lengthwise; open. Right sides together, sew to top of jabot. Fold in half to back, press raw edge under and slipstitch to jabot.

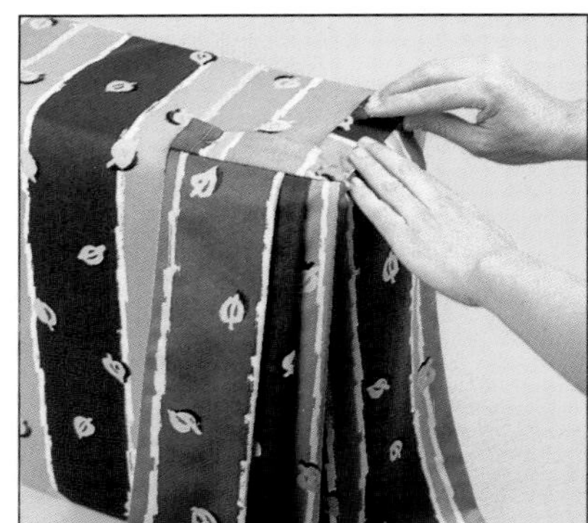

3 Pin each jabot to each side and front of cornice, easing around corners so pleats do not gape open. Secure binding strip to cornice top with "U"-shaped pins, mitering at corner. Finger-press pleats; hang cornice.

Clever Fix-Ups

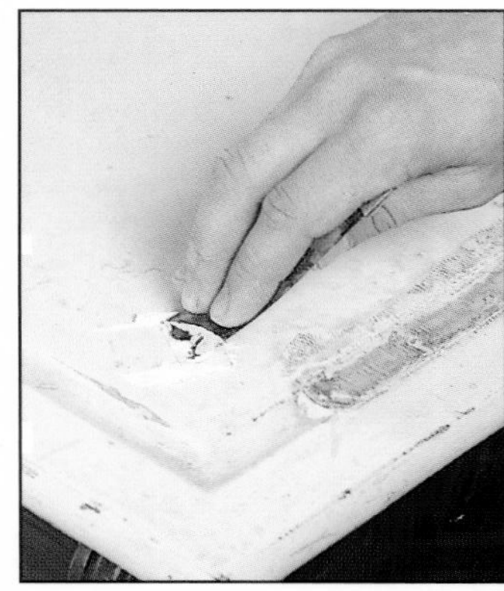

Ideas for trash-to-treasure projects

Decorating Baskets with Potato Stamps

Patterns & Templates

Freshen up an old, plain or painted basket with designs imprinted from stamps made out of potatoes. It's an inexpensive way to revitalize flea-market finds and household castoffs.

Stamping a basket doesn't require any special artistic skills, just a bit of imagination and a desire to create something unique.

The basket featured is painted in spring colors and decorated with bright flowers quickly made by rotating a petal-shaped stamp. Make the leaves from a second potato stamp and add accent dots with a pointed brush.

You can recycle a basket as many times as desired by merely painting over it and restamping.

Paint an old lidded basket and decorate it with tulips made with a petal stamp. To form tulip, apply center petal first, then add a petal to each side. For another folk-art look, stamp an unpainted apple basket with an orchard of apples.

Patterns & Templates *Use the templates from Group 12, Card 1 to create potato stamps for the baskets. Enlarge or reduce the templates as needed.*

One of the best features about potato stamping is the way dramatic designs can be created by simply angling and turning a single motif on a potato repeatedly over a surface.

General Guidelines

Disguise the old basket by sponge-painting it before stamping on the potato designs. Painting with a sponge will add variations of color and texture that a brush cannot.

- Dampen basket with sponge and water so surface accepts acrylic paint more readily.
- Working quickly, use same sponge, wrung out, to apply paint to basket.
- Place pattern face down on cut surface of potato and trace shape onto potato with a pencil.
- Using a small, sharp knife, cut straight down and around motif, then cut away excess potato in chunks.
- If basket has curved or uneven surface, touch up design with paint and a small brush.

You'll Need

- ***Old basket***
- ***Water-based stain***
- ***Artist's brushes: pointed & flat***
- ***Acrylic paints: lavender, light green, dark green, yellow, white***
- ***Flat sponge***
- ***Tracing paper & pencil***
- ***Large potatoes***
- ***Craft knife***
- ***Disposable plates***
- ***Paper towels***

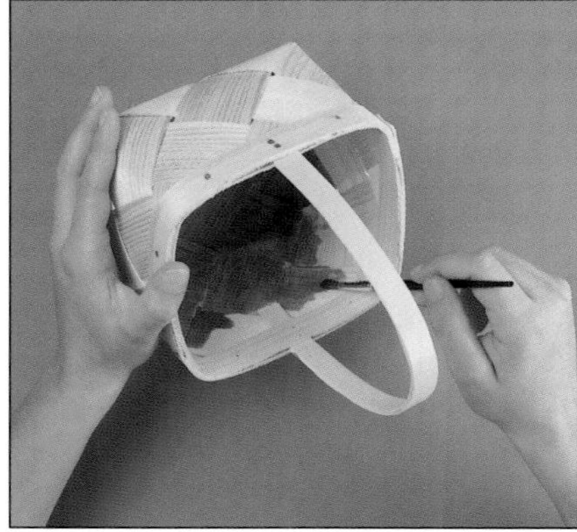

1 Stain inside of damp basket and handle using a flat brush; be sure stain gets into all crevices of basket. Let stain dry completely.

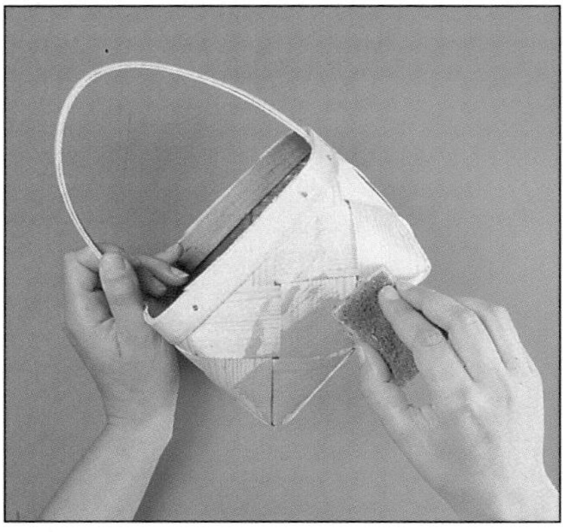

2 Pour lavender acrylic paint onto a plate. Dip sponge into paint and dab it over the lower half of basket. Let paint dry until tacky.

3 Pour light green paint onto a clean plate. Sponge-paint handle and upper half of basket. Overlap colors to gradually blend lavender and green colors. Let dry completely.

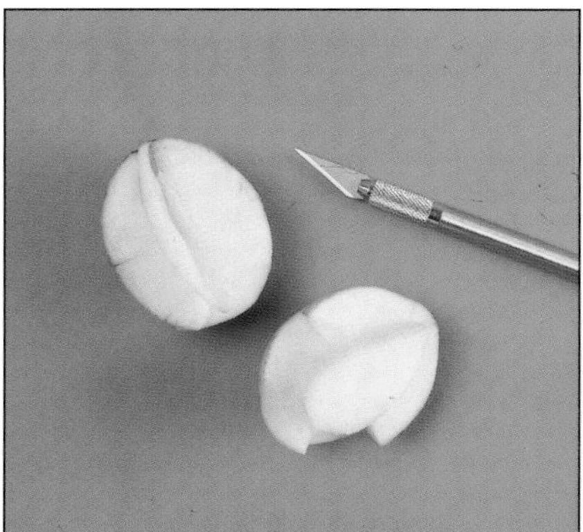

4 Cut a potato in half lengthwise. On 1 potato half, trace and cut petal design using templates from Group 12, Card 1. Trace and cut leaf design on other potato half.

5 Pour yellow paint onto clean plate. Dip potato with petal design straight down into paint for even coverage; test design on paper towel to get comfortable with process.

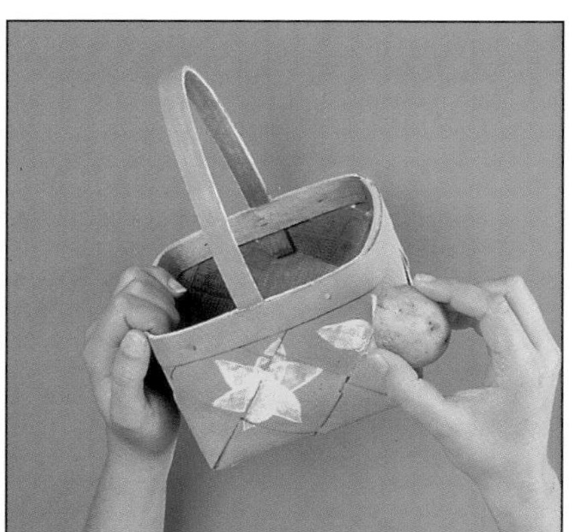

6 Print 5 petals in a circle to create a flower. Print as many flowers as needed to surround basket. Reapply paint to potato as necessary, remembering to test each stamp on paper towel before printing on basket.

For further information: Crafting & Decorating Made Simple™ 1-800-527-5576
International Masters Publishers, 444 Liberty Ave., Pittsburgh, PA 15222-1207

088-055-000 Printed in U.S.A. ©MCMXCVI IMP AB/IMP Inc. Crafting & Decorating Made Simple™
International Masters Publishers AB, produced under license. Packet 0

7 Pour dark green paint onto a clean plate. Carefully dip potato with leaf design into paint. Test on paper towel first, then stamp along side of basket and handle at random.

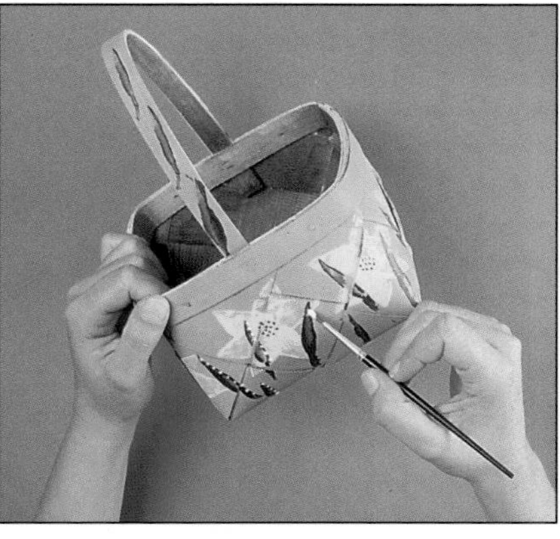

8 Using pointed brush, add a ring of little lavender dots in centers of flowers and white dots along leaves. Let basket dry completely.

Crafter's Secrets

Small cookie cutters make good templates for potato stamps. Push the cutter straight into the cut surface of the potato, and cut away surrounding potato. Press down on the potato to release it from the cookie cutter.

To make the basket as smooth as possible, lightly sand its surface before painting and between each coat of paint. Wipe the basket with a damp sponge to remove any dust.

Try This!

Select a basket large enough to use as a planter and decorate it with potato-stamp prints and simple hand-painted flower petals that you create with single strokes of a small pointed brush. Use a pencil eraser to dab on the flower centers. To make the surrounding dots, use the end of the brush handle dipped in paint. Seal the surface with a clear matte polyurethane and let the sealer dry completely.

Line the inside of the basket with a piece of clear vinyl, then gently lower the potted plant into the basket.

Creating Festive Easter Baskets

A more intricately detailed basket can be created by combining freehand painting and potato stamping. The combination provides greater design freedom than stamping alone, but is still quick and easy. For example, the candy-filled basket at right has stamped flowers and leaves with freehand-painted stems and petal cups. The bordered rim of the basket designed with chicks has stamped flowers and hand-painted details and vines. Although the chicks were drawn, then hand-painted on the basket, the design can also be transferred to a potato and stamped in place, then the painted outline added. Use the templates from Group 12, Card 1 for the motifs shown.

If you are planning to paint a specific detail such as the vine, lightly pencil in a guideline first, then paint over the penciled line.

When combining printing with painting, apply potato print first and let the paint dry completely before handpainting.

Split baskets decorated in traditional spring colors make wonderful containers to take on an Easter-egg hunt or to add a festive look to your holiday table. Line them with excelsior or plastic grass, then fill with an assortment of candies, eggs, and other goodies and treats.

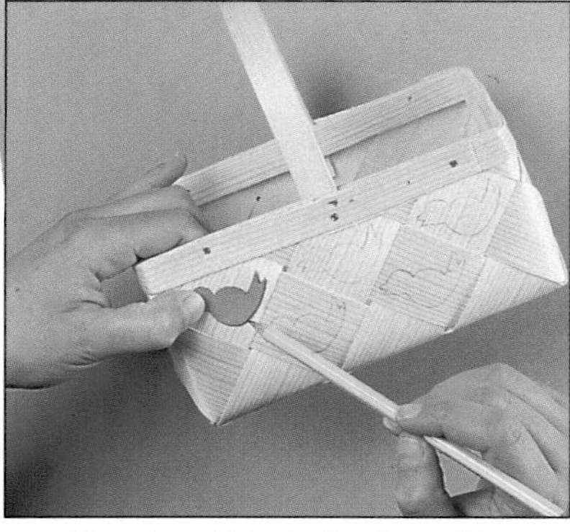

1 Transfer chick design from Group 12, Card 1 onto cardboard and cut out to form template. Hold template against basket and trace around it with a pencil.

2 Paint chicks with matte yellow acrylic paint using an artist's brush. Allow to dry completely. Using orange acrylic paint, outline chick silhouettes and add design details.

3 Paint background as desired with lavender acrylic paint. Use dot-and-dash paint strokes to create green grass beneath chicks. Allow paint to dry completely.

For further information: Crafting & Decorating Made Simple™
International Masters Publishers, 444 Liberty Ave., Pittsburgh, PA 15222-1207 1-800-527-5576

Updating Ceramic Tiles with Stenciling

Patterns & Templates

Freshen those boring ceramic tiles with brightly colored stenciled motifs that add dramatic accent to the pattern of the tiles.

Replacing existing wall tiling is costly. Stenciling is a simple way to liven a wall, an entire room, or just one small section with a border. Choose a motif that is simple in shape, fits the tile size, and can be repeated across multiple tiles to create an overall pattern, such as these vegetable stencils for the kitchen.

Durable gloss enamel paint is used for the motif and then covered with shellac to make the tiles washable. Practice first on surplus or damaged tiles purchased from a home decorating center.

Stencil a single motif or lay down an entire pattern on tile. A border stenciled across plain bathroom tiles wakes up the room with a jolt of contrasting color. One stenciled tile makes a handy trivet. Apply two or more coats of shellac to protect the surface, then stick on cork dots in each corner for cushioning.

Use the templates from Group 12, Card 9 to create stencils for painting cheerful motifs on old tiles and other ceramic objects. Or look for precut stencils at craft and paint stores.

Keep the design simple and uncluttered. Select basic shapes with small details that can be attractively highlighted with a contrasting color.

Preparation Guidelines

Before painting, clean tiles with grease-removing detergent to obtain a smooth surface for paint.

- Use stencil paper with waxed side facing out so paint can be wiped off to avoid transferring it to another tile.
- Use oil-based gloss enamel for colors and alcohol-based shellac for sealer. Do not use polyurethane on glazed ceramic tiles; it won't adhere properly.
- Build up color by applying several coats of paint to motif; let paint dry between coats and before removing stencil.
- Let each painted motif dry before proceeding to next to avoid smudging. Let all motifs dry completely before applying sealer coats.
- When painting tiles over a large area, mark each tile to be painted with a removable label, then peel it off as you work.

You'll Need

- ***Tracing paper, stencil paper, pencil, & craft knife***
- ***Brushes: large & small for paint; flat for shellac***
- ***Oil-based gloss enamel: red, green, & purple***
- ***Alcohol-based shellac sealer***
- ***Masking tape***
- ***Disposable plastic lid or plate***
- ***Paper towels***

1 Cut stencil paper same size as tile for each color in motif. Trace motif. Rub pencil over back of traced outline for transferring. Turn tracing over; outline main vegetable shape onto 1 stencil and stem and leaves onto other.

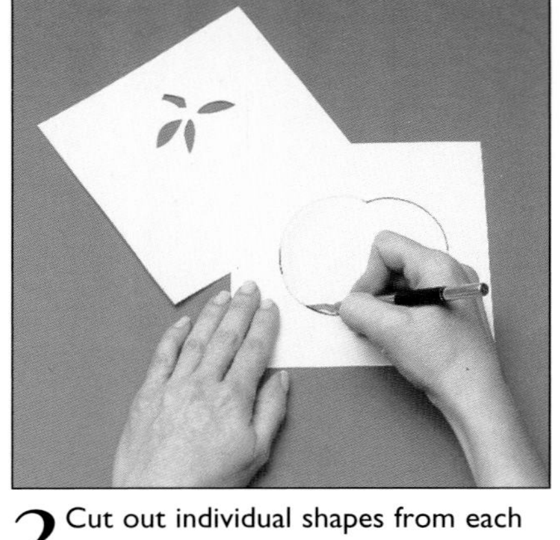

2 Cut out individual shapes from each stencil using sharp craft knife. Carefully cut body of vegetable from 1 stencil and stem and leaves from other.

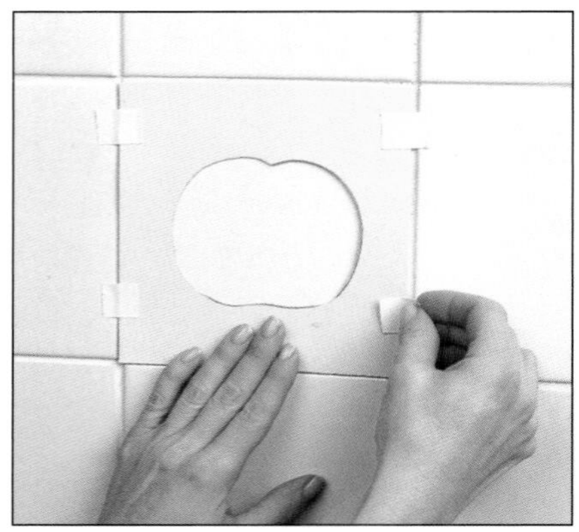

3 Tape stencil with body of vegetable to tile with masking tape, centering design and aligning edges of stencil paper with edges of tile.

4 Pour small amount of red paint onto plastic lid. Dip stencil brush into paint and dab onto paper towel to remove excess; press over cutout area of stencil. Paint entire area, overlapping along cutout edges to obtain sharp outline.

5 Let body of painted vegetable dry completely; remove stencil. Tape stem-and-leaf stencil over same tile, placing it to align with tile edges. Use green paint to stencil over stem and leaves. Let paint dry completely.

6 Remove stencil. Using craft knife, carefully scrape off any paint from tile that may have seeped underneath stencils and blurred edges. Seal tile with 2 coats of shellac, using flat brush; let first coat dry before applying second.

Try This!

Stencil large unglazed terra-cotta tiles with this bold floor design. The templates for creating the stencils can be found in Group 12, Card 9.

Use two colors of exterior acrylic gloss enamel that contrast against the dark tiles. Since unglazed tiles are more absorbent than ceramic ones, high-gloss acrylic enamel will adhere better than oil-based enamel.

Draw stencil pattern to fit the size of the tile, then cut out two stencils, one for each color area of the design to be painted. Stencil each color separately onto every other tile.

It isn't necessary to seal these unglazed painted tiles, but if you're concerned that the paint might wear off in heavy traffic areas, apply 2 coats of polyurethane on all the tiles for a unified look.

Crafter's Secrets

To achieve a uniform look on your tiled area, select a shellac that matches the sheen on your tiles. If the tiles have a matte finish, use a matte or satin shellac. If the tiles are glossy, a gloss shellac is best to maintain a consistent appearance.

Stenciling Kitchen Canisters

Create matching companion accessories that look like expensive designer originals by using the same simple motifs from your newly stenciled walls to paint other ceramic or clay surfaces.

A canister set is the perfect accessory choice for coordinating with stenciled kitchen tiles. Simple tile motifs will look most appealing in smaller sizes transferred onto canisters. Several different sizes of motifs could be used effectively on the same piece if desired.

To make large motifs fit, reduce stencil patterns on a copy machine or use the medium- and small-size versions of the vegetable templates from Group 12, Card 9.

Give your kitchen a decorator look by stenciling smaller versions of the same motifs used on the wall tiles. Use stencil plastic to cut out flexible stencils that will allow you to paint the vegetable designs on a curved surface.

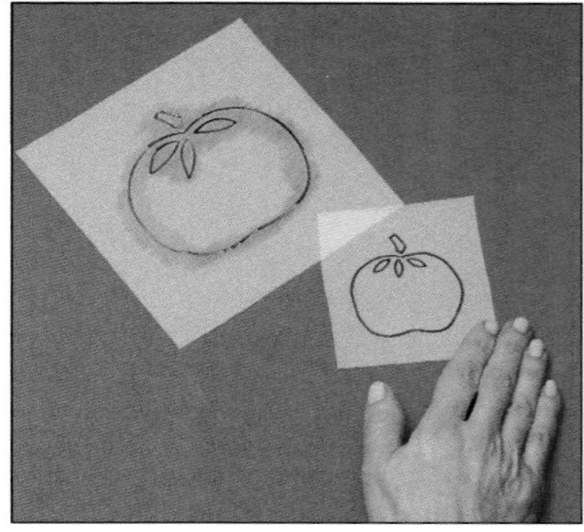

1 Use medium and small vegetable templates provided or reduce size to fit lid and sides of canister. Trace and cut out 2 stencils for each motif, with body on 1 sheet and stem and leaves on other.

2 Tape vegetable-body stencil snuggly around curved body of canister. Stencil with oil-based enamel, applying several coats. Let dry before removing stencil. Proceed using stem-and-leaves stencil. Continue around canister.

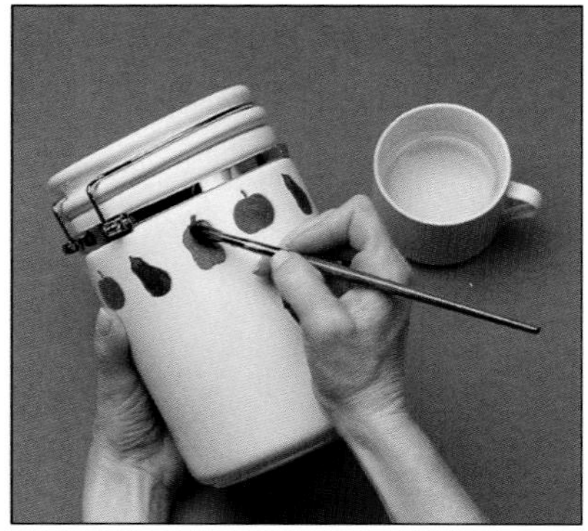

3 Let all stencil paint colors dry completely. Apply 2 coats of alcohol-based shellac over each stenciled motif with small brush to seal surface and protect it. Let dry between coats.

Making Bird Feeders from Recycled Bottles

Recycle empty soda bottles into colorful bird feeders that can accent your patio, deck, or garden. All you need is a simple screw-on attachment, some paint, and a mixture of birdseed.

Select one of the three feeder designs shown here. The "Sunflower" feeder shown above is made from a 2-liter bottle with the centers of the flowers left clear so the amount of feed in the bottle can easily be seen. Save your 2- or 3-liter soft-drink bottles and strip off the labels. Paint your design around the bottle, then complete the feeder by using a bird-feeder adapter kit. Birds tend to scatter small seeds, so use sunflower seeds for the least amount of waste.

Seeds can be seen through the clear window of the 3-liter "Shingled House" (above right). The 2-liter "Night Sky" feeder uses a plastic adapter, which calls for a homemade metal hanger.

The metal adapter kits that form a perch and a tray for the seeds come in two sizes, one for a 2-liter plastic soda bottle and one for a 3-liter bottle.

Materials Information

Look for the adapter kits in stores and catalogs that carry birdseed and feeders.

- A metal feeding adapter comes with its own wire hanger that allows bottle to hang freely.
- Bottle can also be set on top of a purchased hollow ¾"-diameter metal pole that fits under feeding adapter.
- A plastic adapter is also available for 2-liter bottles, but requires a homemade hanger.
- Use waterproof acrylic paints.
- To paint thin lines and small areas, and to create shading effects, use watercolor brushes.

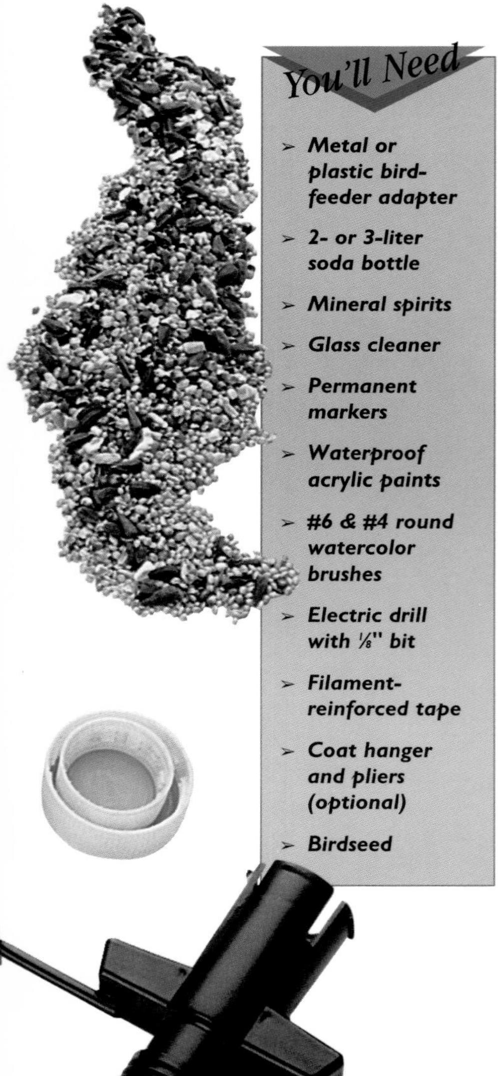

You'll Need

- ***Metal or plastic bird-feeder adapter***
- ***2- or 3-liter soda bottle***
- ***Mineral spirits***
- ***Glass cleaner***
- ***Permanent markers***
- ***Waterproof acrylic paints***
- ***#6 & #4 round watercolor brushes***
- ***Electric drill with ⅛" bit***
- ***Filament-reinforced tape***
- ***Coat hanger and pliers (optional)***
- ***Birdseed***

Making a Recycled Bird Feeder

1 Remove label from plastic soda bottle. Using a soft rag, clean any residual bits of label, glue, and dirt from bottle with mineral spirits and glass cleaner.

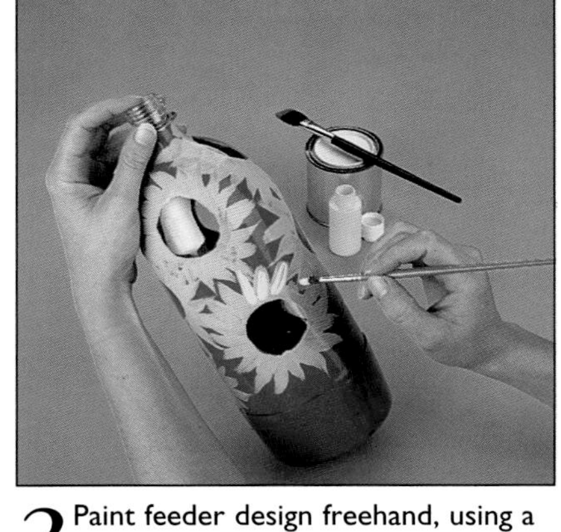

2 Paint feeder design freehand, using a larger brush for background color; do not paint areas where seed is to show through. Add details with permanent markers or round brushes. Allow 1 color to dry before applying next color.

3 When dry, measure 1½" up from bottom and mark on opposite sides of bottle. Stick a small piece of filament tape over marks. Using an electric drill, bore a ⅛" hole through each mark.

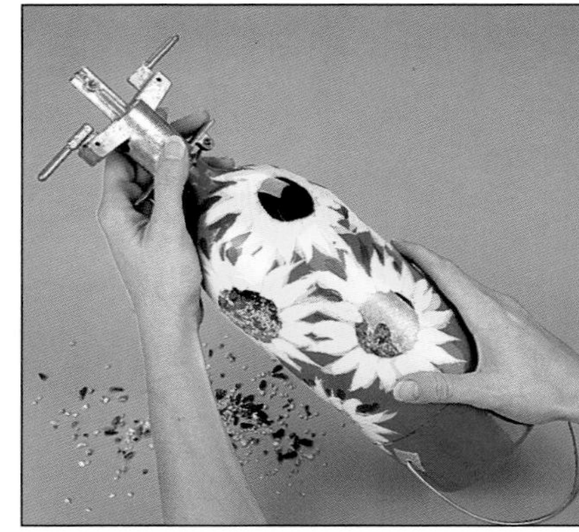

4 Gently spread wire hanger supplied with adapter and insert ends into holes. Fill bottle with birdseed and screw on metal adapter. Hang feeder from a tree branch or under eaves of house.

Making a Wire Hanger

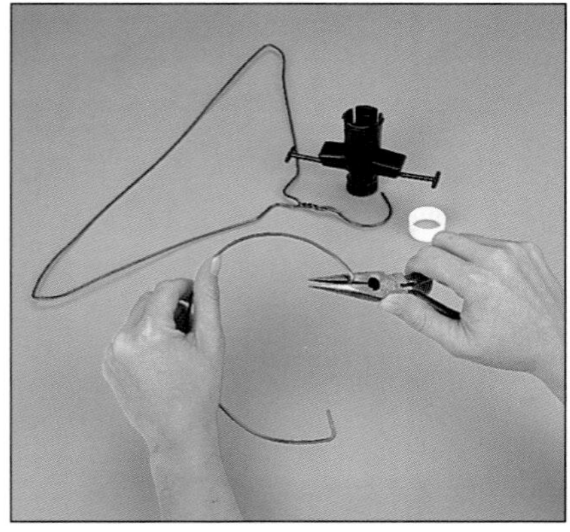

If wire hanger is not supplied, cut a 15" length of coat hanger. Bend into U-shape. Using pliers, lightly bend ends ½" inward. Drill holes in bottle and attach hanger. Screw adapter onto bottle.

Crafter's Secrets

Fine details are difficult to paint on a curved plastic surface; the lines will always be a little wavy. For best results, hold the bottle by its neck with the bottom rested against your thigh. As you paint, rest your brush hand on the bottle to steady it. Rather than trying to draw a straight line freehand, rotate the bottle whenever possible to draw the lines.

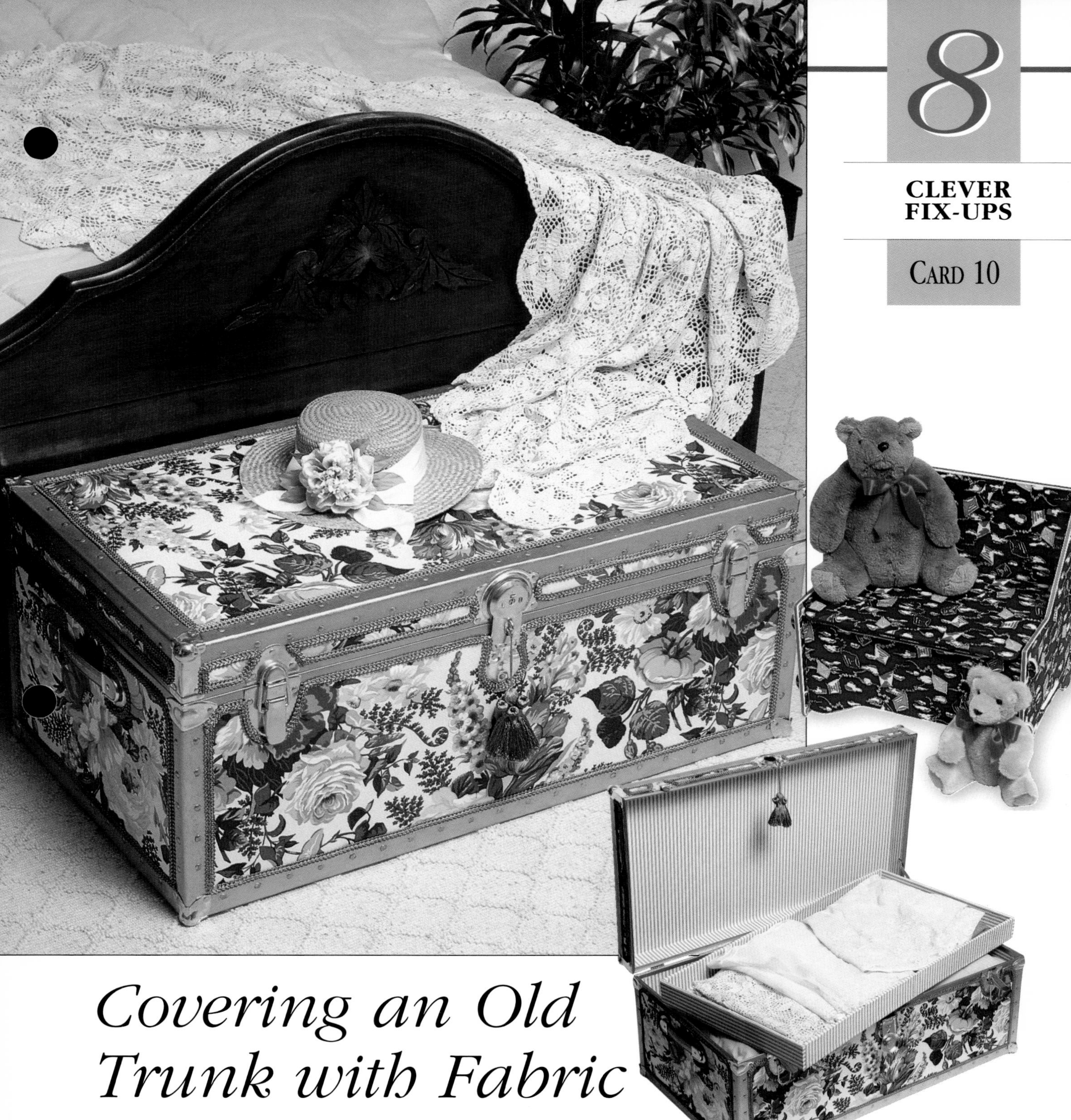

Covering an Old Trunk with Fabric

No one would imagine that this Victorian-style chest was once a plain, black footlocker. Transformed with fabric, trims, and gold paint, it is now fit to be filled with the finest bedroom linens.

There is never enough storage space in our homes today. So create several square feet of additional useful space by turning that unsightly old ugly-duckling trunk into a swan of a storage chest.

Fusible fleece smooths out the exterior surfaces. A decorative fabric that complements your decor is then applied using fusible web. By varying the fabric, you can use this technique to add storage space anywhere in the house, from children's rooms to the family room.

To bring new life to a wooden toy chest, cover it with a juvenile print, paint the edges, then glue narrow grosgrain ribbons of different colors centered along the painted strips. Spruce up the inside and tray of a covered trunk by papering with contrasting wallpaper.

Fusing fabric to wood or metal is not difficult to do. Many fusible products are available that make the job easy. Here are some suggestions to ensure success.

Fusing Guidelines
Always read the manufacturer's instructions before starting a fusible project. While all of the products are applied in a similar manner, there are differences from manufacturer to manufacturer.

- If using both fusible web and fusible fleece, get both products from same manufacturer to ensure compatiblity.
- Be sure the iron heats accurately. Use the manufacturer's specified temperature to create a perfect bond.
- Measure and cut fabric and fusible to size *after* they have been fused together, as fusing process causes a small amount of shrinkage.
- Add trims along edges of finished fused piece to give it a decorator's touch and to help keep edges from fraying.
- Fused fabrics can be treated with dirt-resistant fabric finishes so they remain clean longer and are easier to maintain.

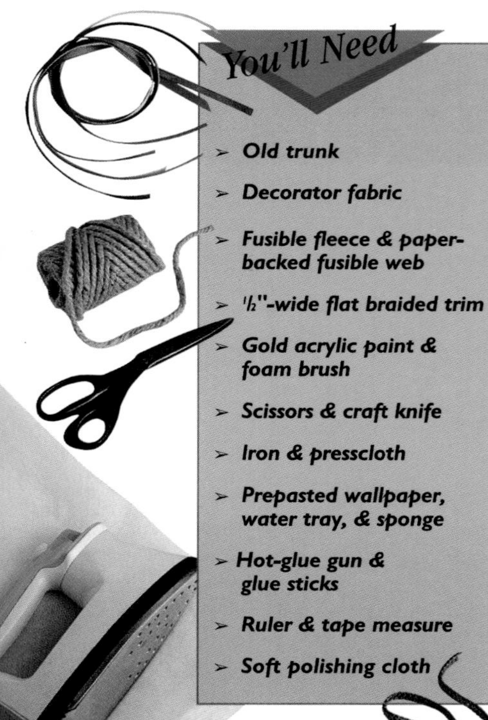

You'll Need

- ***Old trunk***
- ***Decorator fabric***
- ***Fusible fleece & paper-backed fusible web***
- ***½"-wide flat braided trim***
- ***Gold acrylic paint & foam brush***
- ***Scissors & craft knife***
- ***Iron & presscloth***
- ***Prepasted wallpaper, water tray, & sponge***
- ***Hot-glue gun & glue sticks***
- ***Ruler & tape measure***
- ***Soft polishing cloth***

Covering an Old Trunk

1 Clean both inside and outside surfaces of trunk with damp sponge to remove surface dirt or grease. If needed, lightly sand any shiny nonmetal surfaces so fusible materials will adhere properly.

2 Apply thin coat of gold paint to strapping edges of footlocker, painting over nail heads to give their original surface a new shine. Paint handle straps gold as well. Let dry. Apply second coat of paint if necessary.

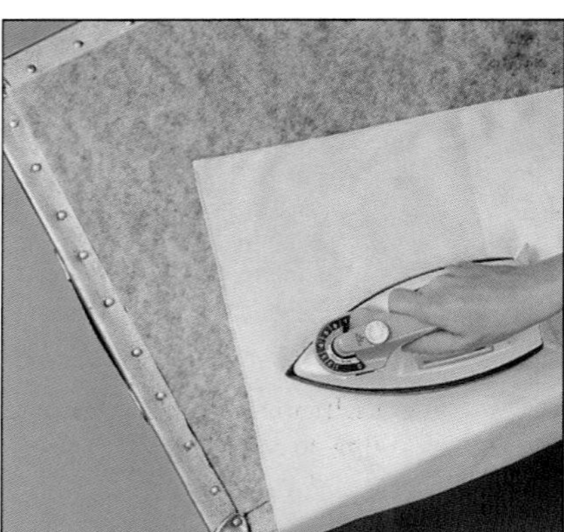

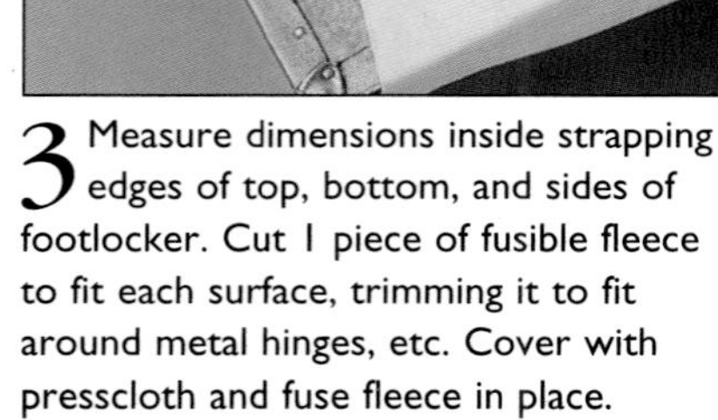

3 Measure dimensions inside strapping edges of top, bottom, and sides of footlocker. Cut 1 piece of fusible fleece to fit each surface, trimming it to fit around metal hinges, etc. Cover with presscloth and fuse fleece in place.

4 Fuse paper-backed web to wrong side of fabric. Using dimensions for fleece, cut 1 fabric piece to fit each footlocker surface. Peel off paper, and with presscloth over fabric, fuse each piece to top of fleece.

5 Glue braided trim over raw edges of each fused fabric piece. Begin and end trim at bottom or back corner and place it to fit inside strapping edges, shaping trim into corners.

6 With soft, clean cloth, polish remaining metal surfaces—hinges, locks, and corners—working carefully around glued braided trim.

Lining the Inside of an Old Trunk

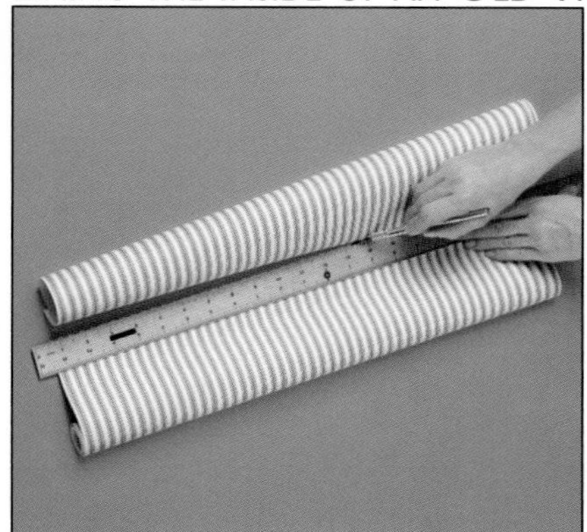

1 Measure tray's surfaces, and using craft knife, cut wallpaper to fit around entire tray, allowing extra for overlapping edges. For fewer seams, use 1 piece to cover more than 1 surface where possible.

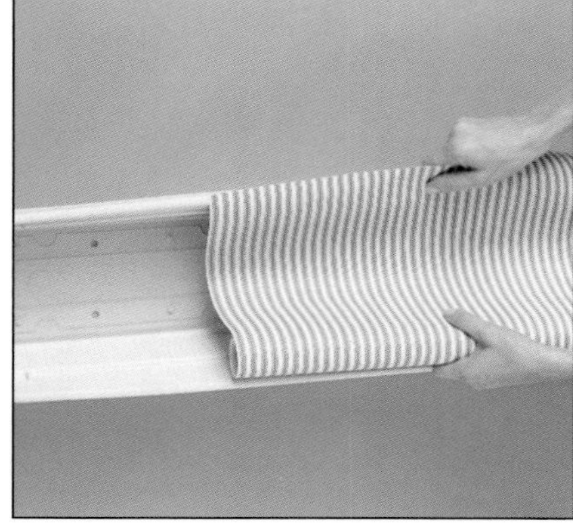

2 Roll up each piece of paper with pasted side out and follow manufacturer's instructions for immersing roll in water tray. Unroll paper and refold, pasted side in, for time specified to activate paste.

Try This!

Cover a plain wooden box with an interesting paisley fabric for a rich, opulent stationery holder. First, paint the exposed edges with gold metallic paint, then fuse the fabric in place, being careful not to rest the hot iron on the painted surface as it might blister the paint. Next, glue flat braided trim along the center of the painted edges and across the top and bottom of the front panel.

3 Unfold paper and lay over short sides of tray; smooth with damp sponge. Fit paper into corners, clipping as neeed so paper lays flat. Cover inside and outside of tray, overlapping first edges. Paper inside of trunk in same manner.

Fusibles can be used on many metal and wood surfaces for instant makeovers. Fuse fabric to old cornice boards, a flea-market-find bedstead or headboard, the top of a vintage dressing table, or to the seat of an old dining room chair. You can even fuse fabric to damaged plaster walls.

Creating Storage for a Family Room

Cover an old wooden trunk or unpainted blanket chest with fabric to serve as a coffee or end table, as well as to provide hidden storage space for games, books, and videos in the family room.

This sturdy wooden piece offers a place to set snacks and to put your feet up as you watch TV or enjoy a chat. It could also be used as a surface for board games and other family activities.

Select an appropriate fabric and a contrasting trim that complement the room's decor, such as the denim and rope that is in keeping with the rustic feeling of the room shown.

While the trunk-table should be viewed first as a furniture asset, don't overlook the fact that it adds about 12 square feet of useful storage space.

With a bit of paint, fabric, and fusible web, an unpainted wooden blanket chest becomes a brand-new coffee table that stores family-room clutter. For an informal country look, choose a sturdy fabric, such as denim, and spray it with a stain repellant; add rope trim and rope handles for a unique touch.

1 Remove original handles and lightly sand wood surfaces. Remove dust with tack cloth or cloth dampened with paint thinner. Let dry. Paint moldings and studs; with lid propped open, paint edges of lid. Let dry completely.

2 Outline surface dimensions and position of studs on paper side of fusible web. Fuse web to wrong side of fabric and cut out fused pieces. Pierce stud marks. Peel off paper, position fabric on surface, and fuse in place.

3 Outline top fabric, base molding, and base below molding with rope. For handles, tie 2 knots 8" apart on 2 (16") pieces of rope; pierce fabric over handle holes. Push rope ends through holes; knot inside trunk to secure.

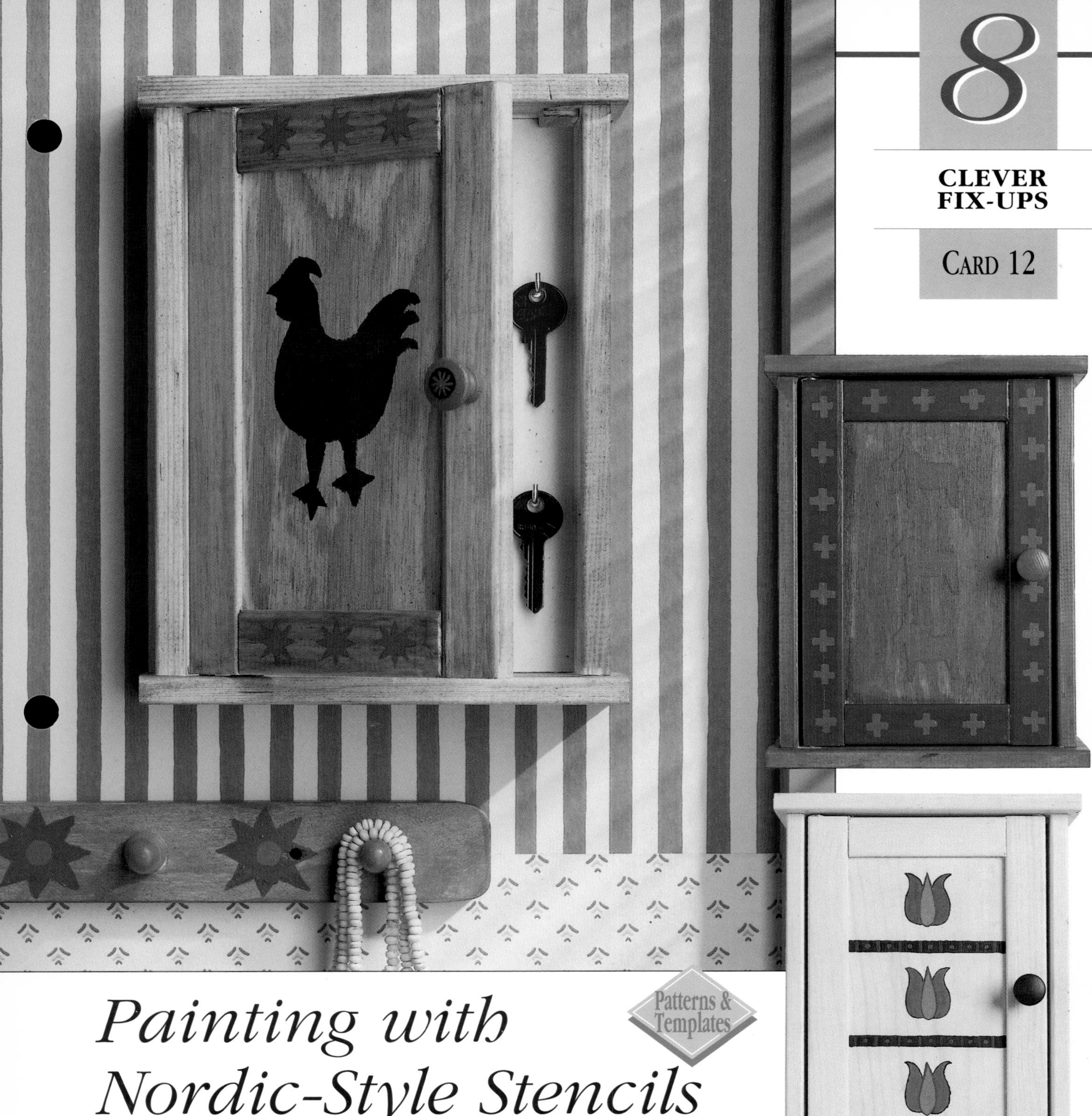

Painting with Nordic-Style Stencils

Patterns & Templates

Recreate the look of a 19th-century farmhouse fixture by stenciling an old wall cabinet or other small wooden pieces with motifs of animals, plants, and other simple shapes from nature.

These homespun Nordic motifs have been popular for generations in many Scandinavian homes for their simple charm and primitive folk-art quality. Painted with traditional bold colors, the country key cupboard featured makes a functional and decorative accessory in a hallway, kitchen, or family room.

Select from the templates in Group 12, Card 10, or design your own motifs. Embellish other room accessories using the same stenciling technique.

Wooden pieces can be painted a color or varnished to emphasize the natural wood finish. Red horses enclosed by a frame of simple crosses are set off against a dark background. Rows of tulips stand out against a natural wood background.

Patterns & Templates *Trace the templates from Group 12, Card 10 onto stiff cardboard to create desired stencils.*

Look for old cabinets, shelves, and other small wooden pieces in your attic, at thrift shops, and at yard sales. Simple styles without intricate carvings or surfaces are more Scandinavian in style and easier to paint.

Preparation Guidelines

For successful results, prepare wood to receive paint and plan placement of motifs before painting.

- Remove any original paint or varnish from wood surfaces with medium and fine sandpapers. Lightly sand new wood to smooth rough edges.
- After sanding, remove excess dust with tack cloth or cloth dampened with solution of equal parts water and vinegar.
- Remove any knobs or hardware to make applying paints for stencils easier.
- To avoid smudging colors, let each painted motif dry completely before proceeding on to next one.

You'll Need

- ***Small wooden cabinet***
- ***Brushes: stencil (foam or bristle), pointed artist's brush, & flat brush for sealer***
- ***Acrylic paints: navy & red***
- ***Craft knife***
- ***Masking tape***
- ***Tracing paper, pencil, & stiff cardboard***
- ***Disposable plastic lid or plate for paint***
- ***Paper towels***
- ***Clear polyurethane sealer***

1 Trace rooster or selected motif onto tracing paper and cut out. Using pattern, outline shape on cardboard. Cut out stencil with craft knife. Trim stencil edges, leaving 1"–2" margins on sides.

2 Position cardboard stencil in center of cabinet front. Trim stencil to lay flat inside any wood moldings of door frame. Tape in place. If needed, tape door to keep it closed while working.

3 Pour small amount of navy paint in plastic lid. Paint consistency should be creamy; if necessary, thin slightly with water. Dip foam stencil brush into paint, then dab brush on paper towel to remove excess paint.

4 Press brush over cutout area of stencil to apply paint to wood, pressing brush up and down and overlapping along cutout edges to obtain sharp outline on motif. Let dry before removing stencil.

5 Mark star positions on cabinet border with pencil. Trace small border star onto paper. Flip paper over and place motif over marked position; outline over drawn lines to transfer image to wood. Transfer other stars in same way.

6 Using pointed artist's brush, paint star with red paint, beginning at tip of star point and pulling brush along 1 edge of point toward center of star. Repeat along each edge of each point to fill in star.

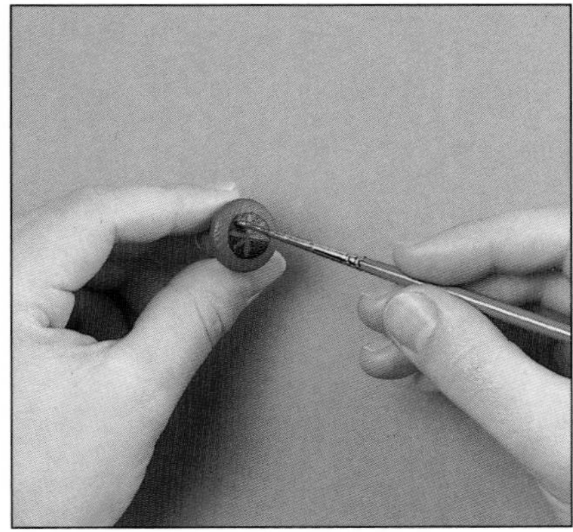

7 Paint cupboard knob with 1 coat of red. When paint is completely dry, paint blue circle in center of knob top and let dry. Finish painting red spoked motif in center of blue circle.

Stenciling a Peg Rack

1 Outline and cut out starburst stencil. Using navy paint, stencil 1 star between each peg on rack; let dry. If desired, paint circle in center of stars with lighter color. Paint each peg red.

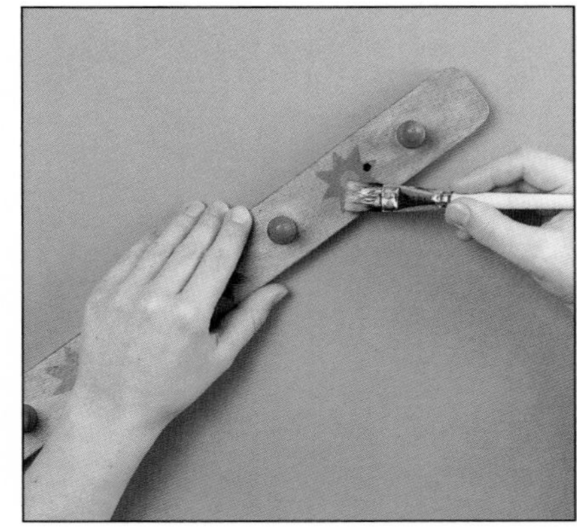

2 Let all paint dry completely. Using flat brush, apply 1 coat of clear sealer to all surfaces, including each peg.

Crafter's Secrets

To prevent paint from seeping underneath stencil, apply a coat of spray adhesive to the back of the stencil and let it dry. Place tacky stencil onto wood, pressing to adhere all edges of cutout area of stencil firmly against wood.

Try This!

Decorate other wooden pieces with Nordic motifs to make matching accessories. Inexpensive unfinished frames or containers can sport similar or complementary motifs and colors. Make straight lines by painting along the edges of masking tape to form framed borders. Then paint or stencil small shapes between the border lines.

Stenciling a Wall Border

Add a colorful focal point to a solid-colored wall or around an entire room by stenciling a delightful Pennsylvania Dutch–style flowered border.

For a horizontal border, especially one that spans several walls, prepare each painted wall by applying painter's masking tape to mark a straight baseline to position the stencils against. Painter's tape can be removed easily without pulling paint from the wall.

Make the stencils from clear stencil plastic or Mylar, so you can easily line up the stencils for the repeat design. Try a few test stencils on paper before stenciling on the wall to determine the correct amount of paint and pressure to use on the brush. Stencil one paint color at a time, letting the paint dry completely before moving on to the next motif and color.

Placing the stenciled border at eye level or just above chair height can add a cozier feel to a room. Choose colors and a style for the border that will complement the room; use sharp contrasts for a bold look or subtle shadings for a more discreet accent.

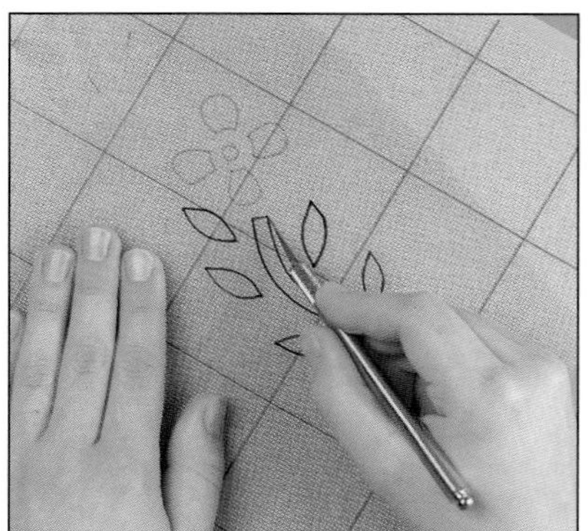

1 Using a fine-line permanent marker, trace entire border motif from Group 12, Card 10 onto each of 2 plastic stencil sheets. Using craft knife, cut out flower shapes on 1 sheet and stalk and leaves on other.

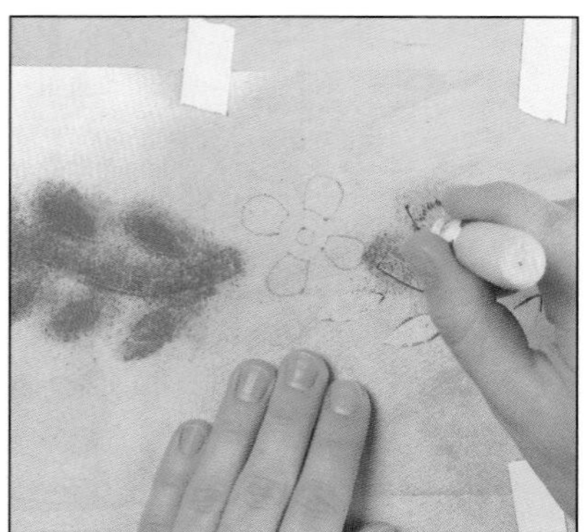

2 Mark motif placements so motifs will align and will be same size at both ends of border. Tape stalk-and-leaves stencil to wall. Apply green paint to cutout area; move stencil to next position; repeat. Let dry.

3 Tape flower stencil in position, matching outlined stalk and leaves to painted motif on wall. Use red paint to stencil flower; carefully move stencil to next position and continue, repeating across wall.

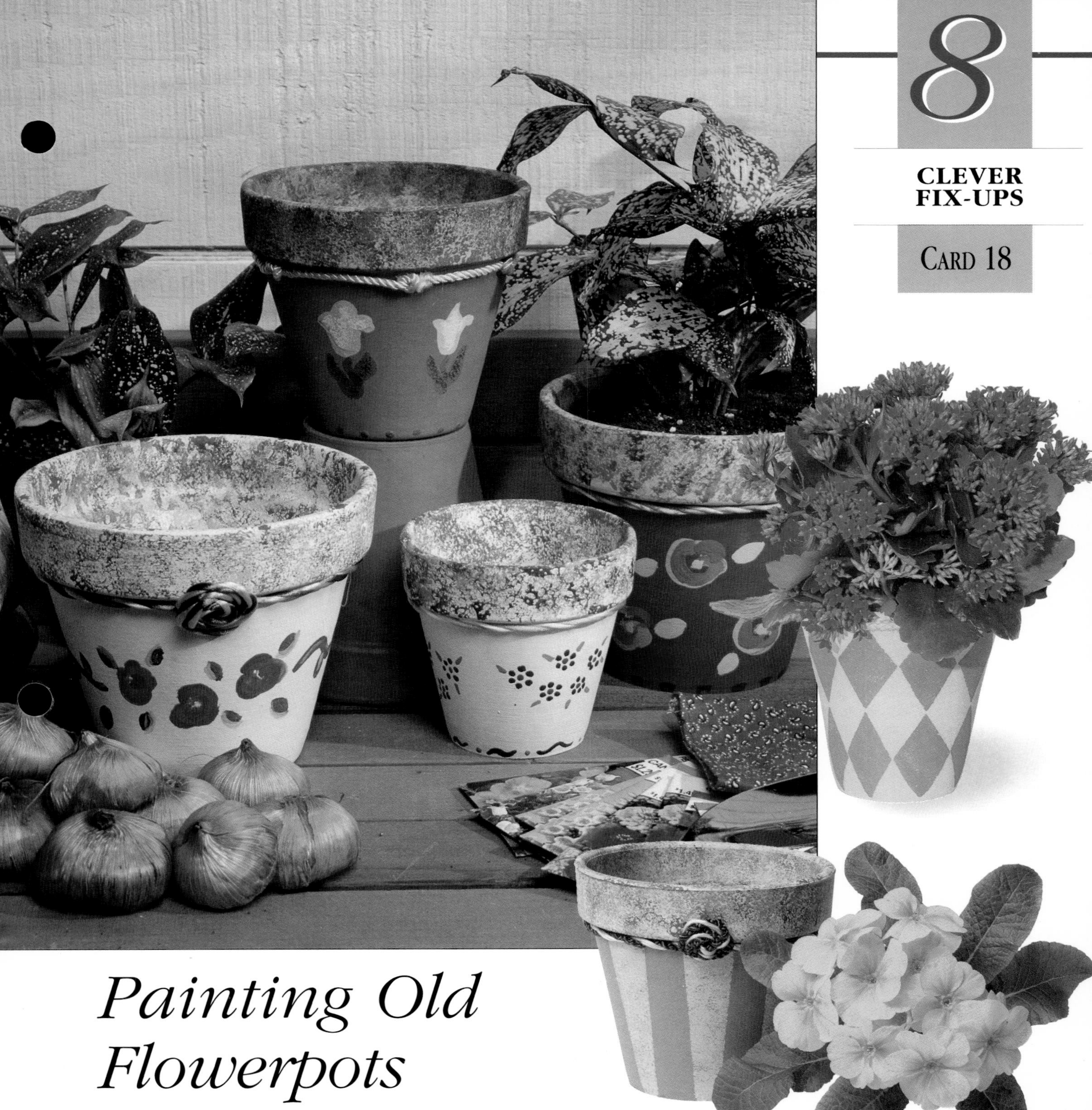

Painting Old Flowerpots

Using simple painting techniques and easy floral designs, you can turn used flowerpots into a gallery of multipurpose eye-catching containers to enliven your patio or windowsill.

Plain terra-cotta pots provide a great surface for decorative painting. A bright base coat becomes the background for hand-painted flowers and leaves and easy geometric or swash borders. The pots are sponge-painted inside and around the rim, then tied with an accent of decorative cording.

Use these cheery vessels for new cuttings, or fill them with packets of seeds and a pair of gardening gloves and present them to friends with "green thumbs."

Create a harlequin design by dipping a sponge, cut into a diamond shape, into green paint and pressing it onto a pot painted yellow. For a bright striped pot, evenly space strips of painter's tape over a blue pot and paint over exposed areas with yellow paint. Let paint dry, then remove the tape. Trim with cording.

Copy the simple designs featured on the pots or invent your own to paint on tired, old clay flowerpots of all shapes and sizes. Check your garage and neighborhood yard sales for pots to paint that are not cracked or chipped. For an added touch, trim the pot with a decorative cording, such as braid, rope, rafia, or even a string of beads.

Paint several pots of the same size to make a delightful set of planters for a shelf or windowsill, such as the trio of cactus pots shown below.

General Guidelines

Wash pots in very hot water and a small amount of bleach to remove chemical salts and to kill any bacteria. Dry thoroughly before painting.

- Spray or brush outside of pot with an acrylic sealer before painting to prevent paint from blistering as result of moisture seeping through clay when plants are watered. If you wish to varnish finished pot, varnish only outside, as some varnishes can be harmful to plants.
- Choose paint colors that coordinate well, such as pinks and greens or blues and yellows. Be sure blooms of plant blend with painted colors.

1 Spray pot inside and out with eggshell paint; let dry. Using light green paint, sponge-paint inside and outside rim; let dry. Allowing eggshell paint to show through, sponge with dark green, then dark pink; let paint dry after each color.

2 Holding pot at an angle, and using dark pink paint, paint 3 or 4 overlapping curves to form a rosette. Paint group of 3 outlined rosettes.

3 Fill rosettes with light pink. Leaving light pink dot in center, blend paints. Repeat around pot. Using dark green, paint vines with sweeping strokes; add 2 or 3 leaves with short strokes. Accent with light green. Let dry.

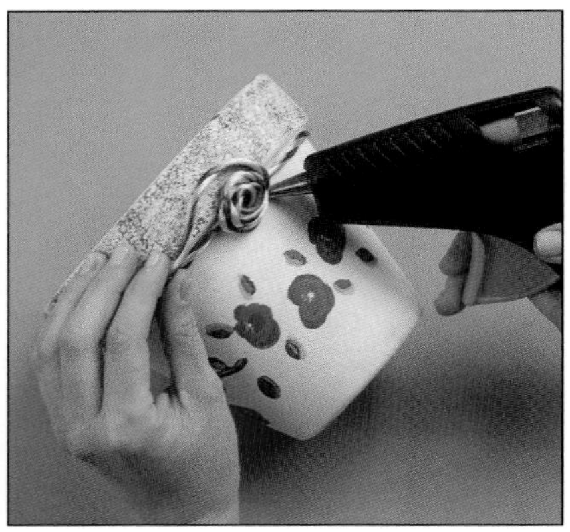

4 Twist together pink and green cording. Using glue gun, glue 1 end under rim; glue around pot. Cut cord; glue end. Cut 12" length of twisted cording. Glue 1 end to bottom of rim. Spiral cord to form rosette; glue end under rosette.

- ***8" clay or ceramic flowerpot***
- ***Acrylic paints: light & dark greens & light & dark pinks***
- ***Spray paint: eggshell white***
- ***Cellulose sponge, cut into 1" squares***
- ***2 small-bristle paint brushes***
- ***1½ yd. decorative cording: pink and green***
- ***Glue gun & glue sticks***

You can create a variety of antiqued effects with painted finishes. A coat of crackling glaze gives the green paint a worn and weathered look. Two contrasting colors, one applied over the other, produce a feathered surface.

Painting an Antique Finish on Furniture

Renew a flea-market bargain or a familiar old eyesore with the patina of an antique painted finish and re-create the country charm of aged farmhouse furniture.

Antique finishes are easily achieved by painting a piece of furniture with one color, then applying a second coat of another shade or color. When the paint has dried, a light sanding in several places will produce the old, distressed quality that is so popular in painted country furniture.

Put on an antique finish to restore the original character to an old washstand or to turn a plain-Jane table into a grande-dame accent piece that will look as if it's been in the family for generations.

To achieve the old and rough-hewn look of a painted "country" antique finish, at least two coats of different paint colors are required. Choose light and dark shades of one color or contrasting colors. Experiment on a scrap of wood or on the underside of the actual furniture piece until the desired look is reached. If the wood is unfinished, apply a clear polyurethane sealer and sand lightly when dry before applying paint.

General Antiquing Tips

Make sure your work space is well ventilated and brightly lit. Use a filter mask to avoid breathing in the wood dust.

- Repair any gouges or dents with wood filler; then sand with medium sandpaper.
- Sand all surfaces with fine sandpaper before applying base color and between coats of paint for better adhesion. Remove dust with tack cloth.
- Apply paint in long, even strokes in direction of grain. Let paint dry between coats.
- To speed up drying, hold hair dryer, set on medium heat, 8"–12" from surface.

- ***Old or unpainted wood funiture***
- ***Screwdriver***
- ***Bucket, soapy water, & sponge***
- ***Fine & rough sandpaper***
- ***Tack cloth***
- ***Latex acrylic paints: sienna for base; yellow for top color***
- ***2 paintbrushes***
- ***Turpentine & boiled linseed oil***
- ***Powdered paint pigment (black or umber)***

This old wooden washstand is in good condition and ideal for antiquing. If finish on your piece has begun to peel, scrape off peeling paint; if finish is in good condition, proceed with following steps.

1 Using screwdriver, remove handles, drawer pulls, and other fittings from furniture. Store them in an organized fashion so you will be able to replace them properly.

2 Wash furniture with a damp sponge and warm soapy water to remove any surface dirt. Sand uneven patches with rough sandpaper, then sand entire surface to prepare for base coat of paint. Wipe off dust with tack cloth.

3 Apply a thin, even layer of sienna base color; let dry. Lightly sand along wood grain with fine sandpaper. Apply second and, if desired, third coat of sienna, letting dry and sanding between applications. Wipe off dust with tack cloth.

4 Over sanded sienna, apply top coat of yellow paint heavy enough to cover, but still allow a hint of base color to show through. Let paint dry completely.

5 With fine sandpaper, lightly sand along wood grain on front and sides where you would like more of the base color to show through. Use long strokes on large areas, such as doors and panels. Wipe off dust with tack cloth.

6 Sand edges of door frame, molding between doors, and any other areas on front that naturally would get worn. Wipe off dust with tack cloth.

7 Continue to sand any edges, moldings, and areas that would naturally wear, so paint looks worn off and furniture has an authentically distressed look. Wipe off dust with tack cloth.

Crafter's Secrets

To further the appearance of a genuine antique, simulate the look of small worm holes, which are a hallmark of old furniture. Dip a toothbrush into black or brown paint and pass your fingers over the bristles to spray flecks of paint onto the wood, giving the surface an authentic-looking effect.

8 Mix equal parts boiled linseed oil and turpentine, plus enough powdered paint pigment to create a soft glaze. Test on scrap of painted wood, adding more pigment if needed. Apply a thin layer over yellow paint to seal surface.

Try This!

Complete the makeover of your old furniture by replacing all the fittings. Select a fixture style suitable to the period or style of furniture being refinished and to the color it will be painted. Porcelain and enamel doorknobs are appropriate to a country-style piece. Brass drawer pulls and fittings are more formal and look great on dressers, chests, and tables. Install the new fixtures when paint is completely dry.

Giving Furniture a Crackled Antique Finish

If you've looked at old painted furniture, you know that the finish is frequently cracked and beginning to peel. This realistic look can be duplicated easily by applying two glazes with different drying times over the finished painted piece. An antiquing glaze adds a patina of age to the base coat of paint, while a crackling glaze causes the painted surface to appear cracked. (Both are available separately and in kits at craft stores and houseware centers.)

Apply the antiquing glaze first and let it dry until tacky; then apply the crackling glaze. You can adjust the amount of crackling by waiting a longer or shorter period between applications. The longer the first layer is allowed to dry, the less visible the crackling will be.

An unpainted cupboard is made to look as though time and use have taken their toll, causing the finish to crack. To darken cracks, rub equal parts of dark oil paint and linseed oil into surface with a soft cloth.

1 If wooden piece is unfinished, sand it smooth with fine sandpaper, wipe with a tack cloth, and brush on a coat of brown stain along grain to seal wood. If piece has a finish, lightly sand and wipe off dust.

2 Apply a base coat of desired paint color. Let it dry completely. If a second coat of same or different color is desired, lightly sand and wipe with tack cloth before applying second coat of paint. Let paint dry completely.

3 Apply thin layer of antiquing glaze; let it dry 5–6 hours or until tacky. Apply a thin layer of crackling glaze; let dry completely.

Marbling a Wooden Surface

With just a few tools you can re-create the luminous look of marble on most wooden surfaces. The technique is so simple, you can achieve great results on the first try.

Marbling is a great way to restore a traditional piece of furniture and give it an entirely new look in your home. Or, have a little fun and create a sense of the unexpected by marbleizing surfaces where real marble could never be used. Dress up a tired and worn-out tabletop, or, transform a dull window or door frame with a colorful marbleized finish.

Before you begin, visit a marble dealer to study the beautiful colors and the intricate and unique veining patterns of real marble.

To simulate the look of real marble, examine an authentic piece and notice how the veins flow and the colors radiate from beneath the surface. Use varying shades of one color, such as the terracotta and lighter peaches, and the mixing of yellow and lemon, to simulate depth and shading.

Marbles come in many different colors. Re-create simple gray and white marbling, or a more colorful design in shades of yellow, green, or pink. You can even try livening things up with an unconventional shade of your own choosing.

Marbling Guidelines

Oil paint is the best choice for marbling. Gather oil paints in desired colors for the base coat and the detailing. Materials are readily available from art supply stores.

- For marbling effect, oil paints need to be mixed with oil paint medium. Choose premixed medium, or make your own mixture of equal parts boiled linseed oil and turpentine.
- Distribute color unevenly to give surface an irregular appearance. Occasionally push lightly on sponge and sweep across surface to create drifts of flowing color.
- When painting veins, vary brush pressure and occasionally roll brush on its side.
- You can use regular sponge, but natural sponge will give a more realistic finish.
- For glossy, more durable surface, finish with clear lacquer varnish.

- ***Wooden surface***
- ***Sandpaper: coarse & fine***
- ***Moist tack cloth***
- ***Paints: oil colors in black & ivory***
- ***Prepared oil paint medium or linseed oil & turpentine***
- ***Brushes: standard, fine, & wide bristle***
- ***Natural sponge & damp cloth***
- ***Varnish***
- ***Putty & wooden putty knife***

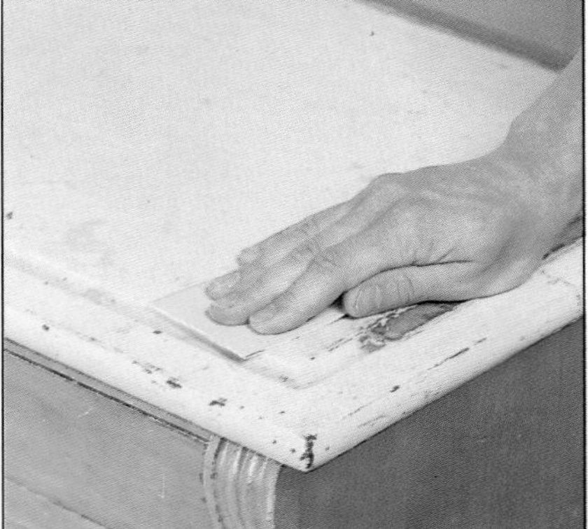

1 Sand wooden surface until smooth. Begin using coarse sandpaper and finish with fine; work in direction of wood grain. When finished, wipe over surface with moist tack cloth to remove dust.

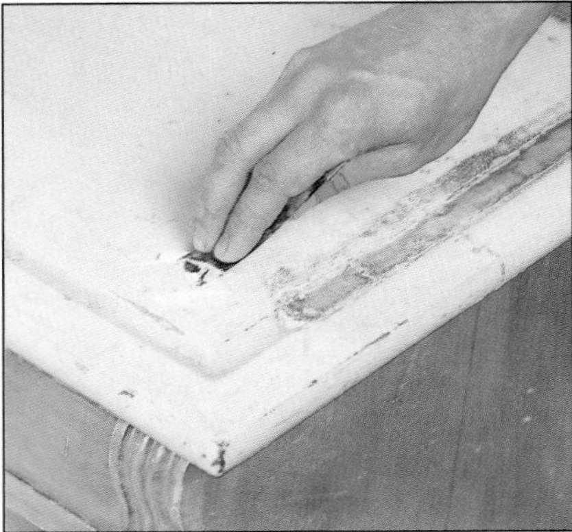

2 Using wooden putty knife, fill in any uneven surfaces and cracks with putty. Let dry. Sand surface with fine sandpaper. If necessary, repeat process. Wipe with moist tack cloth.

3 Apply thin base coat of ivory paint evenly over entire surface with standard paint brush. Let dry. Paint second coat if needed. Select paint color for marble (black is used for this project).

4 Make medium-gray glaze from black and ivory oil paints mixed with oil paint medium. Mix to an even consistency. Dip sponge into mixture and apply thin coat of glaze to surface. Work in diagonal drifts for natural finish.

5 While still wet, rub sponge back and forth diagonally across surface to distribute glaze, smoothing contours as you go. Work along surface with uneven, erratic strokes.

6 To soften and blend sponging lines, lightly stroke dry wide-bristle brush across surface in opposite direction.

7 Mix darker opaque shade of gray. Paint vein pattern with fine paintbrush, holding brush at end for ease of movement. Stagger and vary pressure on brush. Veins should flow in direction of sponging, link up, and occasionally cross.

8 Blend veining immediately by lightly rubbing across surface with slightly damp cloth. Carefully buff back and forth to make pattern appear diffused.

9 To further soften lines, stroke dry wide-bristle brush across veins. Continue treating surface in this manner until veins appear natural. Allow to dry and finish with protective coat of varnish.

Try This!

This simple wooden box was transformed by using a feather to paint the marbling veins. To duplicate this look, pass the feather over the paint and wipe off any excess. Hold the feather lightly and twist it as you are painting. Try cutting out some of the feather spines to obtain a more interesting look. Practice on some paper first until you achieve an effect that pleases you.

Crafter's Secrets

A softer brush, either badger or ox-hair, can be used to diffuse color, creating a cloudy effect like that on natural marble. These brushes can be expensive, so if this is your first attempt, use a regular soft-bristle brush which will provide similiar results. Sweep brush very lightly across painted surface to give it a mottled look. Commercially prepared kits containing paints and brushes are also available.

Marbleizing a Pedestal

It is easier to create marbled effects on flat surfaces, but after gaining confidence you will be ready to tackle more sculptural shapes. Be sure that the objects are not too narrow and that they have enough surface to create a nice image. A pedestal is a suitable shape with enough surface, while a narrow candlestick may prove to be just too small and complicated. A thin coating of green glaze, made by mixing paint with varnish, was applied to this pedestal over the contrasting red shade used in the marbling to give the surface a deep and beautiful luster that simulates the look of aged marble. To re-create the cold, hard polish of authentic marble, apply two coats of a gloss varnish finish after the marbling is completed.

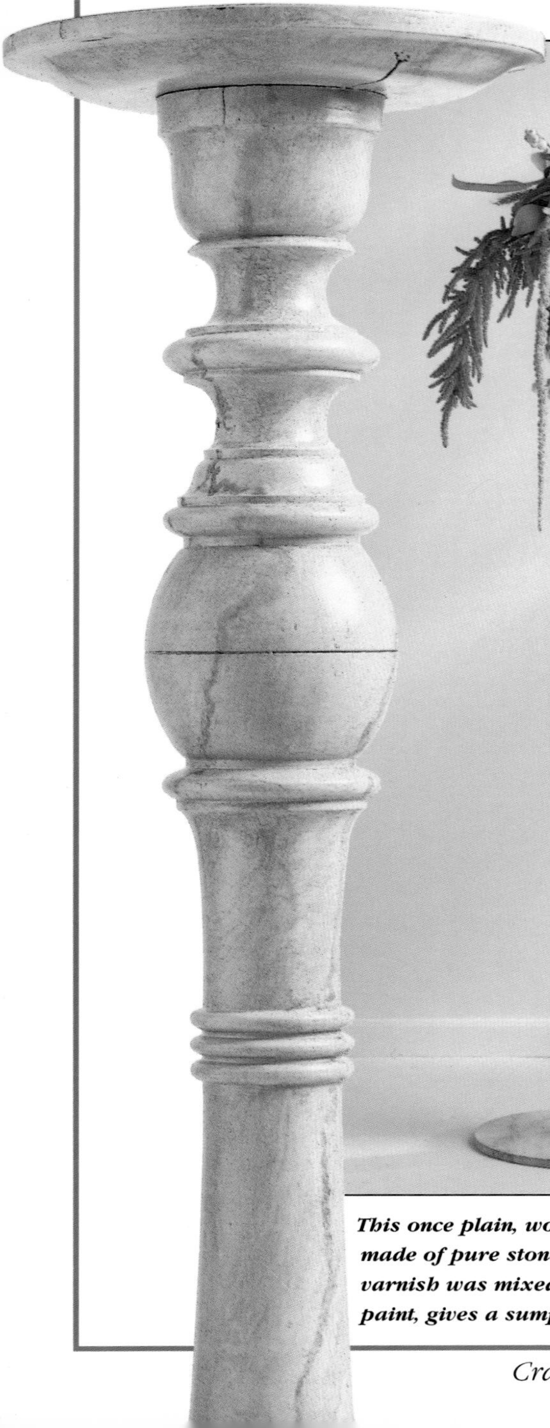

This once plain, wooden pedestal now appears to be made of pure stone. The last coating of color, where varnish was mixed with a very small amount of green paint, gives a sumptuous sheen to the surface.

1 Sand wood surface until smooth and wipe clean with tack cloth. Fill any holes or irregularities with wood filler and sand again. Apply base coat of matte white paint; let dry. Apply second coat for smooth, even surface.

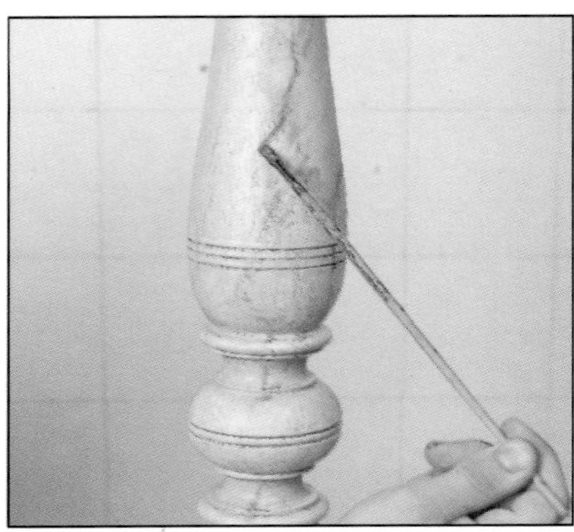

2 Marbleize following basic instructions. Use shades of red earth tones for glaze and veining. Work down the length of the pedestal. Allow paint to dry thoroughly.

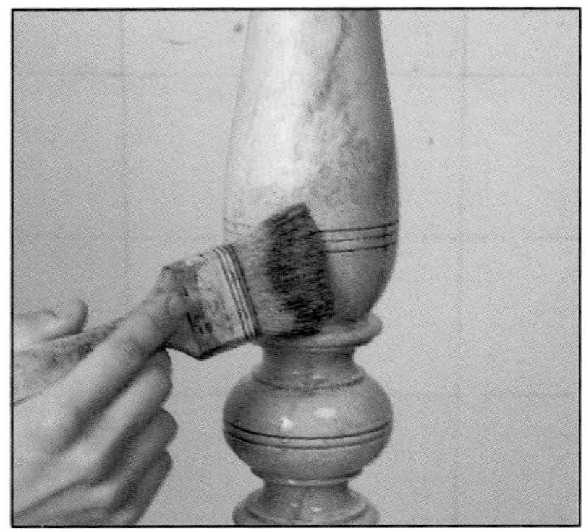

3 Mix varnish with small amount of dark green oil paint. Use turpentine sparingly in varnish to preserve undercoating. Brush thin layer over entire pedestal. Let dry. Finish with 2 coats of clear varnish.

Holidays & Celebrations

Festive ideas for special days year 'round

Creating Festive Christmas Stockings

Patterns & Templates

Santa is bound to be impressed by these opulent stockings filled with gifts galore. The fabrics are luxurious and the metallic ribbons as shiny and bright as the season.

Whether hung by the chimney with care or delivered by hand with love, these glittery Christmas stockings are certain to become favored decorations year after year. Sewing them is very simple, and most of the finishing is accomplished with fusible webs and fabric glue.

The folded ribbon points on each cuff provides the perfect stage for showing off miniature charms or tiny bells. If you are making the stockings as gifts, look for little charms that relate to the hobbies or occupations of the receivers.

Trims are what make each stocking unique. A woven metallic ribbon becomes a luxuriant cuff of points from which to dangle Christmas cherubs. Elegant golden tassels made from metallic cord add sparkle to an already glittery brocade stocking.

Use the templates from Group 12, Card 5 to create these festive holiday stockings. The templates are full size, but you may enlarge or reduce them as desired.

Patterns & Templates

Construction is easy. Simply cut out and stitch up the basic stocking shape. The fun part is choosing the fabrics and trims to be added.

Stocking Guidelines

Before shopping for fabric and trims, have some idea of what you wish the finished stocking to look like. Make a small sketch.

- Take tracing of template with you when fabric shopping. With luck, you'll find a less costly remnant. This is particularly helpful for lining fabric, which is hardly seen and need not be perfect.
- Check everywhere for trims. You might find miniature buttons or charms at a craft or notions shop. Bells might turn up in a pet shop.
- When choosing fabric and trims, consider person for whom stocking is being created. If that person has a country home, he or she would most likely welcome a home-spun look to their gift.
- If using metallic taffeta, cut it on bias to increase its impact.

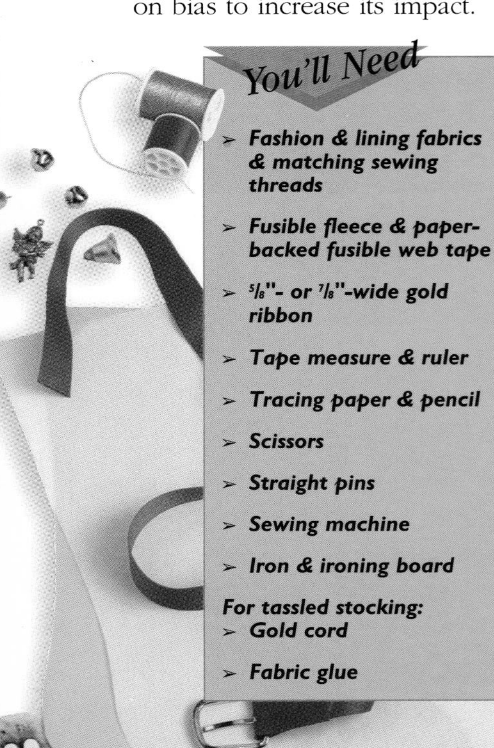

You'll Need

- ***Fashion & lining fabrics & matching sewing threads***
- ***Fusible fleece & paper-backed fusible web tape***
- ***5/8"- or 7/8"-wide gold ribbon***
- ***Tape measure & ruler***
- ***Tracing paper & pencil***
- ***Scissors***
- ***Straight pins***
- ***Sewing machine***
- ***Iron & ironing board***

For tassled stocking:

- ***Gold cord***
- ***Fabric glue***

Making a Ribbon-Point Stocking

1 Transfer stocking pattern to tracing paper and cut out. Fuse fleece to wrong side of 2 pieces of fashion fabric. With wrong sides of fused fabrics together, place pattern on bias of plaid fabric and cut out 2 stocking pieces.

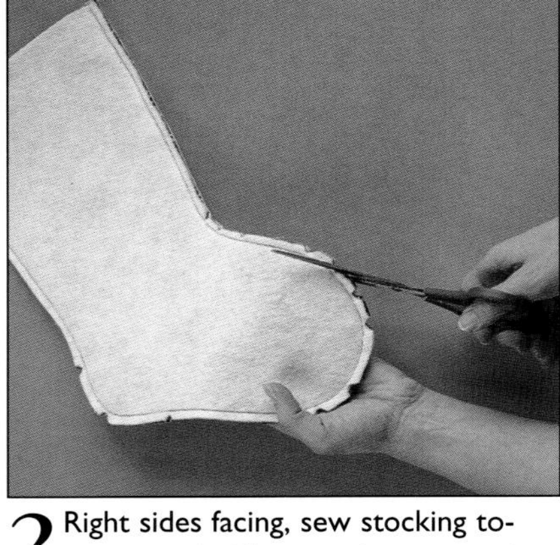

2 Right sides facing, sew stocking together with 1/4" seams; leave top of stocking open. Clip curves and turn to right side. Press under 1/4" along top edge of stocking.

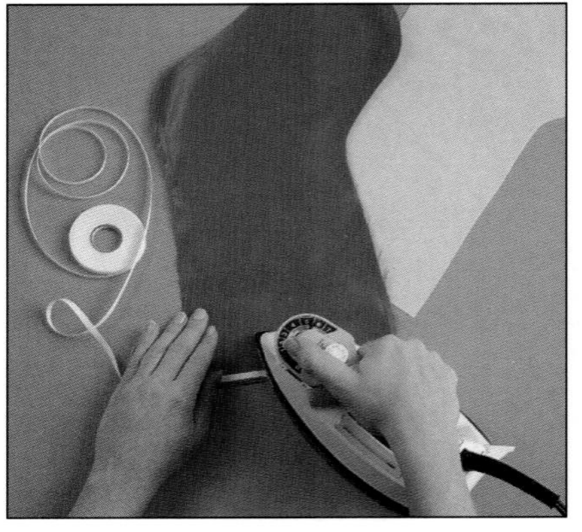

3 Use stocking pattern to cut 2 pieces from lining fabric. With right sides together, sew lining edges as in step 2. Press under 1/4" along top edge and iron strip of paper-backed web to wrong side.

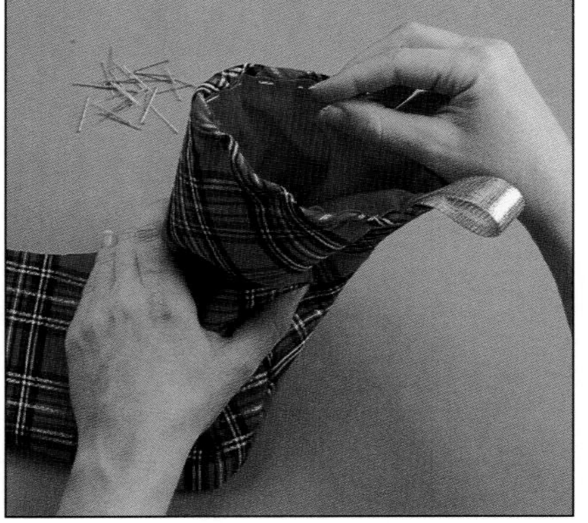

4 Remove paper from web. Cut 6" ribbon; fold in half for loop. Pin ends of loop to back seam inside stocking top. Insert lining into stocking. Match open edges and pin. Fuse edges together, catching loop ends between fabrics.

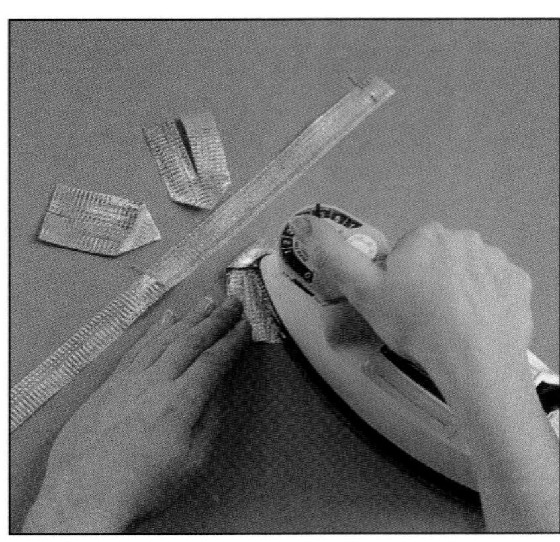

5 Cut a length of ribbon to go around stocking top, adding 1". Pin-mark center and 1/2" from 1 end. Cut a 6" piece for each point and fold in half. Form point as shown and press flat.

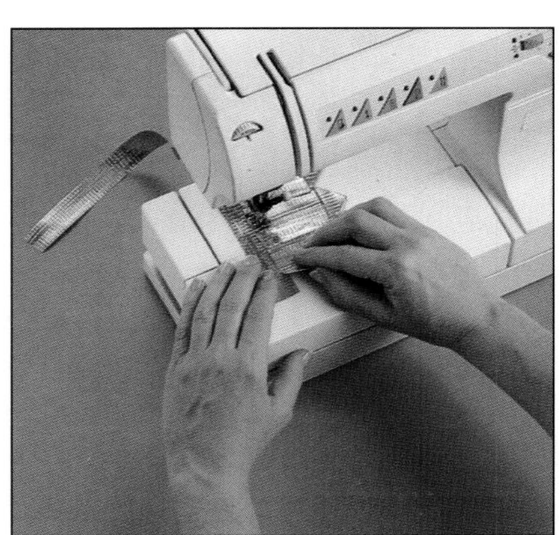

6 Pin ribbon points to wrong side of cuff ribbon, overlapping them 1/4" and fitting them between pin marks. Sew points to cuff; sew ends of cuff. Fuse cuff to stocking with web, matching seams.

Making a Tassel-Trim Stocking

1 Fuse fleece to wrong side of fabric; cut out 2 stocking pieces. Pin-mark lengths of cording "ribs" on 1 piece. Pierce holes at marks; insert and glue cord ends. Glue cords in place. Sew stockings together.

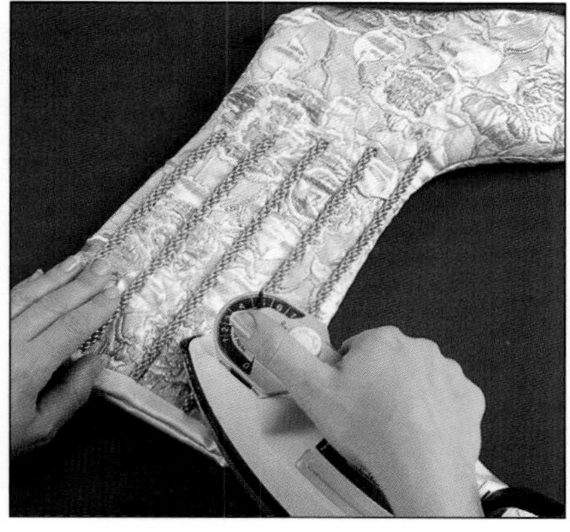

2 Turn stocking to right side. Cut 2 lining pieces, adding 1" at top edges for hem. Sew lining; press under ½" along top edge; iron web over hem. Insert lining, fold hem over to right side of stocking, and fuse.

3 Cut 5"x13" cuff strip. Glue cord along center, then 1½" away. Fold under 1 short end; fold length in half, right sides facing; stitch long edges; turn. Glue raw edges inside folded end. Glue on cuff with 6" loop at back. Make tassels; glue to ribs.

Crafter's Secrets

To make a tassel, wrap colored thread 20–40 times around a cardboard square cut to the size of the finished tassel. With a piece of thread, tie together wrapped loops at 1 end of cardboard square. Cut loops at other end and remove cardboard. Wrap a second piece of thread several times about ¼" below tied end. Tie ends of thread together into a knot. Trim end of tassel to even threads.

Try This!

Using the templates from Group 12, Card 5, compose a winter scene on a checkered stocking. Cut out the main pieces, then stitch the felt appliqués in place. Stuff the snowman with cotton or fiberfill before attaching, if desired. Add a variety of holiday charms to decorate the tree and a two-wheeler or other miniature toy to decorate the toe of the stocking. Finish the cuff with rustic buttons. This design can also be used to personalize a purchased stocking.

No-Sew Stockings for Pets

The four-legged members of the family should have their share of the holiday cheer, especially when it's so easy to create a stocking for stuffing with gifts just for them.

Using templates from Group 12, Card 5, make the stocking from felt, decorate with stenciled paw prints, and trim with appropriate motifs. To personalize the stocking, fuse a strip of contrasting felt in place along the top and with a fabric pen or marker, write the pet's name.

If you decide to trim a doggie stocking with real dog biscuits, be sure to remove them before storing the stocking for the following year.

To attach each ribbon for holding a biscuit, cut two parallel slits in the stocking and thread an 8"-long ribbon through them. Place a biscuit in the center and tie a bow around it.

Kitties leave their prints while playing with balls of yarn. Puppies leave their prints as they whisk away dog-bone yummies. Treat your cat or dog with stocking stuffers such as toys, catnip, a new collar, food treats, and rawhide bones. What a simple way to please the puss or the pup!

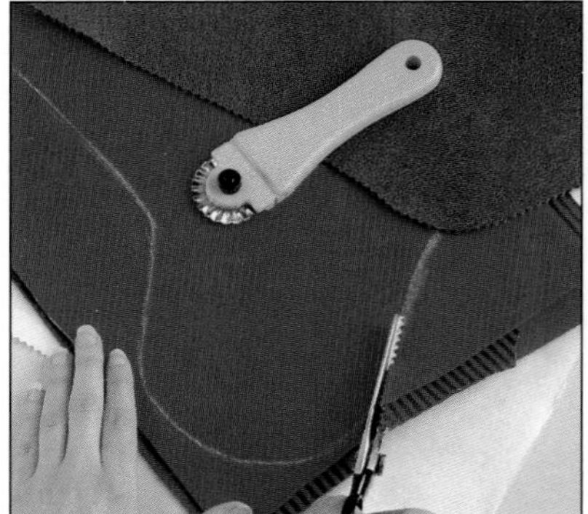

1 Fuse lining to wrong side of 2 felt pieces using paper-backed web. Layer 2 fused pieces together with linings facing together. Outline stocking pattern on felt and cut out with pinking shears or pinking rotary cutter.

2 Transfer paw-print to plastic stencil and cut out. Working from 2" below top edge to end of stocking toe, stencil paw prints on stocking front using black acrylic paint. Allow paint to dry completely.

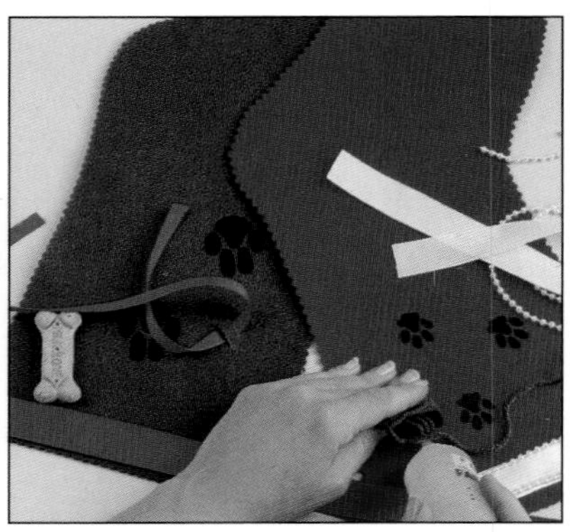

3 Glue on yarn-wrapped felt circles or cut slits for ribbons. Glue 5/8"x6" loop inside top; glue stocking. Measure ribbon to go around top twice; slip on buckle. Glue ribbon around top and pearls along edges. Glue "collar" in place.

9

HOLIDAYS & CELEBRATIONS

CARD 3

Creating an Evergreen Christmas Wreath

Many of us like to start the Christmas season as soon as December arrives. What better way to greet the holiday than with a fresh, fragrant evergreen wreath?

Instead of purchasing a commercial wreath, try making one yourself. They're quick and easy to create and can be made exactly as you desire. Bring in branches of boxwood from the garden, or buy some from a nursery, and wire them to a straw wreath form. Add pinecones or other holiday trims and affix a festive bow. Hang the finished wreath on your front door to welcome your guests. For a traditional colonial look, try hanging small matching wreaths on each of your front windows.

There are as many ways to decorate a Christmas wreath as there are ways to celebrate. Tie on colorful ribbons, or attach pinecones, nuts, cinnamon sticks, and artificial berries—whatever decorations say "Season's Greetings" to you.

If you don't have boxwood evergreens growing in your garden, you can easily find them in most nurseries or flower shops. You can also use other kinds of evergreens, such as various pines and blue spruce. Your florist may also carry straw wreath bases and floral wire on spools.

General Guidelines
Before starting, divide the boxwood into small, even bunches.

- As you start assembling your wreath, be sure to place evergreen bunches close together, so they overlap to make wreath full and uniform.
- Keep back of form free of greens so wreath hangs flat.

Wreath Decorations
Decorate your wreath to reflect your individual Christmas theme.

- Use pinecones, glass balls, bells, and artificial decorations, such as fruits, berries, and little feathered birds.
- Add a cheerful red velvet or satin bow to turn your wreath into a classic beauty.
- Consider using less traditionally colored ribbons, such as bold plaids or shiny metallics.

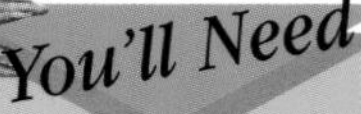

- ***Straw wreath form***
- ***Evergreen boughs: boxwood, pine, blue spruce, juniper***
- ***Spooled floral wire in green & copper***
- ***3 yds. 2½"-wide ribbon (weather-proofed for outdoor use)***
- ***Garden clippers***
- ***Decorations: pinecones, natural & artificial trims***

Making a Boxwood Wreath

1 Fasten end of green spooled wire to wreath form by winding it around form a few times. Gather several stems of boxwood, place on outer edge of wreath, and wrap wire around stems to secure in place.

2 Gather a second group of stems. Working toward inner edge of wreath form, lap second group over first and secure ends by wrapping wire several times around form.

3 Cover inner edge of form with a few boxwood bunches and secure in same way. Do not cover back of wreath form unless it will hang in a place where its back can be seen, such as on a glass door.

4 Continue covering whole form in this manner. Work each row of boxwood stems from outside to inside, always lapping new row over previous one so wreath will be lush and full.

5 When wreath is nearly completed, pull first row of greens up and out of the way, while forcing final row of stems under it to hide wire. Turn wreath face down and cut wire, leaving a long tail.

6 Force end of wire under several strands of wound wire on back to form a loop; twist loop at base to form a small hanger. Make sure hanger will support wreath and not show when hung.

For further information: Crafting & Decorating Made Simple™
International Masters Publishers, 444 Liberty Ave., Pittsburgh, PA 15222-1207 1-800-527-5576

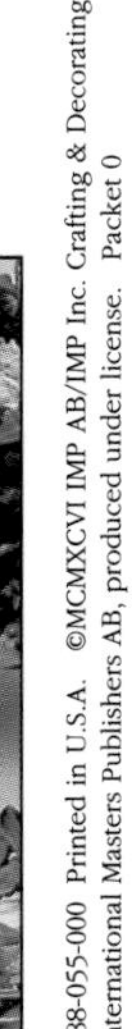

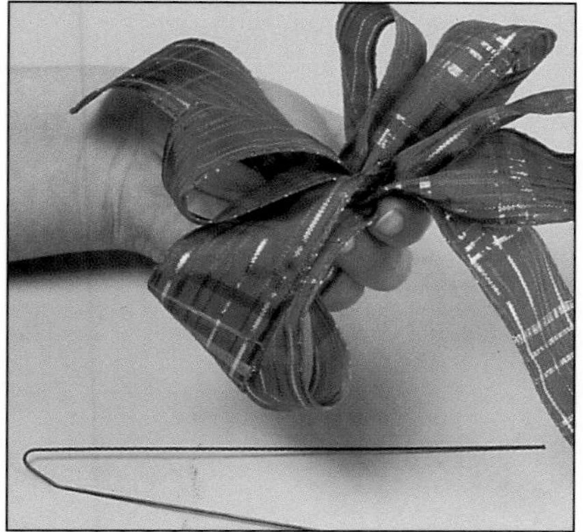

7 Leaving a 10" tail, take ribbon in your hand and make 8"-long loops by running ribbon back and forth, pinching center of loops as you go. Continue until all ribbon is looped.

8 Fasten ribbon loops by wrapping a length of wire at center. Twist wire ends together and push through form at desired bow position. Bend ends of wire against back to secure. Diagonally trim ribbon ends.

Crafter's Secrets

Instead of putting a bow at the top of the wreath, place the bow at the bottom and hang the wreath from a long loop of ribbon. Select a red, green, or metallic ribbon, about 2½"–3" wide. Cut an appropriate length, and loop it around the wreath. Fold in the ends of the ribbon and glue them together. Attach the top of the ribbon to a nail or hook. This treatment is especially effective when hung centered in a window.

Decorating with Pinecones

1 Wind copper spooled wire around each pinecone, beginning at base and winding upward, tucking wire into cone so wire barely shows. Bring wire back to base in same way; twist both ends together.

2 Space pinecones evenly around wreath, placing some in middle and some along edges. Push twisted wire ends through form and bend ends back to secure.

Try This!

By combining different greens, such as pine, blue spruce, and juniper, you can create a wreath with a completely different look. Add a variety of seasonal decorations and you will have a uniquely personal wreath that is guaranteed to be an eye-catcher. Small artificial birds and berries and other amusing decorations can be found in craft stores or flower shops.

Making a Wreath Centerpiece

A very beautiful Advent centerpiece with candles can be made by using the basic wreath instructions, but instead of hanging the wreath, it is placed on a table and decorated with nuts, artificial berries, dried orange and lemon slices, and gold bows. Space candle picks evenly around the wreath and insert picks into the base to hold the candles. You can find candle picks in craft and flower shops.

To make the dried orange and lemon slices for the candle bases, cut fruits into ⅛"–¼"-thick slices and dry them on newspaper. For a quicker method, try drying them in the oven: Arrange the slices on a cake rack and place on top of oven rack. Set the oven temperature to warm, and leave in oven for six to eight hours with the door ajar. Center a dried slice on top of each candle pick and push a candle through it. For safety, use dripless candles and don't allow them to burn down too close to the citrus slices. Spray the wreath with water periodically to keep it from drying out.

The evergreen wreath becomes a charming Advent centerpiece with dried citrus fruits and other beautiful decorations. Light one candle the first Sunday in Advent, two the second, and so on, to count down to Christmas.

1 Using mixed evergreens, make a wreath following basic instructions. Decorate with artificial berries and various types of nuts, attaching them in place with spooled wire or hot glue.

2 Evenly space 4 spiked candle picks around wreath and push them into wreath base. Check to see that they are level and securely attached.

3 Make small bows from gold ribbon and wire and push wire ends into wreath to secure. Center dried citrus slices on candle picks and push candles through slices.

For further information: Crafting & Decorating Made Simple™
International Masters Publishers, 444 Liberty Ave., Pittsburgh, PA 15222-1207 1-800-527-5576

Making Old-Time Tree Ornaments

Gather the family together on a frosty December afternoon to make old-fashioned tree decorations from cake frosting and Victorian motifs cut from old Christmas cards, magazines, and catalogs.

When evergreen trees were first brought indoors as part of the Christmas celebration, trims were homemade. Family members strung popped corn and cranberries, made cookies and candies, and cut out paper ornaments.

A favorite ornament was made by mounting a cutout figure and framing it with simple, piped confectioner's icing. Everyone will enjoy re-creating this time-honored ornament and adding a holiday sparkle to traditional glass balls.

A glitter-paint stripe piped onto the frosting and a gold cord make these traditional cutout ornaments shimmer. Use the same gold or silver glitter paint to turn plain glass balls into holiday treasures. The tree will glow with old-fashioned charm!

Gathering the materials for these ornaments is fun for the whole family. Cut out designs from cards saved from previous holidays or buy antique-looking cards and pictures at card shops and craft and hobby stores. Papers made for découpage are also a good source of designs.

Cover the back of the ornament with a piece of metallic paper to hide the ends of the hanging cord. It will add an attractive homemade touch to the tree.

Icing Guidelines

Prepare the icing by mixing together 1 egg white, $1\frac{1}{3}$ c. confectioners' sugar, and $\frac{1}{8}$ t. cream of tartar until thick and creamy.

- Use a sturdy plastic bag, such as a small, heavy freezer bag, to hold icing. If you have access to an icing tube and points, you might find it easier to use them rather than a plastic bag.
- Practice piping on scraps of plain cardboard until you feel comfortable with the technique.
- Before applying glitter over icing, be sure both icing and sealer are thoroughly dry or glitter will not adhere properly.

- ***Printed holiday pictures***
- ***Plain glass ball ornaments***
- ***Cardboard & metallic paper***
- ***Gold cord***
- ***Gold or silver glitter paint (tube)***
- ***Clear acrylic spray sealer***
- ***Pencil***
- ***White craft glue & glue stick***
- ***Scissors & pin***
- ***Prepared icing***
- ***Sealable plastic freezer bag***

Making Ornaments with Icing Edges

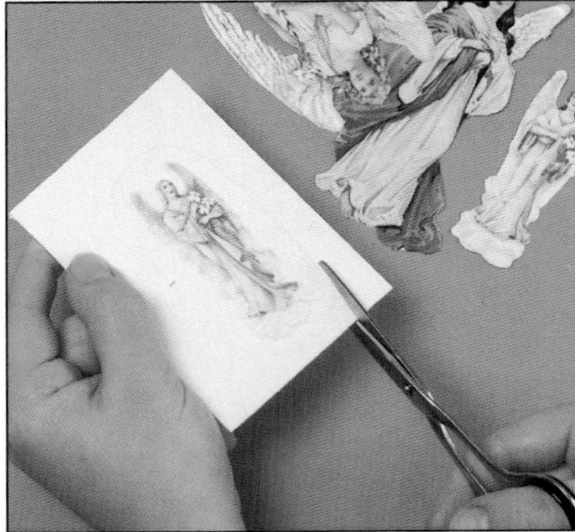

1 Apply glue stick to back of print picture, then paste figure onto piece of cardboard. Trim cardboard into rounded shape, leaving $\frac{1}{2}$" margin around edges.

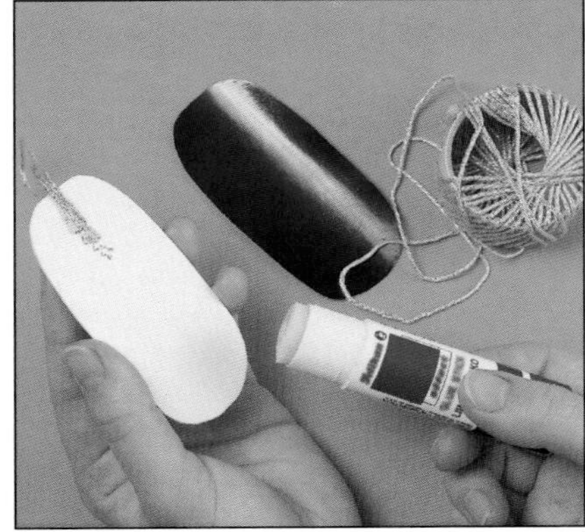

2 Fold a 7" length of gold cord in half. Using craft glue, glue cut ends of cord to back of cardboard to form hanger. Let dry. Use cardboard shape as a pattern to cut out piece of metallic paper. Attach it to back of ornament using glue stick.

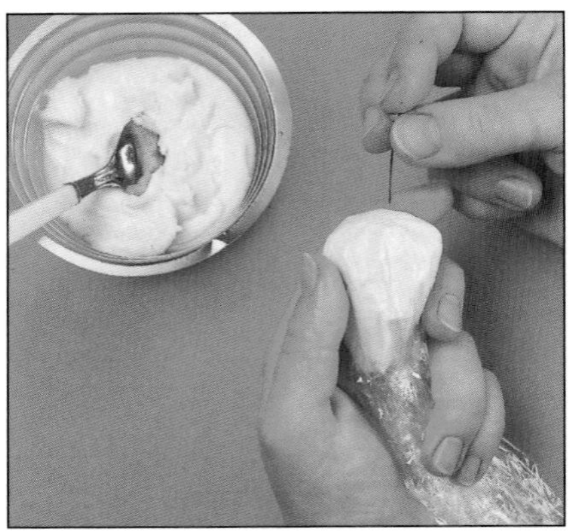

3 Place several spoonfuls of icing into corner of plastic bag. Seal bag, forcing out as much air as possible. Use pin to pierce hole in filled corner of bag to extrude icing.

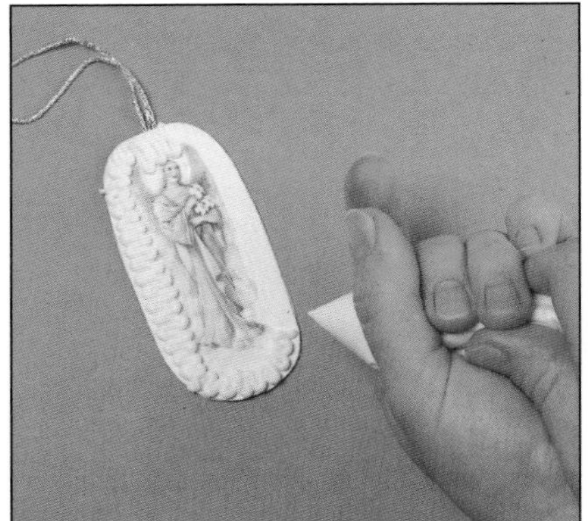

4 Practice on scrap cardboard first to perfect technique of getting smooth, even flow of icing. Squeeze bag to apply bead of icing along edges of cardboard. Let icing dry completely (about 1 hour).

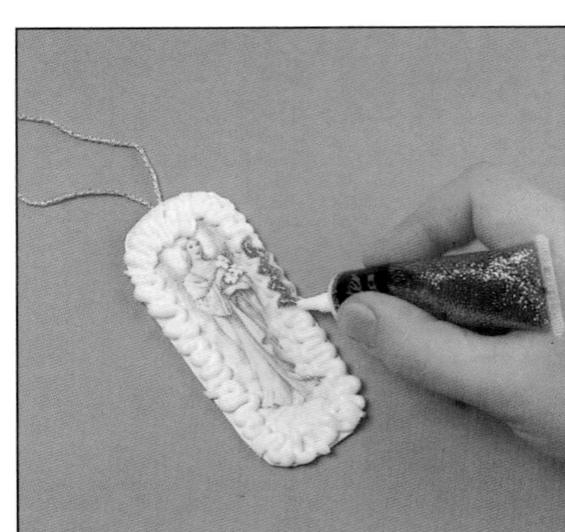

5 Apply thin coat of clear spray sealer over icing and front surface of ornament. Let dry. Finish with thin bead of glitter paint along center of icing edging. Let dry completely.

Decorating Ball Ornaments

Using glitter paint, decorate each ornament freehand with a variety of designs. Work design carefully around ornament. Hang to dry on dowel or hanger, making sure ornaments don't touch.

Painting offers a second option for making a Halloween pumpkin. Or try carving other festive designs, such as a celestial motif of stars and moons. If you are planning a party, carve your name or house number into the pumpkin for a welcoming sign.

Making Glowing Jack-o'-lanterns

Patterns & Templates

Welcome all the little critters, ghosts, and witches who are out trick-or-treating on Halloween with the eerie light cast by spooky faces of hand-carved jack-o'-lanterns.

A few days before the big event, have a pumpkin-carving session to create playfully frightening faces to guide young goblins on their way. Let the kids choose their own pumpkins, then create the faces by mixing the various features from Group 12, Card 4 and tracing the resulting face onto paper. Rely on the shape of the pumpkin to plan a good composition. The kids will enjoy pricking the designs onto the pumpkins, but be sure to supervise the handling of the knives or have an adult cut out the faces.

Use the templates from Group 12, Card 4 to transfer faces to pumpkins for carving. Enlarge or reduce the templates to fit the pumpkin.

Everyone looks forward to decorating Halloween jack-o'-lanterns. To make pumpkin carving easier, use the pricking method described to transfer the design to the skin of the pumpkin. The pricks are easy to see and create a guide for the knife so it doesn't slip and make an unwanted slash. When painting a face on a pumpkin, use waterproof paint in case of rain.

Lighting Guidelines

An electric light bulb is safer to use than a candle and will not char or shrink the pumpkin.

- Make a hole for light in bottom of pumpkin, so top does not shrink from heat of light and fall into its hollow center.
- Tape a short length of dowel or other narrow piece of wood to light socket, so it can be jabbed into base of pumpkin for more stability.
- Afix light socket to cutout base, then set carved portion of pumpkin over it.
- If raining, do not use electrically lit pumpkin outdoors.

You'll Need

- Pumpkin
- #3H pencil
- Tracing paper
- Masking tape

For carved pumpkin:

- Serrated knife
- Spoon
- Purchased light-bulb & socket

For painted pumpkin:

- Graphite paper
- Glossy acrylic paints
- Pointed paintbrush

Carving a Pumpkin

1 Pencil circle at center bottom of clean pumpkin. Use serrated knife to carefully cut out marked circle for insertion of light. Gently remove circle base from pumpkin and set it aside.

2 Clean out inside of pumpkin with spoon, removing seeds, fibers, and any excess pulp. (Rather than discarding seeds, wash and roast them for a tasty snack.)

3 Trace desired face parts from Group 12, Card 4 onto paper and tape it onto pumpkin, pleating edges to lay smooth. Use point of pencil to poke holes ⅛" apart along outlines. Remove paper.

4 Use knife to score pumpkin along pencil-pricked outlines. Cut along lines again, slicing through. Remove cutouts. Tape dowel to base of light socket, insert it into base, and set pumpkin over it.

Painting a Pumpkin

1 Trace design onto tracing paper. Tape piece of graphite paper onto cleaned-out pumpkin. Tape traced design over graphite paper. Pencil along design lines, pressing firmly to transfer design.

2 Using glossy acrylic craft paints and pointed brush, paint larger areas first. Follow with smaller areas of contrast color. Let each coat dry completely before proceeding. Paint fine detail lines last.

Mixing flowers of bold contrasting colors creates visual excitement, as can be seen in this striking arrangement of red-orange Gerbera daisies, lilies, and yarrow mixed with bright purple anemones and punctuated with spiky red gladioli.

Making a Bouquet for a Celebration

Meant for dramatic effect at a special gathering, these bold, sophisticated bouquet-style arrangements are deceptively easy to make.

A variety of large, showy blossoms on long, sturdy stems form a magnificent display for celebratory events. The flower stems are arranged in a tight bunch, free of their bottom leaves, and placed in a narrow-necked vase, which holds them securely without floral foam.

A floor vase of all white flowers, including lilies, snapdragons, and roses, contrasted against bright green foliage, would make an elegant impression at a wedding or anniversary dinner. Or combine only pastel-colored flowers for a christening or confirmation.

Plan your bouquet in advance. Select the colors you want to feature in the arrangement and then decide on the flowers and the greens to go with them. The size of the container should be in scale with the size of the bouquet. Use a deep vase with a narrow neck to hold the stems tightly.

Preparing Bouquet Materials

Use flowers just reaching their peak of bloom to lengthen the life of the arrangement.

- Select flowers with long, sturdy stems for stability. Flowers with large round heads, such as peonies and hydrangeas, add volume to a bouquet. Lilies and other conical-shaped flowers are good for center of arrangement. Tall flowers, like gladiolas, add height.
- Strip leaves from bottom half of flower stems to make flowers bunch more tightly. Recut stems about 1" from ends.
- Fill bottom of container with layer of floral marbles or smooth stones to add weight.

You'll Need

- ***Raffia***
- ***Sharp knife***
- ***Pruning shears or scissors***
- ***Vase***

For White Bouquet:

- ***White lilies, snapdragons, roses, viburnum, & apple blossom sprays; asparagus & maiden hair ferns***

For Colorful Bouquet:

- ***Gladioli, lilies, Gerbera daisies, anemones, yarrow; eucalyptus & tall grasses***

Making a White Bouquet

1 Hold 1 snapdragon stem just beneath its leaves. Add 2 more stems to set height of bouquet, 1 in front and 1 in back of center stem; hold all stems at leaf base, where bouquet will be tied.

2 Add 4 roses, placing them in front, behind, and alongside snapdragons, about 1" below tallest blossom; keep all flower heads pointing outward to form circular-shaped cluster.

3 Continue by adding apple blossom sprays around outside of cluster to height of snapdragons, maintaining firm hold on stems already gathered; turn bouquet as flowers are added to keep symmetrical shape.

4 Add lilies around bouquet, heads facing outward, nestling them amid other flowers and at about same height as lowest snapdragon blossom. Tie raffia around gathered stems to hold them together as bouquet gets larger.

5 Add rings of more roses, apple blossom sprays, lilies, and viburnum, nestling flower heads between leaves on stems for a more natural look. Continue until desired size of bouquet is reached.

6 Surround last ring of flowers with stems of cascading ferns to complete bouquet. Wrap bouquet stems securely several times with raffia; knot. Trim stems even before placing in vase.

Making a Colorful Bouquet

1 Space 3 red gladiola stems evenly around center stem of eucalyptus and about 2" above. Face flower heads outward and hold stems just below lowest branch of eucalyptus.

2 Add evenly spaced rings of purple anemones and yarrow, turning bouquet to maintain symmetrical shape. Fill spaces with tall grasses to form large, compact cluster.

3 Add Gerbera daisies and lilies alternately around outside of cluster until bouquet is desired size. Wrap bouquet stems securely several times with raffia; knot. Trim stems even before placing in vase.

Crafter's Secrets

Include fragrant blossoms in your bouquet to add the sensuous perfume of flowers to the arrangement. Freesias, carnations, and sweet-smelling roses, all available in a variety of colors, look lovely in bouquets. Other scented flowers to consider are lilacs, honeysuckle, jasmine, and sweet peas.

Try This!

Create an eye-catching, exotic bouquet by mixing brilliantly colored tropical flowers and vibrant, unusually shaped leaves with common lilies. Begin with a cluster of several tall, large leaves in the center. Surround the center leaves with exotic red torch ginger flowers and pink lilies. Add spirea sprays, bear grass, eucalyptus stems, and ligularia leaves beneath the base of flower heads to finish the bouquet and cover the rim of the container.

Arranging a Bouquet of Sunflowers

Singularly dramatic yellow sunflowers become the focal point of this large-scale bouquet arrangement. Mixing the more fragile-looking blue larkspur and thin spirea stems with the sunflowers creates a study in contrasting colors and sizes. The large splashes of warm yellow on thick stems balance the small accents of cool blue on wispy stems, and all are pulled together by the solid base of dark green leaves at the container rim. By using larger blossoms for the main flowers, fewer individual stems are needed to achieve the finished size.

You can also use any two types of flowers of contrasting colors, shapes, and sizes. For example, mix full-blossomed peonies and feathery astilbes, spiky snapdragons and conical lilies, or velvety roses and airy Queen Anne's lace. Use as many stems as the mouth of the container can hold for the lushest bouquet.

Spectacular sunflowers make a very striking arrangement for your home during the summer months. Be sure to use a large or tall container that works with the scale of the sunflowers.

1 Holding 3 larkspur stems near bottom, form a fanlike cluster. Add small stems of leaves around base of larkspurs to support the delicate stems and to cushion next addition of flowers.

2 Add 3 sunflowers, evenly spaced around larkspur cluster and facing outward, about 2" or 3" below tops of larkspurs.

3 Add stems of spirea or long, thin sprays of other small-headed flowers. Continue adding stems of larkspur, leaves, and sunflowers until bouquet reaches desired size, turning bouquet to maintain symmetrical shape.

9

HOLIDAYS & CELEBRATIONS

CARD 13

Painting Easter-Egg Containers

Paint and elegant ribbon trims transform ordinary plastic Easter-egg halves into sophisticated holiday gift containers.

Receiving decorated Easter eggs filled with treats is not reserved only for children; adults will covet these tastefully painted eggs too. Finished with a decorative trim of fine ribbon, the eggs are so artful, no one would ever suspect they weren't store-bought.

They are so easy to make, you'll be tempted to make a basketful for your holiday table or to leave one at each place setting. Fill them with mints or hard candies, or use them as little packages for personal Easter presents.

Natural trims, such as straw, dried grasses, and feathers, can be glued onto an already artfully colored egg, or the egg can be presented with just its elegantly painted shell.

These unusual Easter eggs begin with plastic-egg containers from a craft, hobby, or party shop; acrylic paint; and ribbon for the trim. Their uncommon appearance is achieved with a simple sponge-painting technique.

Painting Guidelines

To get the natural-looking dappled effect, a second color is dabbed on over the base color with a sponge, then spattered with gold paint to make the speckles.

- Select any color for base coat, then sponge-dab a second color that is of a similar hue, but is either darker or lighter than first color.
- Mix colors to get exact shades desired. Adding a small amount of another color to base color will produce a new shade that will complement base coat perfectly.
- Test color combinations on scrap paper before committing paint to egg.
- Experiment with colors other than gold for speckled effect. Black, white, brown, and yellow are natural choices, but any color that shows over first two applied colors will work.

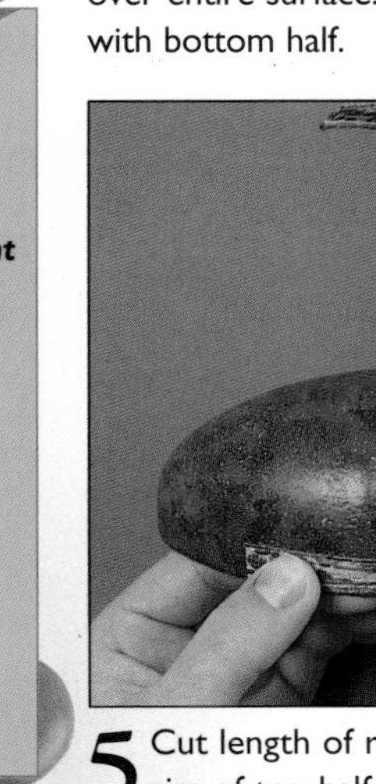

1 Separate plastic egg into its 2 halves. Use paintbrush to apply thin coat of base color to cover entire outside surface of both egg halves. Let paint dry completely.

2 Brush thin coat of gold paint over entire inside surface of both egg halves. Apply gold paint sparingly to keep it from running and collecting in a puddle at bottom of egg halves.

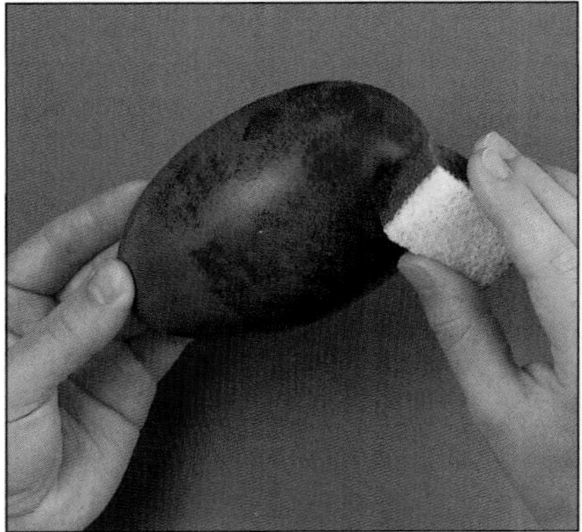

3 Cut a 1"x2" piece from household sponge. Dip into second color and dab sponge against outside surface of top half of egg, creating a marblized effect over entire surface. Let paint dry. Repeat with bottom half.

4 Dip toothbrush bristles into gold paint. Holding toothbrush over outside surface of top half of egg, slide fingertip across bristles to spatter small flecks of gold paint uniformly over entire surface. Let paint dry. Repeat with bottom half.

5 Cut length of ribbon to fit around rim of top half of egg, plus ¼". Glue ribbon to outside of rim, beginning and ending at long side edge of egg half and overlapping ends slightly.

6 Fill bottom half of egg with candy or small gift. Avoid overfilling to protect contents when halves are put back together. If desired, place small amount of excelsior or shredded tissue paper in bottom for cushioning before filling.

9

HOLIDAYS & CELEBRATIONS

CARD 14

Covering Christmas Balls with Cord

Bring a new twist to your holiday decorating with festive cord-wrapped ornamental balls that radiate cheer.

These handsome ornaments are extremely quick, easy, and affordable to make. Simply glue an attractive cord around a foam ball, attach glittering decorations, and top with a bow. You can make casually elegant ornaments with satin cord, shiny bows, and gold-headed pins, as shown, or consider making countrified balls dressed in holiday-plaid ribbon and buttons.

Make a selection of pretty balls in one or more colors to hang on your tree or to decorate windows and doors. Make extra to bring as gifts to your next Christmas party.

Change the cord and decorations to give the ball a totally different look. For traditional simplicity, use twisted red and green twine, spray with a semigloss sealer to add a bit of shine, and top with a red satin bow. For a sparkly natural look, wrap balls in unbleached jute, glue on metallic gold stars, and finish with a gold ribbon bow.

Polystyrene balls are the base around which the decorative cords are wrapped. They are available in a variety of sizes; the project featured uses 2½"-diameter balls. Foam balls and an array of decorative cords and trims can be found in art and craft supply stores. Cord is also often available where sewing notions are sold.

Decorating Guidelines

Use decorative cord that is between ⅛" and ¼" thick. Each 2½"-diameter ball requires about five yards of cord.

- Use clear-drying craft glue.
- When wrapping cord around ball, be sure not to leave any gaps between rounds. Pay extra attention after passing midsection, when sides begin to slope again.
- While wrapping, periodically insert straight pins to keep cord in place until glue has dried. When finished, replace straight pins with decorative gold-headed ones.
- Distribute decorative pins evenly across ball's surface.
- Make hanger from gold thread or string. Tie bow of matching colored ribbon and pin bow and hanger to top of ball.

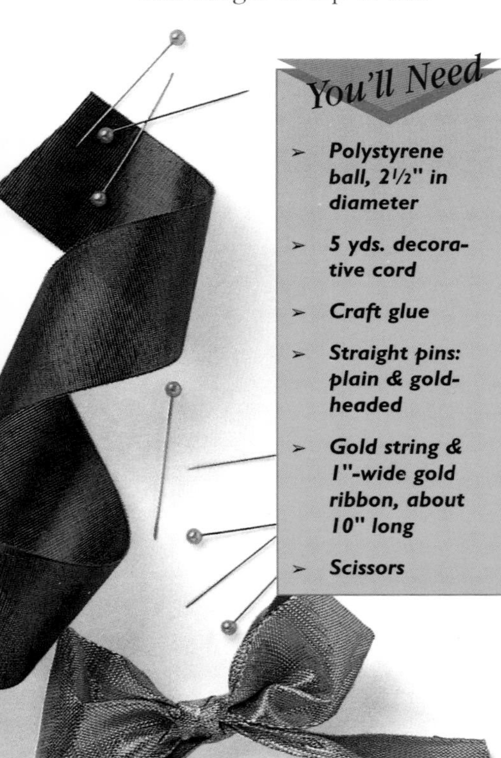

You'll Need

- ***Polystyrene ball, 2½" in diameter***
- ***5 yds. decorative cord***
- ***Craft glue***
- ***Straight pins: plain & gold-headed***
- ***Gold string & 1"-wide gold ribbon, about 10" long***
- ***Scissors***

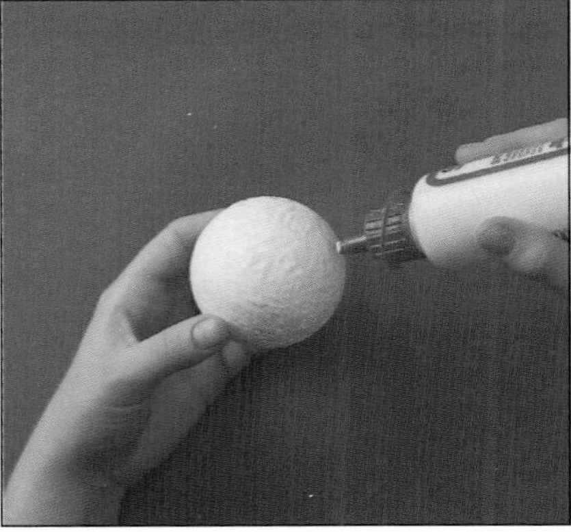

1 Apply glue and spread over upper third of foam ball. Holding ball between fingers, wind cord end into 2 or 3 rounds to make tight coil.

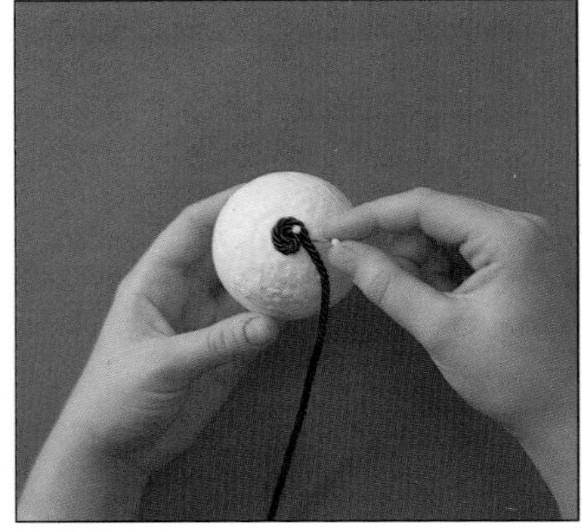

2 Glue wound cord onto top of ball, inserting straight pins through end of cord and at last wrap to hold cord in place. Begin winding cord around ball.

3 Carefully wind cord to cover glued area with no space showing between rounds. Insert pins at each round to hold cord. Spread glue over remainder of ball and continue winding and pinning cord. Let glue dry completely.

4 When glue is dry, remove plain pins and insert gold-headed pins evenly spaced (about 1" apart) around entire ball.

5 Tie gold ribbon into bow and stick gold-headed pin through center knot. Tie 6"–8" length of gold string directly under pinhead for hanger.

6 Dip pin in glue and push it into top of ball. Let glue dry before hanging ball on tree.

Embroidering Christmas Tiebacks

Patterns & Templates

Quick-and-easy holiday tiebacks embroidered with little gingerbread men are an original and festive addition to indoor Christmas decorating as they let the light of the season fill the room.

You don't have to be an expert at needlework to make these lovely contoured embroidered tiebacks. Small holiday motifs are rendered with a simple stem stitch on cotton fabric that matches the color of the curtain fabric.

Because these tiebacks work up so quickly, they are wonderful items to make for a holiday fund-raising bazaar. Or change the motif to make a pair to dress up your windows for Easter, Halloween, or any other holiday.

Coordinate the fabric and trims of the tiebacks to the curtains or use traditional holiday colors. Hand-embroider festive gold stars in running stitches or machine-embroider stylized red hearts.

Patterns & Templates

Transfer the tieback pattern and desired holiday motif from Group 12, Card 25 onto your chosen fabric.

The tiebacks are made with a front and back piece and an interfacing in between. Make the pair of tiebacks from sturdy cotton fabric and use fusible web as interfacing to give them more body. As a time-saving alternative, you can make the tiebacks from felt in a holiday color and glue on a decorative edging.

To fasten the tieback to the wall, sew a small plastic ring to the front end of the undecorated side and one to the back end of the embroidered side. Secure rings to a hook or nail placed in the wall.

Embroidery Guidelines

You need only to embroider the front half of each tieback.

- Use two strands of embroidery floss to hand-stitch small motifs.
- If desired, use small embroidery hoop to hold fabric taut.
- Do not knot thread ends. Secure beginning end under first few stitches; when stitching is completed, weave thread ends through several stitches on wrong side.
- Keep stitching on back flat and smooth so fusible interfacing adheres evenly.

You'll Need

- ***1 yd. cotton fabric***
- ***1 1/2 yds. bias binding***
- ***Embroidery floss & needle***
- ***Tracing and graphite papers & pencil***
- ***Fusible interfacing***
- ***Scissors & pins***
- ***Iron***
- ***Sewing machine & thread***

1 Transfer pattern onto tracing paper. Layer graphite paper and traced pattern face down on doubled fabric; align foldline on tracing with fold in fabric. Pin layers. Trace design to transfer to fabric. Flip pattern to mark second tieback.

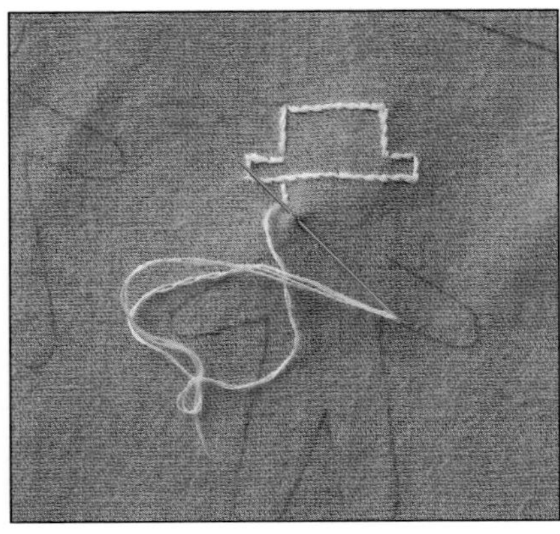

2 Embroider outline of each gingerbread man using stem stitch: Working from left to right, make slightly slanting 1/4"-long stitches, bringing needle up midway along stitch with thread below needle. Repeat sequence.

3 Embroider other details, such as eyes and buttons, using a variety of stitches, as indicated on template in Group 12, Card 25.

4 After embroidery is completed, cut out embroidered tieback fronts along marked lines. Transfer tieback shape to fabric and cut 2 back pieces.

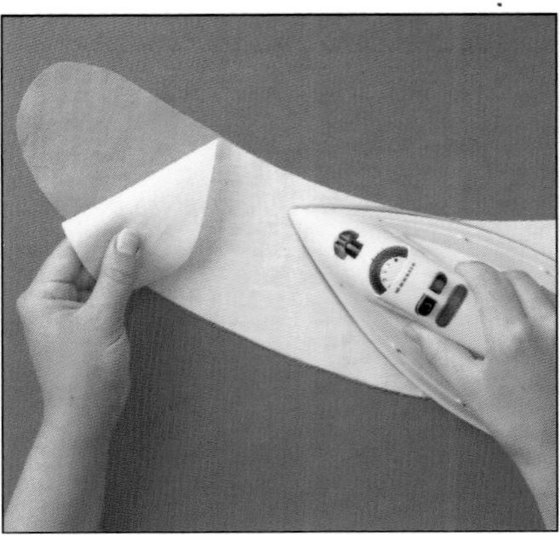

5 Using traced pattern, outline tieback onto fusible interfacing. Cut out 2 pieces; iron interfacing to wrong side of each embroidered piece. Wrong sides facing, place front and back tieback pieces together.

6 Right sides together, pin binding around tieback edge, beginning and ending on unembroidered half; stitch in place. Turn binding to back, encasing raw edges; pin and edgestitch on right side of binding.

Specialties from the Kitchen

Mouth-watering treats for celebrations and gifts

SPECIALTIES FROM THE KITCHEN

CARD 3

Decorating an Animal-Face Cake

Patterns & Templates

Think of the delighted look on the face of that special youngster when he or she is presented with an adorable cake shaped and frosted to look like a bear, a bunny, or even the family kitty.

Kids will clamor to have their favorite animal as the centerpiece of their next birthday party. The hardest part will be choosing the one animal they like best.

Whether you make the cake from your own recipe or from a mix, these confections use standard, round baking pans, easy homemade or store-bought frostings, and purchased tubes of colored icing gels. The simple cut shapes take the mystery out of creating custom-made party cakes.

Cut the bunny's long ears from the edges of an 8" round cake layer and its bow tie from the remaining center portion. Colored icing gels create the faces of the menagerie, including this contented cat. Change the shape of eyes, noses, ears, and mouths to produce different party pets.

Patterns & Templates

Use the templates from Group 12, Card 3 to create faces for the animal cakes.

Assembling and decorating these animal cakes is relatively easy—and a lot of fun. Here are some useful suggestions for attaining professional results.

Cake-Decorating Guidelines

Before cutting out the shapes and beginning the assembly process, be sure that everything you will use—cake layers, frosting, icing gels, utensils, etc.—is at room temperature.

- Brush cake layers with a pastry brush, before and after cutting shapes, to remove all crumbs so the frosting remains smooth.
- To get clearly defined cut edges, use a sharp knife when cutting layers.
- When rounding edges, slice cake from top toward bottom to keep edges well defined and free of crumbs.
- Mark design lines for icing gel on frosting with tip of a wooden skewer, toothpick, or chopstick. If you make a mistake, smooth frosting over and start again.

- *Cake mix for 3 (8") round layers*
- *3 (8") round cake pans*
- *Pastry brush & metal spatula*
- *Long, serrated knife & sharp kitchen utility knife*
- *Colored frostings & tubed icing gels for 3(8") round cake layers*
- *White paper & scissors*
- *Plastic straw*
- *Wooden skewer or toothpick*

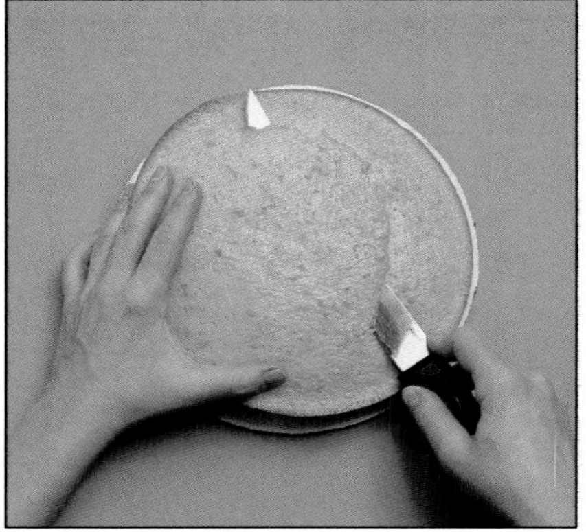

1 Bake 3 round cake layers of same size; let cool. With serrated knife held horizontally, carefully slice across top of 1 cake layer to make top surface level.

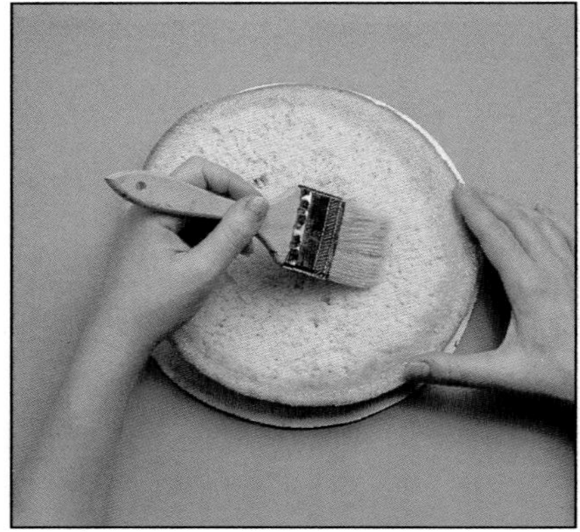

2 Using pastry brush and broad strokes, brush gently across cut surface of cut cake layer to decrumb, taking care not to tear cake as you brush.

3 Dip spatula in warm water to make spreading frosting easier, then spread smooth layer of frosting evenly over entire top of cut cake layer and out to edge.

4 Using serrated knife, level off another cake layer as in step 1. Handling second layer carefully to avoid breaking it, place it cut side down on frosted layer, so bottom of second layer forms top of cake.

5 Using spatula dipped in warm water as before, cover sides of both cake layers evenly with frosting. Spread generous amount of frosting evenly over entire top of cake and out to edge.

6 Trace ear and snout onto paper using templates from Group 12, Card 3; cut out paper patterns. Use utility knife to cut 4 ear pieces and snout from third cake layer. Frost 2 ear pieces; top each frosted ear with unfrosted ear.

7 Spread frosting over sides and top of snout piece. Slide spatula under frosted snout and transfer snout just below center of frosted cake, lowering 1 side of piece onto cake as you slowly remove spatula from underneath.

8 Cut plastic straw into 2" pieces. Insert 1 end into edge of bottom layer at position of ear. Push lower edge of cake ear onto other end of straw to hold ear in place. Repeat with other ear. Frost ears, then paint semicircles with icing gel.

Try This!

Turn a plateful of ordinary cupcakes into a miniature zoo in no time flat. Make the cupcakes in colorful paper muffin cups and frost. Then round up the kids to help make the faces: Add small color-coated chocolate candies, gumdrops, candy corn, and other small candies for eyes, ears, or noses; use icing gel for mouths and other features. Shredded coconut and candy sprinkles can be added for texture if desired.

9 Use pointed end of wooden skewer or toothpick to draw on outlines of facial features in cake frosting. Fill in outlines with tubed icing gel.

Crafter's Secrets

It isn't necessary to be a skilled baker to turn out these charming animal cakes. Use ready-made, packaged cake mixes, frostings, and colored icing gels. Mix equal parts chocolate and vanilla frosting to achieve a lighter brown frosting, or mix food coloring with white or cream frosting to produce a variety of custom colors.

Creating Texture with Frosting

Frosting can be made to duplicate a surface that is lusciously smooth or richly textured.

While the basic technique of applying the frosting with a spatula will result in a smooth appearance, to create a textured effect, use a pastry tube with a round tip. This piping method requires at least twice as much frosting as a cake covered with a smooth layer of frosting.

Before creating the textured effect, cover the cake with an even layer of smooth frosting and apply the animal's features. Practice squeezing out the right amount of frosting on a piece of waxed paper before starting on the cake.

Beginning at the outer edge, pipe in a circle and work around the features, filling in around them as necessary. Pipe around the sides last.

This spotted bear's textured coat was created with a pastry tube and a round tip. The same technique can be used to create any rough-coated animal you might want to duplicate. You don't have to apply texture over the whole cake; if desired, texture only specific portions, and save both time and frosting.

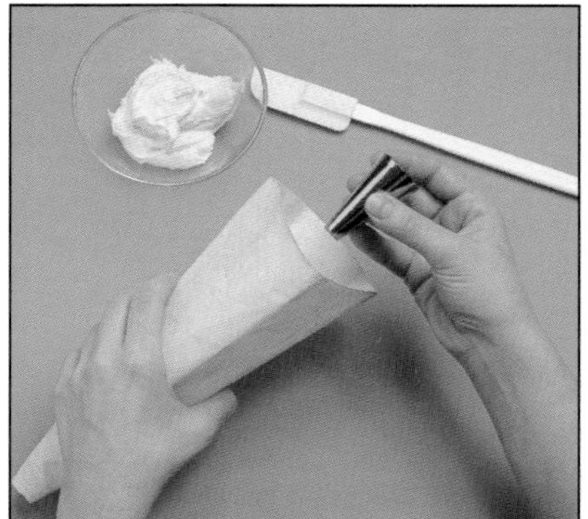

1 Push round tip into narrow end of pastry bag until tip is firmly in position. If pastry bag and tip come with a coupler, follow manufacturer's instructions to join pieces.

2 Fold top of pastry bag down to form a cuff. Using spatula, fill bag with frosting. Pull up cuff. Twist top of bag until all frosting is pushed toward tip end and bag feels firmly filled.

3 Hold tip end of pastry bag with one hand, and placing tip against cake surface, squeeze filled end of bag slightly with other hand; lift to form small point of icing.

Piping Festive Meringue Shapes

Surprise and delight your guests at dessert time with elegant, imaginatively shaped meringues. These crisp, lighter-than-air confections are easy as pie to make and just as versatile.

Beautifully shaped meringues, artfully arranged and topped with sherbet and fresh fruits make a dramatic finale to a special dinner party. Sweeten up a Valentine's celebration or wedding brunch with sherbet-topped meringue hearts floating in a sea of raspberry sauce. Add a joyful flourish to a birthday party with floral-shaped meringue cookies, or surprise and delight guests by sandwiching thin disks of meringue between the birthday cake layers.

There are endless ways to use meringue in delicious and attractive desserts. Try filling piped meringue cups with whipped cream and garnishing with chocolate shavings and nuts. Or design a beautiful dessert plate with a meringue flower, fresh fruits, and ice cream.

Meringues are made basically from egg whites and sugar whipped until very stiff, then baked at a low temperature until they become dry and firm.

Avoid making meringue on a rainy or humid day as the meringue will absorb moisture from the air and not harden properly.

General Guidelines

Separate the egg whites from the yolks and bring whites to room temperature; make sure bowl and beaters are dry and free of grease.

- Keep yolks from getting mixed in with whites or meringue will never stiffen.
- Beat egg whites with electric mixer to incorporate more air and increase volume.
- Use purchased piping bag and piping tip. Or twist waxed paper into cone shape and tape to hold shape; cut tip for hole.
- Do not open oven at end of baking time. Allow meringues to dry in oven for one hour with door closed.
- Meringue can be made in advance and stored in sealed container in dry place for about a month. Do not freeze.

You'll Need

- ***4 eggs***
- ***1 c. sifted sugar***
- ***1/8 t. cream of tartar***
- ***1/8 t. salt***
- ***Electric mixer***
- ***2-qt. glass or stainless-steel mixing bowl***
- ***Round drinking glass***
- ***Pencil & scissors***
- ***Baking parchment***
- ***Baking sheet***
- ***Large spoon***
- ***Piping bag***
- ***Oven***

Making Meringue Cups

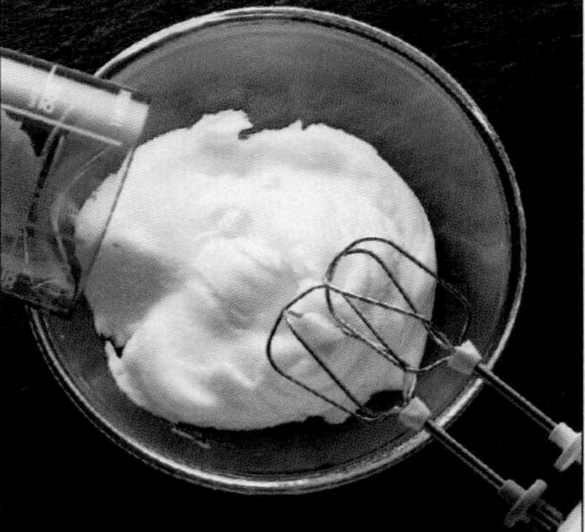

1 Separate eggs. In bowl, beat egg whites, cream of tartar, and salt at high speed until soft peaks form. Slowly add sugar and continue beating until whites are stiff.

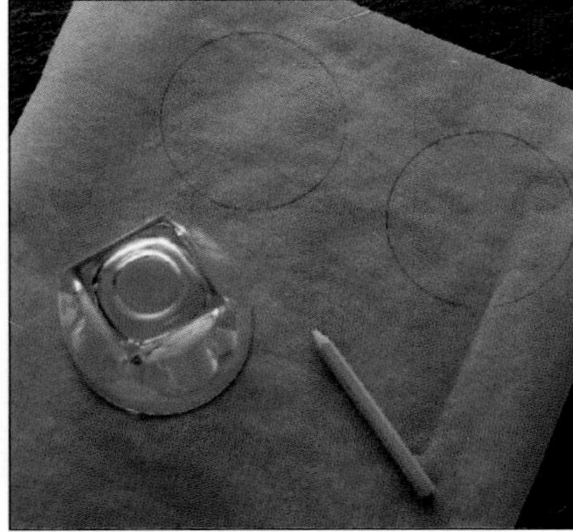

2 Using pencil, outline around mouth of round drinking glass onto parchment-lined baking sheet to make 12 circles about 1" apart.

3 With spoon, drop dollop of meringue onto center of each circle. Using back of spoon, spread meringue evenly to outline of circle. Repeat for all circles to make bases for meringue cups.

4 Fill piping bag with meringue and pipe border around each base. Bake in 225° F preheated oven for about 45 minutes. Turn oven off; let dry in oven for 1 hour. Fill as desired.

Making Meringue Hearts

Draw and cut out heart-shaped pattern. Outline pattern 12 times onto parchment-lined baking sheet. Pipe meringue along outlines; continue piping inward to fill center. Bake as directed in step 4.

Making Meringue Flowers

Draw and cut out a simple 4-petal flower pattern. Trace pattern 12 times onto parchment-lined baking sheet. Pipe meringue along outline of flowers. Bake as directed in step 4.

Making a Decorative Ice Bowl

A frosty ice bowl glistening with cut fruit or beautiful flowers is a splendid way to keep the chill in a fresh fruit salad, a sparkling punch, or a refreshing cold summer soup.

As functional as it is pretty and simple to make, this distinctive server preserves in ice the beauty and freshness of flowers and fruit slices at the peak of their perfection.

Match the icy decorations to the bowl's contents. For example, a selection of mixed berries looks glamorous brought to the table in an ice bowl of fruit slices. An ice ring of colorful vegetables gives a refreshing shimmer to a salad of crisp greens; or help ice-cold punch keep its cool in a frosty halo of summer flowers.

Decorative ice floats conform to the shape of the containers in which they are frozen. A ring-mold pan turns out an icy fruit wreath for a punch bowl, while rows of edible flowers frozen on a baking sheet create a floating garden.

To make an ice bowl, you will need two bowls of the same shape and about the same height, with the inner bowl slightly smaller to fit inside the outer bowl.

Ice Bowl Guidelines

The decorative ice bowl is constructed quickly, but must remain in the freezer at least 8 hours to harden properly.

- Make sure there is at least 1" of space between outer and inner bowls. To make a thicker ice bowl, use a smaller inner bowl and freeze longer.
- Have lots of ice cubes and fruit slices ready when you begin.
- Whole flowers, petals, and leaves can be used as decorations, but they must be edible. Pansies, rose petals, and mint or lemon verbena leaves are good choices.

Making Decorative Ice Cubes

You can also make party ice cubes in an ordinary ice-cube tray.

- Fill individual compartments of tray with water, then place a small flower, mint leaf, berry, or slice of fruit into each compartment. Freeze until solid.
- Add decorative ice cubes to a party punch bowl or glasses of lemonade or iced tea.

You'll Need

For ice bowl:
- ***Glass or metal bowls: 1 large, 1 small***
- ***Freezer-safe weight (such as unopened canned good or heavy measuring cup)***
- ***Ice cubes & water***
- ***Sliced fresh strawberries & starfruit***
- ***Mint leaves***

For ice ring:
- ***Punch bowl***
- ***Ring mold***
- ***Whole strawberries & cherries***

Making an Ice Bowl

1 Place 1 layer ice cubes in bottom of large bowl. Place small bowl inside large bowl to check if there is at least 1" of spacing between bowls. Remove inner bowl. Arrange sliced starfruit on top of cubes. Replace small bowl.

2 Pour cold water into large bowl to cover ice cubes. Arrange sliced fruit and mint leaves inside large bowl above ice-water line. Add more ice, then water to hold fruit and mint in place. Continue layering to just below rim of bowl.

3 Place a freezer-safe weight inside small glass bowl to anchor it in place. Fill large bowl with water to rim. Carefully place bowls in freezer and leave overnight or until frozen solid.

4 Remove bowls from freezer. Remove weight and pour tepid water into small bowl, twisting it until it can be removed. Dip large bowl into tepid water. Remove ice bowl and fill as desired.

Making Floating Ice Ring for Punch Bowl

1 Add water to height of ¾"; freeze. Remove from freezer. Arrange sliced fruits on top of ice ring. Add water to just cover fruit; freeze. Fill rest of mold with water; freeze until solid.

2 Remove mold from freezer and dip in bowl of tepid water or run warm tap water over bottom of pan to loosen ice ring. Unmold ice ring and float, bottom up, in punch bowl.

Decorating Tops of Pie Crusts

The mouth-watering aroma and eagerly awaited first forkful of a freshly baked pie are treats for the senses. A golden top crust, festive with cutout dough motifs, delights the eyes as well.

When decorating your home or serving a meal, it is often the small details that can make the difference, whether it be a perfectly placed plant, an invitingly plump pillow, or a decorative garnish.

Add a creative touch of your own to your next pie crust by decorating the top with fanciful patterns and shapes. Use cookie cutters or a sharp paring knife to make leaves, flowers, fruits, or any other motif as charming dough accents for your crust.

Meat pie, chicken pot pie, fruit pie, or tart—all are fun to garnish with cutouts made of pie dough. If desired, make the motifs to correspond to the pie's contents, then apply the dough decorations directly onto the filling or to the top crust.

A decorated crust on a freshly baked pie is both a tasty and visual delight. Use ready-to-bake pie shells or make your own crust from scratch. A light, flaky crust is not difficult to achieve but does require a bit of patience. Bake according to the directions on the pie crust package or according to your own pie recipe.

Making the Crust

The following recipe yields enough dough for a top and bottom crust and some extra for decorations.

- Mix together 2½ c. flour and ½ t. salt. Using pastry blender or two knives, cut in ¾ c. vegetable shortening until mixture resembles tiny peas. Sprinkle 6–7 T. cold water over mixture, 1 T. at a time, until pastry holds together when gently pressed into a ball.
- Roll out dough on a lightly floured board to about ⅛" thick and 2" larger than pie pan, then lift loosely and fit firmly into pan.
- Press dough against sides of pie pan; crimp or flute edges. Chill for half hour while preparing desired filling.
- If using top crust, flute edges of both crusts together to seal; prick with fork or cut vents to release steam that builds up during baking. Brush top and cutout decorations with lightly beaten egg.

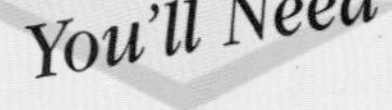

- ***Unbaked, filled pie shell***
- ***Prepared pie dough for top crust***
- ***1 egg, lightly beaten***
- ***Rolling pin & flour for rolling***
- ***Sharp knife***
- ***Cookie cutters***
- ***Pastry brush***
- ***Cookie sheet***

Decorating a Pie with Apple Motifs

1 Lightly flour flat work surface. Roll out prepared dough into ⅛"-thick circle large enough to drape over filled pie shell. Roll dough onto pin, then lift and unroll dough over top of filled pie.

2 Use knife to trim off excess dough; save trimmed pieces for decorations. Moisten dough edges with water; press edges of top and bottom crusts together to seal. Pinch and flute crust edges.

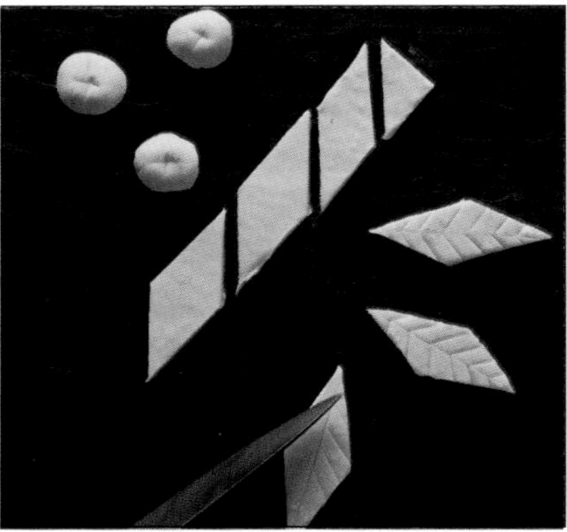

3 Roll out dough scraps and cut into long strips. Cut strips diagonally into pieces for individual leaves. Use back of knife blade to score veins on leaves. Roll small pieces of dough into little balls for "apples."

4 Lightly brush crust with beaten egg. Twist narrow strip of dough for branch and arrange on crust. Place leaves and apples along branch. Brush dough motifs lightly with beaten egg. Place pie on cookie sheet and bake as directed.

Making Decorations from Cookie Cutters

1 Roll out prepared dough on lightly floured work surface to about ⅛" thickness. Use small cookie cutters of various shapes to carefully cut out pieces of dough.

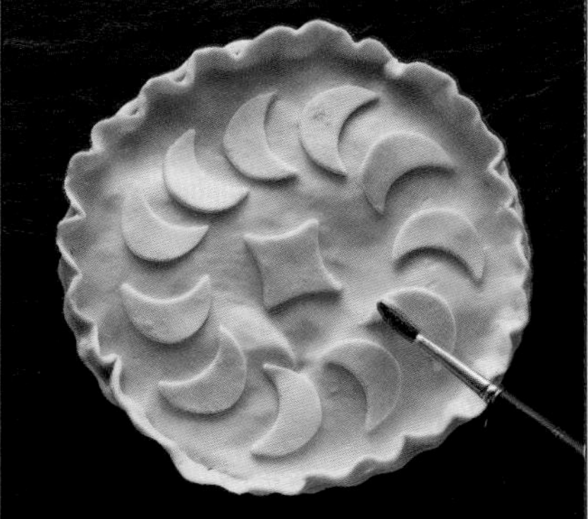

2 Lightly brush crust with beaten egg. Arrange cut dough shapes on pie crust top in a pleasing manner. Brush cutouts lightly with beaten egg. Bake pie as directed until crust is golden.

Techniques & Tools

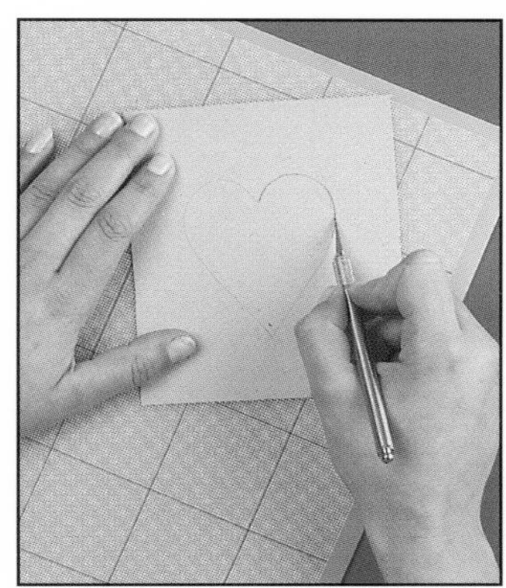

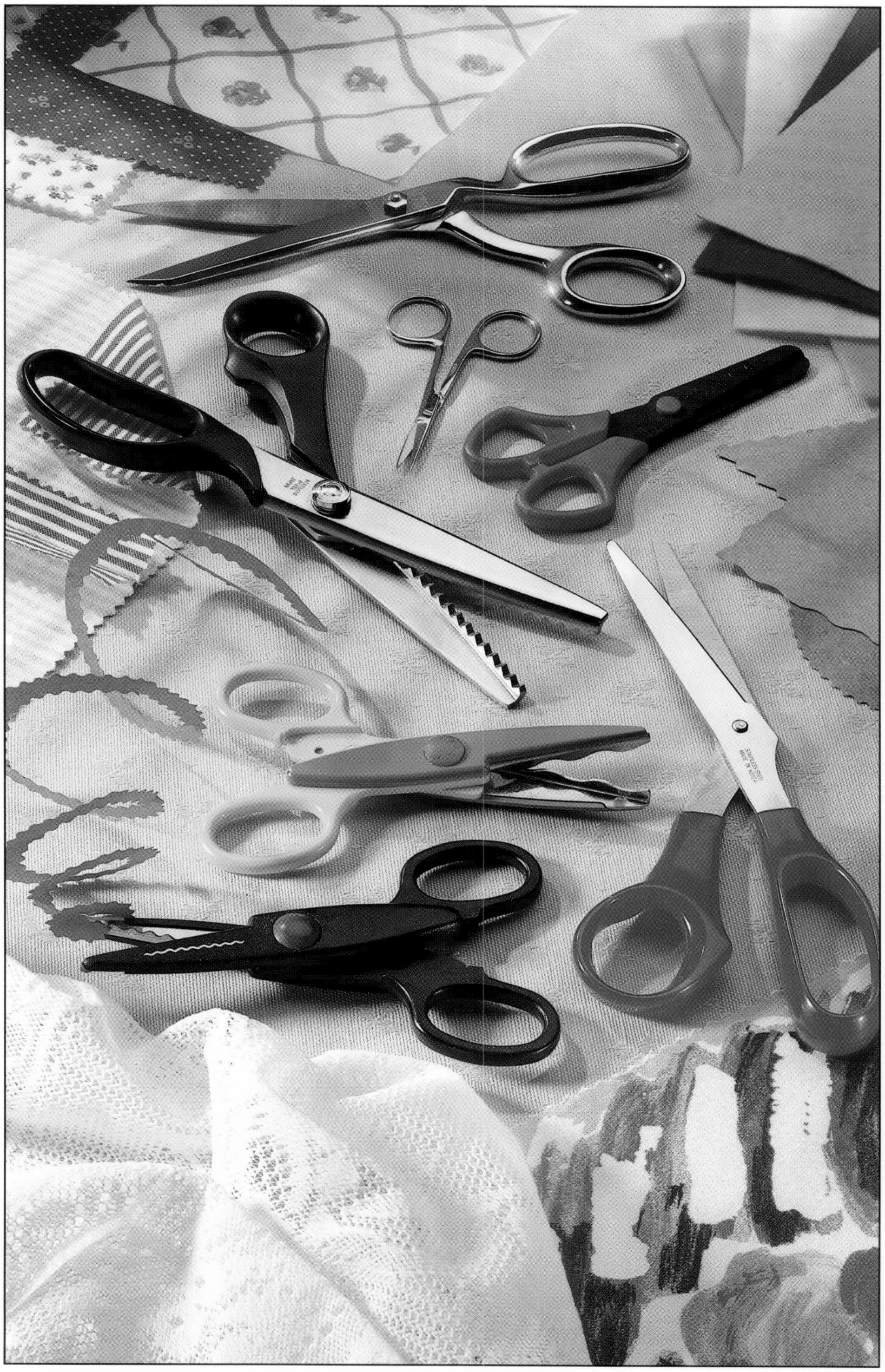

A crafter's guide to basic skills and materials

Painting a Still Life with Watercolors

Patterns & Templates

Bring out the artist in you by trying your hand at the fine art of painting with watercolors. The water-based colors lightly applied to paper create images with a transluscent quality.

Learning basic watercolor techniques will open up a wonderful new world of creativity and expression. You don't need previous art training to master this medium, but you do need to put in a little practice. Carefully follow the steps, one at a time, perhaps repeating them on practice paper, until you feel confident to proceed on to the watercolor paper.

Before long, you'll have a beautiful original still life to proudly hang in your home.

Before starting an actual painting, test the brush, technique, and intensity of color on a scrap of watercolor paper. There are three basic types of watercolor brushes. Use a flat brush when covering large areas and a small pointed brush to add details. For textured effects in a wide area, use a fan brush and sweeping strokes.

Patterns & Templates

Use the template from Group 12, Card 4 to re-create this charming watercolor still life. If necessary, enlarge or reduce the template to fit the frame you have chosen or the paper size you have selected.

Watercolor paints are readily available as dry cakes or in tubes. Both need to be mixed with water before painting. The amount of water used will determine the intensity of the color, and colors can be mixed to achieve new shades.

Use special highly absorbent watercolor paper, which is thick and rough-textured. The paper absorbs the water in the paint, leaving only a wash of color when dry.

Watercolor Painting Guidelines

Keep a scrap of your selected watercolor paper handy to try out different brush strokes and colors.

- Because water in paint is absorbed by paper, colors dry lighter than they first appear when applied. Apply watercolors in layers to achieve darker shades. Let previous coat dry before adding a new color over it.
- Brush water onto paper before painting when you want paint to "bleed" and colors to blend.
- Work with a minimal amount of paint and a light hand. It is easy to add more paint, but once applied, it cannot be removed.
- Keep paper towels handy to absorb excess water from brushes.

You'll Need

- ***11"x14" sketch or tracing paper***
- ***11"x14" watercolor paper***
- ***Graphite transfer paper***
- ***Watercolor paints in cakes or tubes***
- ***Flat & pointed bristle brushes in assorted sizes***
- ***Charcoal pencil***
- ***Water container***
- ***Paper towels***

1 Using charcoal pencil, lightly draw design onto sketch paper, or trace templates provided onto tracing paper, centering design and allowing sufficient margins for any individual framing needs.

2 Place watercolor paper face up on surface. Place graphite transfer paper carbon side down onto watercolor paper, then place pencil sketch on top. With pencil, trace over design lines on sketch to transfer design onto watercolor paper.

3 Using broad, flat bristle brush and water, moisten surface of paper in background area to be painted. This prepares surface for blending colors from dark to light tones.

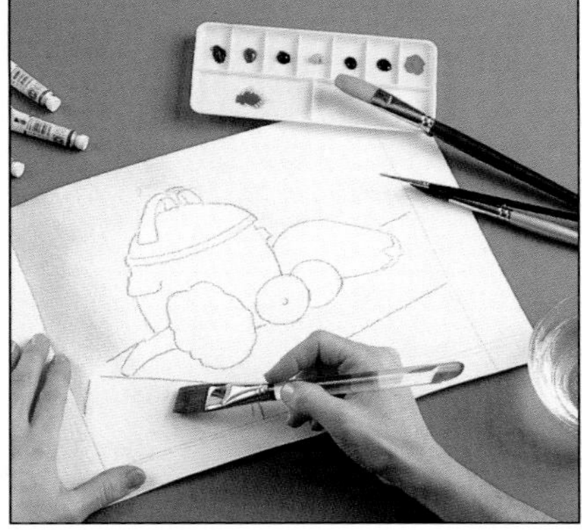

4 Mix red and purple paint with water to obtain mauve color; test on scrap paper, then apply pale mauve wash to upper background. Work around objects to avoid spreading. Mix red with water and apply to foreground in same manner.

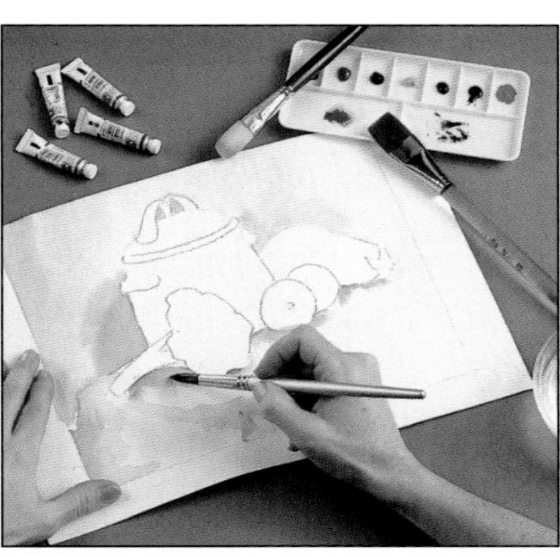

5 While pale washes are still wet, apply second coat of each color to increase intensity. Use broad, sweeping strokes and blend paints close to objects to create darker shadows of desired color depth.

6 Using small, round brushes and bold, sweeping strokes, paint each basic shape with pale wash of appropriate color to create highlights: Paint pot tan, eggplant purple, tomatoes red, and broccoli green.

7 Working shapes farthest in background first, and while pale tone of each shape is still wet, apply darker tone of same color over shape, blending around lighter, highlighted areas. Allow paints to dry.

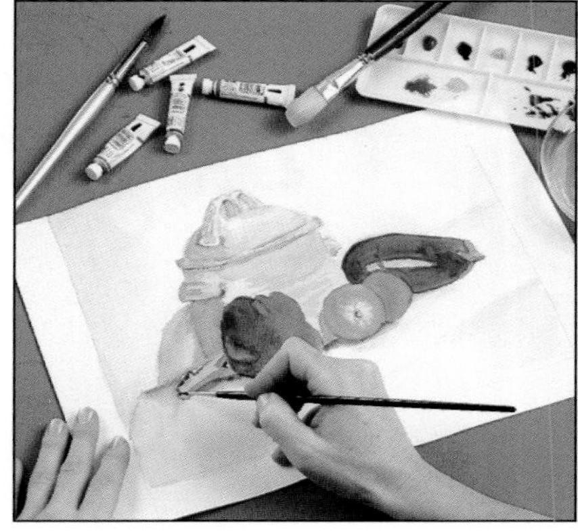

8 Using small, pointed brush, add details: stem ends to tomatoes and eggplants and florets to broccoli. Using darker tones, add contours to broccoli stem and pot; outline edges of each shape to define them and to separate them from other shapes.

Crafter's Secrets

The amount of pressure that is applied to the brush determines how wide a painted line will be. Very little pressure, with the brush just barely touching the paper, results in a very fine line. Keeping the brush on the paper and firmly pressing down on the brush creates a thicker, darker line.

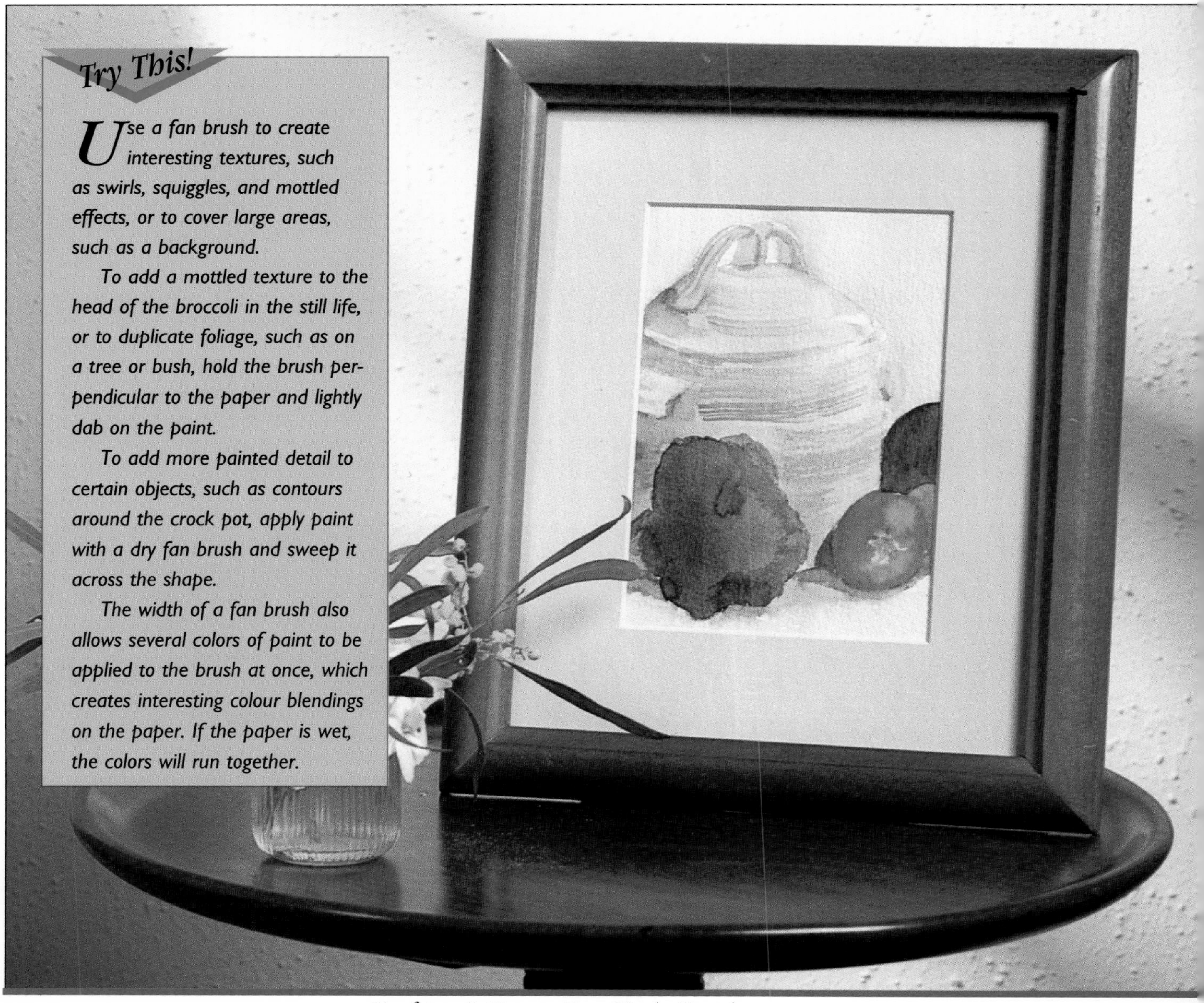

Try This!

Use a fan brush to create interesting textures, such as swirls, squiggles, and mottled effects, or to cover large areas, such as a background.

To add a mottled texture to the head of the broccoli in the still life, or to duplicate foliage, such as on a tree or bush, hold the brush perpendicular to the paper and lightly dab on the paint.

To add more painted detail to certain objects, such as contours around the crock pot, apply paint with a dry fan brush and sweep it across the shape.

The width of a fan brush also allows several colors of paint to be applied to the brush at once, which creates interesting colour blendings on the paper. If the paper is wet, the colors will run together.

The delicate mix of colors applied to the background of this still life is achieved by gently dabbing watercolor paints onto paper with a wet sponge, rather than applying color with a brush. By dabbing color on firmly, details, such as the florets on the head of broccoli, can be made.

Sponging on Watercolor for Texture

Sponges can add texture to a watercolor painting. Experiment with natural and synthetic sponges, some with small, even holes and some with large, irregular holes. To apply the paint, dip the sponge into water, then into the watercolor paint. When dabbed onto the paper, the holes contrast with the thick membranes to create a light and dark pattern of varying density.

Dabbed lightly, a sponge can mimic the look of a textured wall or dappled sunlight. Pressed more firmly, a sponge can simulate the leaves on a tree or the bush in a landscape.

Using even pressure to dab on paint with a sponge that has been cut straight across will yield a regular pattern, while the surface of a torn or natural piece of sponge will create a mottled, shadowy effect. Mix two or more colors together to create interesting effects.

1 Mix green paint with water on plate to desired shade. Dip damp, squeezed-out sponge into paint; test first on scrap paper, then dab paint onto dry paper to fill in drawn shape.

2 Mix blue and green paint with water for a pale tone, then dip sponge lightly into paint. Using broadest sponge surface, dab lightly and color large background area with pale wash, allowing paper to show through.

3 Mix more paint into background color to create darker tone. Dip sponge into paint and dab over paler color, darkening areas behind objects to create shadows. Keep dabbing same area to blend more solid field of color.

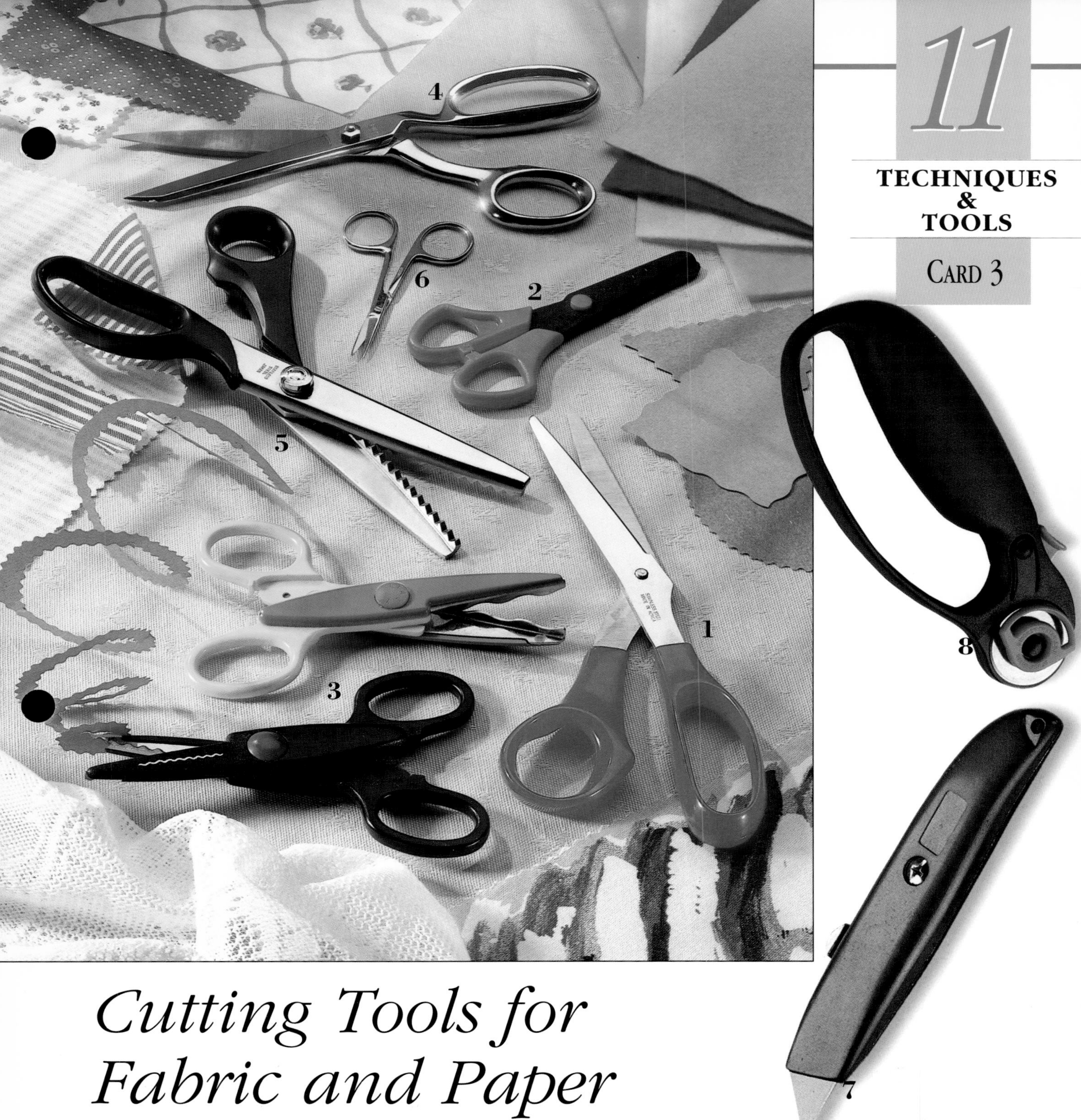

Cutting Tools for Fabric and Paper

When working with fabric or paper, select the right cutting tool to make crafting easier.

Cutting tools come in a variety of sizes and designs for different craft materials and jobs. While it is not necessary to keep every possible kind of cutting tool on hand, it is best to have a few basic ones that are suited to the crafts you perform most often. Choose the appropriate cutting tool for your particular task from the general selection shown above: **1** All-purpose scissors; **2** Blunt-tipped scissors; **3** Contour-edged specialty scissors; **4** Large dressmaker's shears; **5** Pinking shears for fabric; **6** Embroidery scissors; **7** Utility razor knife; **8** Rotary cutter.

A utility knife with a retractable and replaceable blade is the most useful all-around craft knife. The rotary cutter, often used by quilters, has a circular blade that is also retractable and can cut through many layers of fabric.

All cutting tools require some amount of care if they are to last a long time. Scissors are no exception.

General Care Instructions

To keep your scissors in top working condition, be sure to clean and oil them regularly. Send your good pairs of scissors to a qualified expert for sharpening and any screw adjustments.

- Wipe better-quality dressmaker shears and embroidery scissors with a soft, dry cloth after each use.
- Wipe blades of all-purpose scissors periodically, and be sure to remove any residue left by cutting tape or other adhesives.
- Add an occasional drop of oil on pivot point. Open and close scissors a few times to work in oil, then wipe off excess. Test scissors on scrap material to make sure no oil remains on blades.
- To keep pinking shears working smoothly, occasionally rub a lightweight oil over blades and remove any remaining fibers or dust after each use.
- To keep rotary cutters in good working order, change blade as it gets dull. Follow directions on packaging to properly reassemble parts.

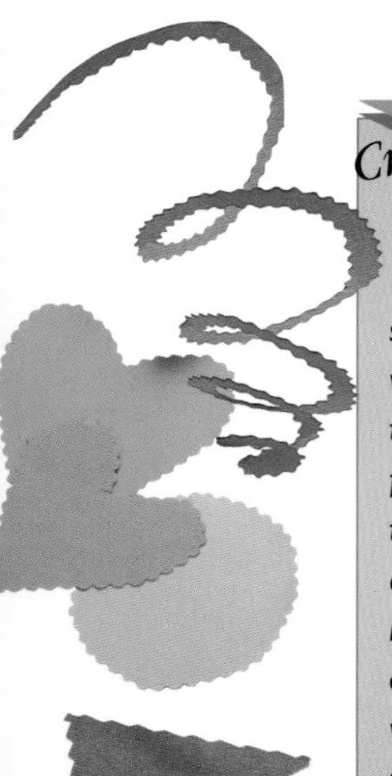

Crafter's Secrets

To keep your fabric shears sharp and in good working order, use them only for cutting fabrics. If you use the same pair to cut other types of crafting materials, including papers of various weights, the shears will quickly become dull.

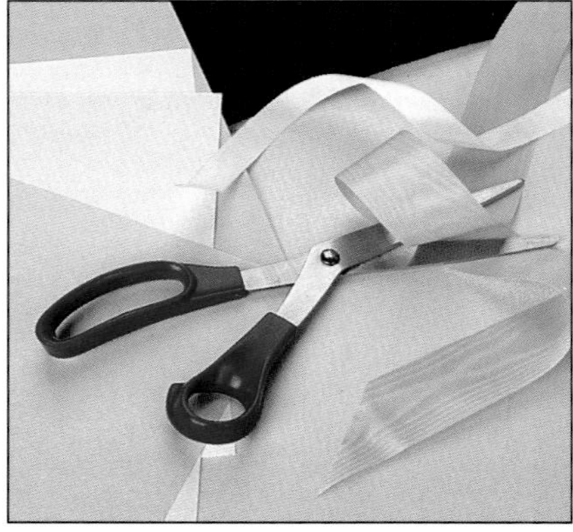

Keep all-purpose scissors in a central location such as a kitchen or family room. Use them to cut paper, felt, ribbon, string, and other similar items.

Blunt tips and large handles make these scissors easy to use on items such as construction paper or felt. Specialty paper scissors with scalloped edges are great for customizing paper crafts.

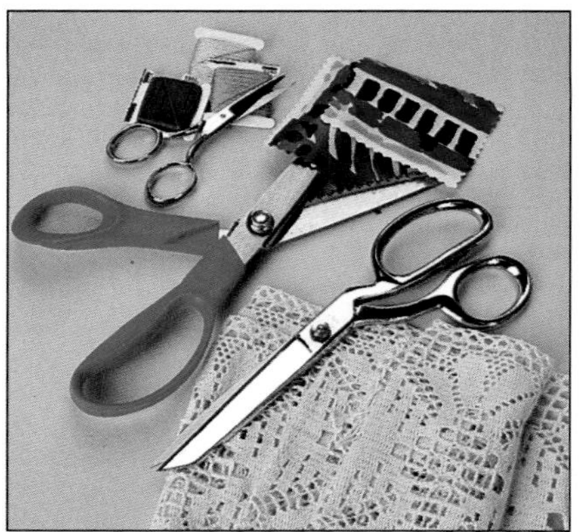

Often used by sewers, large dressmaker's shears easily cut through fabric and patterns, while a small pair of embroidery scissors are ideal for detailed work. Use pinking shears to finish edges and seams.

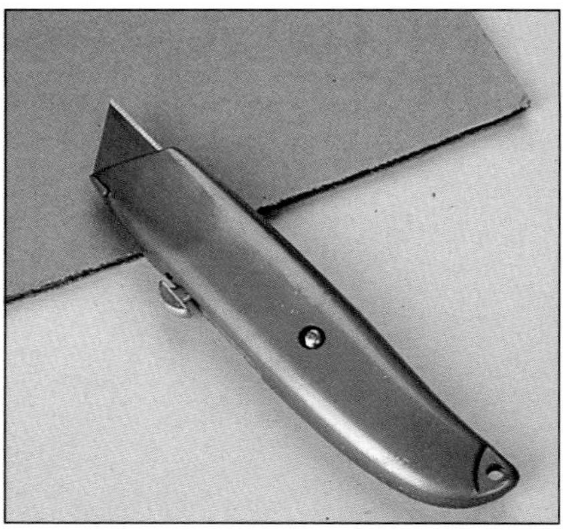

The common utility knife or utility cutter is ideal for heavy-duty cutting jobs, such as cartons, packages, twine, and foam board. The retractable blade is an important safety feature.

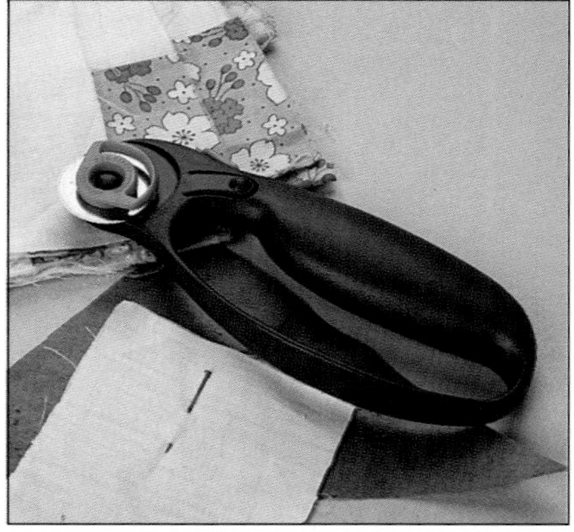

The rotary cutter is perfect for cutting through multiple layers of fabric. Its compact size makes it especially useful when precise cutting is needed. The circular blade retracts to shield its sharp edge when not in use.

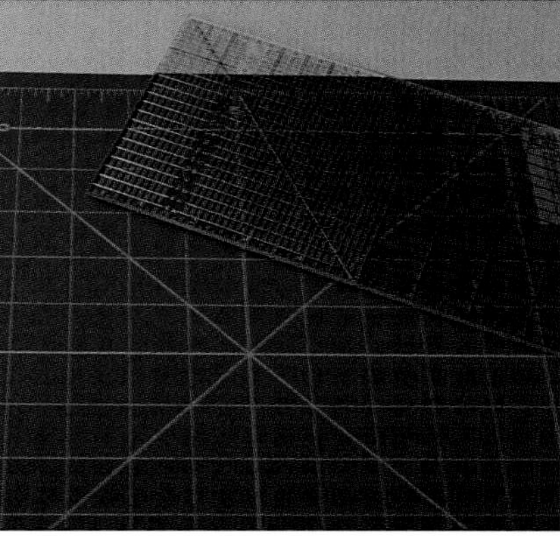

When cutting with a rotary cutter, use a self-healing cutting mat underneath. The mat is made in such a way that cuts mend automatically. For precision and accuracy, cut against an acrylic ruler as pictured here.

Patterns & Templates

Learning to Oil Paint on Canvas

Even a novice painter can create a pleasing oil painting with just a basic understanding of the techniques and a few materials.

As with any art or craft, practice is important. Fortunately, oil painting is quite forgiving because you can easily wipe out or paint over unwanted areas.

The foundation of the painting is first established by determining shaded areas of light and dark. Different brush strokes create texture and other effects. In the tower study, the sky is painted with broad sweeping strokes, the foliage by dabbing and dotting. Controlled sweeping strokes create the water, and the tower is produced with paint applied in layers.

In addition to the canvas, 8–10 paint colors and a palette for holding and blending the paints are essential for beginning painters. Bristle brushes in varying shapes and sizes are also needed. Look for flat, round, and fan brushes, as well as a palette knife for blending paints and a painting knife for more advanced techniques.

Patterns & Templates

Use the line drawing from Group 12, Card 15 as your painting subject. Or, if you prefer, use a photograph or painting from a book, magazine, or any other source.

Novice painters should invest in a ready-stretched canvas that is already primed with a pastelike coating that allows the oil paint to glide on, and in student oil paints, which cost less than professional oils. About 8-10 basic paint colors are adequate, since blending produces a wide variety of colors.

General Guidelines

Oil paints dry very slowly. Thickly applied paints take longest to dry, while paints thinned with turpentine dry quicker. Allow several days for finished work to dry completely.

- Divide subject into graphic sections to simplify painting. In this project, sky, foliage, water, and tower are separate sections, requiring different color paints, brushes, and brush strokes.
- If painting will continue over a few days, it is not necessary to clean paints from palette; they will stay wet for several days covered with plastic wrap.
- Use palette to lay out paints from warmest to coolest colors. Blend paints on palette, not on canvas.

You'll Need

- ***11"x14" primed canvas board***
- ***Oil paints: white, black, ultramarine & cerulean blue, burnt sienna, raw umber, orange, vermilion, ochre, yellow, dark & light green***
- ***Brushes: flats & rounds in 3 sizes***
- ***Palette board***
- ***Odorless turpentine***
- ***Charcoal pencil***
- ***Tracing & graphite papers & pencil***

Starting Oil Painting

1 Using tracing and graphite paper and pencil, trace outline of template onto canvas. Darken design with charcoal pencil, making outlines strong enough to use as guidelines for painting.

2 Prepare palette by squeezing small globs of paints around outside edge of palette. Thin paints with turpentine on palette as needed for painting.

3 Mix some black and white paint and thin with turpentine to make a wash. Apply wash across canvas using flat brush. Thin some black and white paint separately with turpentine to use for shading.

Establishing Shaded Areas

1 Determine direction of light. In example, light is coming from right, so tower's shadows fall to left. Using thinned black paint and flat brush, establish shadowed areas of subject with broad strokes.

2 With thinned white paint and broad strokes, fill in light areas: front of tower and gatehouse, portions of foliage and water, and clouds. Allow to dry overnight.

Painting Details

1 Start actual "painting" of colors and details 1 section at a time. Blend blue and white paints and paint sky with broad, sweeping strokes, working around painted white clouds.

2 Blend variations of green, orange, red and yellow. Beginning with darker colors, use broad dabbing brush strokes and a round brush to paint foliage of different hues. Highlight with lighter colors.

3 Using 2 darker blends of blues and white paints, paint water with slightly smaller flat brush than sky. Use smaller sweeping strokes, then go over first strokes with smaller brush and white paint to create illusion of waves.

4 Using small brushes and a dabbing stroke, paint tower with thick application of shades of gray and brown paint. Add details and texture to roof by dabbing blends of yellow and orange over background.

5 Go back over entire painting and, with small brushes add highlights and details to foliage in blends of yellow and orange and to stonework in grays. Allow painting to dry over several days.

Try This!

Oil paintings benefit from a variety of different brush techniques. One specific technique is called impasto, which is the process of applying paint thickly enough to the canvas to retain the marks of the brush or painting knife. Using this technique allows you to introduce texture and dimension to a painting. Do not thin paint for this type of painting.

The natural and rugged feeling of the tower is drawn out with the impasto technique. Several layers of paint in blends of earth tones and grays were used to build up and add dimension to the tower.

Painting with a Knife

Using a paint knife, either alone or with brushes, produces rich, colorful, and very dimensional oil paintings. Knife painting is used for compositions in which color and texture take precedence over details.

A painting knife should not be confused with a palette knife. A palette knife is straight and is used only for cleaning a palette and blending paints, while a painting knife has a bent handle that keeps the hand away from the surface of the canvas, making it easier to manipulate. Painting knives are available in a variety of sizes and blade shapes, including pear, trowel, round, and diamond shapes.

For this technique paints are kept thick and opaque or semi-opaque. The knife is used to squeeze the paint onto the canvas to create smooth areas of paint bordered by ridges or lines.

When using a knife to apply paint, keep the paint's thickness to a maximum of ¼"; thicker application may crack upon drying.

Knife painting is a slightly more advanced technique. Practice applying paint with a variety of painting knives to become familiar with the depth, richness, and unique sense of dimension created by this method of application.

Crafter's Secrets

Apply two or more coats of varnish to a completed dry painting to protect and add luminosity. Clean painting materials to keep them in good condition.

- *Cleaning a palette is a tedious job, which can be eliminated by using throw-away paper palettes.*
- *Clean brushes at end of each painting session: Wipe off excess paint with paper towels. Rinse brush in turpentine and wipe with rag. Finally, wash brush in warm soapy water. Store brushes with bristle ends up.*

1 Draw charcoal outline of subject on canvas. Eliminate application of wash and lights and darks, which will be covered with thick paint. Use a painting knife to thickly lay paint onto canvas in blocks of color as in previous steps.

2 Squeeze or squash paint onto canvas in ridges for texture, such as for clouds, foliage, and water. Use side of knife to add details and linear marks, as for leaves and waves.

Patterns & Templates

Full-size patterns and templates for projects with a personal touch

APPLE-BASKET MOTIFS

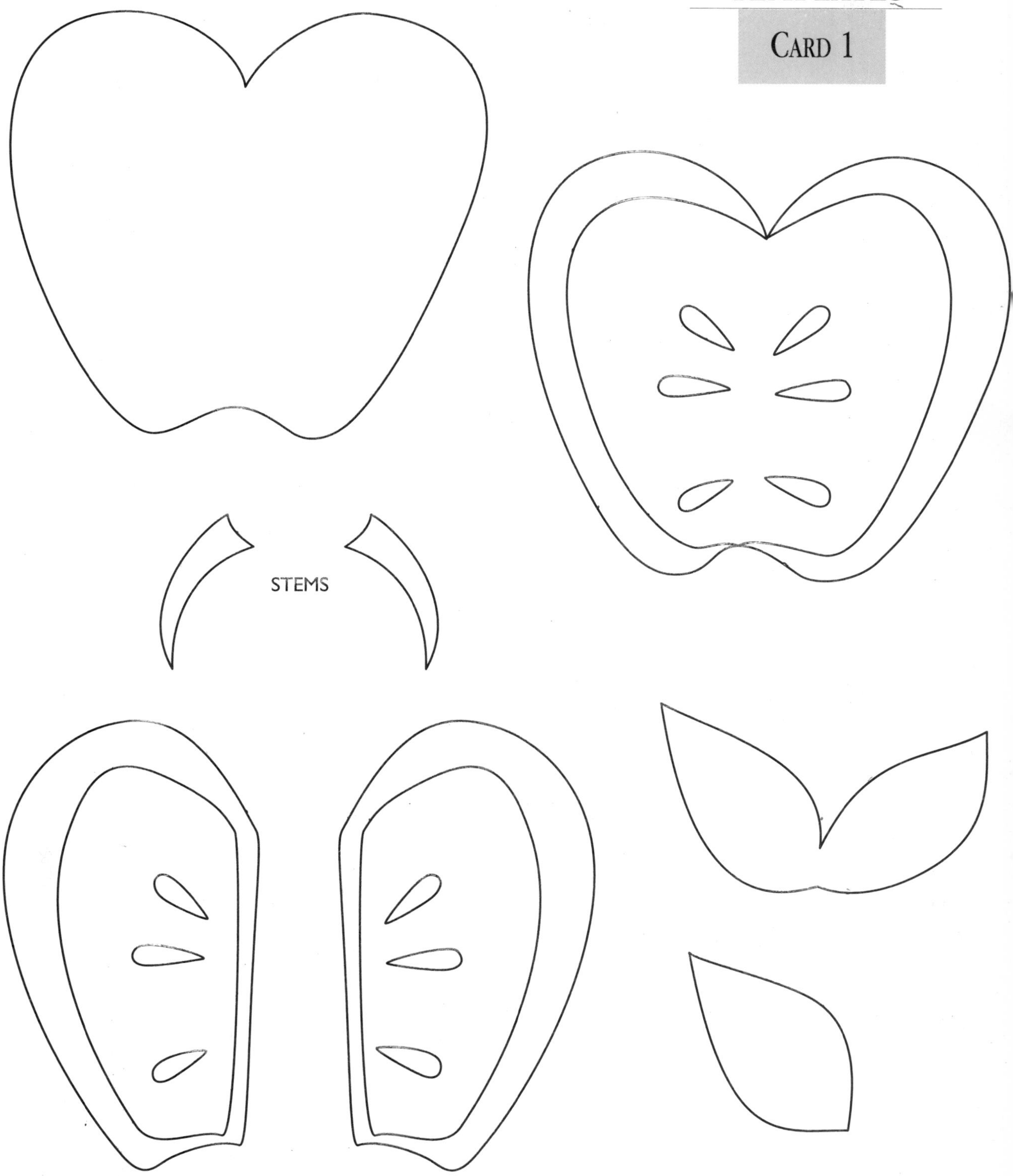

STEMS

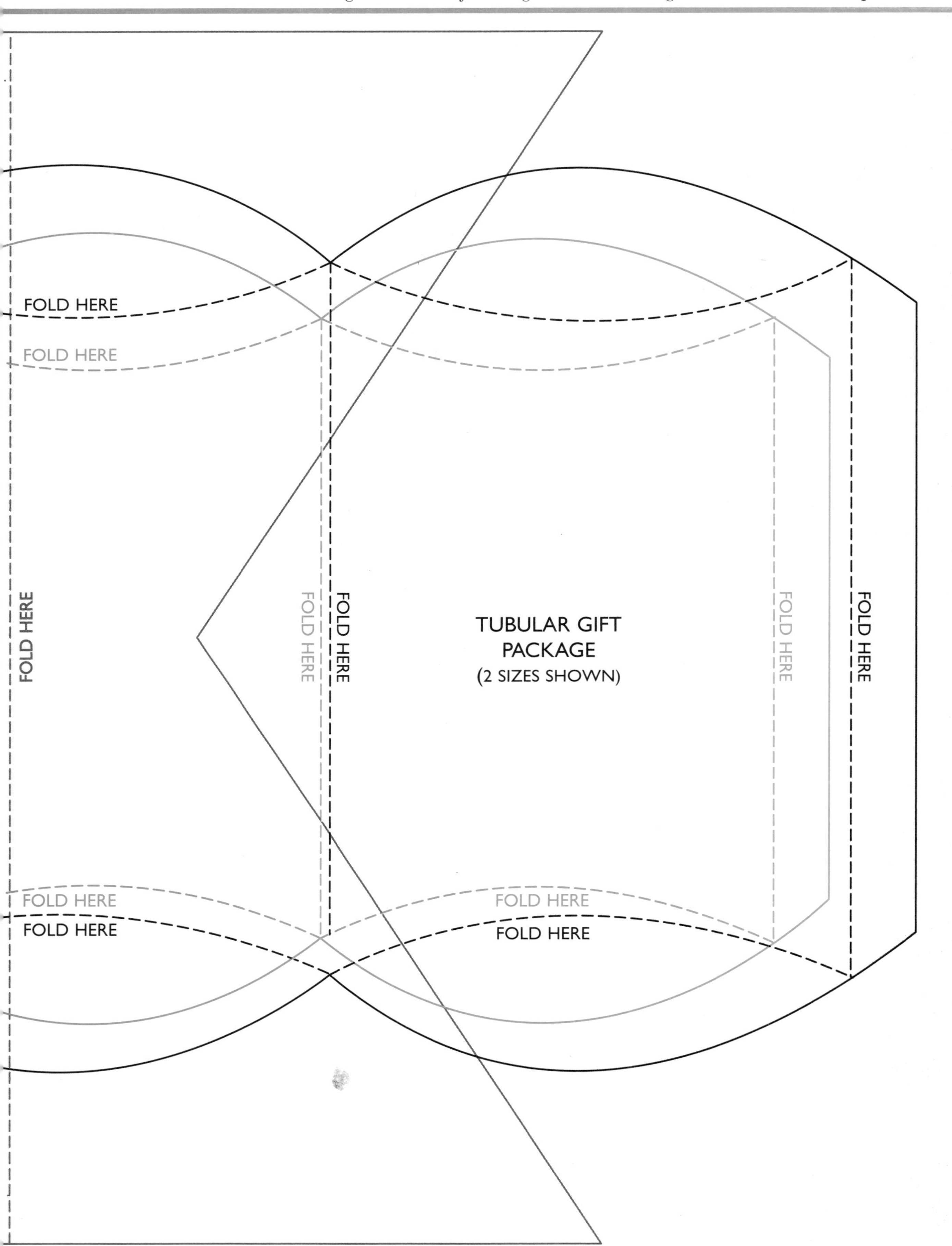
FOLD HERE
FOLD HERE
FOLD HERE
FOLD HERE
FOLD HERE
TUBULAR GIFT PACKAGE
(2 SIZES SHOWN)
FOLD HERE
FOLD HERE
FOLD HERE
FOLD HERE
FOLD HERE
FOLD HERE

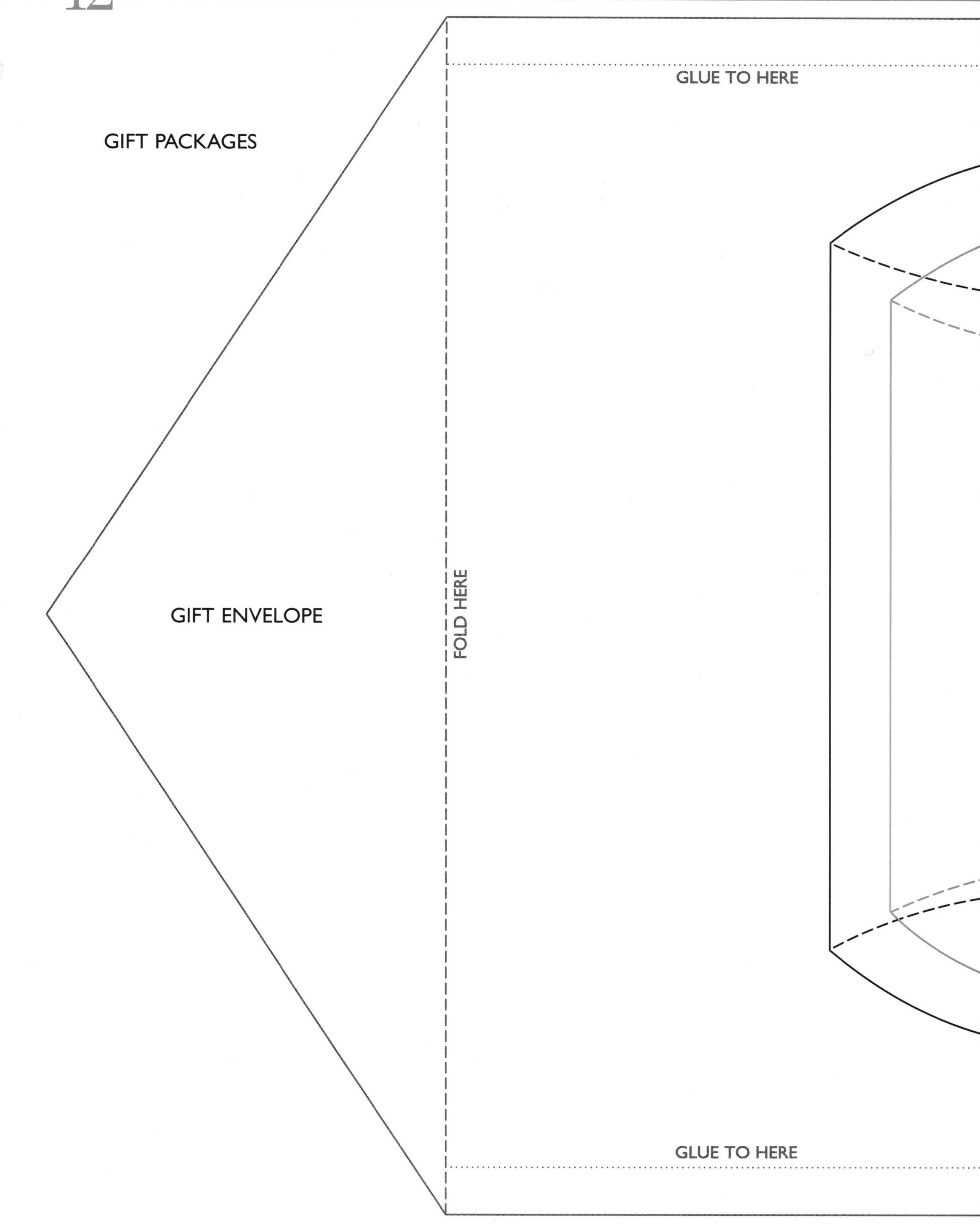
GIFT PACKAGES
GLUE TO HERE
GIFT ENVELOPE
FOLD HERE
GLUE TO HERE

EASTER-BASKET MOTIFS

GIFT-PACKAGE MOTIFS

For further information: Crafting & Decorating Made Simple™ 1-800-527-5576
International Masters Publishers, 444 Liberty Ave., Pittsburgh, PA 15222-1207

PAPER STENCILING MOTIFS

SACHET MOTIFS

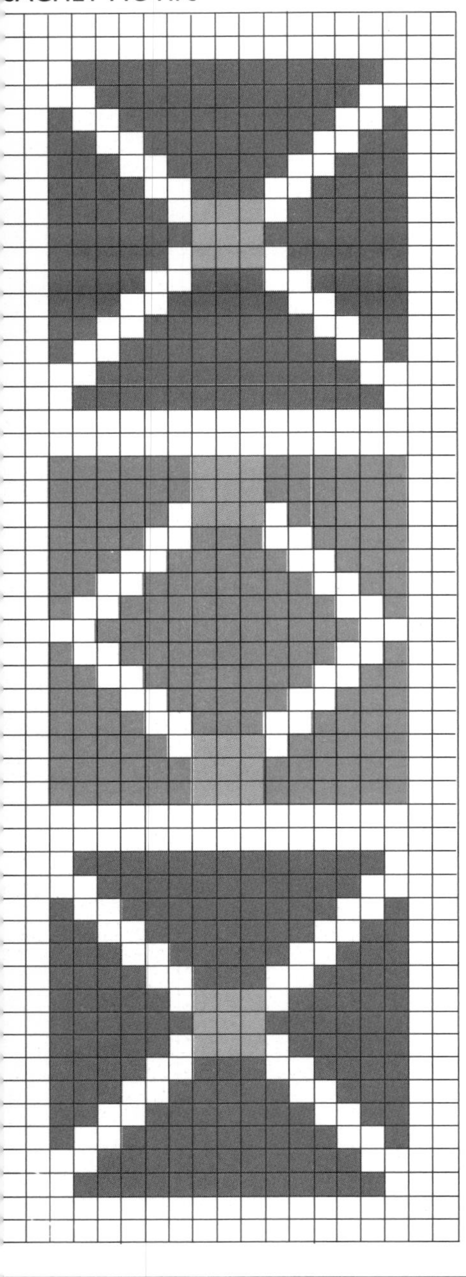

VARIATIONS OF GEOMETRIC MOTIFS

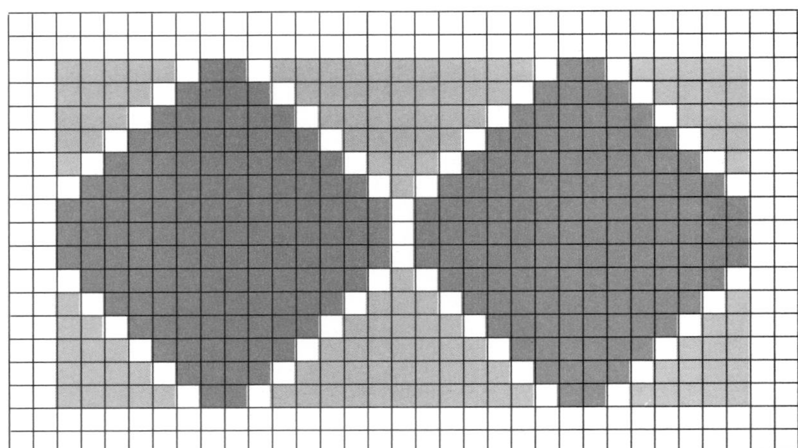

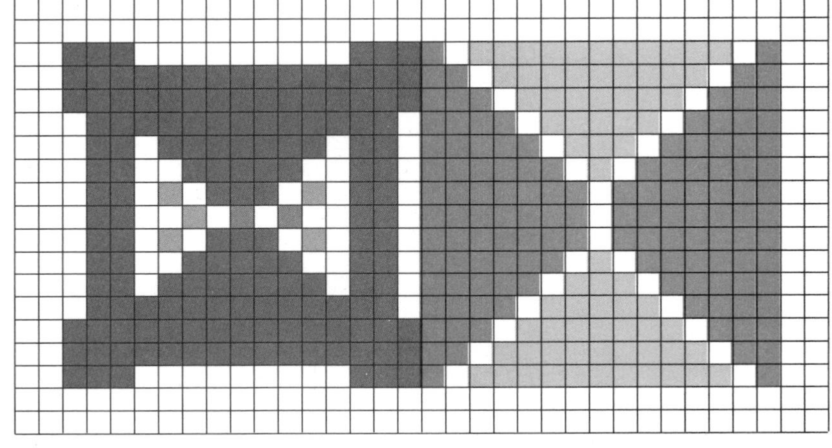

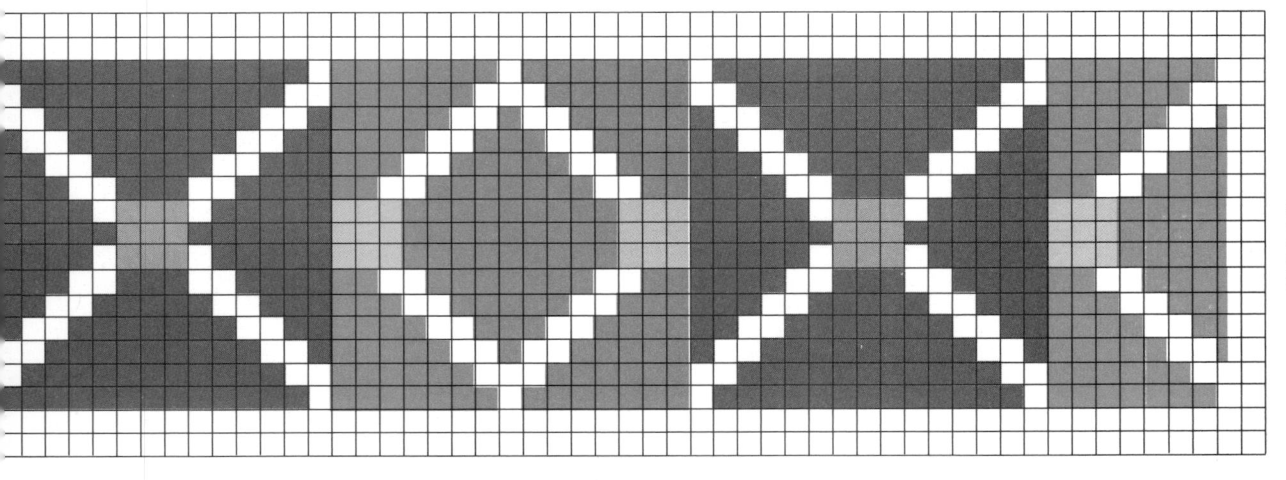

Legend for cross-stitch charts
1 tinted square = 1 cross-stitch; each tinted shade represents a separate color.
1 white square = 1 unstitched area equal in size to 1 cross-stitch.

Calculating finished size of completed cross-stitched design

- Count number of tinted and white squares within length of charted design (example: 15 squares).
- Determine number of fabric threads to be used for each square (example: 3 threads).
- Multiply both numbers to determine number of fabric threads covered (example: 45 threads).
- To determine length of completed cross-stitched design, divide number of covered fabric threads by thread count-per-inch of fabric (example: 45/20 = 2¼"-long motif).
- To determine finished width of cross-stitched motif, repeat previous steps with charted width of design.

CROSS-STITCH MOTIFS

TOWEL MOTIFS

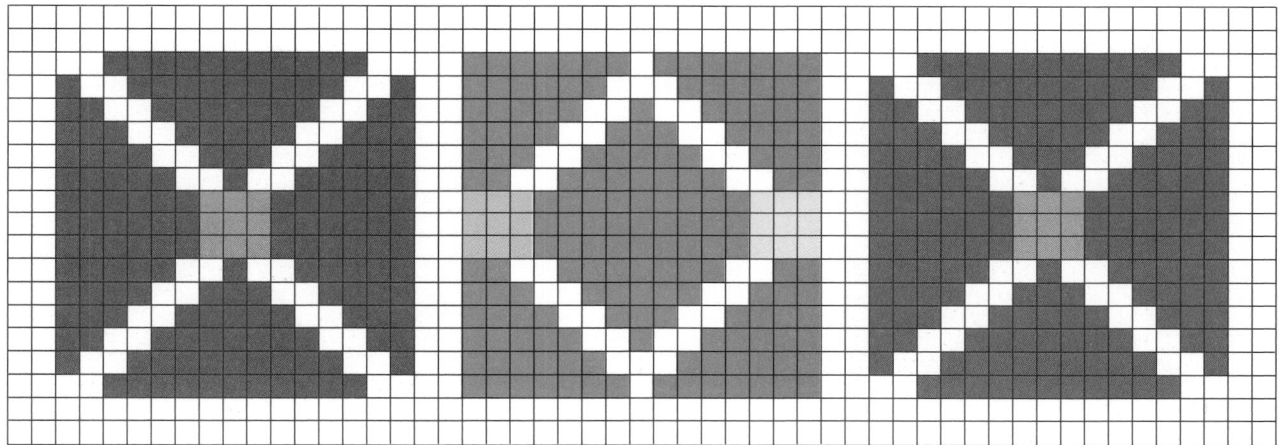

NAPKIN-RING MOTIF

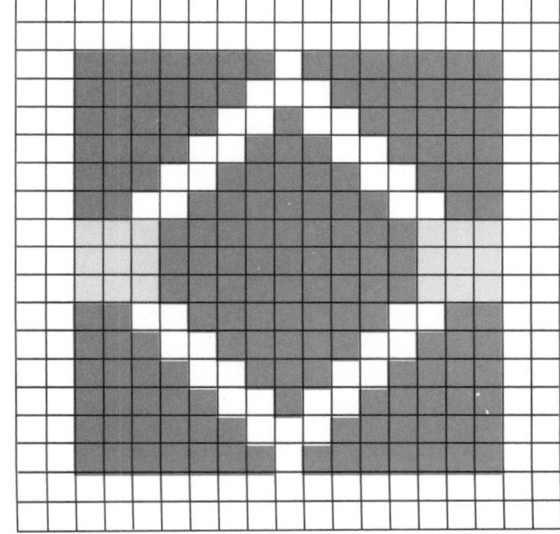

TIEBACK MOTIFS (REPEAT FOR FULL TIEBACK)

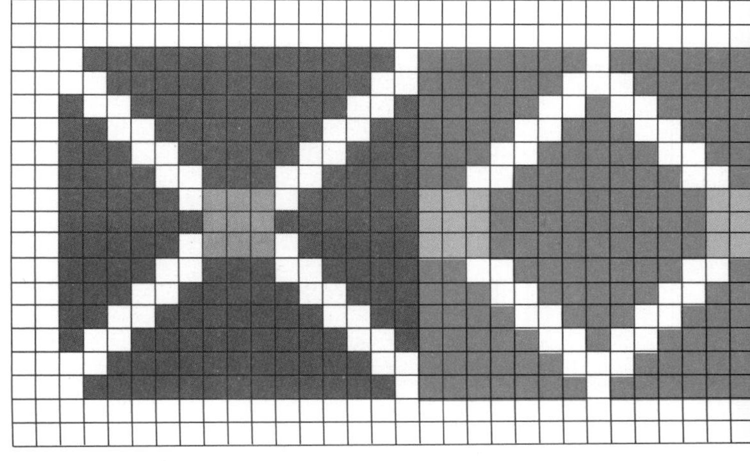

MOTIFS FOR GREEN-HERB POTS

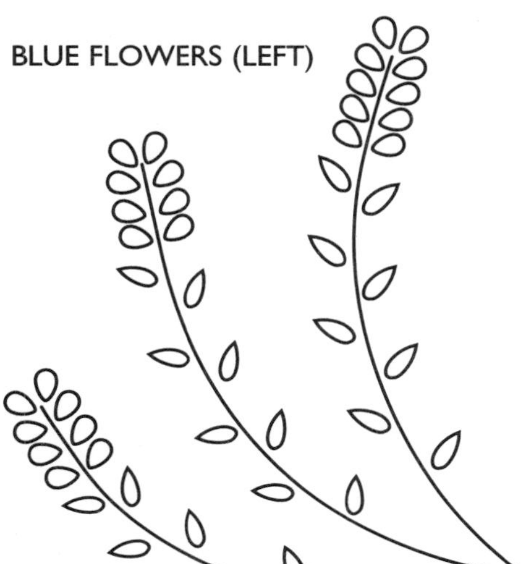

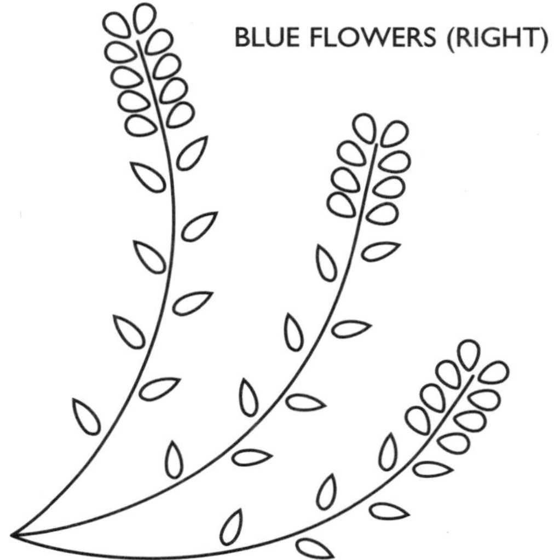

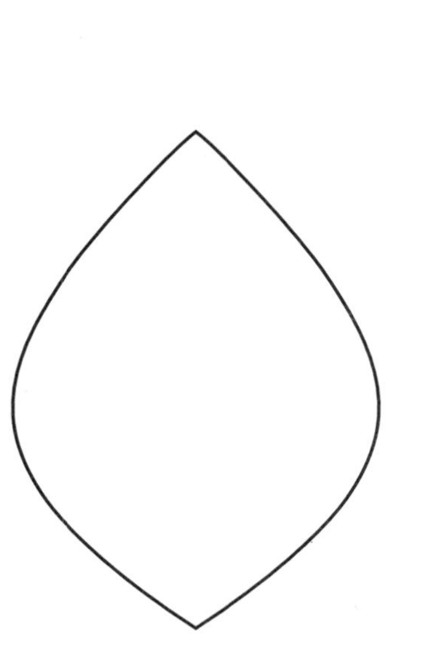

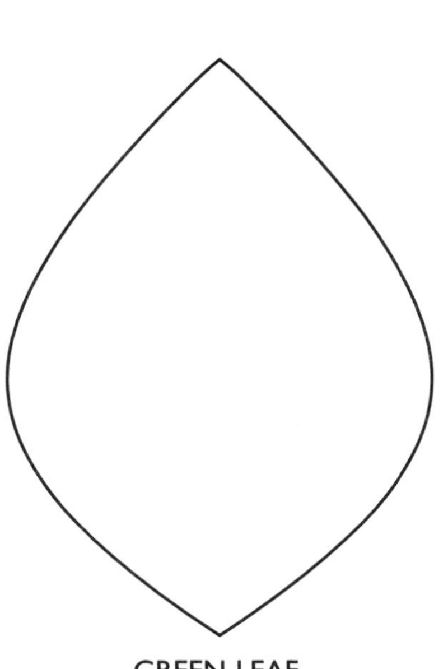

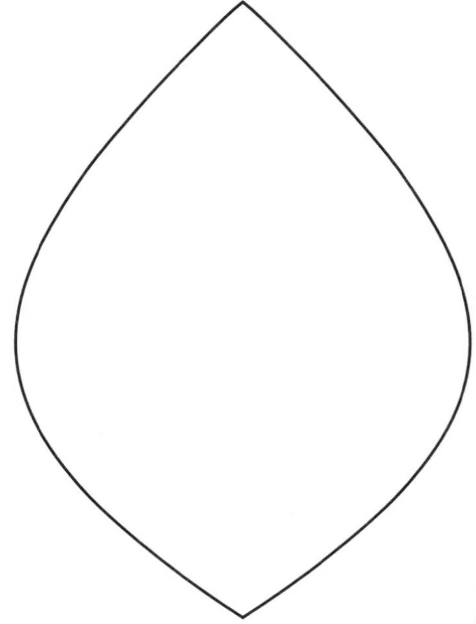

GREEN LEAF

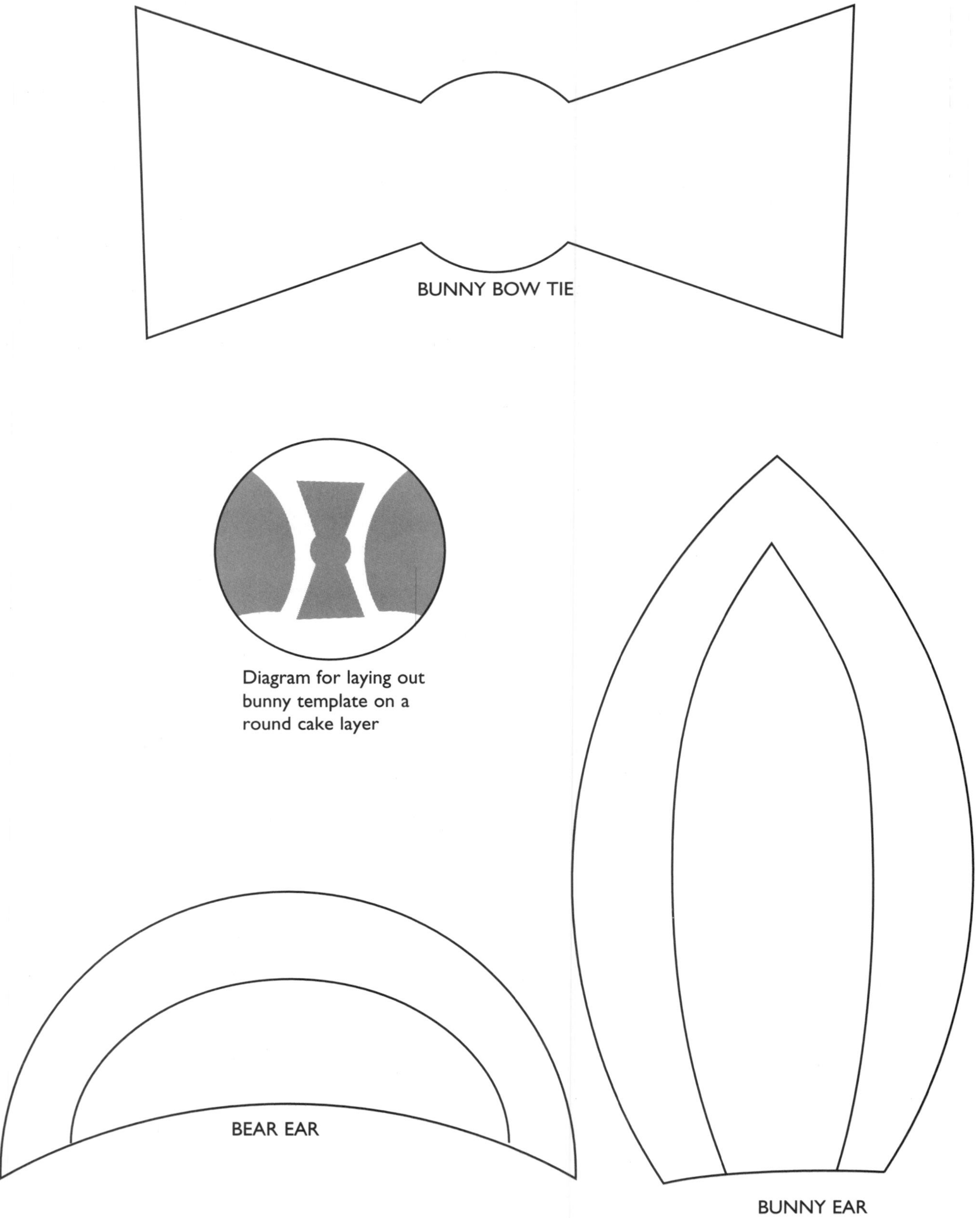

Diagram for laying out bunny template on a round cake layer

SHAPES FOR ANIMAL FACES

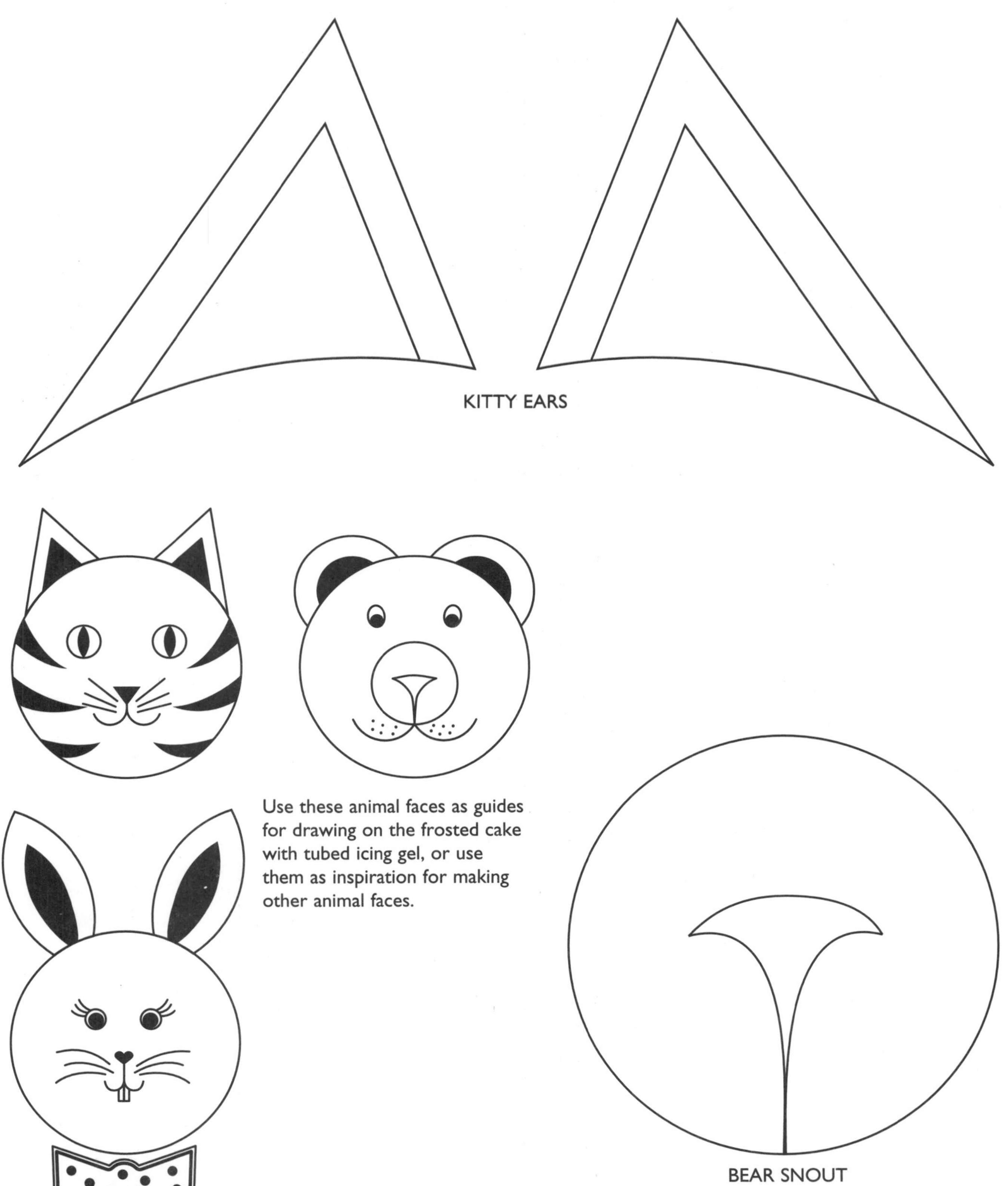

Use these animal faces as guides for drawing on the frosted cake with tubed icing gel, or use them as inspiration for making other animal faces.

FLOWER TRIM

VINE

US P 8801 11 002 Printed in U.S.A. Packet 2

Making Glowing Jack-o'-lanterns Group 9, Card 6
Painting a Still Life with Watercolors Group 11, Cards 1 & 2

MOON AND STARS

NOSES

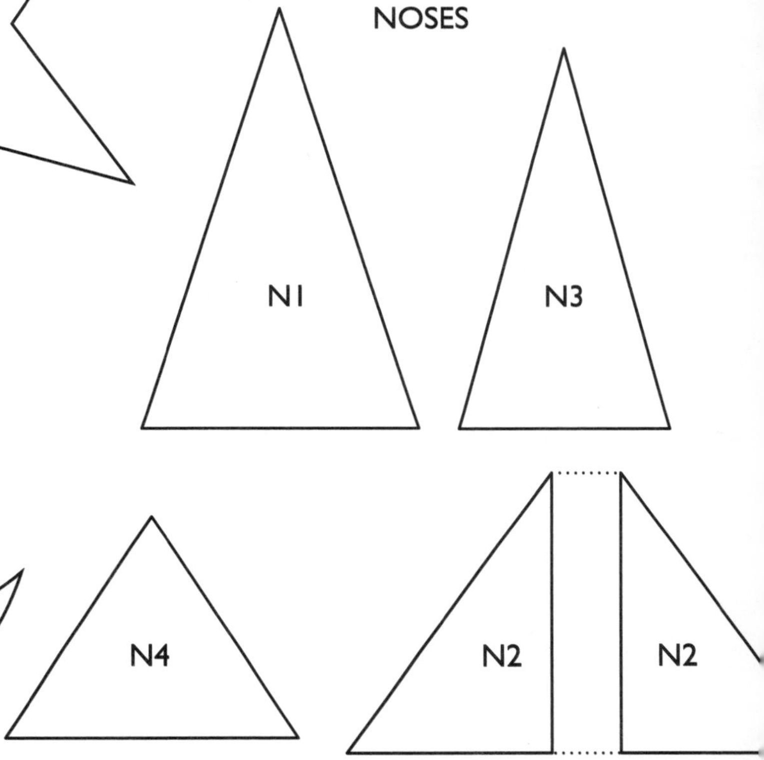

N1

N3

N4

N2

N2

EYES

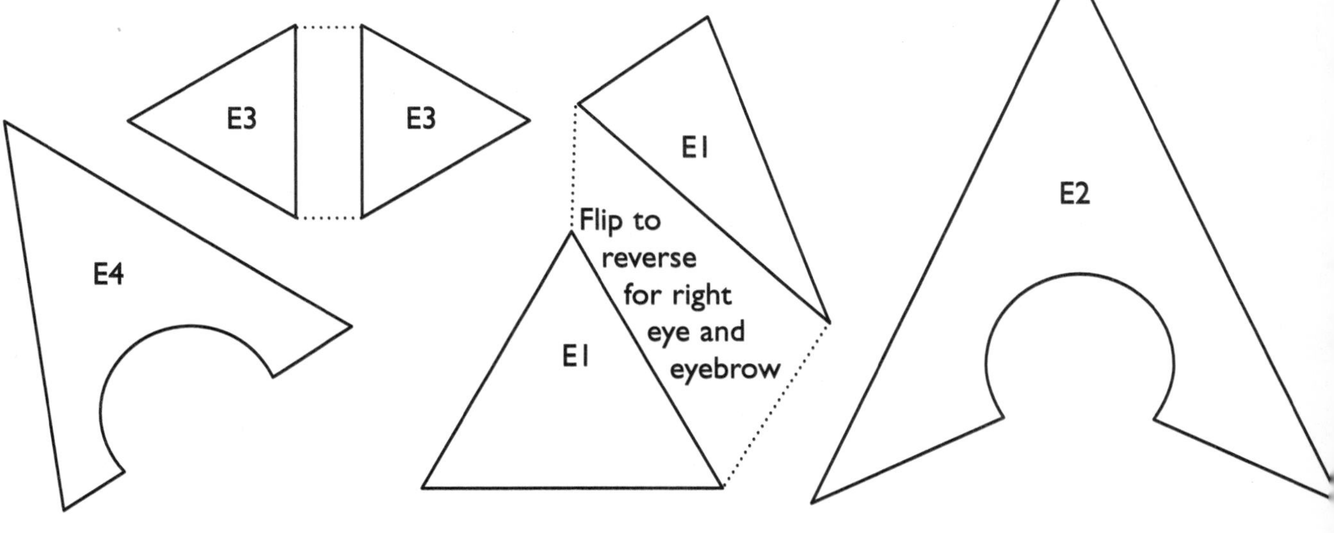

E3

E3

E1

E2

E4

Flip to reverse for right eye and eyebrow

E1

STILL LIFE LINE DRAWING

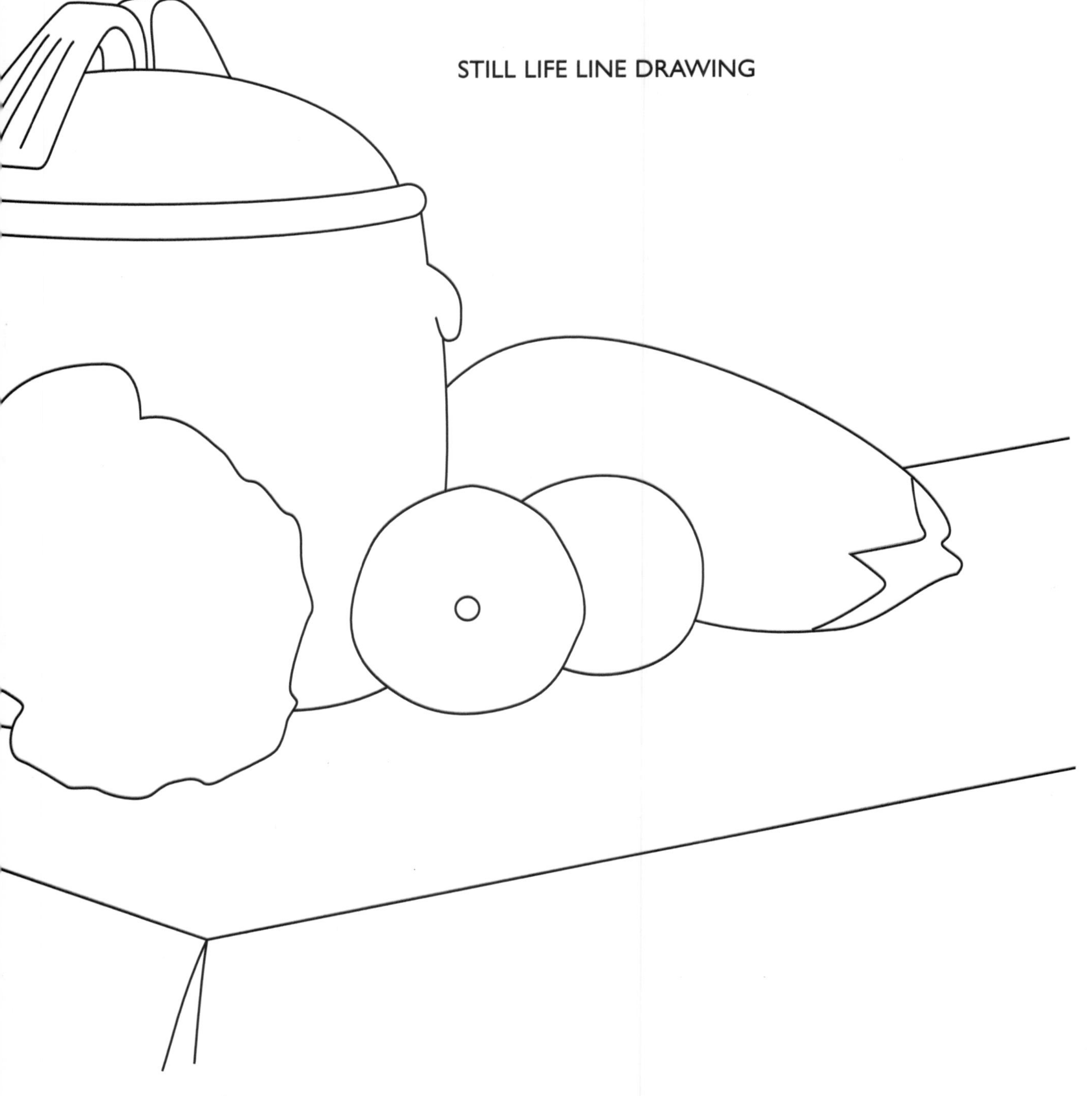

PAINTED PUMPKIN FACE

Carved pumpkin faces below are keyed to templates for face parts, or select different eyes, nose, and mouth combinations for another pumpkin face variation.

MOUTHS

M1

M2

M2

M2

M2

M2

M3

M4

T-SHIRT DESIGNS

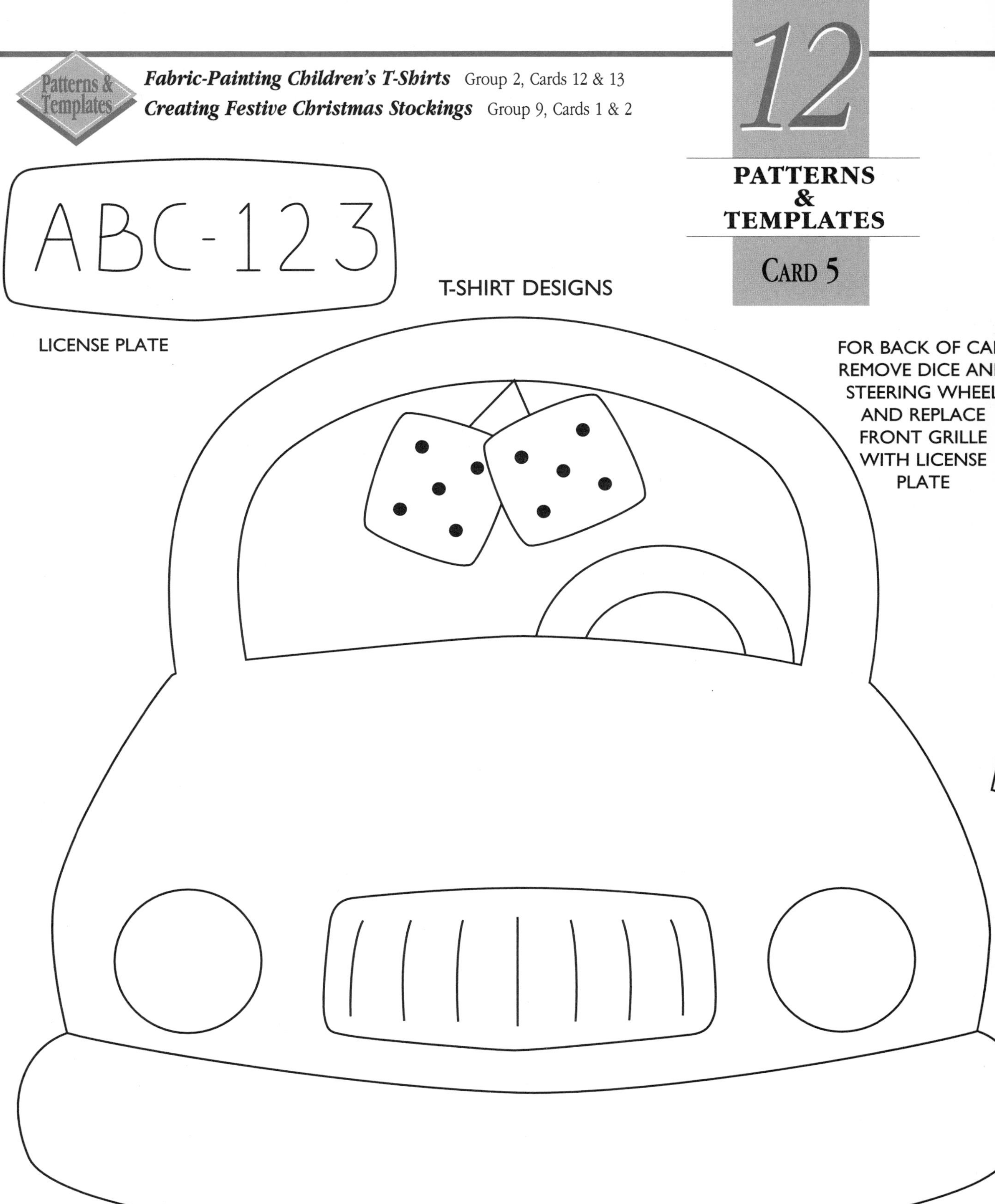

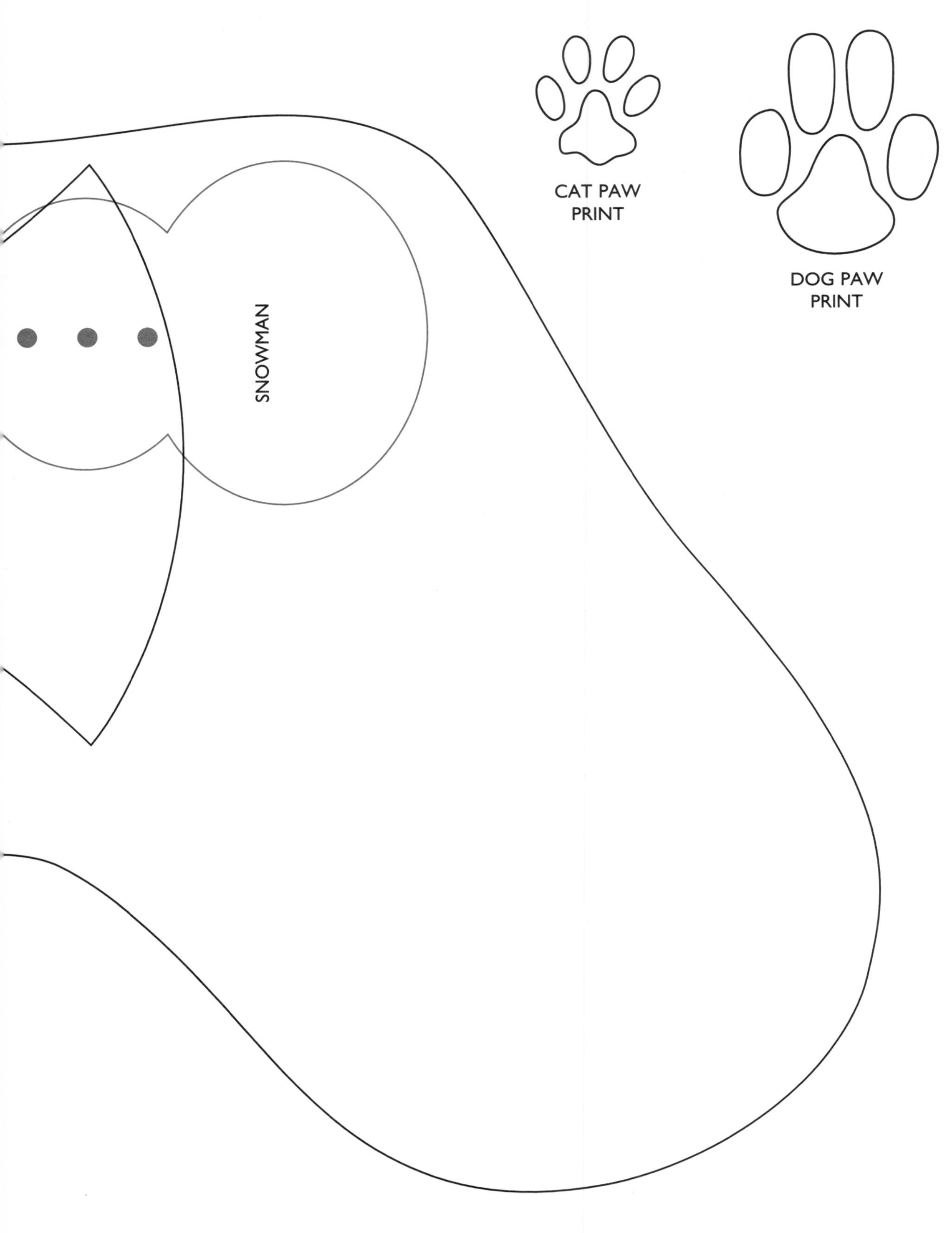
CAT PAW PRINT
DOG PAW PRINT
SNOWMAN

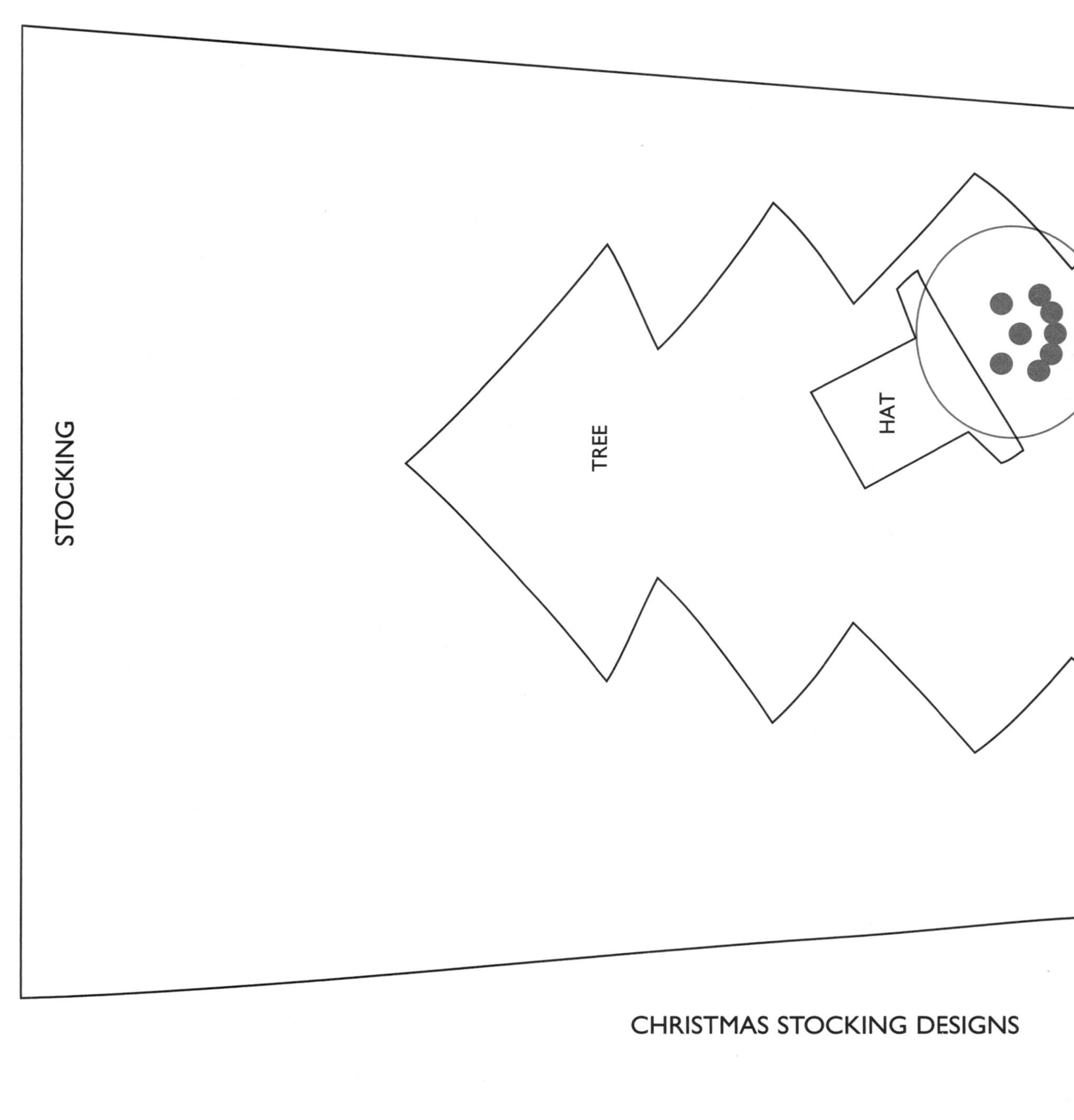

CHRISTMAS STOCKING DESIGNS

SCARF

US P 8801 12 004 Printed in U.S.A. Packet 4

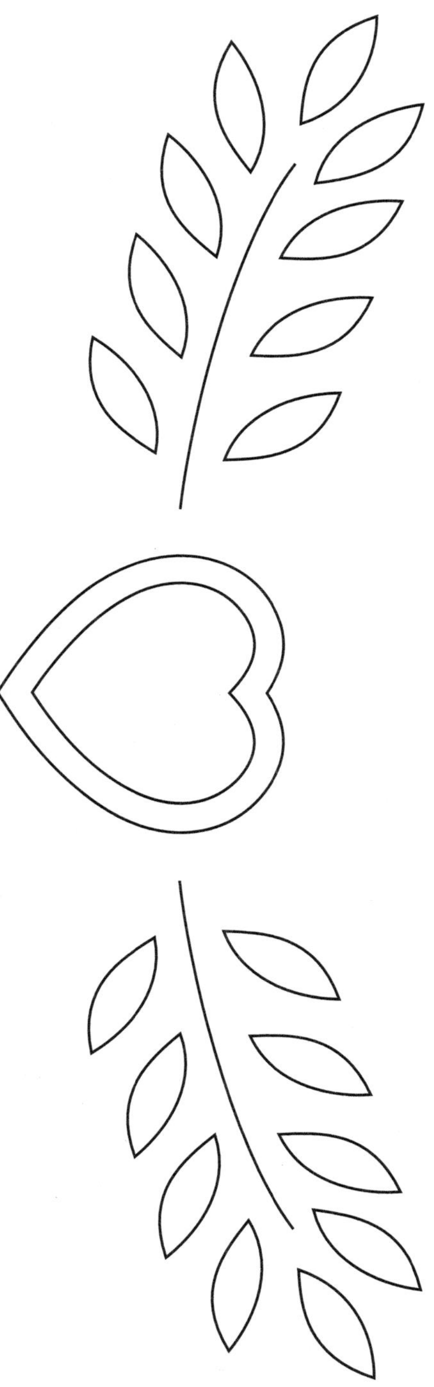

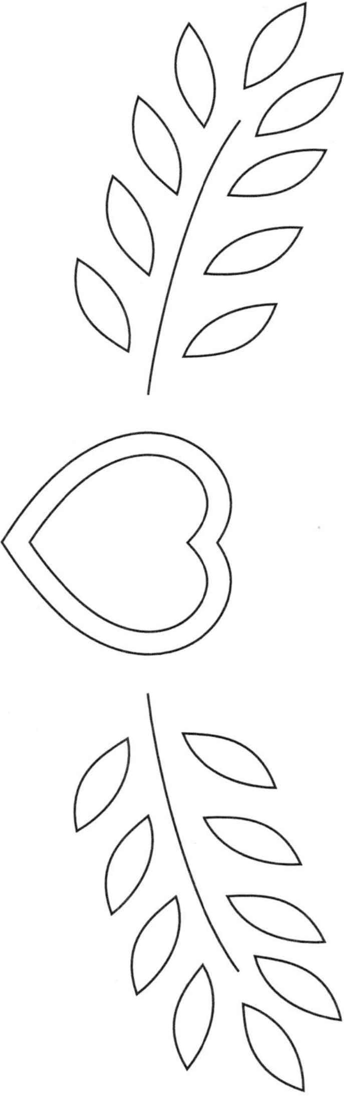

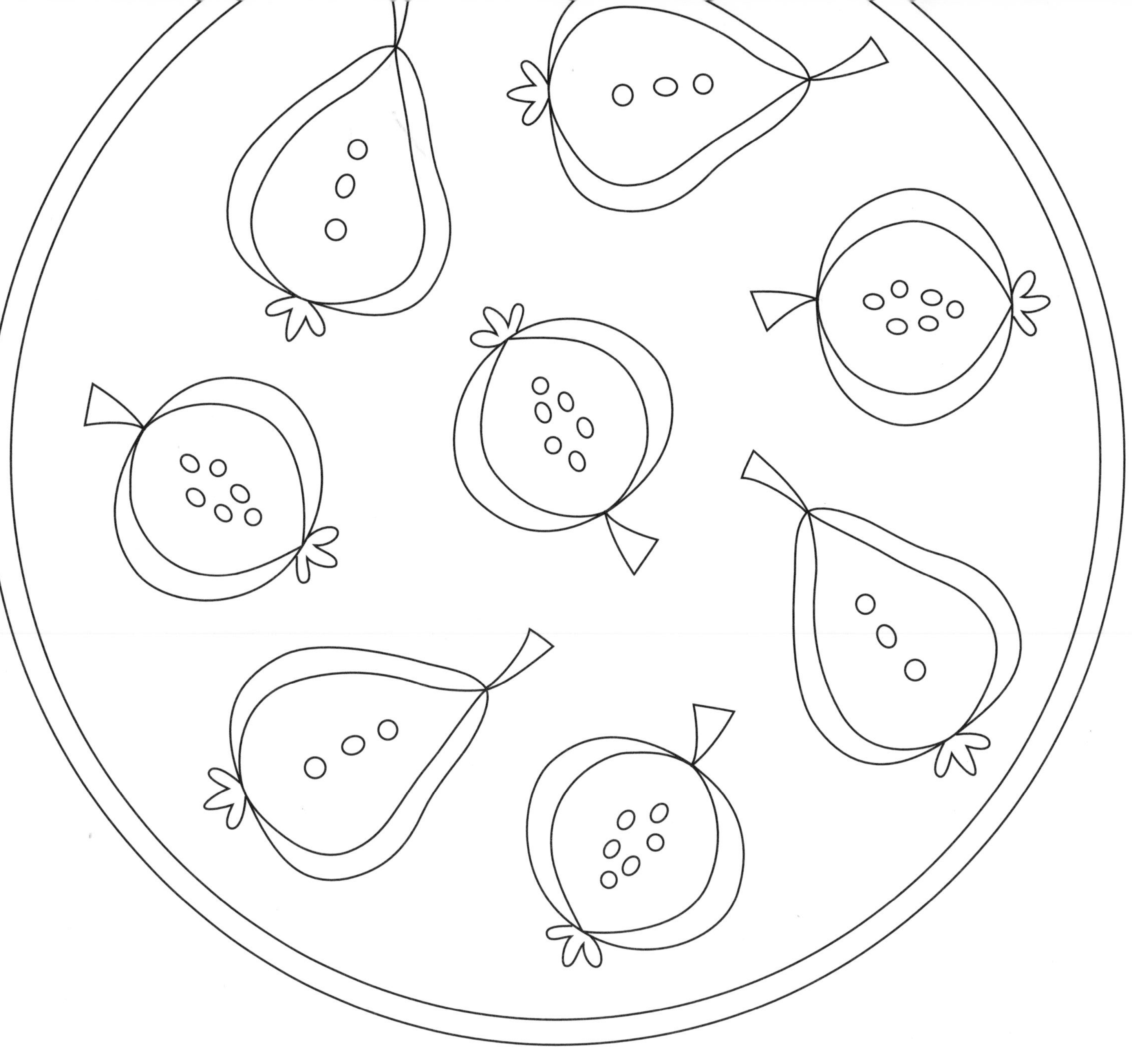

Dressing Up Hangers and Towels, Group 2, Cards 4 & 5
Making a Pillow with Fused Appliqués, Group 6, Cards 11 & 12

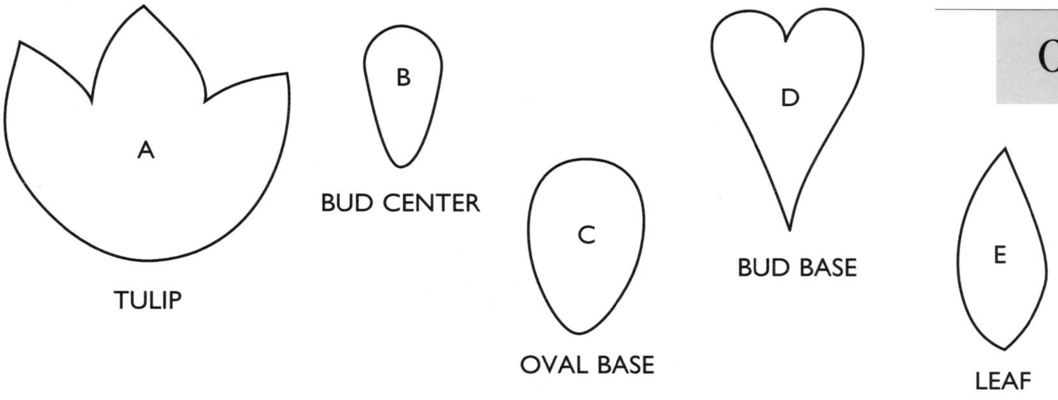

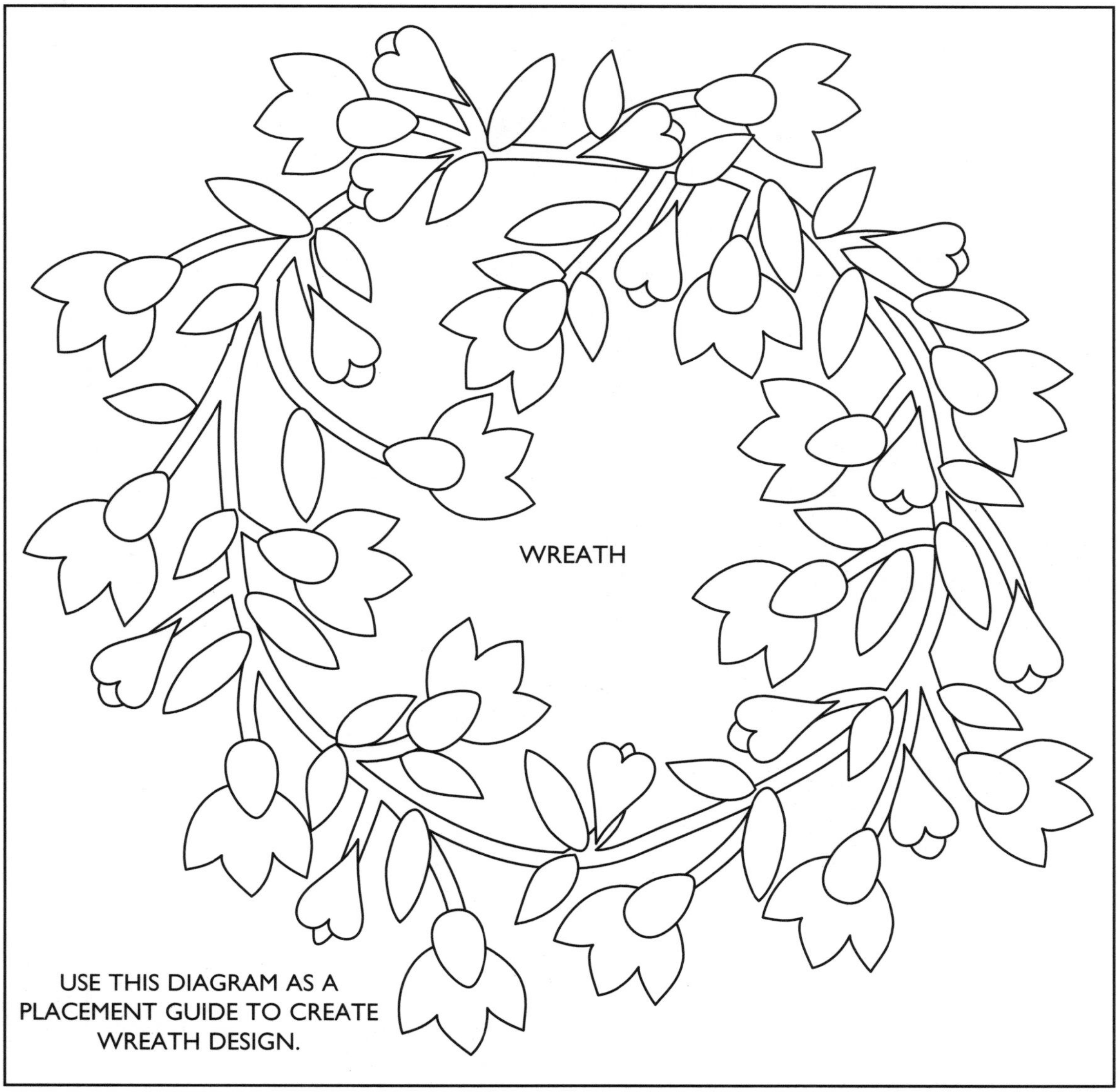

PATTERNS & TEMPLATES

CARD 7

A

TULIP

B

BUD CENTER

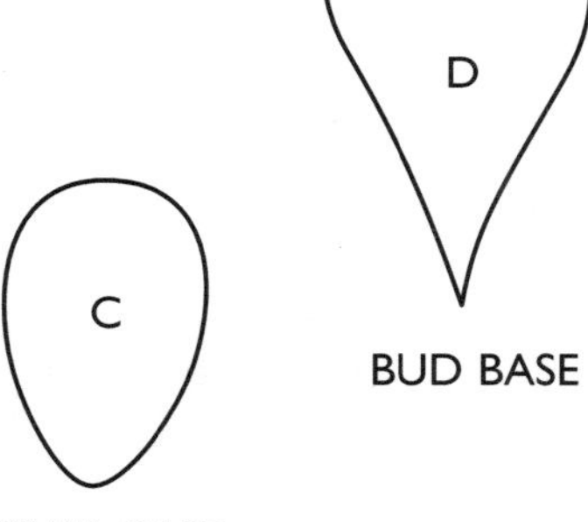

BUD BASE

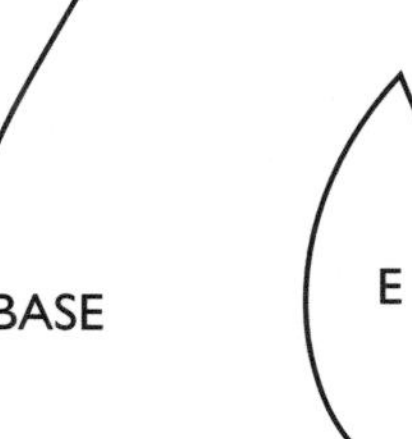

LEAF

WREATH

USE THIS DIAGRAM AS A PLACEMENT GUIDE TO CREATE WREATH DESIGN.

DEFG

LMN

RSTU

KYZ

LETTERS ARE SIZED FOR A SMALL HAND TOWEL. ENLARGE OR REDUCE LETTERS TO COMPLEMENT THE SIZE OF YOUR BATH TOWEL SET.

ABCD

HIJK

OPQR

VWX

BUD CENTER
B
D
BUD
BASE
A
TULIP
C
OVAL
BASE
E
LEAF
FLOWER BASKET

ETCHED GLASSWARE MOTIFS

VICTORIAN RAG DOLL PATTERNS

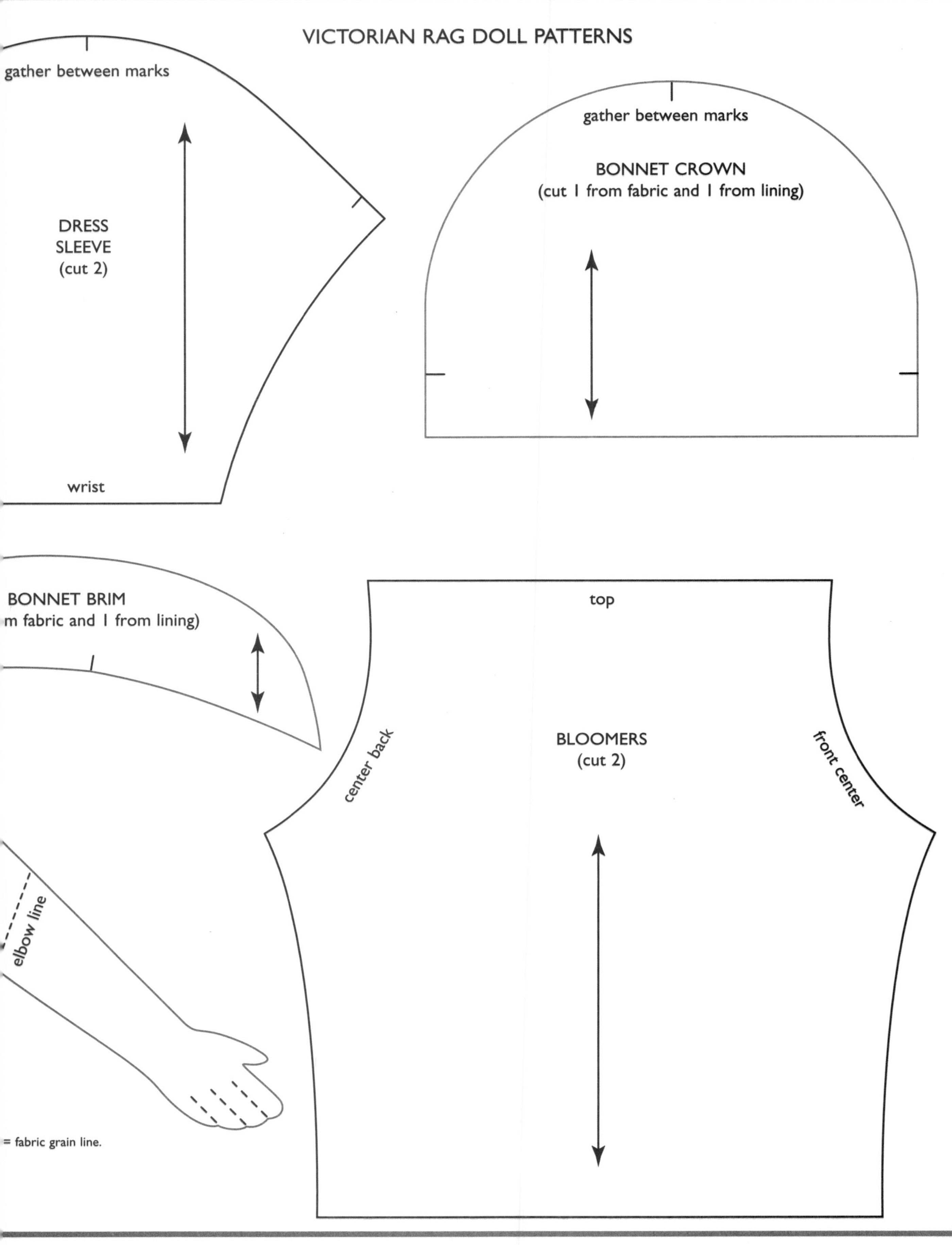

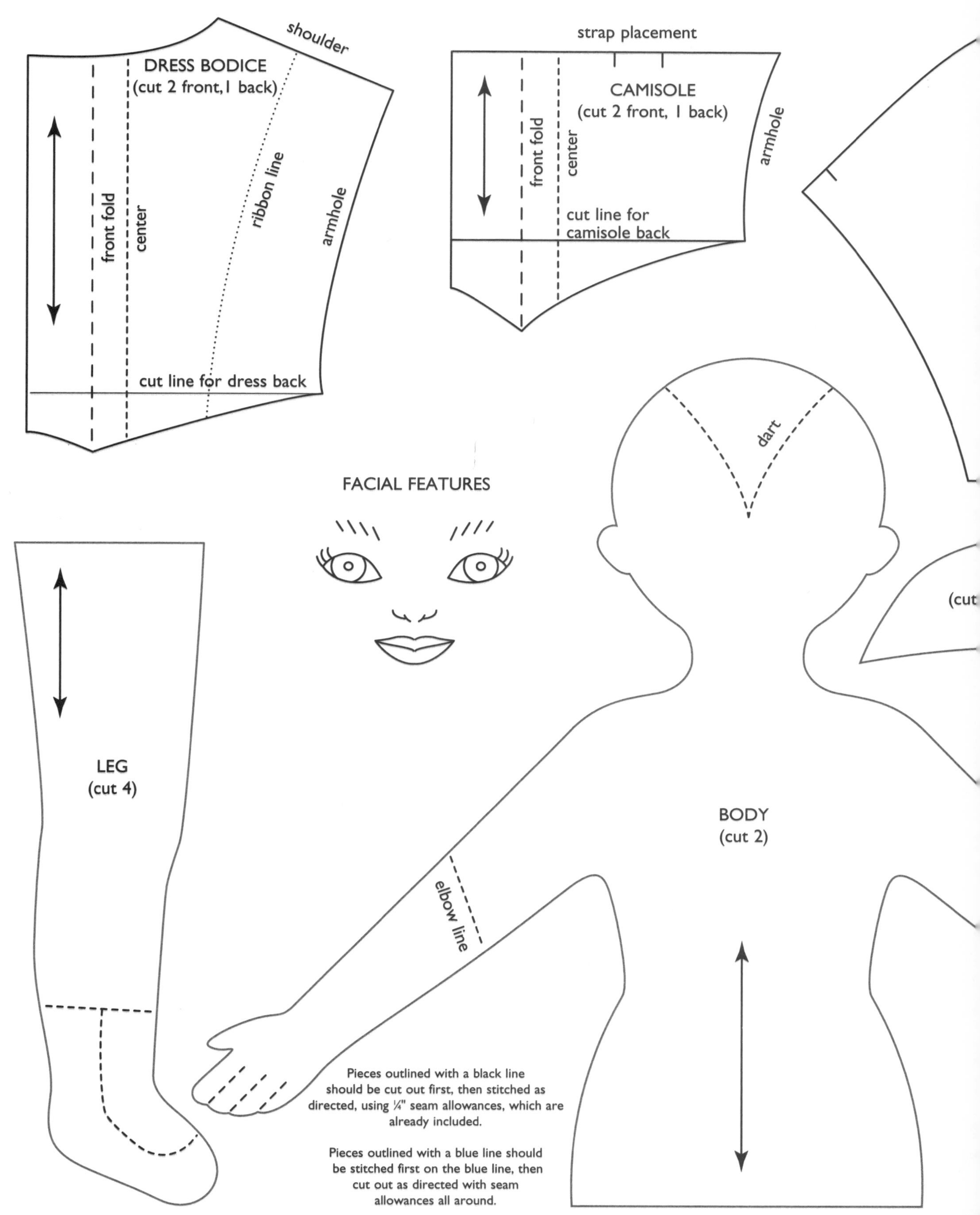

Pieces outlined with a black line should be cut out first, then stitched as directed, using ¼" seam allowances, which are already included.

Pieces outlined with a blue line should be stitched first on the blue line, then cut out as directed with seam allowances all around.

PHOTO-ALBUM COVER TEMPLATES

all details in felt

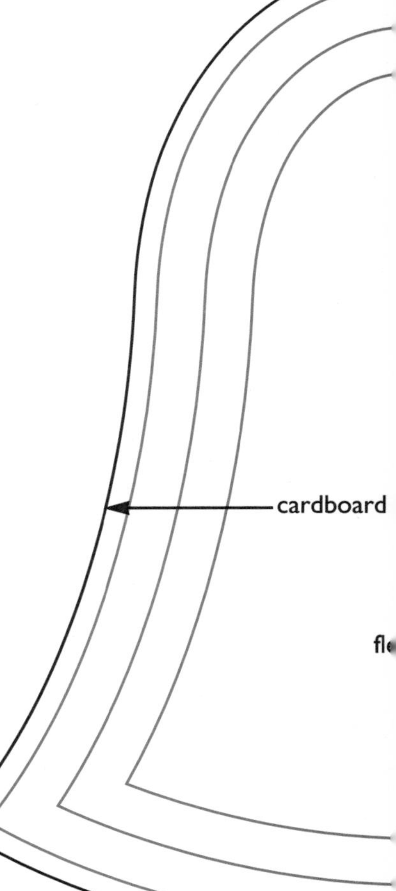

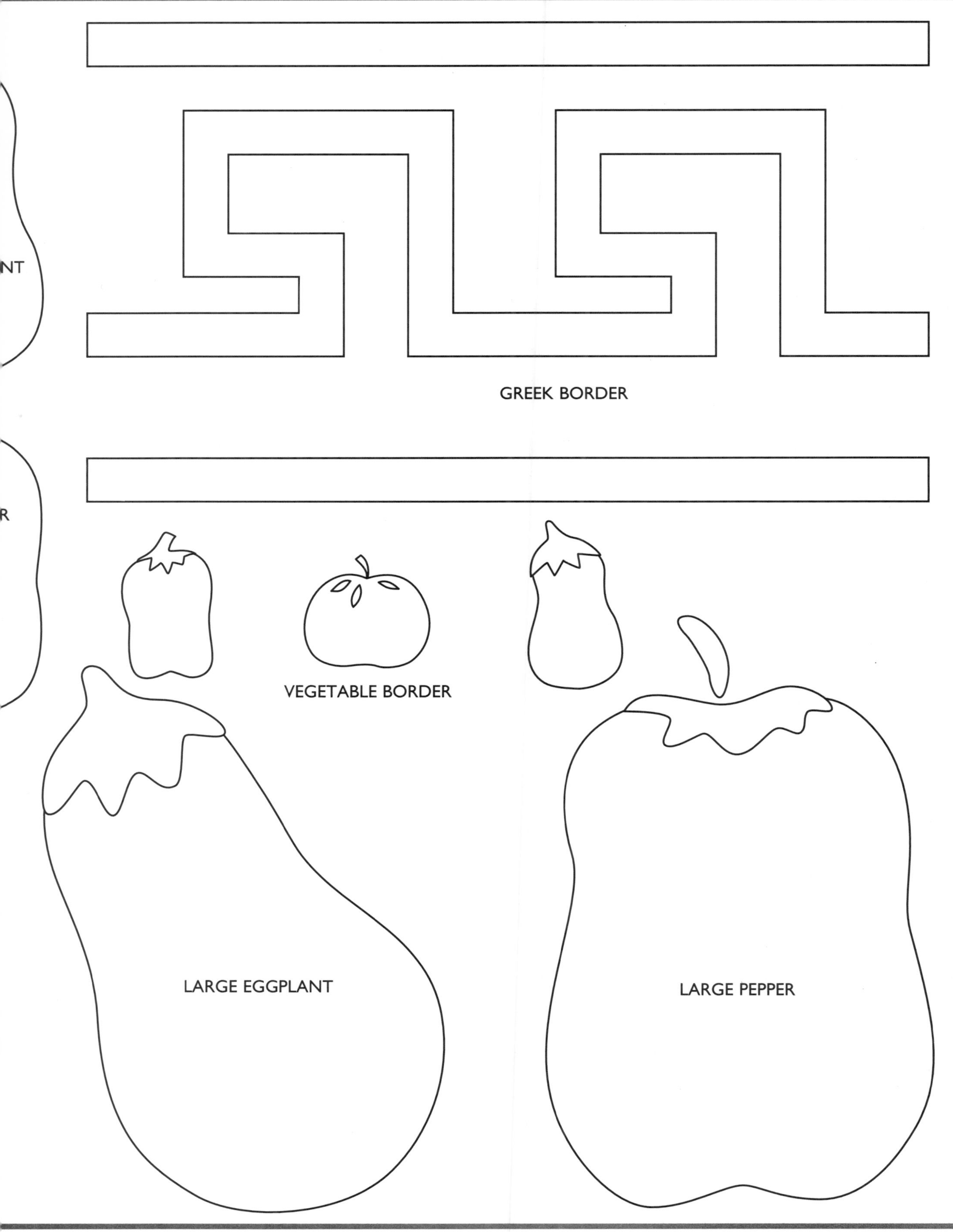
NT
R
GREEK BORDER
VEGETABLE BORDER
LARGE EGGPLANT
LARGE PEPPER

UPDATING CERAMIC TILES WITH STENCILING

FLOOR TILE

MEDIUM EGG

MEDIUM PE

LARGE TOMATO

MEDIUM TOMATO

LARGE BELL

cardboard outline

fleece outlines

BELL

tline

e outlines

Making Teddy Bears with Pile Fabric Group 2, Cards 10 & 11
Painting with Nordic-Style Stencils Group 8, Cards 12 & 13

NORDIC MOTIFS

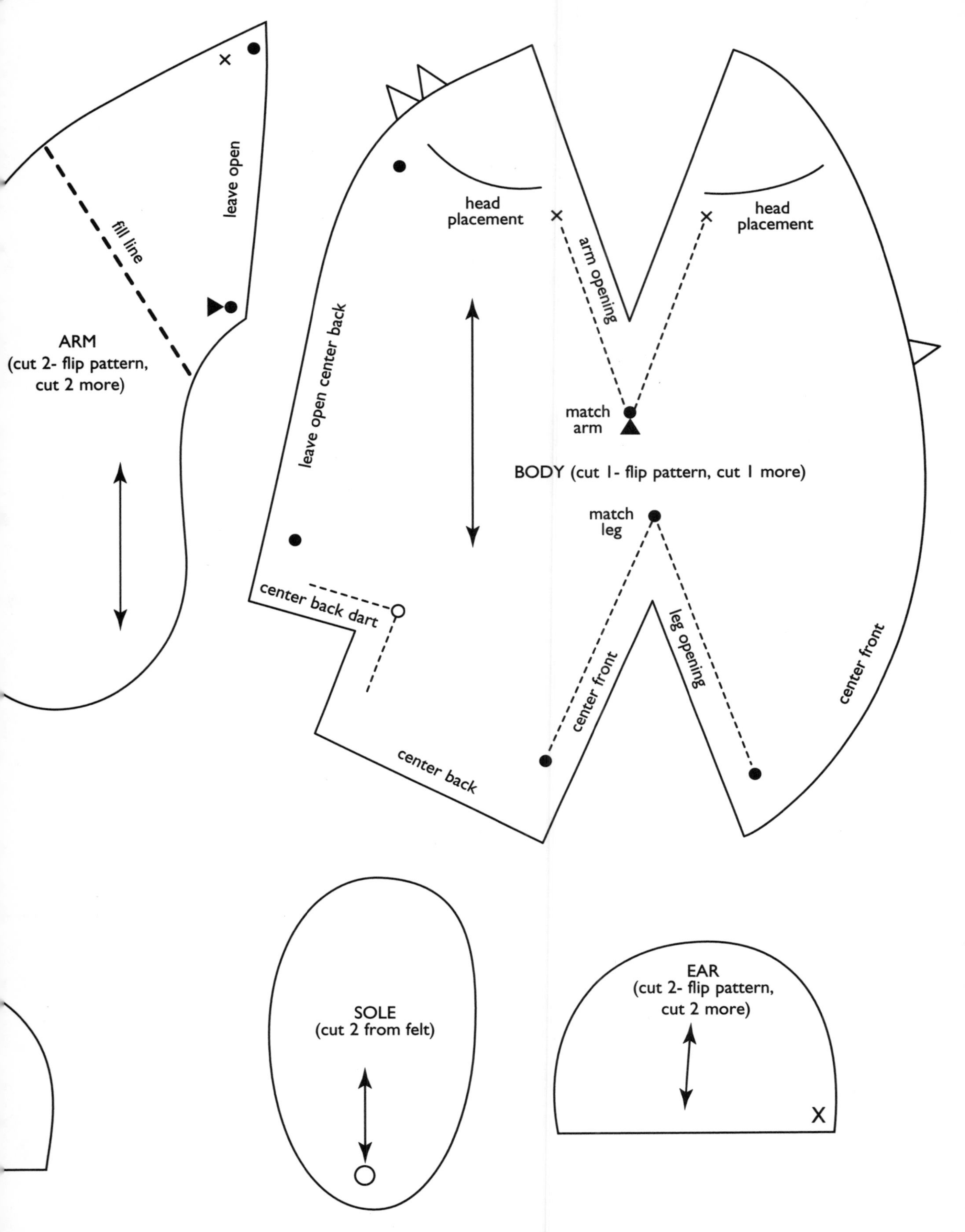
leave open
fill line
ARM
(cut 2- flip pattern,
cut 2 more)
head
placement
arm opening
head
placement
leave open center back
match
arm
BODY (cut 1- flip pattern, cut 1 more)
match
leg
center back dart
leg opening
center front
center front
center back
SOLE
(cut 2 from felt)
EAR
(cut 2- flip pattern,
cut 2 more)
X

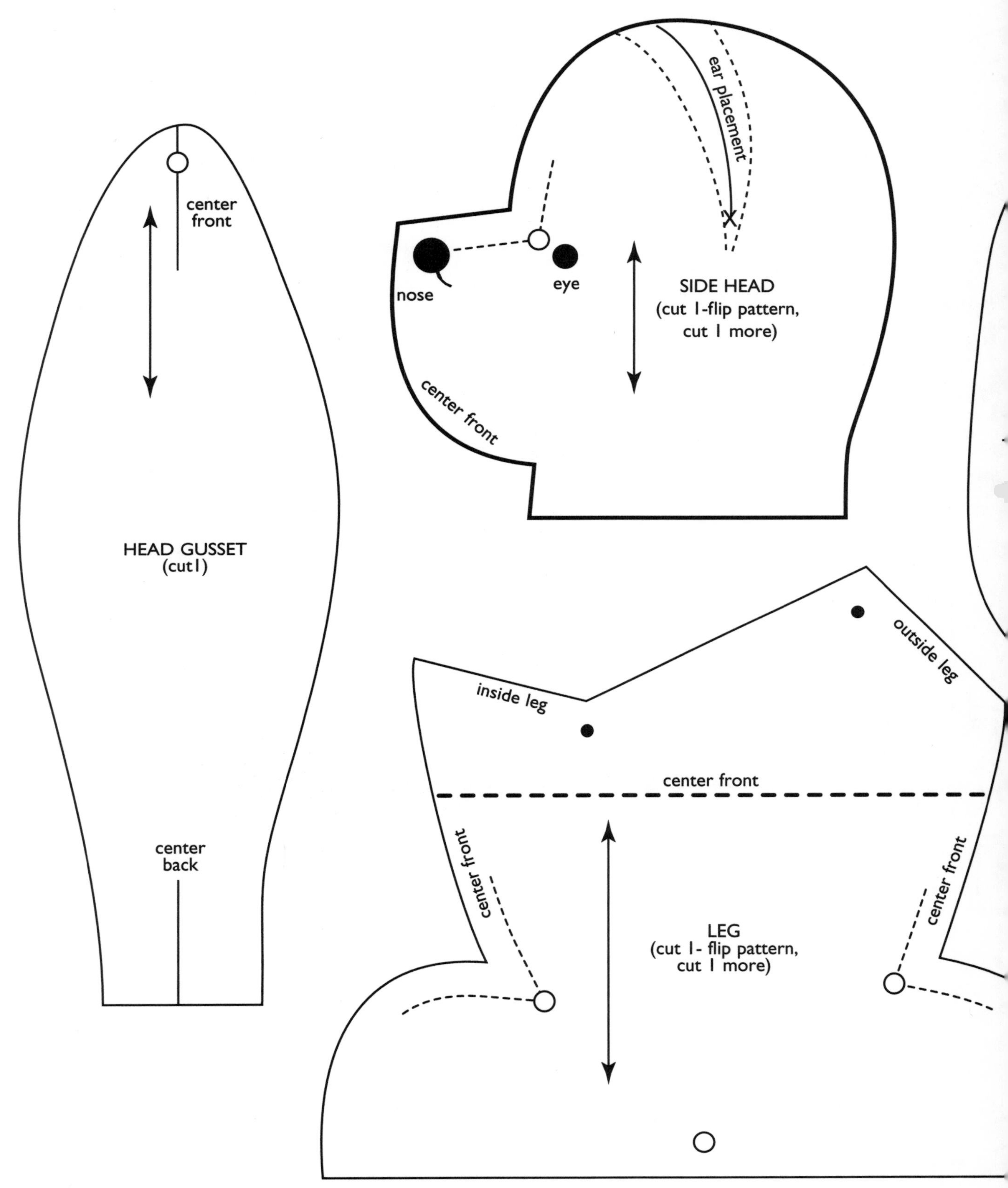

center
front
HEAD GUSSET
(cut1)
center
back
ear placement
nose
eye
SIDE HEAD
(cut 1-flip pattern,
cut 1 more)
center front
outside leg
inside leg
center front
center front
center front
LEG
(cut 1- flip pattern,
cut 1 more)

US P 8801 12 009 Printed in U.S.A.

OIL PAINTING LINE DRAWING

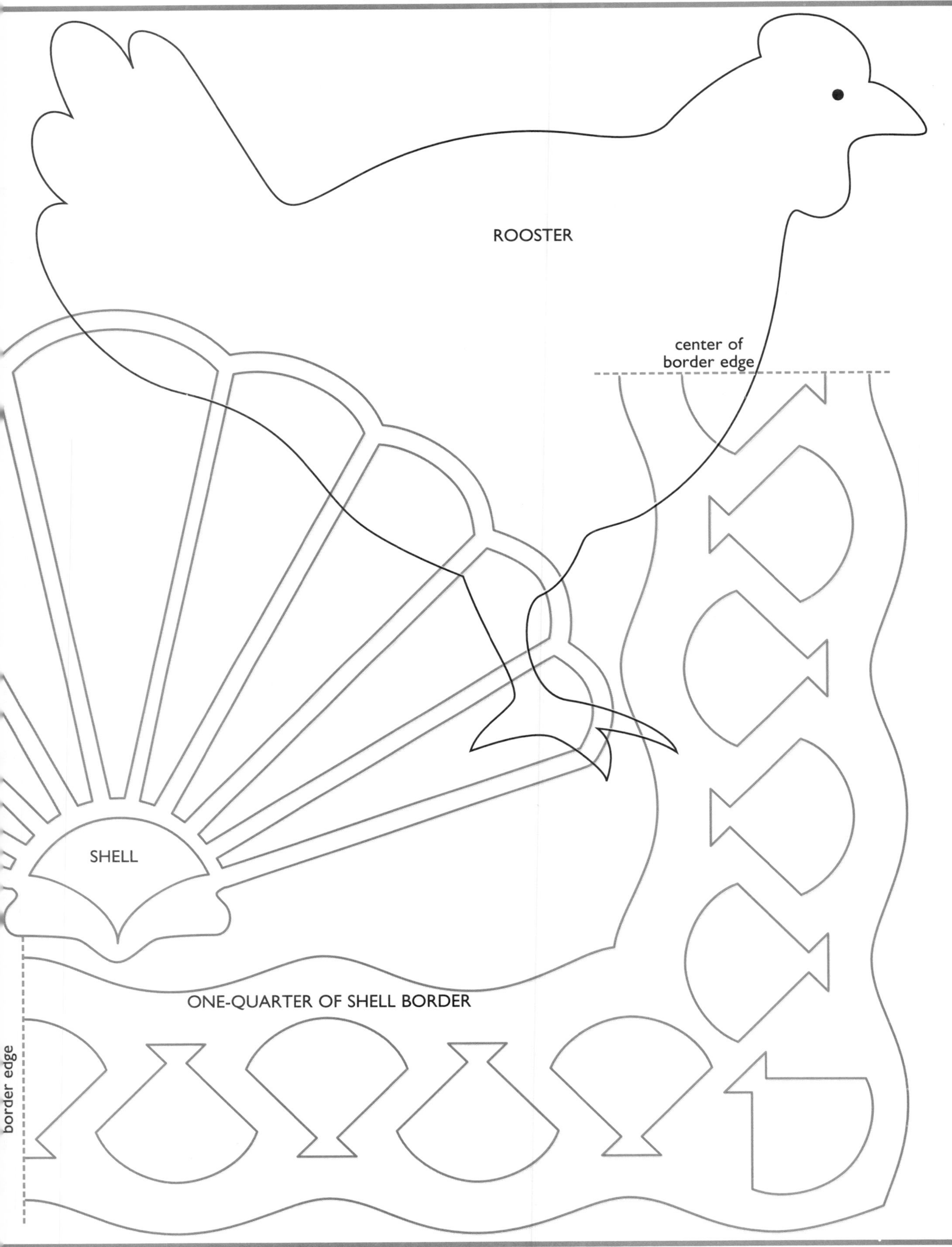
ROOSTER
center of
border edge
SHELL
ONE-QUARTER OF SHELL BORDER
border edge

COW

PIG

Copy and join four one-quarter shell borders to create complete pillow border.

CELTIC KNOT
QUILTING MOTIF

Painting a Plain Roller Shade Group 7, Card 9
Stenciling Chair-Rail Borders Group 7, Cards 15 & 16

SWIRL AND BLOCK CHAIR-RAIL BORDER

Shaded area of swirl is cutaway portion.

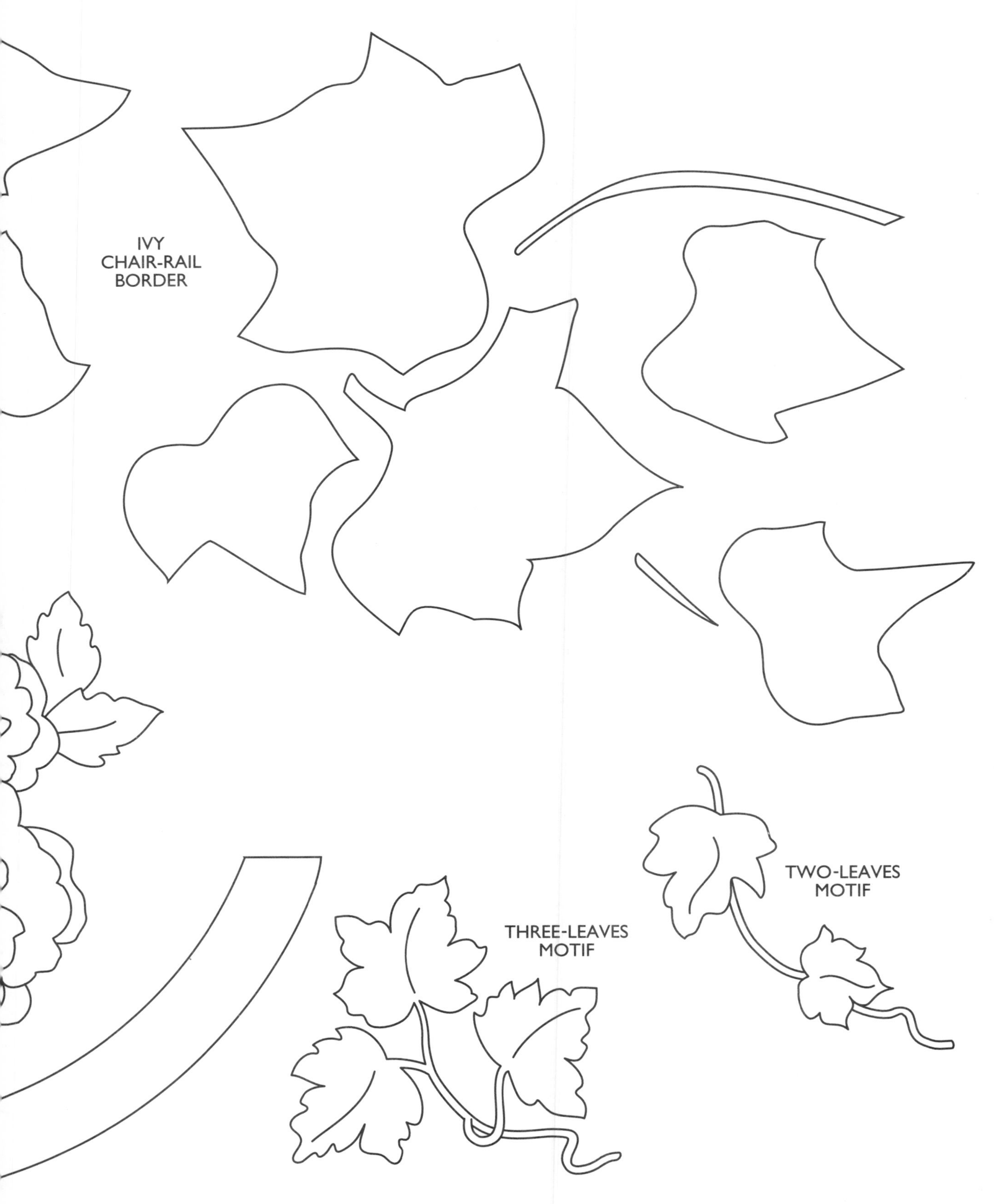
IVY
CHAIR-RAIL
BORDER
THREE-LEAVES
MOTIF
TWO-LEAVES
MOTIF

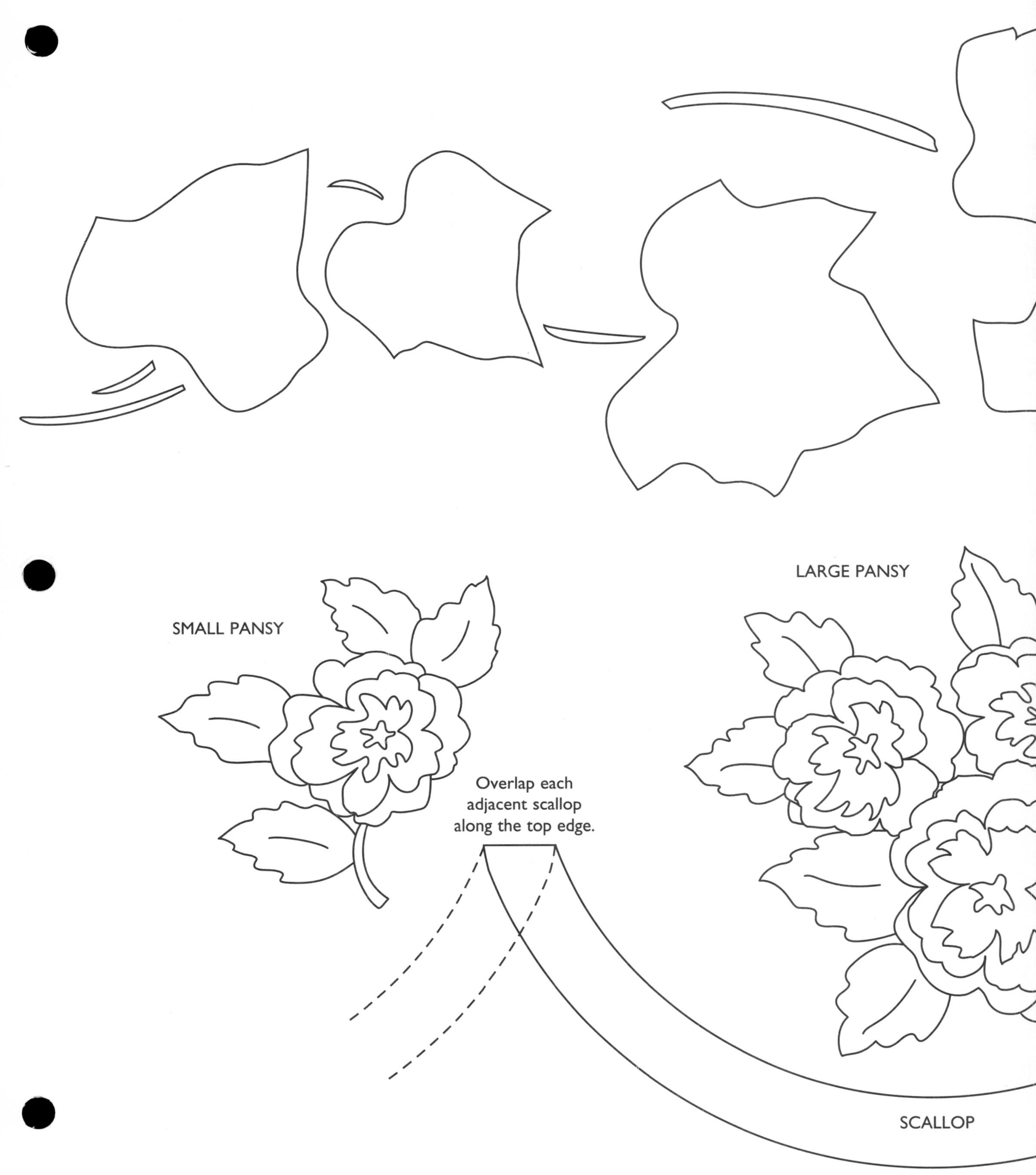
SMALL PANSY
LARGE PANSY
Overlap each adjacent scallop along the top edge.
SCALLOP

TEAPOT
EACUP
STARFISH AND WAVE
CHAIR-RAIL BORDER

Stenciling Holiday Wrapping Papers Group 3, Card 16
Making a Fabric-Covered Cornice Group 7, Cards 21 & 22

LARGE TREE

SMALL TREE

SMALL DOT

LARGE DOT

LARGE HEART

SMALL HEART

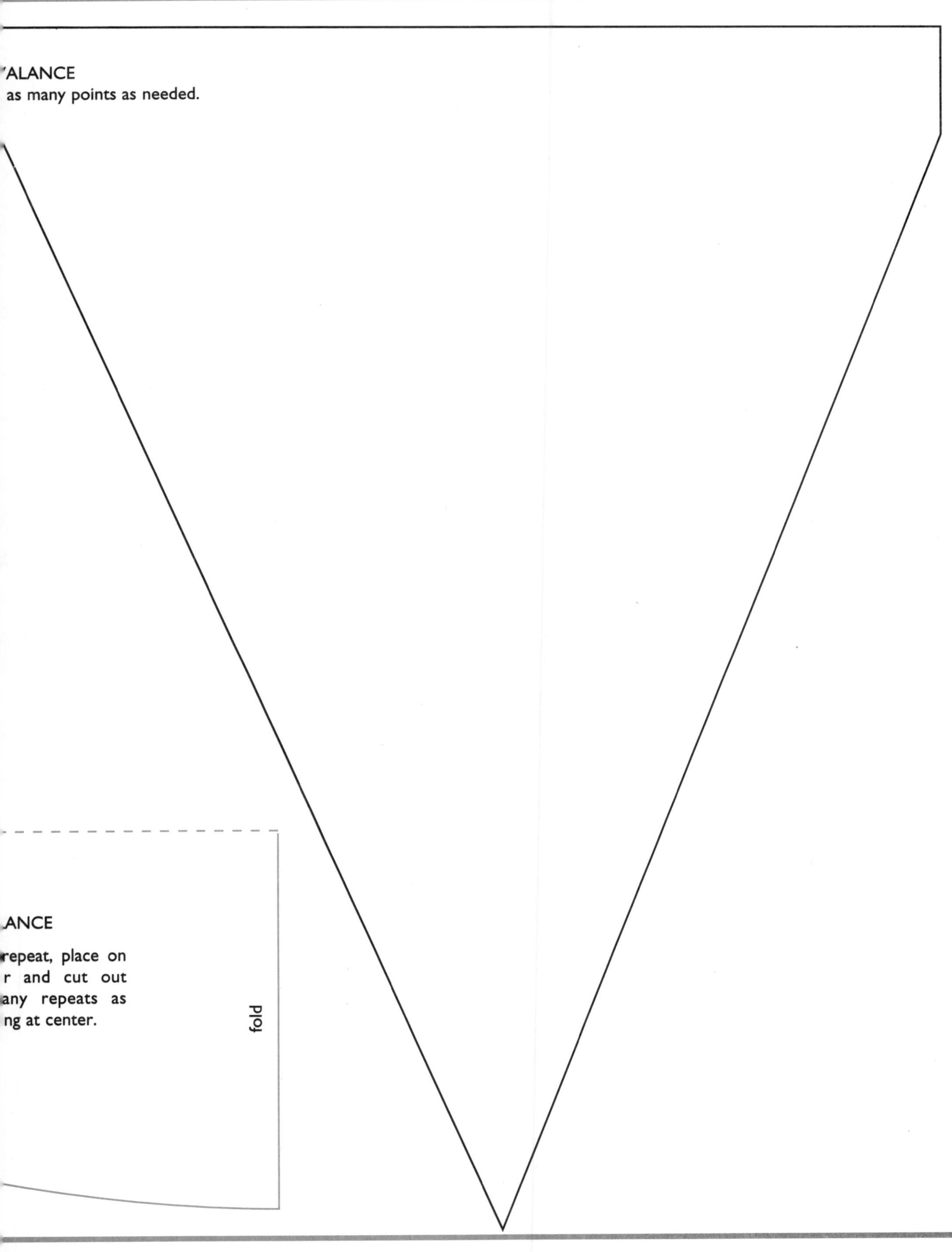
'ALANCE
as many points as needed.
.ANCE
repeat, place on
r and cut out
any repeats as
ng at center.
fold

POINT

Use pattern to mark ar

CURVED

To make full pat
fold of tracing
pattern. Mark a
needed on fabric,

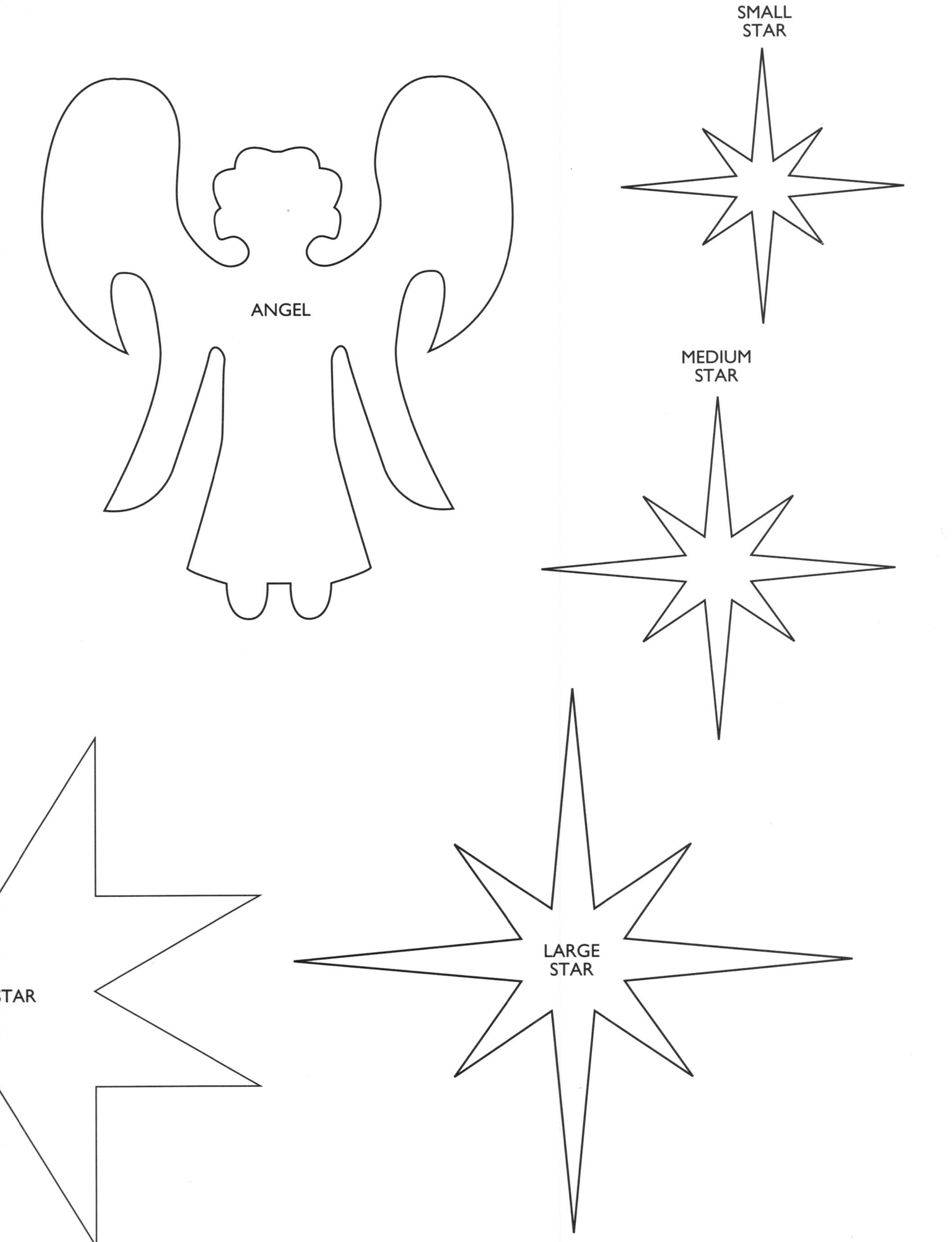
SMALL
STAR
ANGEL
MEDIUM
STAR
LARGE
STAR
STAR

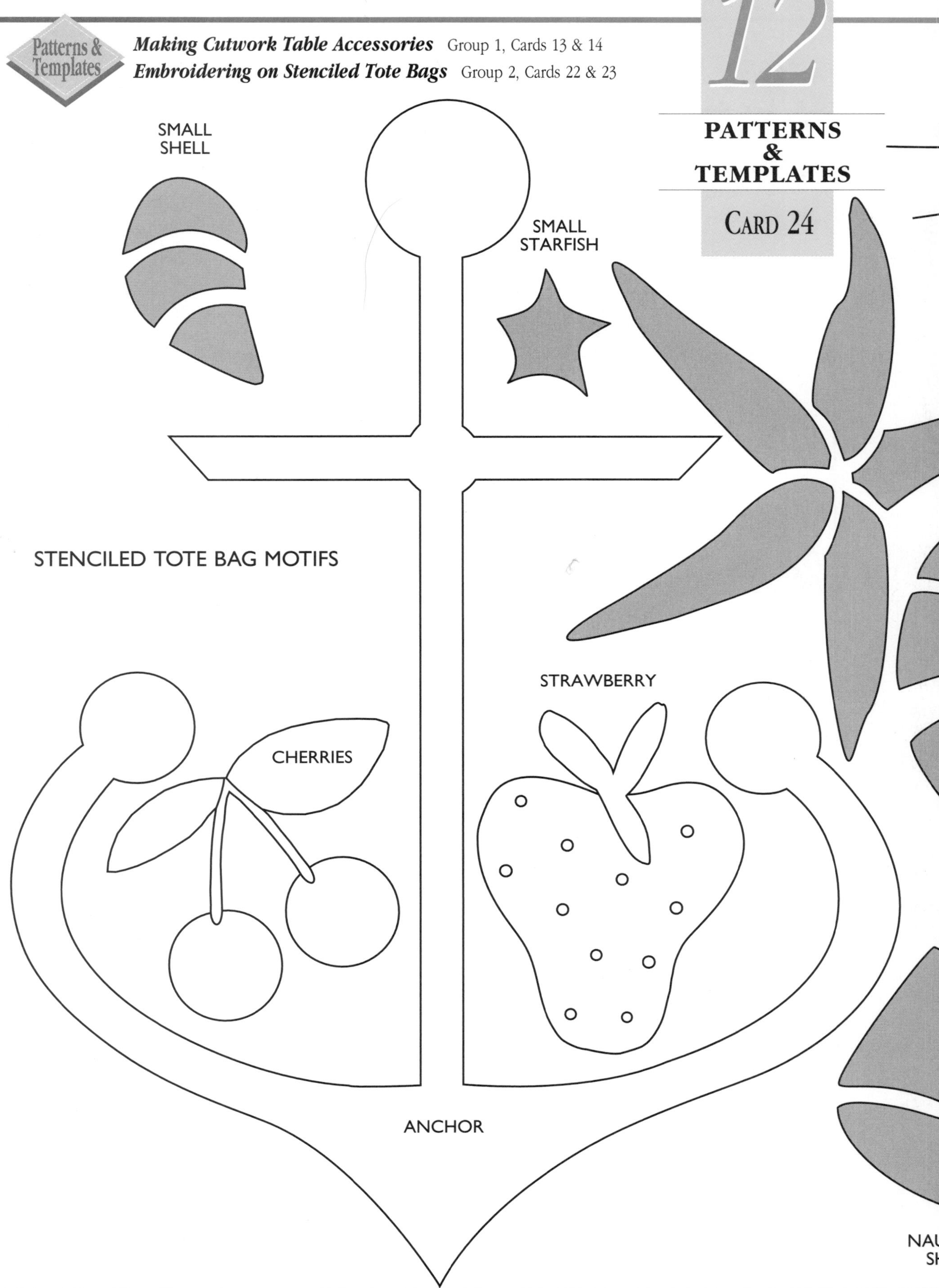
SMALL SHELL
SMALL STARFISH
STENCILED TOTE BAG MOTIFS
STRAWBERRY
CHERRIES
ANCHOR

CALLA LILY
SHELF DOIDLY
BARS
COASTER
BARS

SCALLOP GUIDE FOR TABLECLOTH

FAN

Note: Use only center flower for napkin.

TABLECLOTH CORNER

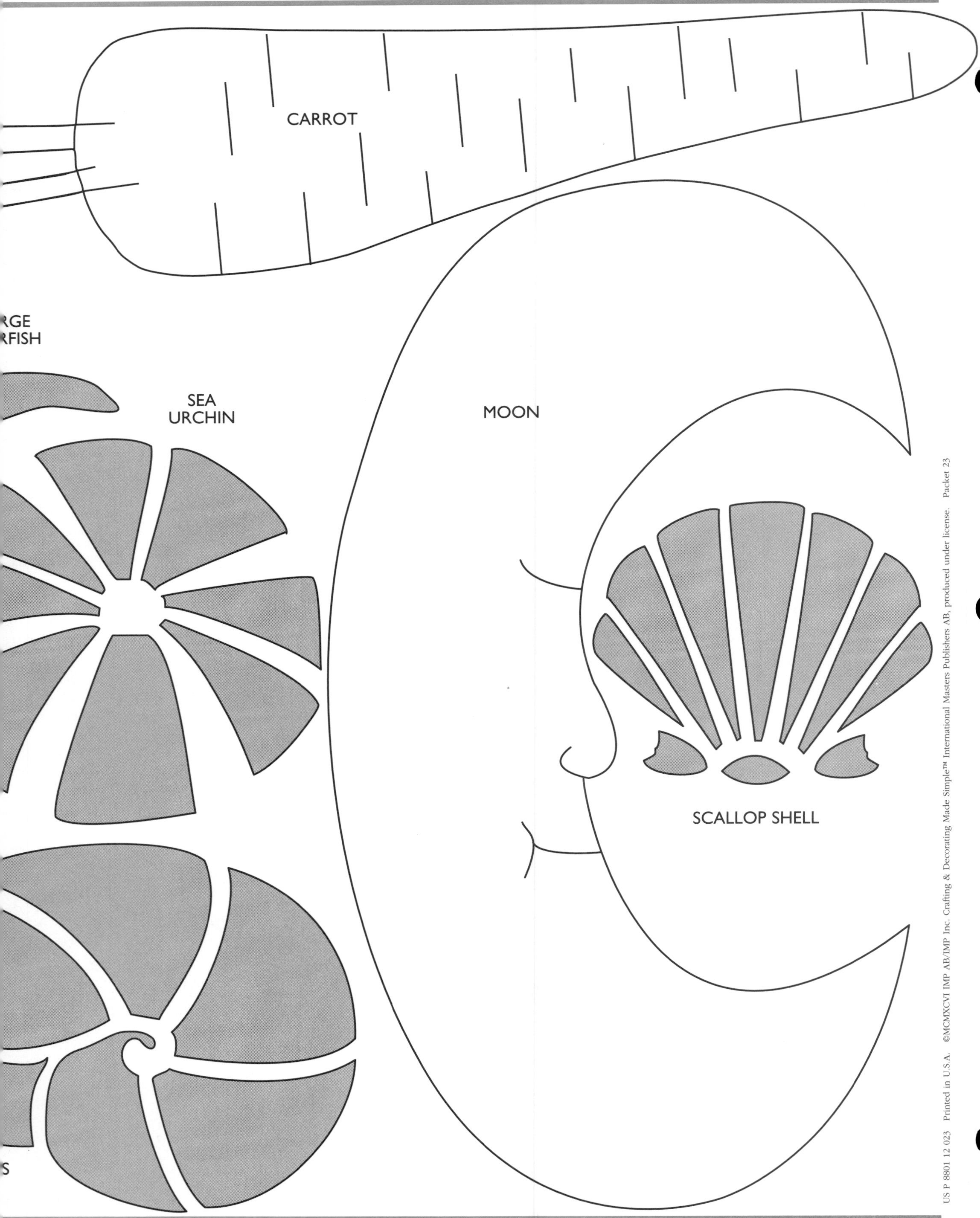
CARROT
RGE
RFISH
SEA
URCHIN
MOON
SCALLOP SHELL
S

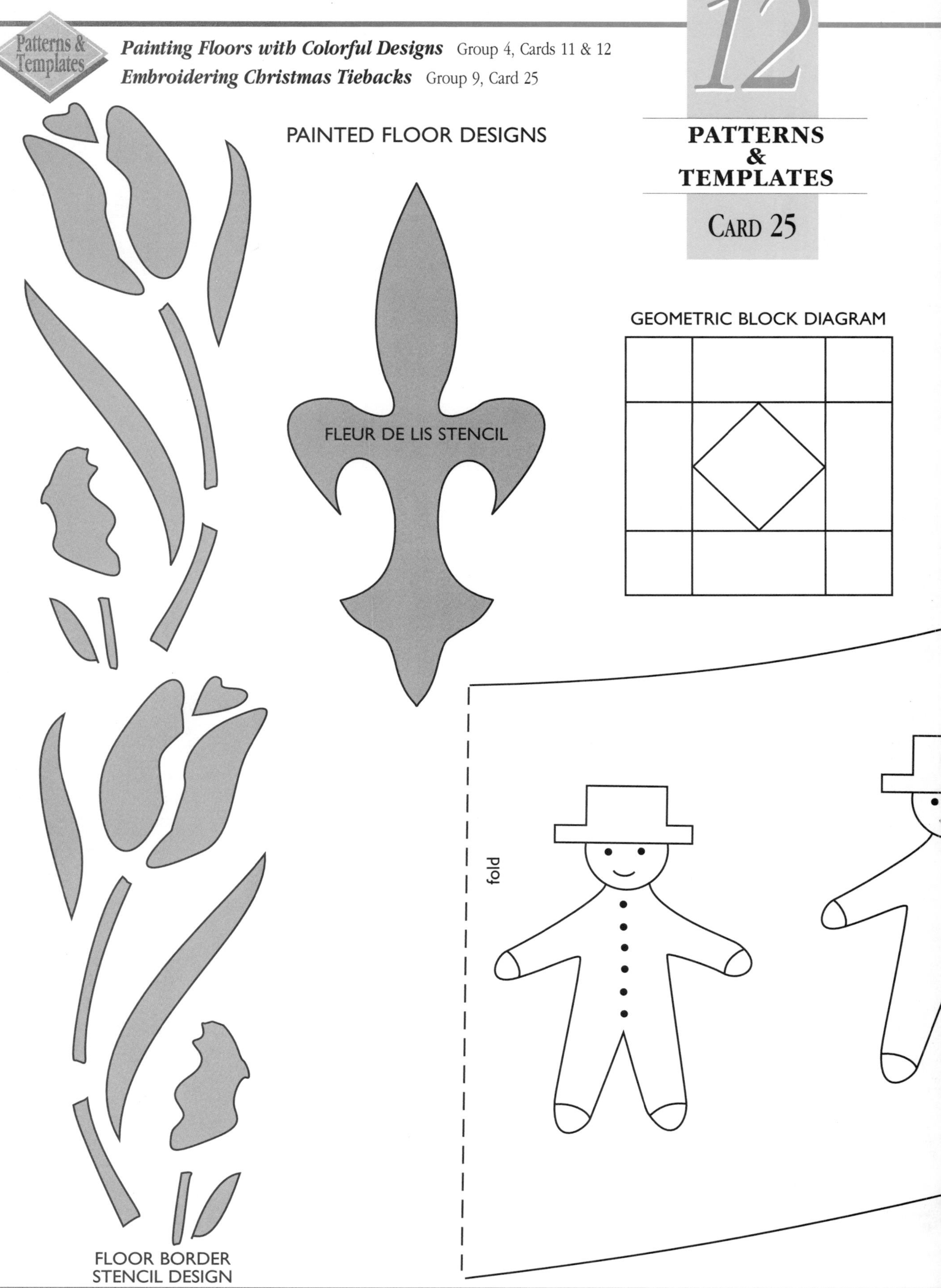
PAINTED FLOOR DESIGNS
FLEUR DE LIS STENCIL
GEOMETRIC BLOCK DIAGRAM
fold
FLOOR BORDER
STENCIL DESIGN

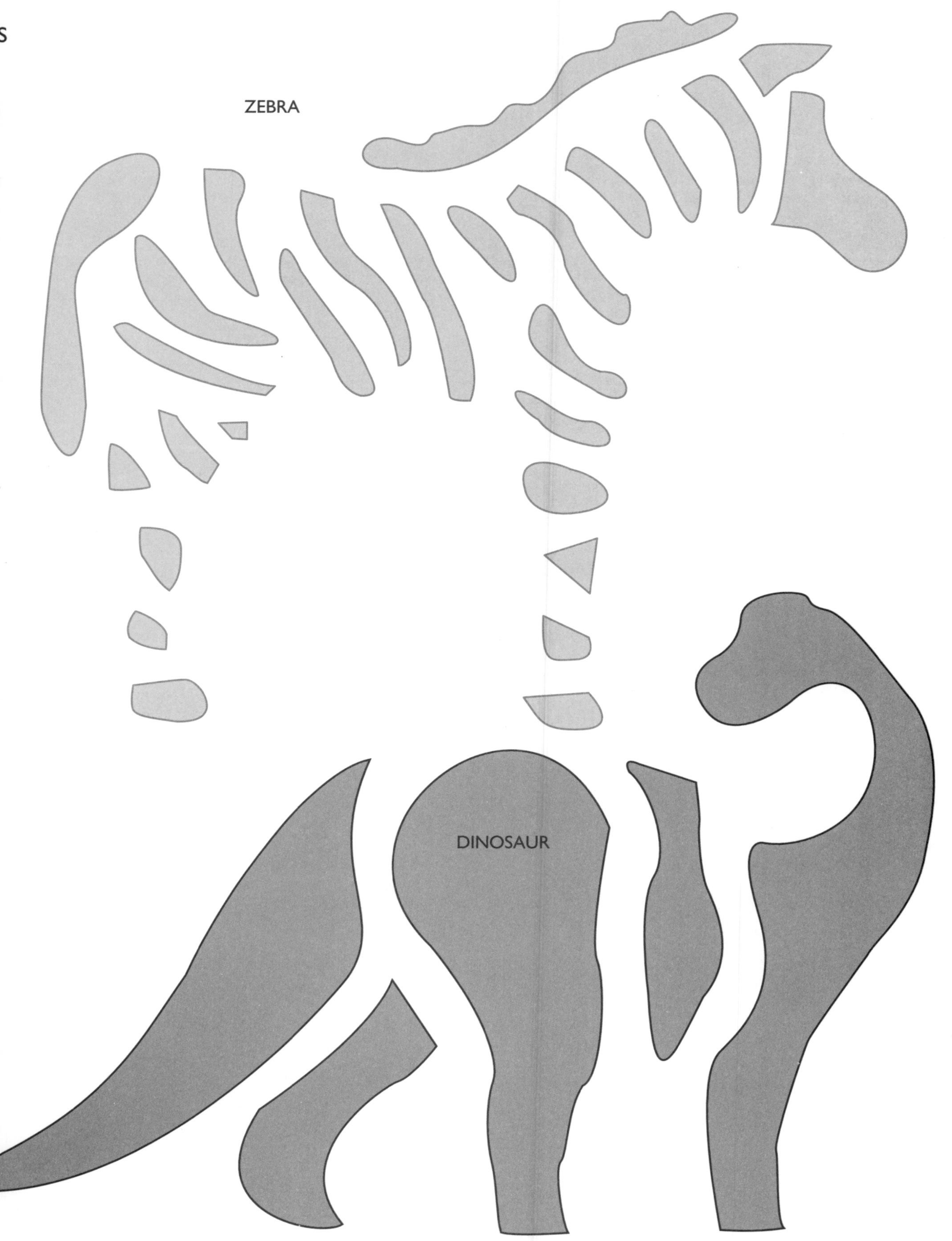
S
ZEBRA
DINOSAUR

ELEPHANT

LION

EMBROIDERED TIEBACK DESIGNS

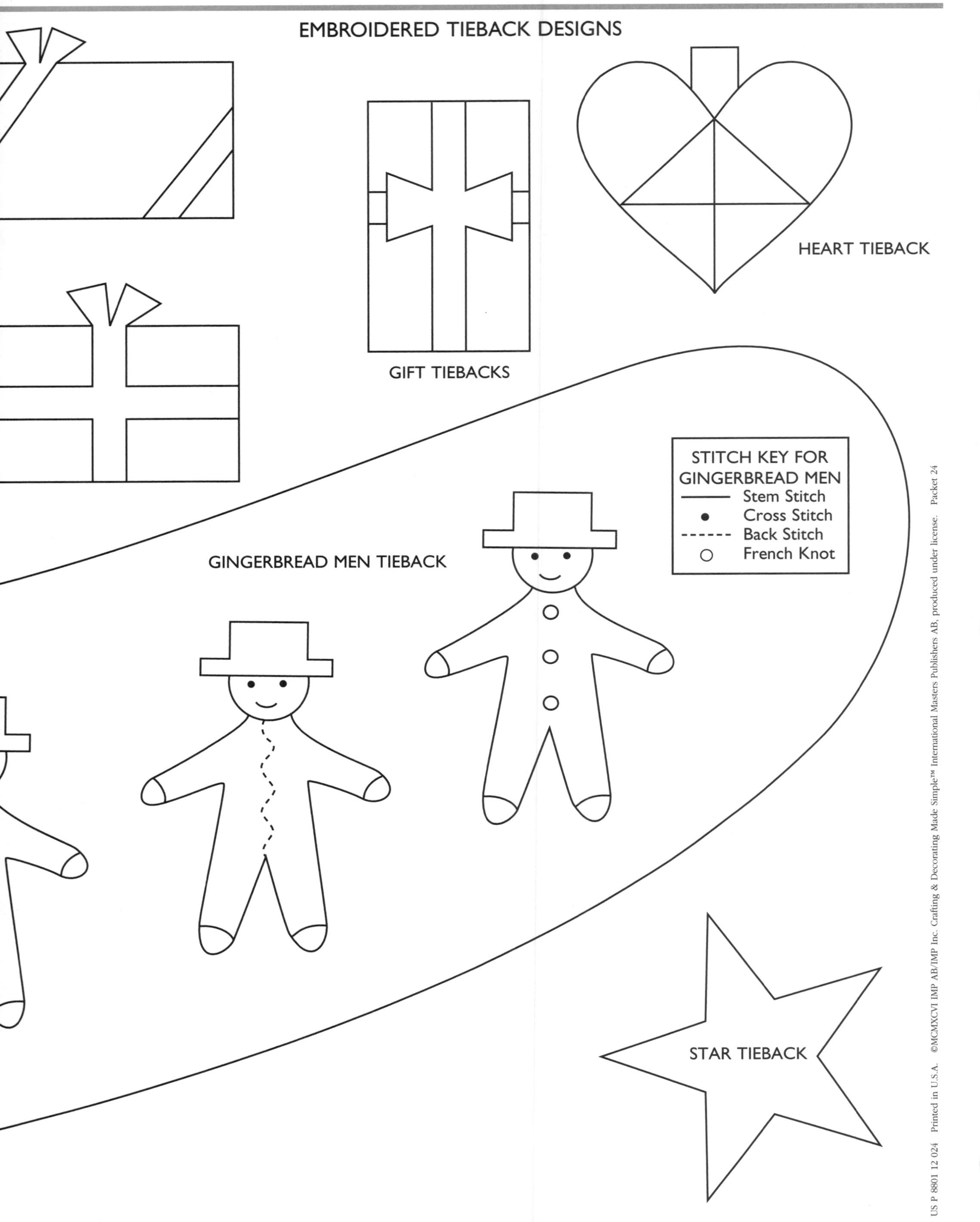

GARDEN CHAIR TULIP

Flop template to turn tulip in opposite direction.

FROG STOOL MOTIFS

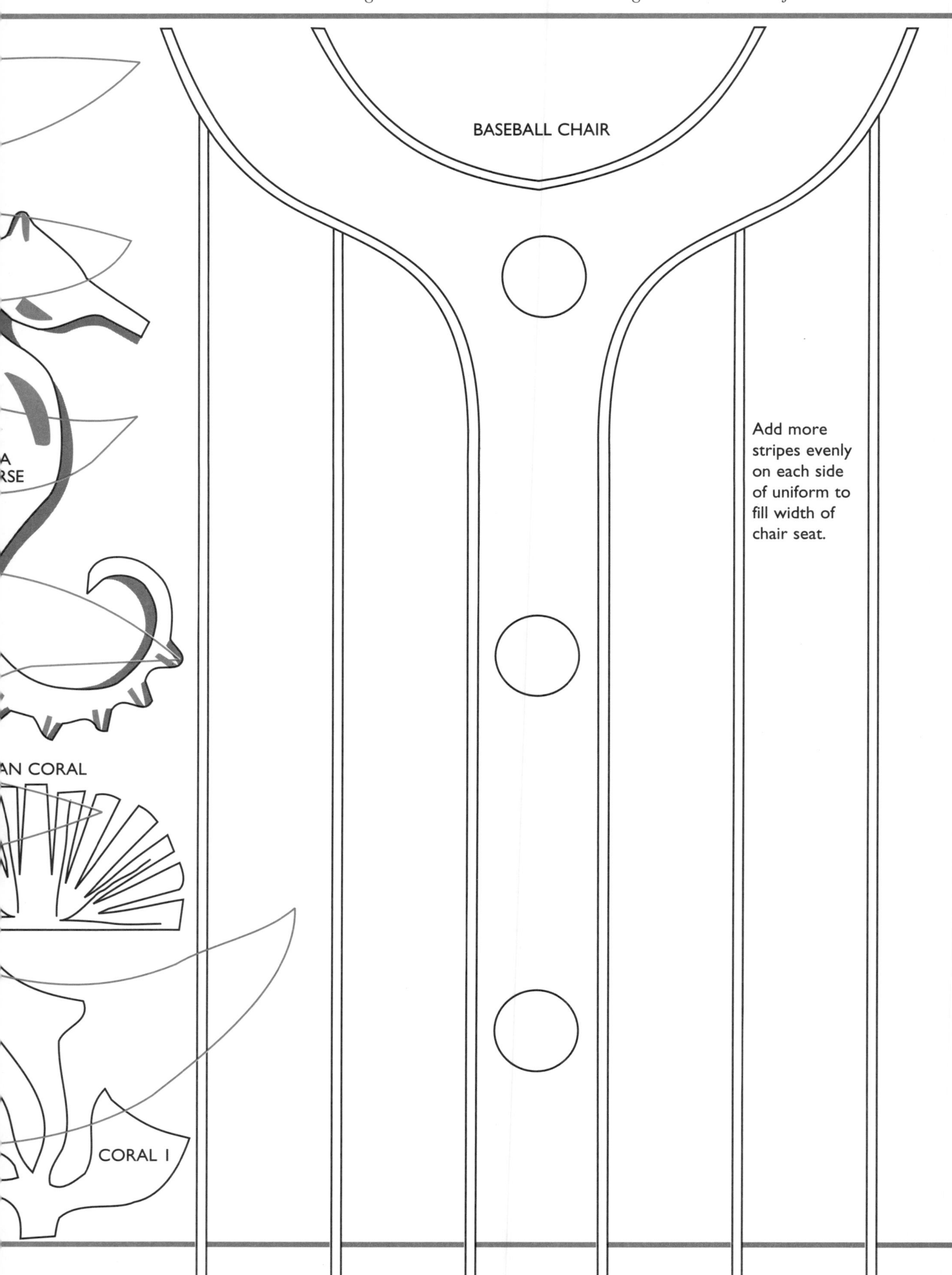

A
RSE
AN CORAL
CORAL I
BASEBALL CHAIR
Add more stripes evenly on each side of uniform to fill width of chair seat.

SEASIDE BATHROOM MOTIFS

THEME CHAIR MOTIFS
LARGE CLOUD
SMALL CLOUD
CENTER GARDEN CHAIR FLOWER
SMALL GARDEN CHAIR FLOWER
STAR
INNER SUN
OUTER SUN
INNER MOON
OUTER MOON